The RoutledgeFalmer Reader in Teaching and Learning

In this new Reader, E. C. Wragg has carefully selected contributions to reflect enduring and contemporary trends in the field of Teaching and Learning. Focusing on the major issues confronting education today, this lively and informative Reader provides a rich hand-picked resource of some of the most influential writing from leading books and journals within education today. The following topics are included:

- early learning
- teaching and learning strategies
- teaching the wider curriculum
- education for all
- managing teaching and learning
- teaching and teacher education

With a specially written introduction from the editor, providing a much-needed context of the current education climate, students of education will find this Reader an important route map to further reading and understanding.

E. C. Wragg is Professor of Education at Exeter University and author of numerous books on education practice.

Readers in education

The RoutledgeFalmer Reader in Higher Education
Edited by Malcolm Tight

The RoutledgeFalmer Reader in Inclusion
Edited by Keith Topping and Sheelagh Maloney

The RoutledgeFalmer Reader in Language and Literacy
Edited by Teresa Grainger

The RoutledgeFalmer Reader in Multicultural Education
Edited by Gloria Ladson-Billings and David Gillborn

The RoutledgeFalmer Reader in Psychology of Education
Edited by Harry Daniels and Anne Edwards

The RoutledgeFalmer Reader in Science Education
Edited by John Gilbert

The RoutledgeFalmer Reader in Sociology of Education
Edited by Stephen J. Ball

The RoutledgeFalmer Reader in Teaching and Learning
Edited by E. C. Wragg

The RoutledgeFalmer Reader in Teaching and Learning

Edited by
E. C. Wragg

RoutledgeFalmer
Taylor & Francis Group

LONDON AND NEW YORK

First published 2004
by RoutledgeFalmer
11 New Fetter Lane, London EC4P 4EE

Simultaneously published in the USA and Canada
by RoutledgeFalmer
29 West 35th Street, New York, NY 10001

RoutledgeFalmer is an imprint of the Taylor and Francis Group

© 2004 E. C. Wragg for editorial matter and selection

Typeset in Sabon and Futura by
Newgen Imaging Systems (P) Ltd, Chennai, India
Printed and bound in Great Britain by
MPG Books Ltd, Bodmin

British Library Cataloguing in Publication Data
A catalogue record for this book is available from the British Library

Library of Congress Cataloging in Publication Data
A catalog record for this book has been requested

ISBN 0–415–33375–X (hbk)
ISBN 0–415–33376–8 (pbk)

May 12, 2006

CONTENTS

ILLUSTRATIONS

Figures

Tables

ACKNOWLEDGEMENTS

The following articles have been reproduced with kind permission of Taylor & Francis Journals, www.tandf.co.uk

Moyles, J. (2001) 'Passion, paradox and professionalism in early years education', *Early Years*, Vol. 21, No. 2, pp. 81–95.
   <http://www.tandf.co.uk/journals/carfax/09575146.html>
Coltman, P., Petyaeva, D. and Anghileri, J. (2002) 'Scaffolding learning through meaningful tasks and adult interaction', *Early Years*, Vol. 22, No. 1, pp. 39–49.
   <http://www.tandf.co.uk/journals/carfax/09575146.html>
Stephen, C. and Wilkinson, J. C. (1999) 'Rhetoric and reality in developing language and mathematical skill: plans and playroom experiences', *Early Years*, Vol. 19, No. 2, pp. 62–73.
   <http://www.tandf.co.uk/journals/carfax/09575146.html>
Baumfield, V. and Mroz, M. (2002) 'Investigating pupils' questions in the primary classroom', *Educational Research*, Vol. 44, No. 2, pp. 129–140.
   <http://www.tandf.co.uk/journals/routledge/00131881.html>
Peacock, A. (2001) 'The potential impact of the "Literacy Hour" on the teaching of science form text material', *Journal of Curriculum Studies*, Vol. 33, No. 1, pp. 25–42.
   <http://www.tandf.co.uk/journals/tf/00220272.html>
Smith, G. F. (2002) 'Thinking skills: the question of generality', *Journal of Curriculum Studies*, Vol. 34, No. 6, pp. 659–678.
   <http://www.tandf.co.uk/journals/tf/00220272.html>
Fenstermacher, G. D. (2001) 'On the concept of manner and its visibility in teaching practice', *Journal of Curriculum Studies*, Vol. 33, No. 6, pp. 639–653.
   <http://www.tandf.co.uk/journals/tf/00220272.html>
Reay, D. (2002) 'Shaun's story: troubling discourses of white working-class masculinities', *Gender and Education*, Vol. 14, No. 3, pp. 221–234.
   <http://www.tandf.co.uk/journals/carfax/09540253.html>
Dudley-Marling, C. (2001) 'School trouble: a mother's burden', *Gender and Education*, Vol. 13, No. 2, pp. 183–197.
   <http://www.tandf.co.uk/journals/carfax/09540253.html>
Rudduck, J. and Flutter, J. (2000) 'Pupil participation and pupil perspective: "Carving a new order of experience" ', *Cambridge Journal of Education*, Vol. 30, No. 1, pp. 75–89.
   <http://www.tandf.co.uk/journals/carfax/0305764X.html>
Chamberlin, R., Wragg, E. C., Haynes, G. S. and Wragg, C. M. (2002) 'Performance-related pay and the teaching profession: a review of literature', *Research Papers in Education,* Vol. 17, No. 1, pp. 31–49.
   <http://www.tandf.co.uk/journals/routledge/02671522.html>

Harris, A. (2000) 'Effective leadership and departmental improvement', *Westminster Studies in Education*, Vol. 23, No. 1, pp. 82–90.
<http://www.tandf.co.uk/journals/carfax/01406728.html>

Coleman, M. (2000) 'The female secondary headteacher in England and Wales: leadership and management styles', *Educational Research*, Vol. 42, No. 1, pp. 13–27.
<http://www.tandf.co.uk/journals/routledge/00131881.html>

Wilkins, C. (2001) 'Student teachers and attitudes towards race', *Westminster Studies in Education*, Vol. 24, No. 1, pp. 13–27.
<http://www.tandf.co.uk/journals/carfax/01406728.html>

Jones, M. (2001) 'Mentors' perceptions of their roles in school-based teacher training in England and Germany', *Journal of Education for Teaching*, Vol. 27, No. 1, pp. 75–94.
<http://www.tandf.co.uk/journals/carfax/02067476.html>

Kyriacou, C. (2001) 'Teacher stress: directions for future research', *Educational Review*, Vol. 53, No. 1, pp. 27–35.
<http://www.tandf.co.uk/journals/carfax/00131911.html>

The following have been reproduced with the kind permission of Taylor & Francis Books:

Wragg, E. C. (2001) 'The two Rs – rules and relationships' in E. C. Wragg *Class Management in the Secondary School*, London: RoutledgeFalmer, pp. 37–49.

Bentham, S. (2002) 'Learning and teaching styles' in S. Bentham *Psychology and Education*, London: RoutledgeFalmer, pp. 97–117.

INTRODUCTION

E. C. Wragg

Two related topics run right through this reader on teaching and learning. First is the need to prepare all children, irrespective of background, for the long and complex life lying ahead of them during the twenty-first century. The second and related challenge is to improve the quality of teaching and learning in primary and secondary schools, which in turn requires the highest quality of professional training. The quintessence of classroom competence, whether of pupil or teacher, lies in their ability to understand what is involved in learning something, and then to be able to act intelligently on that understanding.

There are numerous ways of defining whether this has eventually brought 'success' in education. For some it is determined by test scores, for others it is a broader issue, involving the whole child. While skilful teachers ensure that their classes learn something worthwhile, unskilful ones may turn off that delicate trip switch in children's psyche which keeps their minds open to lifelong learning.

Teachers and pupils engage in hundreds of exchanges every day, tens of thousands within a term or a year. Both teaching and learning consist of favoured strategies that become embedded in our most deeply rooted internal structures, for there is no time to rethink every single move in a busy classroom. Much of what occurs is not consciously appraised by either teacher or learner, it simply happens naturally on a daily basis. Decisions are often made by teachers in less than a second, so once these *deep structures* have been laid down, they are not always amenable to change, even if a school has a significant professional development programme.

Pupils similarly develop learning styles of which they may be unaware until asked. Reflecting on practice alone, or with colleagues, does at least allow teachers to think about what they do away from the immediate pressures of rapid interaction and speedy change, and this collection of readings is intended to facilitate that vital and valuable professional process. The topics covered are all centrally important in education. The first is early years education: that vital period during which young children establish good or bad habits, when they tune in to the vast repositories of knowledge available to them or, tragically, switch them off. Skilful teaching and learning strategies can help keep their minds open, and this is the focus in the second part.

Once in school, children are subjected to a curriculum which may be narrow or broad. Teaching the wider curriculum is the theme of the third part. The fourth concentrates on the vital notion of education for all children, not just a select few, as was the focus earlier in our history. In the final two parts attention switches to the management of teaching and learning, and training. Were these two essential elements in education ineffective, everyone's efforts would gradually slither into the sand.

This general introduction gives an overview of the whole field covered in the collection of eighteen readings, and each of the six parts then has its own preface setting the context in which the three chapters it contains are located. All the topics should be of interest to experienced and trainee teachers, because teaching and learning are fascinating topics that bear endless scrutiny, reflection and discussion.

Early learning

As a species we are capable of learning from cradle to grave. Consider the wide-eyed curiosity of a baby, eagerly scanning facial features, observing the great phenomena of our universe: objects that fall to the ground, rather than rise up to the ceiling; or human behaviour, such as people helping or hindering each other. Skilful teachers capitalise on curiosity, as it is not only a powerful driver of children's learning, but also an indicator that their learning switch has not been tripped into the 'off' position.

It is during these early years that teaching and learning first begin to interact. Many parents are intuitively clever teachers, sensing their child's needs and responding appropriately, through conversations, games, activities. Children learn to talk, think, imagine, create, move, imitate, through interactions with their parents, family and others they meet. Once in a nursery or pre-school they receive further teaching from adults, perhaps offered in a systematic way, though it is not necessarily more effective than what they had before, if their teachers are not skilled.

Adults possess, or have access to knowledge that has been painstakingly acquired over centuries. Life existed on the planet for millions of years before someone discovered how to construct electrical circuits, but teachers can pass elementary versions of that knowledge on to young children in minutes. Imagine a world where every generation had had to start again from scratch, constantly reinventing and rediscovering what others had already resolved. We would never have emerged from primitive squalor. The word 'progress' would hardly exist.

That is what education can achieve for young children: give them a flying start and lay a firm foundation for what should be many decades of further learning, so that they too can contribute their increment to the improvement of the human race and its manifold ways of life. Thereafter they should be partially liberated, capable of studying on their own, as well as under guidance.

If young children are to learn what may be quite difficult concepts, then their teachers must understand how to develop their understanding. This involves a combination of approaches, including graded structuring of what they need to know, harnessing children's own natural learning modes and strategies, stimulating and satisfying curiosity, capitalising on their boundless enthusiasm at this early age. The three chapters in this part of the reader reflect these concerns. They show how skilful and committed teachers can develop important skills, devise meaningful activities, and help children become more competent in key areas like language and mathematics.

Teaching and learning strategies

When teaching and learning work in harmony, the results are far more impressive than when they conflict and grate against each other. The teacher who knows how to use the right language register for a particular child or group stands a better chance of explaining successfully than one who patronises with simplicities, or baffles with unnecessary complexities. Even highly proficient teachers can improve what they do, because nobody will ever reach the state of perfection that would render further improvement impossible.

In order to discharge their duty towards the next generation of adults, teachers need a vast repertoire of personal qualities and professional skills. These include the ability to ask intelligent and appropriate questions, to explain things clearly, to set interesting and absorbing tasks, and to manage their classes effectively. That is the theory, but achieving such goals in practice, especially in schools that operate in a difficult environment, is not a simple matter. Both hard work and reflection are necessary.

Yet many practitioners are unaware of their predominant teaching patterns. In my own research and teacher training, I have often fed back to teachers the results of my observations. Some are surprised to discover that none of the answers to their questions lasted longer than three or four seconds; that only six pupils took part in an interactive oral session, when they were convinced it was about half to two-thirds of the class; that children in tests and interviews reveal they do not understand something the teacher thought was crystal clear; or that a transcript of the lesson shows they never mentioned key elements of a topic they thought they had taught thoroughly.

Learners are similarly ignorant about how they learn. It is often only in retrospect that people realise they have personal preferences that might differ from others, such as liking orderliness and precision, rather than something more diffuse; wanting to learn, or focus on, each element of a concept separately, instead of perusing the whole; preferring to follow a syllabus and tick off each completed topic, while others enjoy freewheeling. How can young people see such features of their inner selves without a metaphorical mirror?

Despite the difficulties, teachers can unscramble the habits of many years, as can learners. People need to be convinced, of course, that it will be worthwhile to reshape the way they teach or learn, but it can be done to good effect if participants are first of all insightful into what is working well and badly for them, and second, if they give it the necessary time and energy. The chapters in the second part of the reader address key classroom strategies, like questioning, class management and preferred teaching and learning styles.

Teaching the wider curriculum

When a new group of student teachers start their course I usually ask them to define the word 'curriculum'. Some describe ten or a dozen familiar school subjects, like mathematics, science, geography, art. Others offer a bigger concept and include activities that take place officially, but during lunch breaks and after school. A small number are prepared to embrace virtually everything that happens in a school, intended and programmed, or not, what is sometimes called the 'hidden curriculum'. For example, if some children are intimidated by more aggressive pupils and a teacher intervenes, then this can be seen as part of what is being learned: that bullying the vulnerable is unacceptable.

This broader concept of a curriculum is often quite fashionable and there are periods when society seems to like the idea that the curriculum should go well beyond traditional school subjects, though there are also times when it retrenches. This happened in England and Wales in 1988, when the Education Reform Act established a nine (primary) or ten (secondary) subject traditional curriculum in schools. Under the more liberal interpretation of 'curriculum' there may be space for personal, social, moral, and health education, or 'thinking'. The usual choice a school faces is between giving such domains a timetabled slot and assuming that every teacher will cover them as part of their subject teaching.

Interdisciplinary study is also an issue. School subjects are often linked whether we like it or not. Physical geography overlaps with scientific aspects of geology. Mathematics has numerous applications. Should children study separate sciences, or an integrated version? Ought young children to learn history and geography separately, or might these be combined into a single 'humanities' programme covering topics like 'canals' or 'water'. To what extent is every teacher a language teacher, since children will learn the specialist language of subjects where it makes most sense, in the lesson concerned. Science and maths teachers are not likely to tell pupils they must wait until the appropriate English lesson to learn what 'inversely proportionate' or 'congruence' mean.

The debate about curriculum is never closed, because the world around is dynamic and changing, and to some extent schools must reflect this flux. No-one can, or should, put a moratorium on change. The issues raised in the three chapters under this heading, science and literacy, the teaching of thinking, and the role of teachers in children's moral education will return several times during the coming years, as they have done in the past.

Education for all

In an ideal society all children would be educated to their full potential. Indeed, many schools state such a Utopian aspiration explicitly in their 'official' literature, though rarely with any guarantees attached, nor much information about how this blissful state of perfection will be achieved. Helping even one or two pupils to achieve the best that is possible for them would be an easy promise to make, but a devilishly difficult one to fulfil.

It is not difficult to identify those groups that are disadvantaged in the formal education system, because they represent a long tradition. If you are born a girl you will probably do significantly better at school, at all ages, than you would if you were a boy, and this will apply especially in subjects with a strong language component. A black working class boy is more likely to be put in a lower set, be excluded from school for 'bad' behaviour, or find difficulty getting into an elite university than a white middle class girl. When a number of African Caribbean parents in Birmingham complained about what they saw as inadequate education for their children, the city set up a working party to investigate their complaints. This led to changes in the conventions for pupil exclusions and other reforms.

Education exists partly to rectify any unfairness. In theory it is a fundamental human right, encouraging schools to offer high quality education to all, irrespective of their religion, racial or social group, gender, physical state, or family income. In practice, it does this very well for many but fails a significant number who slip through the net. Poverty alone is a deadly killer of educational opportunities, even though some people have sought to deny this. Those who believe poverty does not count should try it. They would have to live in a leaky attic, perhaps a single room for the family, sharing water facilities and toilet, with no books, computers, or graduate parents, breathing leaden fumes, coping with the absences from school that ill health will inevitably bring.

Deprivation can, of course, bring out the best in some people, but far more are buried by it. Adversity is a merciless tyrant, robbing whole groups of children of their birthright, simply because they were not born into the best environment.

The three authors who write graphically about the topic in this book describe some of the key factors – social conditions, school pressures, lack of an effective voice – which still today prevent too many children from fulfilling their potential.

Managing teaching and learning

Society often claims to admire the people who actually do a job more than those who manage them, yet managers are usually much better paid and enjoy higher status. Indeed, one of the prime concerns, whenever salaries and pay incentives are discussed, is how to persuade highly competent teachers to stay in their classroom, rather than seek promotion out of it. Good management can enhance what teachers do, while bad management is debilitating and can even drive them out of the profession.

There are probably as many styles of management as there are of teaching and similar principles apply to those described here. Like teachers, heads are under pressure from the demands of a rapidly changing job, so they can easily become set in their ways, as they engage in more and more repeats and rehearsals of their favourite strategies. They may fail to adapt when they ought to, finding out too late that a style which might have been successful a few years ago is no longer adequate in a changed world.

Heads and other senior managers also have to fill out many different roles, not all of which have a direct relationship to teaching and learning in their school. Some may even impede them in discharging their duty to ensure that high quality education is being offered. Heads in particular may be curriculum expert, public relations officer (selling the school to parents, sponsors, or the press), lawyer, counsellor (of teachers, pupils, and even parents), finance director (handling size-able budgets), chief executive, diplomat, jailer (keeping in reluctant pupils), caterer and fund-raiser, to name but a selection. They may founder on just one of these, having succeeded in the others. It is a high risk, high stakes job.

Most secondary heads have learned to delegate some of their responsibilities and this is where middle managers, like heads of departments, can offer valuable service and support, since they have direct access to improving teaching and learning in a particular subject area. In primary schools, by contrast, especially in the many small ones with only two to five teachers, almost every responsibility falls directly on the headteacher, and primary heads have been more frequent victims of stress than their secondary counterparts.

Even teachers who have no intention of becoming heads or taking up a position of middle or senior responsibility, need to think carefully about management. Teaching is a job where even complete novices are expected to manage budgets, resources like books and equipment, some of which may be expensive, time, space, people and relationships. In this section of the reader the three chapters cover many of the key issues in school management, like what happens when managers can offer pay incentives to teachers, the role of the head of department, and the nature of female headteachers' leadership styles.

Teaching and teacher education

From time to time there is a recruitment crisis in the teaching profession, often when the graduate jobs market is buoyant. Subsequently there is an over-supply, usually when pupil numbers are falling, or in times of recession when larger numbers embark on training and then find that securing a good post is not easy, as the competition is fierce. The graph of teacher trainee numbers over a thirty-year period, therefore, will go up and down like a roller coaster. Yet the health of the profession depends heavily on the quality and quantity of newcomers, especially after a particularly large incidence of retirements or defections.

Student teachers are in a curious position. They often identify closely with learners when they begin their course. After all, they are themselves learning something new, and they are usually closer to their own schooldays than older teachers, so they can empathise with anyone struggling to master a new concept or skill. After a while they become more socialised into the profession and increasingly adopt the beliefs and values of their experienced colleagues and mentors, whose 'reality' thus becomes their own, as idealism gives way to pragmatism.

Yet their initial attitudes to children, teaching and learning have often been strongly conditioned by their own experiences and the values and beliefs of the society in which they grew up. Training to teach can be a painful period, during which much individual soul-searching takes place, and people may not like the person they find within themselves when they introspect.

This is where skilful mentors can make a significant contribution. Good mentors may have done the job for some time, but they do not seek to impose their own personal styles and strategies on others for whom they may not work. Helping newcomers discover their own ways, albeit under guidance, is one of the most valuable services the experienced can offer the novice. The mentor–novice relationship is an interesting mirror to the one between teacher and pupil. Adult teaching adult can be just as fascinating an event as teaching and learning among the young.

Firm foundations are necessary in training because the demands on teachers, new or old, can be fierce. They can also exact a high price if not met. Consider the many sources of strain, the stressors that can destroy even the robust. They include: a rapidly changing environment, little time to think, external and internal pressures to achieve the maximum, numerous novelties and fresh demands, difficult behaviour from some pupils, frustration over lack of control, conflicting forces, difficult personal relationships. Add universal stressors like bereavement, marriage breakdown, house move, financial crisis, personal or family illness, and it is not surprising if someone disintegrates under the combined forces.

Good quality support for teachers is vital, therefore, whether they are in the initial or later stages of their career. In the final part of this reader the three chapters address matters of widespread concern, like student teachers' attitudes to controversial issues such as race, the role of the mentor in nurturing the talents of newcomers, and what causes stress in teachers, a major cause of their quitting the profession early.

PART I

EARLY LEARNING

Few would doubt the significance of learning during the early years of life. It was known before child development was studied systematically, and its importance is reflected in the various versions of a frequently quoted Jesuit saying 'Give me a child for the first seven years and you may do what you like with him afterwards.'

In most developed countries it has become increasingly common for young children to be offered a place in some kind of nursery school or kindergarten. The *écoles maternelles* in France are renowned for their work with children before formal schooling begins, and some of the most interesting developments in education have been stimulated by the so-called great thinkers, like Maria Montessori, the first woman to qualify as a doctor in Italy, who went on to become very influential in early years education.

The three chapters in this part address some of the key teaching and learning issues in the education of the young. The first, by Janet Moyles, explores the dilemma faced by a mainly female profession when confronted with powerful forces from outside, such as government prescriptions, or external inspections. Should they back their own judgment about what they do in their classes, or simply collude and provide what is expected? The author is concerned that many teachers of this age group have a low self-image, saying 'I'm only a nursery teacher'. She argues that they can and should reflect profoundly on their own practice and take responsibility themselves for improving it.

Although many of the best-known figures in early years education, like Montessori and Froebel are from Western Europe, two psychologists from a different tradition, the Russian Lev Vygotsky and the American Jerome Bruner, have also been extremely influential. In the second chapter in this section Penny Coltman and her colleagues describe an experiment in which they show how teachers can help children learn quite complicated mathematics if the structure of what they do is appropriate. Using Poleidoblocks, an integrated set of fifty-four coloured wooden shapes, such as cube, cone and pyramid, children were helped to higher levels of understanding based on Bruner's notion of 'scaffolding': they worked with an adult who offered suitably graded guidance. Vygotsky's 'Zone of Proximal Development', the higher area of learning that children are about to enter when they are ready, was also influential. With such graded help the experimental group showed better understanding of the next stages than the unaided.

Finally, Christine Stephen and Eric Wilkinson relate how they observed children in a range of nursery settings to show differences in practice and also how there could be a mismatch between stated aims and what teachers actually did. For example, they did not always have the opportunity to cover their supposed language, mathematics or science curriculum. When they did have such opportunities, they were not always exploited. This occurred when children were in a book corner, but not reading. Sometimes they played with sand and water, but teachers talked to them about clearing up or not getting wet, rather than developing their understanding of the activities.

CHAPTER 1

PASSION, PARADOX AND PROFESSIONALISM IN EARLY YEARS EDUCATION

Janet Moyles

Introduction

Research into early years and primary teaching has shown that those who teach this age group often express a 'passion' for their role and for children which it is perhaps difficult for those in other phases of education to understand. Various research teams and individuals have written of teachers who 'love' teaching and who find teaching 'worthwhile and rewarding' because of the children, their spontaneity and the sheer joy of working in a job which brings them so close to children, families and communities (e.g. Saltzberger-Wittenberg *et al.*, 1983; Nias, 1989; Pollard and Thiessen, 1996; Woods, 1996; Woods and Jeffrey, 1996; Galton *et al.*, 1999; Pollard and Filer, 1999).

Paradoxically, such 'emotional' responses to young children and teaching appear vital to the very role practitioners fulfil, while, at the same, being capable of restricting early years practice to a low-level operation in which children receive care but which negates or rejects education (Sugrue, 1997; Edgington, 1998). Teaching young children also rests paradoxically on something of an intimate relationship with children, yet on a recognition that these are someone else's children. It is difficult to separate out the mother/formal teacher roles, yet imperative to combine them if the individual needs of the child are to be fulfilled (Dahlberg *et al.*, 1999). Having responsibilities and emotions centred on the child can, of itself and paradoxically, displace practitioners' own motivations, generating passivity on their part and encouraging them to 'manage' problems rather than to try to solve them, engendering a sense that responsibility and power lie outside the domain of the practitioners (Moyles and Suschitzky, 1997a).

The very 'professionalism' which is called into question through such practices is, of itself, under scrutiny for teachers and other public sector workers. The government's Green Paper, 'Teachers: Meeting the Challenge of Change' (DfEE, 1998), is a strange mixture of demanding supposed professional thinking and expertise on the part of teachers, and levels of prescription, combined with performance-related pay, which sit in an uneasy juxtaposition. This 'new professionalism' (McCulloch *et al.*, 2000) demands more of teachers than ever before: set in a climate of unprecedented change, however, questions need to be raised as to how teachers and, increasingly, those who work with them in classrooms can develop the understanding necessary to adapt to the impact of such change.

Each of the three 'p' words – passion, paradox and professionalism – will be explored in this chapter, together with their unique and often interrelated characteristics in the education of children under the age of 7 years. An attempt will be made to show how they are each distinctly integrated into the work of early years practitioners, drawing particularly upon collaborative, interventionist and constructivist research undertaken with practitioners over several years, in which partnership between the researchers and the researched has been one key to promoting reflective and effective practice and the development of enhanced professionalism.[1] The focus of each study is given at a relevant point in the text.

Throughout this chapter, early years educators will be referred to as 'practitioners', in order to reflect the diverse backgrounds of those who work and play in the early years. Some of these people are teachers, some are nursery nurses, some are variously qualified or unqualified personnel: the vast majority are also women.

P is for passion

Disraeli (1804–81) suggested that 'Man (sic) is only truly great when he acts from the passions'. The *Oxford English Dictionary* suggests that to be passionate is to be 'dominated by strong feelings' or 'having strong enthusiasm' and to possess 'intense love', 'devotion', 'warmth', 'fervour' and even 'anger'. Most people who are 'work enthusiasts' become, by this definition, passionate about what they do: this passion is part of the nature of professionalism within and outside education and, as such, is continuously challenged within the current climate of accountability, particularly in the public sector.

In the early years, the link between effective and affective dimensions has become an accepted part of the practitioner's role, as responses to interview questions concerning the comparative roles of Key Stage 1 (KS1) teachers and classroom assistants, and nursery teachers and nursery nurses evidenced (Moyles and Suschitzky, 1997a,b) the following:

> We want [to employ] the right people for the children, such as those who've been childminders. (Head)
>
> We must accept that these people primarily work for the kick they get from the job. (Head)
>
> Let's face it, I do this job because I love young children . . . the way they make you laugh and everything. You certainly wouldn't do it for the money would you? (Teacher)
>
> I really find working with young children worthwhile and so rewarding . . . they are so trusting and responsive. (Nursery Nurse)

Practitioners and politicians alike may not be so pleased to learn that one headteacher in the KS1 study (who was not alone in this view) asserted that in interviews for classroom assistants:

> I look for a love of children first and foremost, rather than any real academic ability.
>
> (Headteacher)

Herein, however, lies one of the many paradoxes of early childhood. The role of carer and educator becomes enmeshed and confused. Schools, teachers and parents become satisfied that being 'happy' and socially adjusted are satisfactory in themselves as the basis for early years education (Hughes *et al.*, 1994), at the same time as politicians and society in general are demanding more extensive outcomes from children's early learning experiences (QCA, 1999, 2000).

Experiences of comparative research in China gave a different but related picture. Three in-depth case studies of kindergartens in the Shaanxi province were carried out with an academic in support, as knowledgeable colleague and translator, with the intention of comparing practice with that found in three matched comparisons of early years settings in one region of England. Whereas all kindergarten staff were expected to have a 'love of young children', care and education roles were carefully divided between specially appointed staff trained for the role. They worked in harmony to provide the best possible combination of care and education both for children and for families. However, kindergarten teachers – under rather strict appraisal systems – were, paradoxically, still assessed for performance-related pay purposes, on their ability to care for children, communicate at an appropriate level with families and ensure children's educational welfare and happiness (Moyles and Liu Hua, 1998).

There are many contradictions in the way people outside the early years phase perceive both children and practitioners who work and play with them. Reactions ranging from: 'I wouldn't work with young children if you paid me!' to '. . . It's only childminding!' inspire a range of passions from those whose role (and professionalism) is challenged by such statements. The comedian, Bob Monkhouse, makes the point that 'We all like children . . .', but goes on to suggest '. . . we don't particularly like the children we know!' (Monkhouse, 1999). To be an early years practitioner carries the expectation that you will like all of the children all of the time and respond to them as unique individuals: in this way, operating from the emotions is positively expected by society (Drury *et al.*, 2000). It is hard to imagine how one could deal with the behaviours, reactions and idiosyncrasies of young children day-in and day-out by dealing only with lesson planning, curriculum delivery and outcome measures. With very young children, the expression 'You can take a horse to water but you can't make it drink' takes on a whole new dimension, as anyone will know who has tried to 'persuade' young children to do something they do not particularly want to do! The very nature of the work demands strong feelings towards both protecting and supporting young children and engaging empathetically with these wider family and community aspects of the child's life (Katz, 1995).

The other side of emotional responses is that, in society in general, we are always ready to use images of children and childhood to make social comment (Holland, 1992). The horrendous and heart-wrenching images of children starving in Biafra or Rwanda or the appalling conditions in which children were housed in the orphanages of Rumania, for example, leave few people without passion about the plight of these children. Documentary makers and advertisers know only too well the emotional strings which can be tugged by the images they present of children. Even politicians ensure they are photographed with children to illuminate a caring side to their roles.

The reason is simple: young children are 'pre-programmed' to ensure that potential carers respond favourably to them (Holland, 1992). Without ensuring that adults feel nurturant towards them, babies and young children could not survive. It is a strategy used to good effect by nature and capitalised upon by others and it is hardly surprising, then, that early years practitioners are equally drawn to young children through emotion.

Contemporary research is increasingly establishing that feelings and emotions such as passion are acceptable, and indeed desirable, as part of educational thinking and practice. A few examples include the following:

> *Paolo Freire* (1999) whose work generates a powerful vision for education which capitalises on the very nature of humanity and emotions (the book is even called *Pedagogy of the Heart*);
>
> *Guy Claxton* (1999) writes of the importance of 'intuitive practice'. It is known that teaching demands rapid decision making, immediate apprehension and the use of familiar behavioural patterns in order to respond to the sheer wealth of incoming information from whole classes of learners.
>
> *Daniel Goleman* (1996) produced work about 'emotional intelligence' which has prompted greater acknowledgement and understanding of thinking based in the emotions as a vital component of all human relationships and learning.
>
> *Steinberg and Kincheloe* (1998, p. 228) report on research into students' responses to analysing their experiences which found that 'Little . . . learning takes place until . . . our passions are engaged [and] . . . intellect, academic knowledge and personal experience are brought together. At this point of intersection pedagogical magic takes place – the kind of magic that produces genius, that keeps the romance of teaching alive for great teachers'.

Gardner (1993) reminds us of the many intelligences including emotional with which we are all endowed and Edwards *et al.* (1998) write inspiringly of the feelings and emotions of children – and the necessary emotional responses of adults – as part of their 'hundred languages'. The message from these and many other writers is that passion is never *mindless*, but rather very *mindful*. To operate emotionally at a mindful level equates with significant deep level, higher-order thinking, as shown by this practitioner in attempting to consider her role in developing play and learning for young children:

> I think it's very easy to provide play activities, but whether the children are learning anything from what they're doing is a completely different matter. I think the whole process of having to explain what we understand by play, and to describe what play is . . . I don't think we've reached an understanding yet, but part of the excitement . . . is . . . we have to define it. That's been hard because originally I felt quite secure in what I felt play was . . . but . . .

When the circumstances surrounding the lives of young children in our society and, in particular, in our education system are examined, it is perhaps clear that there are other very fundamental reasons why practitioners should, and do, embrace a 'mindful passion' in their roles.

- Young children themselves respond from feelings and emotions. What 'I want' and how 'I feel' now is what is important to a child. This generates a level of immediacy for practitioners to be responsive and reactive and to understand their work from a basis of developmental knowledge (Fisher, 1996; Moyles, 2001).
- Early childhood is focused upon the individual child as a unique and developing person. New neuroscience research is showing how the emotional experiences are significant in patterning the child's brain (e.g. Kotulak, 1996).

- Relationships in early years are founded on the basis of 'educare' and, very specifically in law through '*in loco parentis*' responsibility.
- Parents and carers themselves frequently react through emotion to everything to do with young children and in particular to separation, a key feature in children's early days in nursery or other pre-formal school education (Hurst and Joseph, 1998).
- All practitioners work in multidisciplinary contexts: this demands certain sensitivities and thought for how others feel and respond. Some practitioners are highly qualified teachers with qualifications up to doctoral level. At the other end of the continuum are practitioners who have little by way of qualification and who are struggling for recognition of their skills and capabilities (Moyles and Suschitzky, 1997a).
- The workforce is mainly female: women are known to work more collaboratively than men (Farrell, 1998) and to use communication as a significant feature of their working relationships. Talking to each other, sharing thoughts and feelings on issues of concern, has been found to be a key 'liberating' experience for women practitioners (Moyles and Adams, 2000).
- Inequalities in society are often epitomised in the lives of young families, especially the current government's demonised 'lone mothers', who often struggle to balance working life and family life to do their best for their young children and rely heavily on early years practitioners for moral and physical support with child-rearing (Anning, 2000).
- Society's general lack of value associated with young children and with care roles (Martinez, 1996) means that low salary and low status go hand-in-hand, at a time when there are, in fact, very high expectations placed on early years practitioners to generate life-long learning potential in all future citizens.

Our society lacks a clear perception as to what kinds of values, respect, funding or time that young children's education and care should demand. Resolving this multi-faceted and affectively dominated role presents challenges to early years practitioners which are not faced similarly by others in the statutory schooling system. Coupling a political mindedness to value for money and pinpointing 'performance' as the basis of value, compounds the difficulties faced by early years practitioners in clearly articulating their roles to less knowledgeable others and retaining their own sense of value within the communities they serve. Mindful passion also brings its own controls, concerns and conflicts.

P is for paradox

So perhaps practitioners need to be passionate about early childhood education and care. As has been indicated, passion seems to be a powerful and necessary, mindful emotion. Practitioners' culture of passion, however, can also carry associations with being anti-intellectual, idealistic, subjective, indecisive and 'feminine' (see, e.g. Stone, 1994; Yelland, 1998). It can be thought that allowing the heart to rule the head diminishes objectivity and logic, yet, paradoxically, a main characteristic of the role of early years practitioners is their ability to handle a range of events, and sometimes potential crises, in a clear-headed, rational way. Working 'not rationally but paradoxically' (Farson, 1996, p. 7) can, then, be a positive strength.

Heart and head can operate in tandem and, indeed, a main argument in dealing with young children is that they must if practitioners are to care sufficiently to do the job well (Anning and Edwards, 1999). What we should expect is that practitioners will reflect upon and evaluate both their role and their responses to it and to the children in their settings (Eraut, 1994) and feel professional (McCulloch *et al.*, 2000). Instead, what has been increasingly happening is that, on the one hand, practitioners appear to feel they are regularly criticised for female caring roles inclining them towards 'non-professional' and 'woolly' thinking and, on the other hand, they are constantly urged to take on many of the perceived ills of society (e.g. low income families), high level assessments of children's existing and potential capabilities, work with a wide range of other people, for low salaries and within a context which they feel is antithetical to their role in educating and caring for small people.

Little wonder that practitioners feel a range of emotions against an education and political system which appears to demand they be all things to all people:

> *Powerless*
> What can you do against the might of OfSTED?
>
> *Vulnerable*
> You just have to keep your head down and do what you can . . . damage limitation.
>
> *Exposed*
> All the while you're told young children should sit still and work – it's just not right!
>
> *Lacking a professional 'voice'*
> Whatever we say, and however right we are, they won't listen to us, so what's the point of arguing?

There is evidence that qualified teachers in the early years sector tend to work 'down' to the level of their variously trained and qualified colleagues rather than raising the standards within their settings through acknowledgement of different roles, experience and expertise (Moyles and Suschitzky, 1995). Again, however, they do this from the best of intentions: keeping the working relationships in the close environment of early years running smoothly for the sake of the children and parents. They perceive that by 'dominating' the context with their views, experiences and expertise, they will be marginalising those of others. Conversely, mentors of early years students and newly qualified teachers expected that somehow, by osmosis or other means, their intuitive skills would automatically be adopted without recourse to them having to offer any detailed guidance (Moyles and Suschitzky, 1998).

Should practitioners be rebuked for this behaviour or be provided with opportunities to explore the issues implicit within this essentially managerial role and be offered professional development opportunities to help them understand this aspect of their role more fully. A clear paradox exists here between a 'shame and blame' culture and a supportive, developmental culture in which everyone may benefit from sharing specialised knowledge at different levels (Abbott and Pugh, 1998; Smith and Langston, 1999).

Other politically based paradoxes face early years practitioners:

- diversity or individuality: working from the basis of knowledge of child development alongside the imposition of common standards;
- the need for flexibility in a future workforce against constraints imposed by curriculum prescription;

- the need for discipline, high literacy and numeracy standards, set against parents and other members of society who are not always models of such socially acceptable behaviours themselves;
- the low level of salaries for early years practitioners against expectations of 'professionalism' (which for many early years workers can appear to mean doing long hours in an unpaid capacity – see Moyles and Suschitzky, 1997a,b);
- education, education and education – usually meaning tests, exams and formal *schooling* – set alongside the very exuberance of young children and their need for very different styles and forms of teaching which support and enable them, rather than 'delivering' pre-determined knowledge which can have little meaning to a young child.

Paradoxically, passion is not always powerful enough to prevent passivity amongst early years practitioners as we saw in the earlier quotations. It is difficult to fight for what one believes in if one has a relatively fragile self-concept and self-confidence, and easy to give up and simply do as one is 'told' by politicians and parents (Dadds, 1997). It is easy to feel disempowered and inadequate in these circumstances and this can readily reduce any appropriate passion. It was just this kind of feeling which drove practitioners in the StEPs Project (Moyles and Adams, 2001) to sink into what they eventually called 'the black hole' (see Figure 1.1).

The 'black hole' represents what this project group of nine practitioners, together for nearly three years, explored with two researchers: the issues for them in trying to work playfully with young children in nursery, reception and KS1 settings.

'Black hole' type pressures are felt not only by early years practitioners but by teachers in other phases. The problems are highlighted for early years practitioners because of the very nature of young children and the close relationships with

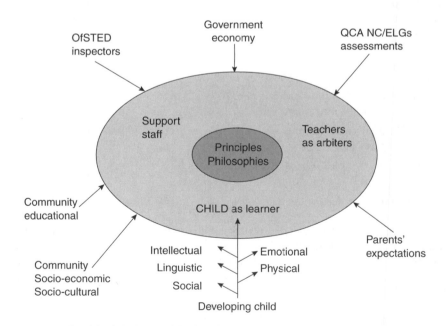

Figure 1.1 The 'black hole' model of early years practitioners

parents and communities which the whole spectrum of providers – nurseries, reception classes, playgroups, crèches and childminders – has in common. Not only do practitioners need to make everything meaningful for young children, but they have to explain to a not always knowledgeable group of outsiders (e.g. OfSTED inspectors of primary schools) the basis of effective early years teaching and learning practices and the implicit differences between pedagogy in this phase and in other phases of education. Teachers in particular have found themselves as arbiters between all these various factions – it is no wonder that they have some-times found themselves lacking in the relevant skills, particularly given that early years as a specialism in teacher training has only just been authenticated, and acknowledgement and validation of their expertise appears still to be some way off for other practitioners in the early years sector.

As an example, there are some well-rehearsed arguments in early years, such as should young children be conceived of as the future workforce and, therefore, be taught mainly a diet of skills which will serve society's economic needs, or do they have a 'right' to be happy and free to play and learn about being part of the wider social society which (arguably) provides the best foundation for future learning? Without being afforded the opportunity to consider such paradoxes in an open and empowering context, promoting passionate discussion and debate of the critical issues, it is difficult for a majority of early years practitioners – with their practical day-to-day educare roles – to find time to stand back and engage in discourse at a professional level. This raises the question of professionalism and how that is defined in multidisciplinary contexts.

P for professionalism

The *Oxford English Dictionary* offers several definitions of 'profession': vocation/calling involving advanced learning/science; body of people thus engaged; and of 'professional': having or showing skills of a profession; worthy. These are exemplified in descriptions of being 'professional' by practitioners and early years employers (which arose in several projects) thus:

> I am a professional – conscientious and experienced. (Nursery Nurse)
>
> [Classroom Assistants] are not here to wash the paint pots. These people are professional but untrained. (Headteacher)
>
> Any differences in training are equalized, in professional terms, by experience. (Nursery Teacher)
>
> We want people whom we can treat like teachers, who can speak knowledgeably about children. (Headteacher)
>
> Gosh, we're professionals here – we should know about learning! (Teacher)

There are indications here that 'professionalism' is related to thinking about the facets of one's role rather than a more proletarian view of teaching potentially espoused in prescribed educational practices (Furlong, 1999). The danger with thought is that it challenges – and not only those doing the thinking! It challenges the very nature of prescription in education (Kompf *et al.*, 1996; Parker, 1997), but it requires high levels of professional knowledge coupled with self-esteem and self-confidence, paradoxically lacking in many early years, female, practitioners, as was hinted earlier. Female practitioners are often convinced that what is 'inside' them is not valid, 'only personal' (Dadds, 1997, p. 31) and equated with emotional responses. They frequently perceive themselves as powerless against (often male) 'authority' (Noddings, 1994). Partly because of insecurity about professional status – after all, everyone has been a young child and therefore knows about young children! – many practitioners have learned to feel that others' visions and experiences are somehow better than their own, mindful responses. They distrust and underestimate their own insights, thus devaluing what Claxton (1999) has called their own 'intuitions' which, in professional practice, he equates with expertise, implicit learning, judgement, sensitivity, creativity/problem-solving and rumination (p. 40), skills which a partnership with researchers appeared to help practitioners to develop.

Encouraging male perspectives in early years settings is perceived as desirable by many in society. This issue is too great to be included here, but a small point worth making is that, ironically, the only male early years teacher (out of ten practitioners in a longitudinal study – Moyles and Adams, 2001) left after only 5 weeks because he gained a place on a management promotion course (National Professional Qualification for Headteachers).

In a partnership of mutual trust and respect, practitioners on one particular project (see Moyles and Adams, 2000) shifted from an initial awe of academic and professional knowledge to a situation in which they were able to surface, analyse and evaluate their own professional views in a 'collaborative culture' (Hargreaves, 1995):

> You don't necessarily like to identify it but you're really not happy with what you're doing and once we'd got past the fact that there are elements none of us were happy with, that gave us a feeling that there's an empathy between us, everyone . . . we're all searching for something . . .
>
> At the beginning of the project I thought 'I'm far too structured. I interfere far too much in what children are doing'. But I didn't know if that was the best way to get the learning to move forward . . . now . . . I'm not here to set the things up and hope that learning happens . . . it is actually down to you to make it happen.
>
> When one begins to analyse them, some of the Desirable Outcomes are as woolly as our learning objectives on our planning sheets [referring to SCAA/QCA 1996]
>
> . . . we have evolved, shared and vocalised a pedagogy that represents how we seek to challenge young learners . . . at an appropriate level and pace.

If we want professionals, then professional understanding itself needs to be nurtured, to be allowed time to develop and opportunity to be applied. Educational improvement depends upon practitioners feeling that they *want* to make a difference; upon them feeling empowered and professional. Performance-related pay, for example, has to be anathema for those who teach young children, for how can educational progress in children be separated from development, care and family circumstances, other than at simplistic levels? As one practitioner (passionately) remarked:

> League tables implying that any move forward – or not – is entirely due to what the school or educational setting has 'put in' rather than it being a 3-way process – child/school/home – well, it's just nonsense!

For practice to reach professional status, both head and heart need to meet at the interface of reflection. It is necessary to think about the components of the role of the 'new professionalism' (Furlong, 1999) in order to resolve its many issues. Without this, then my experience is that the cycle of supposed 'learning' for practitioners about their own practice is one of practice driving practice, itself driven by more prescribed practice such as, for example, that handed down in the National Literacy and Numeracy Strategies (which themselves have impinged heavily upon the new Foundation Stage Guidance – DfEE/QCA, 2000). Whatever the political rhetoric, a diet of evidence-based practice is likely only to inform practice and *not* underlying professionalism.

As has been shown, practitioners have revealed themselves capable of significant thought on their own practice once provided with a context in which this is made acceptable, desirable, necessary and inspiring. As professionals, these practitioners have been willing to engage in a number of important processes which surface their passions, help to resolve some of the paradoxes they face and show them to be highly professional. In the StEPs project (Moyles and Adams, 2001) these processes were revealed as follows:

- deconstruction of practice and thinking, whatever the emotional costs to themselves;
- openness to challenge, conflict and paradox, however painful this may have been, for example, in the case of the 'black hole';
- analysis of practice and, more importantly, their views on their own and other's practices and intentions;
- reconstruction of practice and theory, following a period of affirming the validity of their own knowledge, beliefs and values and the support available from other sources;
- development of thinking and articulation, leading to greater justification of practice and values.

Exploring their passions gave 'voice' to practitioners – 'Like a dried-out sponge put in fresh water, I was excited about learning for myself'. Exploring professionalism gave credence to their beliefs and values:

If you say to someone [e.g. a colleague] 'Look – children learn like this and this is the way they need to learn', then they've got much less chance of coming back at you and saying 'No, I want you to do worksheets'.

Other evidence of finding one's voice lies within what practitioners report in interviews and in writing about the process:

I struggled with my inability to articulate, to argue my corner with more than platitudes and correspondingly felt a deep loss of self-confidence and self-esteem. I was not the practitioner I thought I was . . .

This [analysing practice] has been a complete challenge to everything I have ever thought about to do with early years . . . it's made me stop and think and question everything I do . . . but it's kind of liberating!

In watching video of her own practice, one practitioner faced head-on the difficulties of resolving one's own feelings with the value of self-analysis:

> I found the video horrifying, but it was probably useful at the same time. I think people ought to be videoed . . . everybody baulks at the idea of being assessed or having someone watch and appraise them and yet the video, where you do the appraising yourself, is very valid as an alarming way of perhaps seeing what you don't want to see or do want to see!

There was other significant change in practitioners' views about the products of the professional, research-based partnership:

> I've got more confidence to tackle the head, and the parents; more confidence in myself – self-belief and what I believe in.

> I've got more confident intervening in children's play and doing it without feeling guilty . . . I can justify my actions.

> I've got more knowledge. I've changed practice in the nursery . . . I think [I've] grown. I didn't think I knew anything before.

> It's certainly been challenging in terms of thinking! I mean you come out and your head is buzzing and you feel as if it's ten times the size . . . Research certainly isn't easy. In fact, you feel more tired after a [research] session than at school, to be quite honest.

> . . . I feel that the group has already helped me a lot, to reflect . . . because I think we all probably started thinking we were practising well in play, but we've had to question ourselves and how we approach it and what we assume, what we don't assume, and I think I have to keep on that reflecting, and to keep this communication, this bouncing of ideas and I think now I feel prepared to be torn apart!

There were a number of fears practitioners had to overcome, particularly in terms of working with colleagues who, for example, perceived professional vocabulary such as 'pedagogy' to be threatening, highbrow or unduly 'academic'.

> At first, I wanted to avoid the 'pedabogey of academia' but now I realise its importance in speaking and acting professionally.

It takes strength as an early years practitioner to stand up to senior colleagues who signal anti-theoretical stances. The evidence that practitioners are able to do so from engagement in the research partnership lies within analysis of their own written and spoken words. From what could be perceived as 'lay' language – that of describing everything in emotive (and sometimes emotional) terms, early years practitioners were able to report at a highly professional and more sophisticated level:

> I now KNOW our principles [of play] don't sit easily alongside a prescribed curriculum. How can we carry on with what is so centrally important to us [and young children] when we are pressured into making sure children attain at certain arbitrary levels . . . themselves inappropriate to children's current developmental needs?

The research partnerships lasted over a period of at least one academic year and up to three years in the case of one project. The critical factor – and the key to changing levels of professionalism – appears to have been the opportunities presented by being part of funded research (and, therefore, freed occasionally from teaching responsibilities) to 'wallow' in the issues as perceived by the practitioners and to engage in supported challenge leading to change. A framework of partnership and trust between the researchers and the researched was critical, providing a context in which the challenge shifted from researchers challenging practitioners to the researchers themselves eventually being challenged by the practitioners. One teacher-practitioner felt passionate, comfortable and secure enough to write in the two-way notes kept as part of a project on interactive teaching:

> I was a bit concerned about your write-up of my reflective dialogue, Janet, where it said in italics 'Researcher note: I find that JL does not stick to interactive teaching when she watches the video but focuses on what individual children are doing'. This surely shows that what I feel about my quality of teaching is reflected in the responses I see in the children? This is not seen in the Literacy Hour videos where teaching techniques are demonstrated but not the reactions or the quality of learning the children receive.

This ability to reflect on and evaluate practice, prescription and one's own thoughts about it must be the key to professionalism in the early years – and arguably elsewhere in the education system. However, change takes time while, paradoxically, practice (and politics) is grounded in an immediacy of response and reaction which is unsympathetic to achieving depth in professional thinking and vision, and 'magic' in teaching and learning.

So what did practitioners achieve within the various research partnerships? Analysis of qualitative data shows practitioners exhibiting significant ability to

- clarify their passions;
- value their own appropriate instincts and intuitions;
- analyse and interpret practice;
- surface and understand their automatic responses to children/teaching;
- have confidence in their own convictions by being able to justify appropriate practices;
- learn that other forms of passion (e.g. anger and outrage) are acceptable when channelled towards issues about which they can justify their professional views;
- understand and evaluate their own responses to situations;
- extend the practice > informing > practice cycle to include theoretical justifications and considerations;
- critique their own thinking about practice in a reasoned way;
- engage in extended dialogue and critical discourse;
- re-educate themselves through the process of reflection and continue to want to learn more about theory and practice relationships in the early years.

They also learned to acknowledge and celebrate the specialness of early years practice rather than apologising for it.

Drawing it all together

The point has come to question the 'Ps' of early years practice that have been presented.

Q Do we want a passionate early years workforce?

A Yes, it is difficult to operate with young children without accounting for feelings but analysing practice and thoughts is clearly a potent combination of passion linked with reason. As E. M. Forster (1879–1970) once wrote 'Only connect the prose and the passion and both will be exalted'.

Q Can research really contribute in the ways suggested to advanced professionalism?

A In itself this appears to me to be a powerful way of providing practitioners with the means to extend and develop their own practices and cope with the many paradoxes with which early years – and education in general – is currently imbued. We must assert the legitimacy of early years as an academic discipline in its own right rather than as the 'also ran' of the education system. To do this, we need a professional body of practitioners who can speak with authority on the special nature of the education and care of young children and their own roles in those processes.

Q Should we urge professionalism?

A Going through the motions of delivering a curriculum to young children can take no account of the variation between the delivered and the received curriculum. This reminds the writer of the story of the young child who flew home from school informing his parents, 'I can write, I can write'. When they asked him what he had written, he declared 'Well, I don't know. I haven't learned to read yet!' Seeing the world from the point of view of the child is vital to early years professional practices, but young children's logic is almost always different from that of adults and thus 'tuning into children' is a very critical process in which practitioners must engage (Costello, 2000).

This process is not something which will happen overnight. Change takes time, particularly, in a climate where balancing your own views against those of political prescription requires strength of mind and in-depth knowledge of such a complex area as young children and their education. Early years practitioners possess a specialised body of legitimate knowledge for which they frequently become apologetic – 'I'm only a nursery nurse/teacher'. This knowledge may be about small children but it enables children to cope with, progress, and enjoy their early steps into the education and schooling system outside the home.

The sixth-century Chinese philosopher Lao-tzu (the founder of Taoism) once wrote: 'The journey of a thousand miles begins with a single step'. Those who work with young children take many 'single steps' every day – both with children and in advancing their own knowledge and expertise. This potentially gives them very unique insights into the way young children perceive and conceive of the world, but the very nature of this 'closeness' also brings with it an emotional and affective dimension which is not replicated elsewhere in the education system. Extended partnership between practitioners and researchers can make each step more productive and pleasurable, benefiting children and future society.

Passion for young children is part of the culture of practitioners. Passion must be allowed, both as a panacea for coping with challenging paradoxes and also for inspiring professionalism in those who work and play with the youngest members of our society.

Note

1   See, in particular, Moyles (1989, 1991), Moyles and Suschitzky (1995, 1997a,b, 1998), Moyles *et al.* (1998), Moyles and Adams (2000), Adams *et al.* (2000), and Moyles and Adams (2001).

References

Abbott, L. and Pugh, G. (eds) (1998) *Training Issues in the Early Years* (Buckingham, Open University Press).

Adams, S., Medland, P. and Moyles, J. (with Sian Adams) (2000) Supporting play-based teaching through collaborative practice-based research, *Support for Learning*, 15(4), pp. 159–164.

Anning, A. (2000) New Deals and Old Dilemmas: Lone Parents of Young Children Balancing Work and Parenthood. Paper presented at BERA Conference, Cardiff, September.

Anning, A. and Edwards, A. (1999) *Promoting Children's Learning from Birth to Five: developing the new early years professional* (Buckingham/Philadelphia, Open University Press).

Claxton, G. (1999) The anatomy of intuition, in: T. Atkinson and G. Claxton (eds) *The Intuitive Practitioner: on the value of not always knowing what one is doing* (Buckingham, Open University Press).

Costello, P. (2000) *Thinking Skills and Early Childhood Education* (London, David Fulton).

Dadds, M. (1997) Continuing professional development: nurturing the expert within, *British Journal of In-service Education*, 23 (1), pp. 31–38.

Dahlberg, G., Moss, P. and Pence, A. (1999) *Beyond Quality in Early Childhood Education and Care: postmodern perspectives* (London, Falmer Press).

Department for Education and Employment (DfEE) (1998) *Teachers: meeting the challenge of change* (Cm 4164) (London, Stationery Office).

Drury, R., Miller, L. and Campbell, R. (2000) *Looking at Early Years Education and Care* (London, David Fulton).

Edgington, M. (1998) *The Nursery Teacher in Action: teaching 3, 4 and 5 year olds* (London, Paul Chapman).

Edwards, C., Gandini, L. and Forman, G. (1998) *The Hundred Languages of Children: the Reggio Emilia approach to early childhood education*, 2nd edition (New Jersey, Ablex Publishing).

Eraut, M. (1994) *Developing Professional Knowledge and Competence* (London, Falmer Press).

Farrell, A. (1998) Gendered settings and human rights in early childhood, in: N. Yelland (ed.) *Gender in Early Childhood* (London, Routledge).

Farson, R. (1996) *Management of the Absurd: paradoxes in leadership* (New York, Simon and Schuster).

Fisher, J. (1996) *Starting from the Child* (Buckingham, Open University Press).

Forster, E. M. (1910) *Howards End* (Richmond, Hogarth Press).

Freire, P. (1999) *Pedagogy of the Heart* (New York, Continuum Publishing).

Furlong, J. (1999) Intuition and the crisis in teacher professionalism, in: T. Atkinson and G. Claxton (eds) *The Intuitive Practitioner: on the value of not always knowing what one is doing* (Buckingham, Open University Press).

Galton, M., Hargreaves, L., Comber, C. and Wall, D. (1999) *Inside the Primary Classroom: 20 years on* (London, Routledge).

Gardner, H. (1993) *The Unschooled Mind: how children learn and how schools should teach* (London, Fontana).

Goleman, D. (1996) *Emotional Intelligence. Why it can matter more than IQ* (London, Bloomsbury).

Hargreaves, A. (1995) Renewal in an age of paradox, *Educational Leadership*, 52 (7), pp. 1–9.

Holland, P. (1992) *What is a Child? Popular images of childhood* (London, Virago Press).

Hughes, M., Wikeley, F. and Nash, T. (1994) *Parents and their Children's Schools* (Oxford, Blackwell).

Hurst, V. and Joseph, J. (1998) *Supporting Early Learning: the way forward* (Buckingham, Open University Press).

Katz, L. (1995) *Talks with Teachers of Young Children* (New Jersey: Ablex Publishing Corporation).

Kompf, M., Bond, W. R., Dworet, D. and Boak, R. T. (1996) *Changing Research and Practice: teachers' professionalism, identities and knowledge* (London/Washington, Falmer Press).

Kotulak, R. (1996) *Inside the Brain: revolutionary discoveries of how the mind works* (Kansas City, MO, Andrews and McMeel).

Martinez, L. (1996) Gender equity policies and early childhood education, in: N. Yelland (ed.) *Gender in Early Childhood* (London, Routledge).

McCulloch, G., Helsby, G. and Knight, P. (2000) *The Politics of Professionalism: teachers and the curriculum* (London/New York, Continuum).

Monkhouse, B. (1999) *Just Say a Few Words*, 2nd edition (Harpenden, Lennard Publishing).

Moyles, J. (1989) *Just Playing? The role and status of play in early education* (Milton Keynes, Open University Press).

Moyles, J. (1991) *Play as a Learning Process in Your Classroom* (London, Cassell).

Moyles, J. (2001) *Playful Children: inspired teaching* (Buckingham, Open University Press).

Moyles, J. and Adams, S. (2000) A tale of the unexpected: practitioners' expectations and children's play, *Journal of In-service Education*, 26 (2), pp. 349–369.

Moyles, J. and Adams, S. (with others) (2001) *StEPs: A framework for playful teaching in the early years* (Buckingham, Open University Press).

Moyles, J. and Liu Hua (1998) Kindergarten education in China: reflections on a qualitative comparison of management processes and perceptions, *Compare*, 28 (2), pp. 155–170.

Moyles, J. and Suschitzky, W. (1995) A matter of difference: nursery teachers and nursery nurses working together, *Education 3–13*, 23 (3), pp. 41–46.

Moyles, J. and Suschitzky, W. (1997a) *Jills of All Trades . . .? Classroom assistants in KS1 classes* (ATL and University of Leicester).

Moyles, J. and Suschitzky, W. (1997b) *The Buck Stops Here . . .! Nursery teachers and nursery nurses working together* (Esmée Fairbairn Charitable Trust/University of Leicester).

Moyles, J. and Suschitzky, W. (1998) Painting the cabbages red? Training for support staff in early years classrooms, in: L. Abbott and G. Pugh (eds) *Training Issues in the Early Years* (Buckingham, Open University Press).

Moyles, J., Suschitzky, W. and Chapman, L. (1998) *Teaching Fledglings to Fly: mentoring in the primary school* (London, The Association of Teachers and Lecturers/University of Leicester).

Nias, J. (1989) *Primary Teachers' Talking* (London, Routledge).

Noddings, N. (1994) An ethic of caring and its implication for instructional arrangements, in: L. Stone (ed.) *The Education Feminism Reader* (New York/ London, Routledge).

Parker, S. (1997) *Reflective Teaching in the Postmodern World: a manifesto for education in post-modernity* (Philadelphia, Open University Press).

Pollard, A. and Filer, A. (1999) *Social World of Pupil Career: strategic biographies through primary school* (London, Cassell).

Pollard, A. and Thiessen, D. (1996) *Children and their Curriculum: the perspectives of primary and elementary school children* (Lewes, Falmer Press).

Qualifications and Curriculum Authority (QCA) (formerly Schools Curriculum and Assessment Authority) (1996) *Desirable Outcomes for Children's Learning* (London, Stationery Office).

Qualifications and Curriculum Authority (1999) *Early Learning Goals* (London, DfEE).

Qualifications and Curriculum Authority (2000) *Curriculum Guidance for the Foundation Stage*1 (London, DfEE).

Saltzberger-Wittenberg, I., Gianna, H. and Osborne, E. (1983) *The Emotional Experience of Learning and Teaching* (New York, Routledge and Kegan Paul).

Smith, A. and Langston, A. (1999) *Managing Staff in Early Years Settings* (London, Routledge).

Steinberg, S. and Kincheloe, J. (1998) *Students as Researchers – Creating Classrooms that Matter* (London, Falmer Press).

Stone, L. (ed.) (1994) *The Education Feminism Reader* (New York/London, Routledge).

Sugrue, C. (1997) *Complexities of Teaching: child-centred perspectives* (London, Falmer Press).

Woods, P. (1996) *Researching the Art of Teaching* (London, Routledge).

Woods, P. and Jeffrey, B. (1996) *Teachable Moments: the art of teaching in primary schools* (Buckingham, Open University Press).

Yelland, N. (ed.) (1998) *Gender in Early Childhood* (London/New York, Routledge).

CHAPTER 2

SCAFFOLDING LEARNING THROUGH MEANINGFUL TASKS AND ADULT INTERACTION

Penny Coltman, Dinara Petyaeva and
Julia Anghileri

Background

With the current focus on teaching and learning number skills, aspects of mathematics relating to shape and space have recently received rather less attention. Anghileri and Baron (1999) established that children's self-directed play with wooden building blocks provides valuable opportunities for extending learning related to 3D shapes, including such aspects as the characterisation of properties, the awareness of relationships between 2D representations and 3D structures and the development of intuitive awareness of aspects of symmetry, measure, stability and balance. Anghileri and Baron (1999) carried out their observations on children engaging in free play with Poleidoblocs and on tasks completed without adult intervention. This study investigates the role of adult interaction in improving the effectiveness of such learning.

Poleidoblocs are brightly coloured wooden blocks in a range of geometric shapes, widely available in primary school classrooms. The full set consists of fifty-four blocks in six basic 3D shapes (cube, cuboid, cylinder, triangular prism, cone and square based pyramid) which are mathematically interrelated in their size. They were devised and described as 'materials of play' by Dr Margaret Lowenfeld (Lowenfeld and Anderson, 1963) who used them to study aspects of children's non-verbal communications. In the classroom, Poleidoblocs are traditionally used for both free play, and as exemplar materials to support the teaching of early aspects of 3D geometry. They can provide tactile and visual opportunities for children to develop a dynamic awareness of shapes, including topological relationships (Piaget and Inhelder, 1956), and 'to form schemas on the basis of feature analysis of visual forms' (Clements *et al.*, 1999).

Although spatial ability may not appear to be the most vital component of mathematical ability (Orton, 1992) within a classroom situation 'an appropriate balance is needed of different kinds of activity to cater for the varying degrees of this potential that children may have and to accommodate their learning patterns' (Nickson, 2000, p. 51). It is suggested that many powerful and abstract ideas have their origins in experiences with 3D shapes, such as 'moving small objects, rotating them and rearranging them into patterns' (Davis, 1986).

Research framework

Learning theories

This study is largely framed by the 'cultural–historical theory' of Vygotsky which has provided the basis for a wide range of work by researchers and writers that has resulted in different understandings of the learning process (Elkonin, 1971; Vygotsky, 1978; Hedegaard, 1999; Lompscher, 1999). The guiding principle for this research is taken as a 'cultural–historical approach' (Hedegaard, 1999) in which learning is characterised as a process which results from an interaction between the individual, and both social and cultural conditions. Lompscher (1999) discusses the importance of considering 'the widespread efforts of designing new conditions and forms of teaching and learning based on ideas of learners as subjects co-operating with others, actively acting upon learning objects and each other, regulating and forming their activity under guidance and becoming more and more independent and self-responsible in the process' (p. 143). Both the adult interactions and the design of playful contexts for the activities will be considered as key considerations in this study for enhancing the learning process.

Spatial ability

In founding this study in children's learning about shapes it is informed by van Heile's (1986) theory of children's geometric concept development in which different stages are characterised, from an initial Gestalt-like visual understanding through increasingly sophisticated levels of description, analysis, abstraction and proof. Although level 1 involves children's ability to recognise shapes as wholes without identification of the properties or determining characteristics, Clements *et al.* (1999), working with children from 3 to 6 years of age, found that children of this age were generally operating at the 'pre-representational' van Heile level (0) with experience and language limiting their ability to refine or demonstrate understandings related to geometric shapes.

Adult interaction

The notion of social interaction as a key to learning is seen in the social-constructivist theory described by Pollard and Tann (1997) as a form of constructivism 'which strongly suggests the importance for learning of the social context and of interaction with others' (p. 124). Within this paradigm, the example is used from Rowland (1987) who describes a model in which 'a reflective agent scaffolds children's understanding across their zones of proximal development'. Activity is followed by support and instruction and a cycle is established which takes the learning forward beyond the level which the child would have reached alone. Eventually a point is reached at which the child has constructed an understanding with support.

In any activity with children the social environment, and particularly adult involvement, can increase the effectiveness of the learning process (Donaldson, 1978; Vygotsky, 1978; Wood, 1986; Edwards and Knight, 1994; Bruner, 1996; Anning and Edwards, 1999). The role of the adult can be taken at its most fundamental level: the management of the learning environment, the presentation of materials, the design of a task and its placement within a context. This is then extended to a subsequent level of adult involvement, that of providing supportive interaction during the learning process itself, sometimes referred to as *scaffolding*

(Wood *et al.*, 1976; Pollard and Tann, 1997). Although the evidence of scaffolding in the classroom is inconclusive according to some studies in mathematics (Bliss *et al.*, 1996), others find it useful to characterise classroom activities. Tanner and Jones (2000) use the terms 'dynamic scaffolders' to describe teaching styles and showed this approach was effective in 'accelerating the development of active metacognitive skills' (p. 27).

When children play freely with materials they may serendipitously solve a particular problem without being aware of the relationship between their actions and the solution. Hence they would be unable to transfer their method to new situations or to another task. It could be said that there is no evidence of metacognition (Flavell, 1976). Adult interaction has a benefit in promoting the child's awareness of the significance of the acts which were carried out in successfully completing a task. The child is aware not only of the found solution, but of the processes which led to its discovery. Gallimore and Tharp (1990) describe a process in which children become self-regulating, and thus independent of adult help, through the provision of feedback.

In this study, a significant aspect of the role of the adult will be the design of checking or feedback procedures within the task, which encouraged children to reflect on their success in meeting goals.

Playful context

Among the social and cultural conditions for consideration are the activities to be engaged in and the ways in which they are presented. Vygotsky highlighted the role of play within the learning process of young children when he wrote that 'the child moves forward essentially through play activity' (1978, p. 103). This view, which has subsequently been supported by the findings of many researchers and educationalists working within a number of theoretical perspectives (Edwards and Knight, 1994; Moyles, 1994; Bruner, 1996; Anning and Edwards, 1999), is taken as another key consideration in this study.

Leontiev (1981) used the term 'leading activity' to describe an activity with which the child was especially eager to engage. This activity 'contributes in a decisive way to the development of the child by promoting new actions and psychological processes that anticipate a new episode of development' (p. 485). Chaiklin (1999), working within the framework of cultural–historical theory, asserts that 'the theoretical assumption is that development occurs when teaching is formulated in relation to the pupil's leading activity'. Following the work of Elkonin (1971), van Oers (1999), who worked with children from 4 to 8 years of age, assumed that within the context of a school setting, play was a leading activity and hence learning would be most effective when it occurred through play. Indeed he considers that 'play activity is fundamental for young children as a context for learning and development' (p. 272).

Closely linked to an acknowledgement of this fundamental role of play is the understanding that children should perceive a motivational component that corresponds to their own needs and facilitates their own comprehension. This is often described as a requirement for a meaningful context within which the child sees both purpose and relevance (Donaldson, 1978).

Zone of proximal development

In this study, it is acknowledged that there are limits to the learning which may be achieved even with adult support. At any particular stage of development some tasks will require individual children to use intellectual processes which are beyond their Zone of Proximal Development or ZPD (Vygotsky, 1978; Rowland, 1987; Tharp and Gallimore, 1998). When working within the ZPD the amount of support needed by a child may vary. Within his model of scaffolding, Bruner proposes a form of intervention in which the adult and child establish a 'co-construction' of meanings through a system of graded help (Bruner, 1990). Within this chapter, we attempt to establish one approach to this grading of the level of support given.

Aims of the study

The main aim of this research has been to study the effect on children's learning of different provisions of adult support for children undertaking problem-solving tasks and the effectiveness of embedding tasks in playful contexts. The hypothesis was that using wooden blocks with appropriate adult interaction would increase the effectiveness of the learning process and lead to an enhanced development of secure and transferable concepts related to shape and space.

Methodology

Materials

A series of problem-solving tasks were designed using selected subsets from a set of 3D wooden shapes, Poleidoblocs. These materials were used as they are typically available in infant classrooms. Additionally, a range of simple props was used including, for example, toy animals and cardboard models which helped to provide playful (and thus meaningful) contexts to the tasks.

Sample

The project involved children aged 4–6 years from two schools ($n = 90$), in the spring and summer terms of their reception year and was developed in three phases – a free play phase, a pilot phase, and an experimental phase. The pilot phase involved children ($n = 30$) from the reception class of one primary school and the experimental phase involved children ($n = 60$) comprising two complete reception classes from a second primary school. In all phases, children were observed individually working on specific tasks. Each session was 10–20 minutes in duration and field notes were taken. Some children were also videotaped.

Free play: the initial phase

All of the ninety children taking part in the research were given the opportunity to become familiar with the Poleidoblocs through periods of individual free play. Observations of this play gave an additional opportunity to characterise the types of activity which children spontaneously initiated (see Anghileri and Baron, 1999) and helped to reduce the possibility of poor responses which could be attributable to working with unfamiliar materials.

Pilot phase

During the pilot phase, a number of practical activities were tested and the responses of children ($n = 30$) were analysed to inform the design of the tasks to be used in the experimental phase. Six different tasks were selected for the main experiment relating to different aspects of learning about shapes. Throughout the experimental phase of the research the tasks related to the following aspects of shape and space:

- matching 2D outlines to the faces of 3D blocks;
- recognising and using alternative orientations of 3D shapes;
- developing an awareness of aspects of balance;
- characterising and classifying 3D shapes;
- recognising equivalence in shape and size;
- constructing a reflective image of a given pattern (using reflective symmetry).

The model of graded support involved the design of contexts for the tasks that would be meaningful for the children and additional interactions which provided cues and prompts of an increasingly explicit nature. These interactions consisted of four levels as listed here.

- *Initial level – design of meaningful task*: changes were made from an abstract/ unembedded mathematical task to a contextualised task which required the same solution.
- *Second level – reflective observations*: the researcher drew attention to the shape of particular blocks in relation to the task, encouraging the child to handle the blocks, examining the shapes of different faces both visually and manually.
- *Third level – intermediate modelling*: the researcher demonstrated the actions necessary to solve the task, using an equivalent but different set of blocks.
- *Fourth level – direct demonstration*: the researcher showed the child how to complete the task.

Experimental phases

Children ($n = 60$) were first given abstract/unembedded tasks presented in a material form. The purpose of the pre-test was to select children who were as yet unable to complete one or more of the tasks. Inability to complete tasks showed that the relevant understanding was not, at this stage, within the capability of the child (the zone of actual development), but could be within the zone of proximal development. These children were thus selected as subjects for the study which focused on the forming of this understanding, working within the zone of proximal development, and proceeded to a 'teaching phase'.

After the pre-test, selected children ($n = 54$) were divided into three groups, each of them including children who had not performed the same two tasks from the six offered at the pre-test (four of the children had completed all but one task). Each of these three groups was then further divided into control and experimental groups, taking into account the gender, age, teacher and baseline assessment scores of the children, to maximise equivalence between the groups. Thus each of the three groups completed a 'teaching phase' for two different aspects of understanding shape and space (Table 2.1).

The experimental procedure was designed to encompass both motivational and cognitive aspects when working within a zone of proximal development. A source of motivation was provided in the use of embedded tasks with contexts meaningful to young children; for example, in order to help 'a prince rescue the princess' children were asked to build a tower from certain blocks using the elements of

Table 2.1 Phases of the experimental programme

Pre-test (unembedded task)
Children who did not successfully complete the pre-test task proceed

---

Teaching phase

Experimental group (*n* = 27)	Control group (*n* = 27)
First Embedded Task A	First Embedded Task A
Success rate recorded	Success rate recorded
Structured adult interaction	No structured adult interaction
until the task is successfully completed	
3 days	3 days
Second Reinforcement Embedded Task B	Second Reinforcement Embedded Task B
Success rate recorded	Success rate recorded
Structured adult interaction until the	No structured adult interaction
task successfully completed	
3 days	3 days

Post-test (unembedded task)

---

balance. The cognitive aspect was supported by the provision of additional graded levels of adult help, and also by the presentation of both the task and the adult help in a material form so that there was hands-on activity. In addition, in order to provide for self-regulation leading to the development of secure and transferable concepts (i.e. a metacognitive level of learning) an element of self-correction with resultant feedback was incorporated into the design of each task. For example, a task requiring 3D blocks to be matched to 2D faces was set in the context of a 'lorry' with recessed frames that the blocks fitted into, remaining in view.

Results

Pre-test

The six unembedded tasks used in the pre-test were considered as being at an appropriate level of challenge and suitable for support as between a third and a half of the reception aged children tested were unable to complete each one of the tasks.

Teaching phase

In the teaching phase, each child dealt with two aspects of shape and space for which they had been unsuccessful in the pre-test. Having been unable to complete the abstract task, the children in both control and experimental groups were presented with the same first embedded task (Task A), that is, with a context that was meaningful to the children. In both groups the children first tried to solve the tasks on their own with no adult intervention. Children in the experimental group then had graded levels of adult support while the control group had no further intervention. After three days the children in each group were presented with a further/reinforcement embedded task (Task B). After a further three days the post-test unembedded task was given. At each stage success rates were noted (Table 2.2).

In every task the experimental group were more successful in the post-test than the control group. The greatest difference between the groups appears in tasks

Table 2.2 Results for different tasks

Tasks	Groups	Pre-test (%)	Embedded task A (%)	Embedded task B (%)	Post-test (%)
Matching 2D outlines to the faces of 3D blocks	Control	0	78	67	44
	Experimental	0	67	55	100
Recognising and using alternative orientations of 3D shapes	Control	0	11	22	22
	Experimental	0	22	78	89
Developing an awareness of aspects of balance	Control	0	44	22	11
	Experimental	0	55	67	100
Characterising and classifying 3D shapes	Control	0	22	44	0
	Experimental	0	44	89	67
Recognising equivalence in shape and size	Control	0	89	55	89
	Experimental	0	89	89	100
Constructing a reflective image of a given pattern	Control	0	33	78	33
	Experimental	0	33	89	89

related to developing an awareness of aspects of balance, the least in tasks related to the recognition of the equivalence in shape and size. Due to the embedded nature of the first teaching Task A, some of the children from both the control and the experimental group could execute activities which they had not been able to do in the pre-test. In the pre-test, for example, children were asked to balance a cuboid on three cones. The children almost invariably were unable to do this as they repeatedly arranged the cones in a linear fashion. The embedded task asked the children to build a rocket from a number of blocks including three cones. The context powerfully suggested a vertical structure and the only way this could be produced incorporating the cones was to group them together. This automatically resulted in a tripod on which another block could be placed. Consequently, the results of the control and experimental groups showed no significant difference. In the control group 46.3 per cent of the children could find a solution and in the experimental group 51.8 per cent ($p > 0.05$).

After engaging in a task, the children in the experimental group were encouraged to check their findings, reinforcing the significance of their solution and the children who could not execute the task received graded help as previously described. An overwhelming majority of children (72 per cent) managed to find a method of solution on receiving the third level of help. The second level of help appeared sufficient in 28 per cent of cases. No-one in fact required the fourth level.

In the control group no adult interaction was offered to the children. The design of the tasks, however, encouraged children to check the effectiveness of their found solutions. For example, when children carried out a task which required them to make a model bridge taller by re-orientating the blocks supporting it, a cardboard bus was either able or unable to pass beneath it.

Three days after the presentation of these first embedded tasks the children in both the control and experimental groups were presented with second, reinforcement

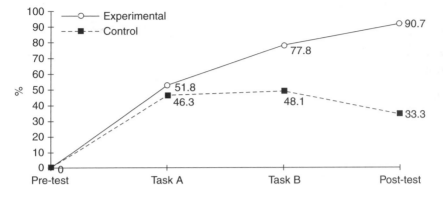

Figure 2.1 Percentages of children successfully completing tasks

tasks (Task B) requiring the same kinds of activity but within a different meaningful context. A second task which required children to re-orient blocks to make a tower taller, for example, involved a 'mouse' and a cardboard 'Christmas Tree'. The mouse was unable to reach the top of the tree to place a sequin star in position. The children 'helped' the mouse by changing the orientation of a triangular prism, standing it on one of the triangular faces to reach the greater height. When the children were asked in the post-test to make a tower taller by re-orienting the blocks they were able to relate back to the story context.

When the results are combined for all tasks, Figure 2.1 shows that success in the post-test in the experimental group is over 90 per cent while the control group remain considerably lower at 33 per cent.

In the control group there was no significant improvement in the results after the first intervention. On the first presentation of an embedded task (Task A) 46.3 per cent obtained a correct solution and for the reinforcement tasks (Task B) 48.1 per cent ($p > 0.05$). Thus, simply increasing the number of tasks appears not to be very effective in promoting learning.

Before the provision of any adult support in Task B, 77.8 per cent of children in the experimental group correctly found the solutions. Such a sharp increase (26 per cent) can be explained by the adult support supplied in completing Task A which enabled the children to acquire a method of action and use it in approaching another, similar problem (Task B). The difference in success between the experimental and control groups in completing Task B was 29.7 per cent ($p < 0.05$). The 22.2 per cent of children in the experimental group who were unable to complete Task B, again received adult support as described earlier, to enable them to do so successfully.

Discussion

In the control group the introduction of a meaningful context at the beginning of the teaching process led to a substantial improvement in the results compared to those of the pre-test (Table 2.2). Reinforcement through an additional task (Task B) did not add anything new to the learning situation as the results showed no significant improvement. In the post-test the success rate of children, working again without the support of a meaningful context, decreased. Following Hughes

(1986) we believe that an increase in the number of concrete tasks alone does not advance the child to new stages of learning (levels of knowledge). In our case the children in the control group, whilst improving their solution of concrete tasks, did not realise the principle of their solution and could not transfer it to another situation.

In the experimental group the children, with the support of an adult, solved the teaching tasks and carried out a self-correction process, with resultant feedback, which raised an appreciation of the actions carried out in order to achieve the successful solution. This, in turn, led to an enhanced ability to transfer the acquired activity to new circumstances (indicating learning at a metacognitive level) and thus to further improvement in the performance of post-test tasks. Moreover, children became self-regulatory (Gallimore and Tharp, 1990) because in many cases of post-tests they carried out their own checking procedures. A particularly striking example of this was seen in a group of children who had carried out a pair of tasks designed to develop an understanding of the characteristics of cylinders. In Task A the children had been shown two cylinders of different proportions and a cuboid of similar size. These blocks were presented in a basket which was introduced as the nest of the 'cylinder bird'. The task for the children was to identify the 'baby' which did not belong to the 'cylinder bird'. It was explained to the children that cylinder bird babies love to roll. Exploring this idea enabled the children to identify the cuboid as the 'intruder'. In Task B the same context was used but this time the 'nest' contained two cylinders and a cone. The additional information given was that cylinder birds play in the sand jumping on their feet and then their heads always making an identical round print in the sand. Investigating this information enabled the children to identify the cone as the intruder. The post-test presented a selection of blocks with children asked to identify the cylinders. Most of the children in the experimental group related this task to that of the cylinder bird babies, and used the concepts of rolling and identical round end-faces as support for checking their solutions.

Although the assumption for this study was that the children were operating at the pre-representational van Heile level (0), the findings of this research suggest that this is not uniform across all the shapes involved. Evidence suggests that their understanding of the cuboid and its properties, for example, was more secure than that of the triangular prism. Their confidence in working with cuboids and their facility in matching their faces to 2D shapes showed awareness of the images that different orientations would give. For the triangular prism, on the other hand, most of the children were unsuccessful at working with different orientations, showing their difficulty in perceiving the shape other than in its holistic sense as a 'roof'.

Conclusions

The results of the experiment support our hypothesis that the provision of graded levels of adult support (scaffolding) substantially improves the effectiveness of learning related to aspects of shape and space. With appreciation of the importance of free play with wooden blocks, there is an element of insufficiency in facilitating the acquisition of early geometrical concepts. Children alone cannot reliably 'discover' all the important and necessary knowledge and methods of action solely through manipulating the blocks. They learn these more effectively through carefully structured joint activity with 'experienced others'.

References

Anghileri, J. and Baron, S. (1999) Playing with the materials of study: Poleidoblocs, *Education 3–13*, 27 (2), pp. 57–64.

Anning, A. and Edwards, A. (1999) *Promoting Children's Learning from Birth to Five: Developing the New Early Years Professional* (Buckingham, Open University Press).

Bliss, J., Askew, M. and Macrae, S. (1996) Effective teaching and learning: scaffolding revisited, *Oxford Review of Education*, 22, pp. 37–61.

Bruner, J. S. (1990) *Acts of Meaning* (Cambridge, MA, Harvard University Press).

Bruner, J. S. (1996) *The Culture of Education* (Cambridge, MA, Harvard University Press).

Chaiklin, S. (1999) Developmental teaching in upper-secondary school, in: M. Hedegaard and J. Lompscher (eds) *Learning Activity and Development* (Oxford, Aarhus University Press).

Clements, D. H., Swaminathan, S., Hannibal, M. and Sarama, S. (1999) Young children's concepts of shape, *Journal for Research in Mathematics Education*, 30 (2), pp. 192–212.

Davis, R. (1986) Conceptual and procedural knowledge in mathematics: a summary analysis, in: J. Heibert (ed.) *Conceptual and Procedural Knowledge: The Case of Mathematics* (Hillsdale, Erlbaum).

Donaldson, M. (1978) *Childrens' Minds* (London, Fontana).

Edwards, A. and Knight, P. (1994) *Effective Early Years Education Teaching Young Children* (Buckingham, Open University Press).

Elkonin, D. B. (1971) Toward the problem of stages in the mental development of the child, *Soviet Psychology*, 10, pp. 538–653.

Flavell, J. H. (1976) Metacognitive aspects of problem solving, in: L. B. Resnick (ed.) *The Nature of Intelligence* (Hillsdale, NJ, Erlbaum).

Gallimore, R. and Tharp, R. (1990) Teaching mind and society: teaching schooling and literate discourse, in: L. Moll (ed.) *Vygotsky and Education* (Cambridge, CUP).

Hedegaard, M. (1999) The influence of societal knowledge traditions on children's thinking and conceptual development, in: M. Hedegaard and J. Lompscher (eds) *Learning Activity and Development* (Oxford, Aarhus University Press).

Hughes, M. (1986) *Children and Number* (Oxford, Basil Blackwell).

Leontiev, A. N. (1981) The problem of activity in psychology, in: J. V. Wertsch (ed.) *The Concept of Activity in Soviet Psychology* (Armonk, NY, Sharpe), pp. 37–71.

Lompscher, J. (1999) Learning activity and its formation: ascending from the abstract to the concrete, in: M. Hedegaard and J. Lompscher (eds) *Learning Activity and Development* (Oxford, Aarhus University Press).

Lowenfeld, M. and Anderson, V. (1963) *Poleidoblocs in the Infant School* (London, E. A. Arnold).

Moyles, J. (1994) *The Excellence of Play* (Buckingham, Open University Press).

Nickson, M. (2000) *Teaching and Learning Mathematics: A Teacher's Guide to Recent Research and its Application* (London, Cassell).

Orton, A. (1992) *Learning Mathematics: Issues, Theory and Practice* (London, Cassell).

Piaget, J. and Inhelder, B. (1956) *The Child's Conception of Space* (London, Routledge and Kegan Paul).

Pollard, A. and Tann (1997) *Reflective Teaching in the Primary School* (London, Cassell).

Rowland, S. (1987) An interpretive model of teaching and learning, in: A. Pollard (ed.) *Children and their Primary Schools* (London, Falmer Press), pp. 128–132.

Tanner, H. and Jones, S. (2000) Scaffolding for success: reflective discourse and the effective teaching of mathematical thinking skills, in: T. Rowland and C. Morgan (eds) *Research in Mathematics Education*, Volume 2 (London, BSRLM).

Tharp, R. and Gallimore, R. (1998) A theory of learning as assisted performance, in: D. Faulkner, K. Littletone and M. Woodhead (eds) *Learning Relationships in the Classroom* (London, Routledge).

van Heile, P. M. (1986) *Structure and Insight* (Orlando, Academic Press).

van Oers, B. (1999) Teaching opportunities in play, in: M. Hedegaard and J. Lompscher (eds) *Learning Activity and Development* (Oxford, Aarhus University Press).

Vygotsky, L. S. (1978) *Mind in Society*, edited by M. Cole, V. John Steiner, S. Scribner and E. Souberman (Cambridge, MA, Harvard University Press).

Wood, D. J. (1986) Aspects of teaching and learning, in: M. Richards and P. Light (eds) *Children of Social Worlds* (Cambridge, Polity Press).

Wood, D. J., Bruner, J. and Ross, G. (1976) The role of tutoring in problem solving, *Journal of Child Psychiatry*, 17, pp. 89–100.

CHAPTER 3

RHETORIC AND REALITY IN DEVELOPING LANGUAGE AND MATHEMATICAL SKILL

Plans and playroom experiences

Christine Stephen and J. Eric Wilkinson

Introduction

This chapter reports on a study to investigate the relationship between explicit descriptions of the curriculum and children's actual experiences in a range of nursery settings. Describing the curriculum of any pre-school setting can be explored by examining relevant formal documents, such as statements of curricular intent or guidelines on curriculum content and by scrutinizing plans for activities. The experience of children can be studied by making observations of children participating in playroom activities using equipment or interacting with adults. This chapter draws on all these approaches to examine whether the rhetoric, in documentation and espoused descriptions of practice, matches the experience of children and the behaviour of staff in pre-school provision with regard to two key aspects of the curriculum, that is, **developing language and literacy skills, and mathematical understanding and skills.**

The observations presented in this chapter and the questions raised arise from the experience of carrying out a research project which tried to describe the salient features of being an adult or child in each of five very different pre-school settings.[1]

It has long been the accepted approach to both formal and informal curriculum planning in pre-school that a broad spread of learning experiences, covering cognitive, emotional, social and aesthetic aspects of development, is desirable. More recently, concern with core literacy and numeracy skills and early intervention in primary education has also focused attention on provision for these particular curriculum areas in pre-school.

There is broad agreement that promoting the development of skills and understanding in language and mathematics is part of the task which those offering pre-school children care and education undertake. In *Quality Targets in Services for Young Children* (1996) the European Commission Network on Childcare proposes that the educational philosophy of pre-school provision should promote (amongst other areas) *'linguistic and oral skills'* and *'mathematical concepts'*. Formal curriculum guidelines such as those developed by the Scottish Office Education and Industry Department (SOEID, 1997), School Curriculum and Assessment Authority (SCAA, 1996) and by the voluntary sector Scottish

Pre-school Play Association (SPPA, 1996) all describe ways of working to promote the development of language and communication and mathematical understanding. The Quality Assurance scheme developed by Stephen and Wilkinson (1996) for the Scottish Independent Nurseries Association (SINA) sets out a standard for the learning environment which makes explicit reference to developing language and communication skills and mathematical concepts (the latter in the context of knowledge of the world and investigating). In offering advice on constructing a curriculum for the under 5s, the Rumbold Report (DES, 1990) refers to language and literacy as '*this fundamentally important area of the curriculum*' (p. 40) and goes on to describe the acquisition of mathematical concepts and the appropriate language to support these ideas as being '*an important competence that young children begin to acquire in pre-school provision*' (p. 41).

The study

The pre-school settings

The data presented in this chapter were gathered in a study of five very different pre-school settings. Each of the five settings was considered by informed 'experts' to be a good example of its kind. The areas in which the nurseries were located differed, as did the service which they offered. Each aimed, however, to meet the needs of children and parents as they perceived them. Four of the nurseries were in England and one in Scotland. Each nursery is described briefly here.

- Windmill, a private nursery offering extended day and all year care. The nursery was part of a large chain and was used by working parents.
- Issacs, a large local authority nursery school with an established tradition which had widened its remit to include childcare for under 3s and some extended hours for 3–4 year olds. The nursery had unusually extensive grounds and opportunities for outside play.
- Losely, a voluntary sector children's centre run as part of a local development programme.
- Rooster, a local authority nursery which had changed from a traditional nursery school model to a centre offering extended day, all year provision, offering flexible hours to working parents and sessional places to other families.
- Tiptree, a former traditional day care nursery for vulnerable children managed by an organisation established by the local authority to set up and run a range of childcare services. While the nursery continued to offer some places to children referred by social workers it also offered extended day, all year places to employers and working parents.

The study gathered data from staff, management, parents and from children. The evidence presented in this chapter draws on data from

- interviews with management;
- interviews with staff;
- documents produced by the nurseries, describing their service and policies;
- observations of children and staff in the playroom.

Interviews with staff and management were semi-structured and were analysed for similarities and differences in content in specific domains. Likewise, the content of the available documentation was examined for evidence in specific domains such as aims and goals for the curriculum. The observations of children and staff were carried out by two experienced researchers following agreed schedules for recording observations and the timing of observations. The observation schedules were developed to focus on particular aspects of children's experience and of the behaviour of staff (not all of which are reported on in this chapter). The observation procedure and schedules were piloted in pre-school environments in England and Scotland which were not included in the main study reported here. For each child-focused observation period, the time of observation was recorded, followed by a description of the child's location and activity, codings for the curricular area involved, the child–child interaction, child–adult interaction, and the intensity of the child's involvement in the task. Further notes on contextual information were added where relevant. For observations of staff, time, location and activity were again noted along with codes for the curriculum area and the nature of adult–child interaction, followed by further contextual notes as necessary. During the pilot phase, inter-rater reliability was checked and the process refined until acceptable levels of reliability were obtained. At the end of each observation visit, the playroom environment was recorded on a prepared schedule listing the activities and equipment available on that occasion.

The espoused perspectives on the curriculum

An examination of the aims and curriculum documentation of the nurseries illustrates the formal espousal of a concern to promote the development of mathematics and language.

For example, when asked about aims for the nursery the manager at *Tiptree* talked of offering a flexible but high quality service. The curriculum was taken from company policy which paid scant reference to learning per se or the role of the adult in children's learning. The guidelines or handbook for staff did, however, have a section on planning which included an aim of working '*towards intellectual development*' and another of working '*towards language acquisition*'. The playroom had been set up by a teacher to deliver a Highscope curriculum (as adapted by the company) and there was a list by each area describing the areas of learning which could be achieved there. There was reference to linguistic and literacy skills in every curriculum activity area. Examples from some of these lists are given in Table 3.1.

Rooster had a more developed rhetoric on learning and educational experiences than Tiptree. The nursery had a development plan, an articulated perspective on learning and development with consideration of process, content and context, a range of policies articulated and a system of staff supervision and non-contact time which emphasises the role of the reflective practitioner. There were, for example, policies on selecting and displaying children's books, on displays and labelling children's work and a policy on learning which incorporated planning for groups and for individual children. Staff aimed to deliver a broad curriculum and to help children to become independent learners. Learning experiences were shaped by the learning environment which was organised to offer a long list of learning experiences. Children spent time choosing their own activity and sometime every day in adult directed small group activities.

The observations

Observations were focused on specific children aged 3–4 years. The sample was selected on the basis of age and from those who attended for 5 half days or at least 2 whole days each week. Across four of the nurseries a total of 52 children

Table 3.1 Examples of 'learning areas' listed by the water, construction, book/listening and mark making activity areas at Tiptree

Water	Construction
Mathematical	Mathematics
volume	orientation
capacity	sequence
counting	correspondence
	classification
Scientific	number
water pressure	proportion
characteristics of materials	addition and subtraction
observing	area
classifying	measurement
concluding	angles
testing	
Book/listening area	*Mark making*
experiencing different texts	symbolic representation
encountering book language	narrative skills
enlarging vocabulary	letter forms
understanding that print has meaning	writing as communication
	sense of authorship
	audiences, contexts, purposes

Table 3.2 Percentage of all observations in each curriculum area

	ac	*hs*	*ll*	*m*	*p*	*s*	*sm*	*t*	*mt*	*h*	*u*
Autumn term observations											
Win.	10.8	12.0	16.6	15.7	21.7	4.8	0	4.8	10.9	0	2.4
Issa.	15.0	15.8	11.6	11.0	20.6	2.0	0	4.8	5.5	7.5	6.2
Los.	10.1	16.5	11.9	17.4	17.4	5.5	0	0	2.8	11.0	7.3
Roos.	12.8	9.2	10.1	7.3	28.4	11.9	0	1.8	16.5	4.6	6.4
Tip.	21.0	9.5	23.2	4.2	7.4	3.2	1.1	2.1	24.2	3.2	6.3
Summer term observations											
Win.	17.5	25.0	22.5	2.5	5	0	0	0	15.0	7.5	5
Los.	5.88	23.5	17.6	7.8	13.7	3.9	2.0	0	15.7	3.9	5.9
Roos.	13.3	0	6.1	5.1	22.4	11.2	7.1	0	19.4	1.0	14.3
Tip.	15.8	5.3	6.3	8.4	15.8	2.1	0	1.0	28.4	7.4	9.5

Notes:
No observations at Issacs in Summer term.
Nurseries: Win., Windmill; Issa., Issacs; Los., Losely; Roos., Rooster; Tip., Tiptree.
Curriculum areas: ac, aesthetic and creative; hs, human and social; ll, language and literacy; m, mathematics; p, physical; s, science; sm, spiritual and moral; t, technology; h, housekeeping; u, other.

were observed for four sessions each, that is, on two separate occasions in the autumn term and on two separate occasions in the following summer term. Each child was observed for a period of 5 minutes six times during each observation session. Unfortunately at one setting (Issacs) observations on 22 children were only possible during the autumn term (see Table 3.2).

Observations on focal children in the playroom covered five aspects of behaviour in all, one of which, the *curricular area* in which the child is engaged, is reported here. The area of the curriculum in which each child was engaged was categorised following the areas outlined in the Rumbold Report (Department of Education and Science, 1990). This classification was chosen as a way of covering the curriculum categories used in both Scotland and England. The curriculum areas were as listed here.

aesthetic and creative   science
human and social   language and literacy
mathematics   physical
spiritual and moral   technology
housekeeping   other

Activities categorised as relating to *language and literacy* included speaking and listening, sustained conversation with an adult, story-telling, tapes, books and writing activities. *Mathematical activities* included working with shapes, spacing, patterning, size, quantity and numeracy such as, bricks, containers, weighing, measuring, counting games and rhymes. Conversations about mathematical ideas, for example, relative size and the use of mathematical symbols and notation were also noted.

The proportion of observations in the areas of language or mathematics is given in Tables 3.3 and 3.4.

Table 3.3 Percentage of all observations – mathematics and science

Location	Autumn term		Summer term	
	Maths	*Maths including science*	*Maths*	*Maths including science*
Windmill	15.7	20.5	2.5	2.5
Issacs	11.0	13.0	—	—
Losely	17.4	22.9	7.8	11.9
Rooster	7.3	19.2	5.1	16.3
Tiptree	4.2	7.4	8.4	10.5

Note:
No observations were made at Issacs during the summer term.

Table 3.4 Percentage of all observations – language and literacy

Location	Autumn term		Summer term	
	Language and literacy	*Lang./Lit. including social/moral*	*Language and literacy*	*Lang./Lit. including social/moral*
Windmill	16.6	16.9	22.5	22.5
Issacs	11.6	11.6	—	—
Losely	11.9	11.9	17.6	18.6
Rooster	10.1	10.1	6.1	11.2
Tiptree	23.3	24.3	6.3	6.3

Note:
No observations were made at Issacs during the summer term.

This evidence suggests that at Rooster and Tiptree in particular in the Autumn term and in all nurseries in the Summer term the children spent relatively little of their time engaged in mathematics activities, although the picture did change, in varying degrees, when science-orientated activities (often involving some mathematical concepts) were included.

Turning to language and literacy, there was only a very limited proportion of observations in some settings where children were engaged in activities designed to promote this area of development. The amount of engagement with language activities was noticeably low at Rooster and Tiptree in the Summer term. However, if social and moral activities (involving listening, recall and speaking) were included the picture changed somewhat at Rooster. Overall, a picture of varying experiences arises across time and nurseries. Children are having very different experiences and engaging in different opportunities for development in different settings.

This observational evidence is in contrast with the evidence gathered from interviews and nursery documentation. Each nursery had planned activities for language and literacy development or had some space allocated to a book corner for example. There was some construction equipment, sequence or shape games available in most settings, and sand or water offering opportunities to learn about volume and conservation of quantity. Each nursery acknowledged the need to promote both these areas of the curriculum in their formal rhetoric.

Experiences and practice observed

The qualitative observation notes made in the playroom, in addition to the quantified, categorised observations given here, also suggested an environment very different from the one set out in the statements of intent. At Tiptree for example, children were engaged in few activities which could be categorised as having mathematical or scientific content in either term and few language activities in the Summer term. While a much higher proportion of observations in the Autumn term recorded children at Tiptree involved in language and literacy activities, the detailed observation notes revealed that these were most frequently large group story times or video watching sessions where stories were read or watched at a particular time of day, such as before lunch or while waiting to go home. Notes made while watching these activities demonstrate that there is little opportunity for children to participate in conversation or recall on these occasions and that the story was often interrupted by the demands of managing a large group of children and the need for some children to move to other activities. These observations point to a gap between setting up an area of activity or of having an allocated time slot in the timetable and children actually engaging in the activity in a way which promotes learning or development. Some specific examples from the detailed notes made at Tiptree serve to illustrate this further.

> The observation focuses on Holly (3 years old): Holly moves to the story area as a member of staff plays a tape and turns the pages of a book. The adult suspends the activity briefly to stop other children fighting. Holly listens to the tape while playing with some spoons in her hand. The boys who had been fighting continue to talk and another member of staff asks questions of the adult holding the book, while the tape is playing. Holly loses interest after 4 minutes and goes back to the house corner with the spoons.
>
> The observation focuses on Jenny, a member of staff: Jenny is in the cloakroom area with all the children (20) while another member of staff is in

the adjacent toilet area. Jenny is about to read to the whole group but is waiting for everyone to be quiet and sit 'properly'. She waits to get their attention but the children find it difficult to settle. Tension rises and the story does not flow. Jenny breaks off to call the children out one by one to the toilet and they then return again to the story area. The playroom door opens and the children are called for lunch. The story is unfinished.

Examples of involvement in mathematical and scientific activities were harder to find but again looking at the details of an observed event illustrates the potential for a mismatch between intention and the children's experience.

The observation focuses on Joanna, a member of staff: Joanna is in a very small room with her key group and is directing the children towards particular activities, that is, a selection of puzzles and games designed to focus on sorting and matching. She has set up a matching game on the computer for Emily and starts her off on the game giving instructions like 'find another bear', 'you need an elephant now'. Joanna has also to keep an eye on the other children in the group and intervenes in their activities saying things like 'put that there' to children working on a wooden colour and shape puzzle. She offers praise when a task is completed. Sally tries a game on the computer too. The task involves counting and matching but Sally cannot count and is not encouraged to count. She remains quietly involved in trying to match by picture alone. By trial and error she manages to complete some matches and is delighted with her achievement.

The observation focuses on two adult-led science activities: During the morning session – a member of staff is talking to the whole group about a plant but the children are diverted by snack being served at the same time and are restless in the large group sitting on the floor.

During the afternoon session – the children are waiting to cut cress which they had grown and make cress sandwiches for snack. The conversation and instructions are about waiting for a turn and using scissors (rather than the transformation of seeds into food).

Looking at the details of each observation at Rooster, rather than the espoused area of learning or category of activity alone, suggests that the quality of the experience there was more likely to promote the development of literacy and numeracy regardless of the number of literacy and numeracy events recorded. Rooster had little that was coded as mathematics by our criteria but the detailed notes did suggest that on at least some of these occasions children were actively engaged in play which offered opportunities for developing concepts that cross both mathematics and science. Activities in the literacy and language categories were strikingly low on occasions at Rooster. Indeed, when some of this data was fed back to staff they were shocked at the low incidence of engagement in language-orientated activities recorded. Yet, this was a nursery where staff did take some time out to observe, though not with the same focus as that adopted by the observers in this study. Nevertheless, there were some positive experiences recorded.

Again some examples serve to illustrate the children's actual experience.

The observation focuses on a group time activity: A science orientated activity is underway at group time with a small group of children. They are making fruit juice ice lollies. There is a discussion about the flow of juice through the funnel. The adult asks the children how juice feels in a bag (soft, squashy, etc.) and what it will feel like when frozen (hard, cold).

The observation focuses on Martin (3 years old): Just before the observation period began Martin is looking very carefully at a book on his own, counting under his breath while pointing. (His key worker had previously explained that Martin was fascinated by train tracks, trains and vehicles with wheels.) The book Martin is looking at involves a line running across the page, not unlike a train track. During the observation Martin sits with a member of staff who is now reading the book he was looking at alone. Martin listens, watching the book intently and offering comments on pictures in the book.

A further example from Rooster demonstrated the difficulty of attending to a variety of requests which can move the focus of the adult or children from the espoused intent of the initial activity.

The observation focuses on the book corner: One member of staff is in the book area with two boys who are choosing a book for her to read. Lee is also responsible for the puzzle table and someone there has a problem. She goes to help and discovers one piece of a puzzle is missing. The puzzle is removed and an alternative found. Lee goes back to the book corner where the boys are still waiting. They sit happily on Lee's lap. Another child asks for help with a puzzle but is asked to wait and instead comes to join the story group. Lee continues to read and sing, pointing out rhyming words.

A final example points to the holistic nature of the pre-school experience and the way in which staff can seize an opportunity to facilitate development, following the current interests of the children.

The observation focuses on the science area: Five children are gathered around a table with magnets. They are in the area designated as a science area. When the staff member joins them the children are having a discussion about pals and what someone's Mum had said. The adult takes up the conversation and prompts a discussion about friendship.

Encouraging children to reflect and plan (activities which involve language skills and an understanding of the mathematical concepts of time and sequence) was also managed differently. While the Highscope programme at Tiptree was designed to encourage children to make independent choices and later recall their involvement and consider new plans the way in which this was delivered militated against the programme's ideals. Planning was done as children arrived with some children each day being asked what they would like to do and this being recorded in a book. There was no formal time or space set aside for this and, as not all staff were present at the beginning of the session (due to the shift pattern adopted), planning for individual children was rather a 'hit and miss' affair. If no adult was readily available when a child arrived then planning did not take place. Recall was done at a whole group gathering, fitting this in with other staff duties such as, preparing the playroom for lunch and staff breaks. All children were asked to listen while one child recalled their morning activities. This recall time frequently broke down when some in the large group fidgeted or talked out of turn and others were called to go to the toilet and wash before lunch. As no member of staff was allocated to a particular area of the playroom there was often no adult who could comment on the child's play and activities that morning.

There were examples at Rooster where similar events were handled very differently.

> The observation focuses on Ailish (3 years old): Ailish is in her morning group welcome time with 5 other children. The group is being led by a student nursery nurse. The children are recalling the week-end and the outing in the previous week. They take turns to speak but Ailish wants to monopolise the conversation repeating 'but I'm not finished'. The student purposefully moves the conversation on to another child and Ailish listens. The student then turns to planning the week. She looks with the children at a diary to see if there were any special events in nursery that week (encouraging the children to think about time and demonstrating the value of written language).

At Tiptree opportunities for planning and recall were not capitalised on due to circumstances of staffing and playroom planning, nor were opportunities for developing literacy offered to children by using labels or symbols to mark the use of a play area, nor was reference made to the planning chart. At Rooster however, time was set aside to discuss planning and recall the weekend and the adult skilfully promoted both expressive language skills, listening, recall and planning and the use of written material to aid the conversation and planning.

Key issues for practice and training

Although only part of the data gathered in this research project, the observations presented here, both quantitative and qualitative, are enough to raise three particular questions that practitioners and those who train practitioners need to consider.

What do staff see as an appropriate curriculum for developing language and mathematical reasoning skills?

Our evidence suggests that they do not in fact address this question directly in terms of the child's experience in the playroom. All five nurseries make reference to language development and the development of mathematical or scientific concepts but none made explicit the way in which this was offered in terms of individual experiences. Rather, they were concerned to offer a curriculum with breadth and balance in the activities offered over a period of time (often a week). Rooster had a growing list of policies and in documentation referred to the needs of the learner and to language and communicative skills. There was not, however, a written curriculum document although areas of the curriculum or areas of development were acknowledged in planning and in the room layout. At Tiptree there were notices by each area listing the learning possibilities but there was no evidence, either in planning or in the staff interviews, that these were ever consulted to chart individual experiences.

Typically, then, either through a timetabled slot (such as the pre-school 'work' time) or allocated space (the science table which might have magnets one day followed by magnifying glasses the next), activities which could be categorised as relating to the development of language and literacy or mathematics and numeracy were offered but this is not the same as having clearly established ways of working as an adult supporter of learning or an adult provider of opportunities or an adult assessor to promote these areas of development in a range of contexts or experiences in the playroom. Having timetabled slots and corners in the playroom may be part of planning for children's development but this does not amount to a comprehensive plan or programme or an explicit awareness of the role of the adult which will allow staff to capitalise on opportunities.

How do staff seek to deliver the curriculum which they espouse?

It has been demonstrated that the nurseries offer language and literacy play opportunities or activities. They set up a book corner, read stories (though not to every child), may sing songs or rhymes or set up a mark-making table. To promote mathematical reasoning they may put out puzzles and games for matching and sorting, there is usually sand and/or water, there are construction toys and sometimes group activities which involve measuring and counting.

Despite this, neither managers nor playroom staff interviewed talked about their role as facilitators in learning and developing these skills. Our observations have demonstrated that staff sometimes facilitate development, for example, by rhyming words or counting cups at snack time but we have also recorded staff behaving in a way which seems contrary to their intentions, for example, asking children to sit in the book corner but not making time to read a story to them. Staff have been recorded putting out sand and water but only having conversations about brushing up the sand or wearing 'pinnies' at the water. Children were invited to watch a video but snack was then passed to them as they watched and listened and adults gave instructions over the sound of the video.

In the course of interviews, staff did not talk about literacy and numeracy skills when describing their work with either the whole group or children in their key worker group. When they mentioned language, the focus was usually on how intelligible the child's speech was or on the appropriateness of the language. Staff at both Rooster and Tiptree were more likely to talk about having behaviour goals for children or some very specific goal, like knowing colour labels.

When staff were observed developing numeracy and literacy skills this was usually, but not always, in the context of a language or science/mathematics area and seemed to be a result of an appropriate adult response to a child's need or exploration not the result of curriculum statements, policies, plans or timetables.

Does the child's experience match staff intentions for literacy or numeracy development?

The observations given as examples here, along with the quantitative data, demonstrate clearly that the child's experience does not always match the adult plans or thoughts about the playroom events. The gap demonstrated between plans and the adults' construction of playroom events suggests that there is a need for adults to spend time in focused observations or careful recording of the child's experience.

Conclusion

Pre-school practitioners have a range of curriculum frameworks available to guide their practice and in many settings staff spend time developing a curriculum and set of learning outcomes for their own provision. This study points to the necessity to observe the way in which these frameworks, which are essentially aspirational goals, are delivered in practice and experienced and participated in by the children. The experience of the curriculum is, like all else in the pre-school environment, a function of conditions and intentions. Organisational factors, the facilitating skill of the adults present and the degree to which the activities capture children's interest will all operate to influence the curriculum experienced by individual children.

An awareness of the potential for a gap between rhetoric and reality in the pre-school curriculum is a necessary first step towards reducing the gap illustrated by the data presented here. Staff in all kinds of provision, no matter how excellent its reputation, need to engage in careful, focused monitoring of the experience of children and adults in the environment and the influence of conditions on intent. There is a need for periodic, formal consideration by each staff group of the curriculum goals (for literacy, numeracy or other areas of development) of their nursery. These goals may be prompted by the requirements of funding bodies and established 'good practice' but should also reflect the aims of each pre-school environment and the needs of the particular children attending there. Staff need to question what balance of curriculum experiences and activities children in that nursery need. Is there a need for, or an established tradition of, focusing on a particular aspect of development, perhaps verbal communication between children, vocabulary building, physical skills or investigating?

Staff then need to go on to consider whether they are delivering a curriculum, as experienced by the children, which meets these goals. Does their programme 'work', do the children experience the curriculum in the way in which adults intended? Answering these questions about the children's experience requires systematic observation by adults who have time set aside to focus on that task and who have the support of the staff group they will report to. Observations may focus on particular aspects of the curriculum as here or on the breadth and balance of the experiences of focal children. Having examined their own rhetoric or espoused goals and their observable practice it is important that a staff group completes the cycle by considering the match between intention and experience, identifying gaps, noting achieved and unachieved or unachievable goals and going on to consider what aspects of staff practice and nursery conditions should or can be amended. Policies, strategies and programmes are clearly necessary but so too are conditions which allow skilful and sensitive practitioners to work at their best.

Note

1   This study was funded by the Baring Foundation and carried out jointly with Dr Helen Penn (Institute of Education, University of London). The study is reported in full in a paper, Early Excellence Centres, Helen Penn and Christine Stephen (1997) given at the Daycare Trust Conference, October 1997.

References

European Commission Network on Childcare (1996) *Quality Targets in Services for Young Children*, Brussels: ECNC.

Department of Education and Science (1990) *Starting with Quality. Report of the Committee of Inquiry into the Quality of Educational Experience Offered to 3- and 4-year Olds* (the Rumbold Report), London: HMSO.

School Curriculum and Assessment Authority (SCAA) (1996) *Nursery Education. Desirable Outcomes for Children's Learning*, London: DfEE.

Scottish Office Education and Industry Department (SOEID) (1997) *A Curriculum Framework for Children in their Pre-school Year*, Edinburgh: SOEID.

Scottish Pre-school Play Association (SPPA) (1996) *SPPA Early Years Curriculum: A Framework for Development*, Glasgow: SPPA.

Stephen C. and Wilkinson J. E. (1996) *SINA Quality Assurance Scheme, A Manual*, Glasgow: University of Glasgow.

PART II

TEACHING AND LEARNING STRATEGIES

Teachers can draw on a rich armoury of teaching styles and strategies, as there is no shortage of possibilities. Every single day children engage in hundreds of interactions with each other, or with the adults they meet inside and outside their classrooms. A teacher may ask 50–100 questions within a single hour, sometimes to an individual, often to a group or the whole class.

This puts a premium on their professional skill. It is not easy to decide what to do when there is little time to make each decision. Classrooms can be like a major railway station: many permanent features, but full of movement, announcements and rapidly changing events. Deep structures need to be laid down, fundamental principles and values that inform practice, so that teachers are operational in the hurly burly of daily classroom life.

The three chapters in this part address fundamental issues of classroom practice. In the first one (Chapter 4), Vivienne Baumfield and Maria Mroz analyse children's questions in primary school lessons, a fundamental driver for teachers who try to respond to their pupils' needs. They show how children were able to ask a wide range of interesting and thought-provoking questions when given the opportunity to discuss a version of the *Three Little Pigs* story. This is a particularly interesting matter, because the evidence cited by the authors shows that most questions asked by teachers tend to be fairly closed, so letting pupils express their own curiosity can both illustrate what they do and do not understand, and also open up the process to wider possibilities.

Effective classroom management lies at the heart of skilful teaching, and Chapter 5 is an extract from my own book on that very topic (Wragg (2001) *Class Management in the Secondary School*). It looks at the two Rs, rules and relationships, showing not only their wide range and fascinating nature, but also how teachers can analyse their own practice. Teachers have many different ways of introducing rules, not always by direct exhortation. Sometimes they will ask questions, negotiate, or operate case law, by responding to something that has just happened. Relationships are crucial in classrooms and they can sometimes be determined, for good or ill, by how teachers respond to key events.

In Chapter 6 Susan Bentham describes different ways of classifying the preferred styles that teachers and learners bring to education. These cover a wide range of possibilities. Some learners are highly systematic, following logic and rules, while others prefer to freewheel. Personality traits and individual preferences about the environment in which they best learn, alone or with others, for example, can play a strong role. Equally, the way people teach is influenced by similar factors. When teachers and learners come together these styles can harmonise, or clash. It may not be possible to match a teacher's teaching style to every pupil's preferred learning style, but it will certainly help to be aware of the many differences and indeed to be sensitive to them whenever this is feasible.

CHAPTER 4

INVESTIGATING PUPILS' QUESTIONS IN THE PRIMARY CLASSROOM

Vivienne Baumfield and Maria Mroz

The importance of pupils' questions for learning

The importance of talk in the classroom is encapsulated in the often quoted 'talk drives learning' (Wells, 1986). Initial research findings of, for example, Edwards and Westgate (1994) continue to generate interest in the structure of teacher–pupil discourse, which they showed to be the means of establishing the extent of shared attention and joint activity in the classroom. Morgan and Saxton (1994) characterize questions as the 'chief agents' by which meanings are mediated in education. However, we also know that the teacher carries out 70 per cent of the talk in classrooms. Furthermore, classroom discourse conforms to a standard pattern characterized by researchers as IRF (Initiation, Response, Feedback) in which talk is initiated by the teacher, usually by the use of a closed question, and pupils are invited to make a short response to which the teacher then gives feedback (usually evaluative). The IRF pattern of teacher–pupil discourse is a persistent feature in classrooms: 'Across two decades, the overall proportions of teacher statements and questions have remained remarkably stable' (Galton et al., 1999, p. 62). It is a pattern of interaction that is resistant to innovation and persists even when teachers are trying to implement new teaching methods (Edwards and Westgate, 1994).

Evidence from studies by Wells (1986) and Tizard and Hughes (1984) demonstrates how few questions children ask of their teachers on entry to school compared to the numerous ones they ask of their parents. Tizard and Hughes refer to children who were asking 50 per cent of the questions at home going on to ask fewer than 5 per cent at nursery school. The questions they did ask were often 'business' or permission questions rather than attempts to understand what was being taught.

Teachers in classrooms ask a lot of questions and it is the most common means of initiating responses from pupils. During episodes of classroom discourse, 11 per cent of teacher communications with the class consist of asking questions (Wragg et al., 1998). Consequently, research on questions in the classroom has largely been concerned with teacher questioning and various attempts have been made to classify the questions asked. One categorization, which is widely accepted, relates to the concept of open and closed questions. In the Leverhulme Primary Project (ibid.) it was noted that the majority of questions (92 per cent) relating to lesson content were closed and only 8 per cent were open questions. This figure is similar to that found by Galton et al. (1980, 1999) where 5.5 per cent of all questions asked by teachers were open questions.

Categorizing questions according to their form (open or closed questions), or on a lexical basis, for example, all 'what' questions would be grouped together, might seem a simple system to adopt but presents difficulties in so far as the surface form of the questions may be similar while the function of the questions may be very different (Young, 1992). Approaches that classify questions based on question purpose try to avoid this problem but can become very complex; Morgan and Saxton (1994) cite one example which generated forty-eight different categories.

Given that attempts to classify teachers' questions must address the issues of the relationship between the form of a question, its intention and the response it elicits, it should not be surprising that formulating a classification system that is robust has proved difficult. Researchers continue to explore the link between questioning and children's thinking, so that they can identify those types of questioning that promote better thinking. Systems based on Bloom's taxonomy of types of thinking make a distinction between 'lower order' thinking, involving basic comprehension and recall, and 'higher order' thinking, consisting of analysis and synthesis, but their effectiveness in linking questioning with thinking is disputed (Dillon, 1990).

The imbalance between the ratio of teacher to pupil questions in the classroom is reflected in the lack of research into pupils' questions. Little reference is made in the literature to pupils' questions as indicators of states of understanding, nor on their impact on subsequent learning. Some work has been done from the perspective of speech and language development that can begin to indicate how the structure of the questions is linked to the child's cognitive development. De Villiers and de Villiers (1979) note that children can only answer those questions that require components of a sentence they use readily; thus children begin by answering 'what', 'who' and 'where' questions because their own sentences can express these relations. Similarly, the child who can use 'when' questions appropriately is likely to be beginning to have an understanding of time relations, and 'why' questions reflect, or build upon, the child's desire to understand cause and effect. The role of pupils' questions in the development of listening and reading comprehension is another area in which some research has been done (Palincsar and Brown, 1984). Results from a review of programmes to encourage question generation in pupils (Rosenshine *et al.*, 1996) indicate that significant improvements in comprehension could be achieved by consistent use of strategies such as signal words (who, what, where) and generic question stems ('How are x and y alike?').

The National Curriculum for primary schools has reiterated the importance of asking questions both in its broad introduction to thinking skills and in subject-specific documentation (DfEE/QCA, 1999, p. 50). Encouraging pupil-generated questions in the classroom offers a number of potential benefits that could promote more effective learning. The pupils' questions can serve as a diagnostic tool to demonstrate the current level of understanding and also highlight areas of confusion. By listening to and discussing one another's questions, pupils can be aware of the range of interpretations and understanding among their peers so that the processes of learning become more explicit. Taking pupils' questions as a starting-point allows for situations where the teacher does not control the questioning and may not know the answer, thus facilitating opportunities for 'real' discourse in the classroom rather than the customary IRF pattern. Young (1992) emphasizes the importance of authentic conversation in classrooms in promoting learning. Hughes and Westgate (1997) found that nursery nurses and teaching assistants were more effective talk partners for young children because they were able to engage in more natural patterns of conversation that reflected the kinds of talk that the children would be involved in outside of the classroom context. We were interested to see if a style of pedagogy based on a community of inquiry could replicate in a whole-class context patterns of interaction and talk associated with these informal learning contexts, in which the teacher was more tentative than authoritative and able to facilitate pupil questioning and discussion.

Lipman *et al.* (1980) developed the community of inquiry approach, derived from the work of Vygotsky and Dewey, as the key strategy in his 'Philosophy for Children' programme. His approach promotes the generation of pupils' questions based on a shared narrative, which then form the agenda for whole-class discussion. The use of a narrative text as a basis for the generation of questions supports the pupils by offering a format which is central to learning, is familiar and can be readily integrated into the curriculum by the teacher (Bearne, 1997). It also takes into account both the cognitive and affective aspects of learning and meets the requirements of researchers, such as Morgan and Saxton (1994), that the whole ethos of the classroom must be conducive to pupils asking questions. Evaluations of the impact of the community of inquiry approach on pupils' learning indicate that significant improvements can be made in tests of reasoning and in standardized reading tests (Lipman *et al.*, 1980). If such a change in perspective were to be possible, the characteristics of a powerful learning environment (De Corte, 1990) could be established. Within this environment high-quality thinking would be a priority, thought processes would be made explicit through discussion and a vocabulary for talking about thinking would be shared by pupils and teachers.

Outline of the study

Four first schools (5–9 year olds) took part in the research in which one teacher in key stage 1 (5–7 year olds) and one teacher in key stage 2 (8–9 year olds) undertook to incorporate the community of inquiry into their work on literacy. The aim was to test whether there were any improvements in pupils' ability to ask purposeful questions and to monitor the impact of the intervention on listening and reading comprehension. In the term preceding the full project, a pilot was undertaken. This was designed to enable teachers in the schools to become familiar with the strategy and to gather questions which would form the basis for categorizing pupils' questions so that any changes in the pattern and frequency of questioning during the project could be analysed.

Question categories

Questions were collected from one class in each school who had all participated in a community of inquiry based on the same narrative text (*The True Story of the Three Little Pigs*: Sczieska, 1989). Each session began with the teacher explaining that the class was going to listen to a story and then think of any questions that they would like to ask. After listening to the story, pupils were given time to write down their individual questions before discussing them with a partner and then in a group of four. During the discussion in groups, they were instructed to decide on one question to share with the class in a whole-class discussion. Questions from the older children from each school participating in the project were selected for analysis as these pupils had been able to write down their own questions; 355 questions in total from three Year 3 and one mixed Years 3 and 4 classes were used to generate the categories.

Table 4.1 Question categories

1a	Single issue from plot of story with a factual answer – usually a closed question, e.g. What did . . .? Who is . . .?
1b	Single issue with a factual answer but incorporating a challenge to the conventions of the plot/narrative, e.g. How could . . .?
2a	Single issue focused on the motivation of characters with direct reference to information given in the text, e.g. Why did . . .?
2b	Single issue focused on the motivation of the characters but incorporating some inference by generalizing across number of instances, or using information implied in the text but not referred to directly.
3	More complex structures using subordinate clauses and using logic to offer alternatives, e.g. If . . . then . . . why not . . .?
4	Summary of plot or key themes in the narrative with open-ended question.
5	Questions exploring what happened before the story starts or what happens next – usually focused on one issue.
6	Incomplete questions.
7	Statements.
8	Misunderstandings – questions that do not take account of specific information provided in the text.
9	Tangential questions.

The questions were used to generate the categories by devising codings linked to descriptors based on the apparent relationship between the questions and the story's plot. By linking the categories to the plot of the story, we were able to suggest a means of distinguishing between those types of questions the teachers were keen to promote as part of improving pupils' literacy and those they would like to change. The categories included references to the structure of the questions in so far as statements and incomplete questions are coded and one of the categories refers to the use of complex syntax to present alternative plot lines; but, in the main, the categories refer to the extent to which the pupils appear to have comprehended the story, its plot and conventions.

Inter-rater reliability of the coding was checked within the research team and with the classroom teachers involved in the research and a schedule for coding agreed (Table 4.1).

Distribution of pupils' questions in the pilot

The majority of the questions were in the categories 1–5 (Table 4.2), denoting a good grasp of the purpose of asking questions, and this is encouraging. The most common types of question are consistent with what the pupils had learned about exploring narrative texts: focusing on the motivation of characters and predicting what is going to happen next, for example. The relatively high incidence of questions of type 1b ('Why did the pigs die when he sneezed?' or 'How can pigs talk?') is interesting. Although pupils are introduced to the skills of critical analysis with regard to exploring the author's intentions or the effectiveness of the techniques used, most of the questions in this category challenged the conventions of the narrative and would not have been modelled or taught explicitly. In fact, in some instances, contributions such as 'How can animals talk?' would not have been encouraged in lessons and could be viewed as distracting from engagement with the story. There are quite a few type 3 questions, that is questions with a complex

Table 4.2 Analysis of questions in pilot phase

Question type	School A Y3				School B Y3/4				School C Y3				School D Y3				Number of questions asked
	Total	Boy	Girl	Anon.	Total	Boy	Girl	Anon.	Total	Boy	Girl	Anon.	Total	Boy	Girl	Anon.	
1a	8	6	1	1	6	5	1		5	4	1		8	3	5		27
1b	9	7	1	1	8	6	2		2	1	1		27	14	13		46
2a	13	7	4	2	10	3	7		35	11	23	1	18	4	14	1	77
2b	5	3	2		5	4	1		1	0	1		9	4	5		20
3	12	8	4		3	2	1		11	2	9		12	0	12		38
4	2	2	0		3	2	1		3	0	3		3	0	3		11
5	13	4	8	1	29	18	11		10	4	6		5	2	3		57
6	8	2	6		0				7	4	3		8	5	3	3	28
7	1	1	0		0				0				3	1	1	1	4
8	2	1	1		3	1	2		7	3	4		3	3	0		15
9	2	1	1		17	9	8		7	3	3	1	6	0	6		32
Total	75				84				88				102				355

structure and suggesting alternatives ('Why didn't the wolf take the sugar when he went to the first house?') but not so many questions that rely on a degree of inference and require the capacity to summarize the main ideas of the narrative (type 2b: 'Was the wolf telling the truth?', and type 4: 'Why did they put the wolf in jail just for eating a dead pig?'). The scarcity of summary questions is consistent with research into children's comprehension of narrative; it has been noted that summarizing the main points is difficult even for 10 year olds (Oakhill and Garnham, 1988).

The findings from the pilot study provided some questions to be explored in the next phase of the project:

1   Would the coding schedule be applicable over a wider range of narrative texts?
2   Would a programme of planned communities of inquiry, over a term, lead to any significant changes in the frequency of types of question?
3   Would the inclusion of pupils from a wider age range be reflected in the distribution of types of question?
4   Could the community of inquiry be developed to include more pupils in the generation and selection of questions?

Distribution of pupils' questions during the development of the project

For one term, the teachers in the four schools developed the community of inquiry using a narrative text to generate and discuss questions. The questions from one class in each school were collected and analysed using the coding schedule. The classes covered a range of ages from Years 1–4 and the teachers were free to choose any narrative text as a focus for the session and to develop the organization of the question generation and selection to suit the needs of their class. The freedom to adapt the approach was essential if the teachers were going to test the extent to which this approach could be integrated into their normal classroom setting and become part of their practice. However, the variations in approach did make it difficult to track changes over time.

We were able to analyse questions from 29 sessions, different texts being used in each case, and chart the frequency of the different types of question. The findings discussed here are generalized across the four schools. (The project report provides more detail regarding the individual classes and includes the teachers' own interpretations of the positive impact of the intervention on pupils' motivation and social development in the case studies: Baumfield *et al.*, 2000.) While needing to exercise caution regarding the significance of any shifts in the relative frequency of question types given the variation across schools, the following observations can be made:

1   the coding schedule was applicable over a wider range of narrative texts;
2   the age of the children did not influence the type and frequency of questions;
3   the most frequent type of question in the pilot (2a – questions focused on a single issue involving the motivation of characters and with direct reference to the text) continued to be the most frequent during the project, as did the least frequent type (7 – statements), with no instances of statements and only one example of an incomplete question;
4   the incidence of single-issue questions that incorporated a challenge to the convention of the narrative remained constant – it was the third most frequent type of question in both the pilot and the project;

5   questions focused on a single issue with a factual answer increased in frequency during the project and were the second most likely category of question;

6   there were few instances of questions referring to what happened before or after the narrative, although these had been frequent in the pilot study based on one text;

7   the incidence of questions requiring a degree of inference and a summary of the plot or main themes of the narrative was not clear-cut during the project, with some types (4 – summary with an open-ended question) becoming slightly more frequent while the complex questions offering an alternative are less common. Questions focusing on the motivation of characters with indirect reference to the text and requiring a degree of inference increased during the project phase;

8   tangential questions continued to occur during the project at a similar level of frequency as in the pilot.

Discussion

Pupils can and do ask a range of questions when given express permission to do so. In both the pilot and the development phase of the project, pupils were willing to ask questions. The structure of the community of inquiry may have prevented some of the barriers to question generation operating. For example, the difficulty pupils may have in detecting their own misunderstandings is reduced by the familiarity even very young children have with narrative structure and the discussion and subsequent clarification within the community of inquiry. The fear of losing face in front of peers is another potential barrier and this was reduced by having the opportunity to have questions discussed in a small group before sharing them with the whole class. It has been suggested that another barrier is the poor model of question generation provided by teachers in most classrooms due to the preponderance of closed and short answer questions; this is discussed at a later point.

One of the teachers' concerns had been to address how the community of inquiry might be developed so as to include more pupils in the generation and discussion of questions. Evidence from our observations suggested that most pupils were able to generate a number of questions during the small group time and therefore the approach was inclusive. For some pupils, it was only towards the end of the project, after a great deal of prior modelling, that they were confident in creating a number of questions. For younger pupils and those with literacy problems, sensitive intervention by the class teacher in terms of careful grouping, the encouragement of 'brave writing' from Year 1 pupils and at times the use of scribes ensured maximum participation.

Pupil expectations of the type of question most appropriate in the context of a narrative text continued to focus on the motivation of characters and this is, as we have seen, consistent with their previous experience of working with text and the model promoted by the teacher before the intervention. However, it would seem that, given the opportunity, pupils are keen to engage with issues in the narrative and challenge the conventions of the story even though this is unlikely to have formed part of their experience of working with narrative in the classroom. There is some slight indication that boys are more likely to ask this type of question than girls and it would be worth pursuing this further. Certainly, there could be implications for the willingness to 'suspend disbelief' and engage with fiction that would resonate with existing research into some boys having a preference for non-fiction (Millard, 1997). While it must remain a matter of conjecture given the limitations of the data from this project, there could be issues regarding the response of teachers to pupils in a more conventional story-telling context when the conventions of the narrative are subjected to critical challenge. Contributions such as 'How can animals talk?' may be welcomed by teachers trying to encourage pupils to ask questions in a community of inquiry but could elicit a very different response at other times, which could actively discourage some pupils.

Careful structuring of the question generation and selection process removed all instances of misunderstandings and tangential questions. Increased facility with the process of discussion and selection of questions could also account for a rather disappointing reduction in the number of complex questions (type 3) as the complexity of these questions may make them less robust and difficult for their advocates to sustain arguments for their retention during the group negotiations. It may also be that the choice of narrative has a part to play in the incidence of this type of question. In the pilot, the narrative text (Sczieska, 1989) relied on interplay between the story and the plot of the original story of the three little pigs; the intertextual nature of the story may have encouraged pupils to pose questions drawing on the two parallel narratives. Our current research in primary schools supports the value of using such stories, with teachers reporting a greater incidence of the more inferential and complex questions from young children. Years 1 and 2 children, for example, engage actively with a story such as 'Beware of the Bears' (McDonald, 1999). Other stories that teachers have found to be successful in stimulating questions are ones that have an intriguing twist or puzzle within them such as most of the writing of Anthony Browne or Maurice Sendak. Folk tales and Aesop's fables, with the moral withheld until later in the discussion, have also been used.

Choice of narrative is the most likely factor in the comparison of the relative incidence of the summary-type questions (2b and 4) both within and between schools. There is no significant correlation between the age of the children and the frequency of these questions and their occurrence is not incremental during the period of the intervention. It is possible to detect a pattern that indicates that, in some instances, the incidence of summary questions is linked to a rise in the number of tangential questions and misunderstandings. Perhaps those stories that promote a high level of inference and speculation in some pupils are also likely to lead others to become confused and liable to miss the point. The impact of the organization of the question selection could also have an impact here as the process that reduces tangential questions and misunderstandings could also discourage inference and speculation.

Conclusion

The study has raised a number of important issues relating to the ability of children to question narrative text and the types of questions asked.

Influence of text type

Texts that were culturally or conceptually 'foreign' to the pupils elicited questions that asked for clarification of vocabulary or the basic plot. Thus, in order to develop questioning which goes beyond basic clarification, one needs to ensure that the choice of text allows children to engage with the subject matter and the story structure. These choices are likely to involve the teacher's in-depth knowledge both of the interests of the class and their prior knowledge, as well as the curriculum content that may need to be addressed.

Benefits to pupils and teachers

If teachers are going to devote the time and effort to this type of questioning approach to a text, they need to be clear about the potential benefits to their pupils. Among the benefits are the importance for pupils' motivation of having control over their own learning and an opportunity to follow their own agenda. It is also valuable for pupils to know that their own questions are seen as important and that questioning is a major means of developing understanding. Rosenshine *et al.* (1996) suggest that question generation as a cognitive strategy offers a guide to pupils which may help them to develop their own ways of, for example, analysing texts which they have heard. The relationship between listening and reading comprehension is high (Rubin, 1980; cited in Oakhill and Garnham, 1988) and so the benefits of a strategy mainly used for reading will be similar for a listening task. While the use of question generation need not link directly to improved reading comprehension, the process of creating questions, such as searching back through text and linking pieces of information, will be useful in establishing understanding. Woodward (1992) highlights the role of pupils' questions in diagnostic assessment. If one accepts the clear links between listening and reading comprehension, then such an approach would help to identify pupils at risk from failure to succeed with literacy and those who would benefit from more challenging reading material.

Other potential benefits to the class teacher include the need to ensure that pupils have a means for engaging critically with a range of spoken, written and visual information across the curriculum. The community of inquiry offers pupils opportunities to state their case and to produce a reasoned argument – both transferable skills that will have benefits in school life and beyond.

Implications for future development

Within the community of inquiry, approach to generating pupil questions there are issues around the possible 'screening out' of inferential and summary-type questions in favour of more limited questions. Although the approach is to encourage pupils to take responsibility for setting the questioning agenda, there is also a need for teachers to offer models of more complex question types and to encourage their use. While this may reduce the democratic nature of the process, it benefits pupils in allowing them to understand that these types of question are valued and that they offer potential for discussion. Texts which produced more complex questions were also those that led to an increase in wild and potentially unproductive speculation. Clearly a balance has to be drawn between the potential for a few children to demonstrate and develop greater understanding at the expense of the majority spending their time uncertain of the content of the text and unable to pose useful questions.

An additional advantage of the teacher carrying out an overview screening of the questions asked by the pupils as a whole could be that a system of monitoring could take place. Thus teachers could be aware of the questioning ability of different individuals and determine to what extent they were benefiting from the modelling of desirable question types. Teachers who took part in this research have since devised a simplified system for recording the categories of questions asked (ignoring those that fell into categories 6, 7, 8 and 9). As a result of this, they hope to be able to monitor the types of questions agreed by the class as a whole and by individuals within groups.

Further study into the place of tangential questions is warranted since what may appear irrelevant may in fact not be so. For some of the tangential questions asked, there was the possibility that these actually reflected a deeper understanding relevant to the text.

In summary

The study into the pupils' use of questions during a community of inquiry has raised a number of areas of interest into the potential for the approach to develop pupils' critical analysis of text. The discussions that flowed from the questions provided opportunities for the pupils to present arguments and to qualify, justify and extend their thinking in the light of others' questions or accounts. In terms of addressing both the speaking and listening and the thinking skills requirements of the curriculum, this approach offers teachers and pupils a way of learning which is different to some of the more prescriptive methods currently in place. The teachers in the project adapted the approach to suit the needs of their pupils and found that they could incorporate the community of inquiry into their classroom practice. The schools are now working to consolidate the understanding of which texts are most conducive to question generation and discussion and how best to organize the class to ensure participation and promote more complex questions.

The teachers involved in developing the community of inquiry to promote pupils' questioning began their work in the early stages of the introduction of the National Literacy Strategy (NLS) and there were, initially, some concerns as to whether the two approaches could come together. We have found that it is possible to incorporate the community of inquiry into the primary curriculum and make links across to the pedagogy of the NLS, with some teachers reporting that they find the emphasis on sharing ideas in the plenary helpful in supporting the development of a whole-class community of inquiry. We find that this is particularly true with more experienced staff who are confident in their delivery of the NLS and are able to explore methods of extending and varying text-level, whole-class work.

References

Baumfield, V., Leat, S. and Mroz, M. (2000). *Thinking through Stories*. Newcastle: University of Newcastle.

Bearne, E. (ed.) (1997). *Use of Language across the Primary Curriculum*. London: Routledge.

De Corte, E. (1990). 'Towards powerful learning environments for the acquisition of problem-solving skills', *European Journal of Psychology of Education*, 1, 1, 5–19.

Department for Education and Employment and Qualifications and Curriculum Authority (DEE/QCA) (1999). *The National Curriculum: Handbook for Primary Teachers in England*. London: HMSO.

De Villiers, P. A. and De Villiers, J. G. (1979). *Early Language*. London: Fontana/Open Books.

Dillon, J. T. (1990). *The Practice of Questioning*. London: Routledge.

Edwards, A. D. and Westgate, D. (1994). *Investigating Classroom Talk*. London: The Falmer Press.

Galton, M., Simon, B., Croll, P. (1980). *Inside the Primary Classroom*. London: Routledge.

Galton, M., Hargreaves, L., Comber, C., Wall, D. and Pell, A. (1999). *Inside the Primary Classroom 20 Years On*. London: Routledge.

Hughes, M. and Westgate, D. (1997). 'Teachers and other adults as talk partners for pupils in nursery and reception classes', *Education 3 to 13*, **25**, 1, 3–7.

Lipman, M., Sharp, M. A. and Oscanyon, F. S. (1980). *Philosophy in the Classroom*. Philadelphia, PN: Temple University Press.

McDonald, A. (1999). *Beware of the Bears*. London: Magi.

Millard, E. (1997). *Differently Literate: Boys, Girls and the Practice of Schooling*. London: The Falmer Press.

Morgan, N. and Saxton, J. (1994). *Asking Better Questions*. Toronto: Pembroke.

Oakhill, J. and Garnham, A. (1988). *Becoming a Skilled Reader*. Oxford: Basil Blackwell.

Palincsar, A. S. and Brown, A. L. (1984). 'Reciprocal teaching of comprehension-fostering and comprehension-monitoring activities', *Cognition and Instruction*, **1**, 117–75.

Rosenshine, B., Meister, C. and Chapman, S. (1996). 'Teaching pupils to generate questions: a review of intervention studies', *Review of Educational Research*, **66**, 2, 181–221.

Sczieska, J. (1989). *The True Story of the Three Little Pigs*. New York: Penguin.

Tizard, B. and Hughes, M. (1984). *Young Children Learning: Talking and Thinking at Home and at School*. London: Fontana.

Wells, G. (1986). *The Meaning Makers – Children Learning Language and Using Language to Learn*. London: Hodder and Stoughton.

Woodward, C. (1992). 'Raising and answering questions in primary science: some considerations.' In: Newton, L. D. (ed.) *Primary Science: The Challenge of the 1990s*. Clevedon: Multilingual Matters.

Wragg, E. C., Wragg, C. M., Haynes, G. S. and Chamberlin, R. P. (1998). *Improving Literacy in the Primary School*. London: Routledge.

Young, R. (1992). *Critical Theory and Classroom Talk*. Clevedon: Multilingual Matters.

CHAPTER 5

THE TWO Rs – RULES AND RELATIONSHIPS

E. C. Wragg

Many human activities are governed by rules, some explicit and often available in written form, others implicit, unwritten, unspoken even. If we were to try to play a game like chess without observing the rules it would either consist of constant negotiation, or it would be chaotic, or it would collapse under a welter of argument. On the other hand, few families have a written set of rules about meal times, television watching or use of the bathroom. Such codes that govern family matters have often been worked out by trial and error, by sustained informal negotiation over a long period of time.

Rules

Life without any rules at all would be chaotic and downright dangerous. Too many pedantic and rigid rules, however, would paralyse a community, which is why workers in dispute with their employer sometimes decide to 'work to rule'. In an unruly society, we would probably be killed crossing the road for how could we know on which side of the road to expect cars and lorries, or indeed whether they might suddenly veer on to the footpath?

Rules in school are of several kinds. There are national rules, many incorporated in Acts of Parliament, which govern such matters as pupil attendance, parental rights, use of punishments; there are local authority rules, such as the code of laboratory safety, or what teachers must do on field trips; there are also school rules which may be similar to or different from those of other schools, and these can concern dress, behaviour in the playground or use of facilities. Finally, there are teachers' rules on matters such as talking, movement, the setting out of work or disruptive behaviour.

The question of rules is closely bound up with, but also distinct from, that of relationships. The relationship between two or more people is to some extent affected by the rule conventions under which it operates. Bantock (1965) stressed that teachers are paid to be present and are therefore different from pupils. They also have legal and contractual obligations, to act as a parent, *in loco parentis*, which means that, to some extent, their relationship with children is affected by what a court might require of them. Should there be an accident, teachers can avoid legal action for negligence by acting as a responsible parent would, summoning help, checking that the child is in good hands, communicating with those who need to know. When sour relationships develop, it is sometimes because rules are perceived to be unfairly or inconsistently applied, or because there is dissent or uncertainty about the rules themselves.

Within the first few days of the school year, dozens of rules are established or reaffirmed in some form or another by teachers. However, although some rules are stated explicitly early in the school year, like the science lab safety issues mentioned above, it is common for others to emerge by case law: 'don't talk to your neighbour when someone is answering a question, listen', 'walk on the left please', 'you're not allowed to play football there', 'show your working clearly and underline each answer with a ruler'. Given the many rules and conventions governing behaviour in schools, it is hardly surprising that teachers do not attempt to read them all out on the first morning – it would be too much to recall and would suggest that school is solely about rules. Some rules may even be expressed through euphemism. When one teacher expressed dismay about someone who 'had big eyes', this was not a slur on Mickey Mouse, but rather a coded message that a pupil had been spotted looking at a neighbour's paper during a test.

One of the most frequent findings in our own research is the importance of *consistency*. Teachers who are consistent seem to have fewer difficulties than those who are inconsistent or erratic, tolerating misdemeanours on certain occasions, or from some pupils, but becoming cross about identical matters at other times. Professor Jerry Freiberg (Rogers and Freiberg, 1994) has worked with some of the most difficult schools in the United States to improve discipline. Consistent implementation of humane rules and the involvement of pupils in managing their own behaviour has been a very important part of his programmes, which have produced not only fewer referrals to the principal or exclusions for poor behaviour, but also a significant increase in performance in English and mathematics scores.

Let us now take, as an example, the common rule, 'Don't call out, put your hand up if you want to speak.' I have observed several different ways of establishing this, including the following:

> *Teacher A*: 'One thing I want everybody to be clear about in my class is that you must put your hand up whenever you want to say something. I don't want anyone calling out. If everyone calls out then we can't hear what anybody is saying.' (Early in the first lesson of the year.)
>
> *Teacher B*: 'What do we always do before we want to speak?' (An odd one this. It happened early on the first day of school, and although teachers sometimes use 'we' when they mean 'you', it seemed especially strange in this context since she never raised her own hand. Moreover, when a pupil called out, 'Put your hand up', she replied, 'That's quite right, Alison', even though Alison had, herself, called out – a mixed set of messages.)
>
> *Teacher C*: 'I'm getting a bit concerned about everybody just calling out, "Miss, Miss," all the time. Let's see you put your hands up and then I'll decide who speaks.' (On the second day, when the class had become noisy.)

There are certain differences as well as similarities here. All three teachers were seeking to achieve the same goal, that of persuading children to raise their hands before speaking, but whereas Teacher A stated this explicitly as a rule clearly on

---

Activity 5.1

1   Write down the three or four most important rules you can think of for your own classroom.

(i)

(ii)

(iii)

(iv)

2   Write down some other, less important rules that occur to you.

(i)

(ii)

(iii)

(iv)

3   Discuss the following:

(i)   How would you classify each of your rules? (Movement? Property? Relationships? School work?)

(ii)   Why is your first set of rules more important than your second set?

(iii)   Take one or two of your more important rules and describe how you established them. (In written form? Did you tell people what you expected? Did you wait until the rule was broken and then react?)

(iv)   What do you do when someone breaks each of your rules?

(v)   How do your rules reflect on and affect your relationships with pupils?

---

the first day, Teacher C waited until some degree of disorder occurred. Teacher A also gave an explanation, self-evident maybe, of why the rule existed.

Interviews with teachers and observations of lessons shows that rules fall under certain clear headings. These included the following, with some specific examples in each case.

Movement
Walk quietly.
No running.
Ask first if you want to go to the toilet.
Don't just wander around the room, unless you're getting something.

Talking
Don't talk when I'm talking to you.
You should only be talking to each other if it's about your work.

Don't talk when someone is answering a question.
Only one person talking at a time.
No shouting out.
Put your hands up, if you want to ask a question.
Silence during registration.
Silence in the library area.

Work-related
Being able to work independently on your own.
Being able to work harmoniously in a group.
Working quietly even if the teacher is out of the room.
Starting work without having to be told.
Not distracting or spoiling the concentration of others when they are working.
No mobile phones, or if permitted they must be switched off during lessons.

Presentation
Knowing how to set out work and when to hand it in.
Taking care with content.

Safety
Care with equipment, particularly in subjects like science, technology, PE.
No swinging on chairs, pushing and shoving.
No playing on slippery banks in wet weather.

Space
Not allowed in classrooms or specialist rooms at break.
Carrying out activities near appropriate facility (e.g. sink, bench, gym equipment).

Materials
Equipment to be handled carefully and kept in proper place.
Keep library books tidy.
Know the correct place for returning equipment or unused materials.
Put things away properly at the end of the day.
Clothing and PE equipment to be kept in the approved place.
No writing on desks or book covers.
Return borrowed items to their owner.
Stack chairs on or under tables or desks at the end of the day.

Social behaviour
Show consideration for others.
Be willing to share things and co-operate.
Don't abuse or take the property of classmates without permission.
Be polite and thoughtful, treat others as you would like to be treated yourself.
Show good manners.

---

1   Consider the sets of rules given here. Which do you find most important and which seem more trivial? Which would you wish to see in operation in your own classroom, and which not?

2   Take some particular rules, perhaps 'safety requirements', 'consideration for others', 'being able to work independently on your own', or 'appropriate dress must be worn' and discuss how a teacher might (a) establish (b) explain the need for and (c) fine tune such a rule.

3   Choose some rules about which different teachers in the same school might disagree:

    (a)   what problems might be caused by different practices
    (b)   what solutions might be found to avoid difficulties. Such rules as 'not being allowed in classroom at break time', 'working quietly even if the teacher is out of the room' and 'knowing how to set out work and when to hand it in' are worth considering here.

4   Discuss the extent to which there should be uniformity and what degree of diversity is permissible in different teachers' classroom rules and conventions within the same school.

Clothing/appearance
Clothing to be neat and clean.
Wear appropriate uniform properly (e.g. shirt tucked in).
All clothing to be labelled.
During hot weather sleeves may be rolled up, cardigans, jackets, pullovers and ties removed.
Hairstyles, jewellery, studs and rings only as approved.

Self-discipline and negotiation

Rules are usually imposed on children by adults. The idea of negotiating rules with them is not as widespread as one might believe. Yet in much of school, and indeed most of adult life, we have to take responsibility for discipline ourselves, in the light of society's established order, without some superordinate telling us what to do every few minutes. Most people agree that self-discipline is important and that pupils in school should master it, but this belief is not always translated into practices which would secure it. There are many ways in which pupils themselves can take more responsibility for their own and their colleagues' behaviour and progress, without the teacher abdicating responsibility.

There is a view proposed by Glasser (1969), in his book *Schools without Failure*, that class management problems are made easier if children can understand why certain rules apply, or are consulted about the sort of behaviour that is desirable in a classroom. Glasser argued that it was worthwhile for teachers to spend some time explaining what rules they believed in, but also asking pupils to suggest adjustments or new rules of their own. Subsequently, other proponents have suggested that teachers should discuss rule-related problems to see who 'owns' it, whether it was the teacher, the pupil, or a shared responsibility. This raises the issue about what *is* open to negotiation – bullying, theft, damage to property and people, for example? The means of prevention, perhaps, but surely not the issues themselves. Ensuring children's well-being and law-abiding behaviour is a legal requirement on teachers, for they must exercise the 'duty of care', as it is called.

Occasionally it may be worth creating the time for discussion of what is happening in the classroom, especially at the beginning of the year, or if there appear to be problems. This ritual is known as 'Circle Time' in primary schools, when pupils sit round and discuss the process of teaching and learning with their teacher. From time to time, it may be a valuable lubricant in a secondary class, though not if it becomes an over-indulgence or begins to predominate.

One teacher, seeking to explain that a laboratory could be a dangerous place, engaged the children's interest by giving them a blank piece of paper first, saying, 'I want you to make up and write down some rules which will help us avoid having accidents.' Most of the local education authority (LEA) rules like 'no running or pushing', 'handle equipment carefully', 'be careful with flames or acids', were anticipated by the class, so that when he gave out copies of the actual rules they were pleased at their success. Matters like 'wearing goggles', which no one had suggested, were then discussed.

One important fundamental question about negotiation is not merely what is or what should be negotiable, but how children can understand the need for rules, such as wearing proper clothing on a field trip, staying away from dangerous places and not taking risks. This does not negotiate away teachers' legal responsibilities, it actually makes them more meaningful. Adolescents need to face up to matters such as self-discipline and respect for others, because these are necessary in families and communities, as well as in schools. Teachers in the end must take responsibility for rules, even if they sometimes endorse sensible proposals from pupils.

There are several ways in which rules can be introduced. These include, with examples:

General explanation   'I want to see you showing consideration for others.'

Specific prescription   'You must put your hand up when you want to say something.'

Rule with explanation   'I don't want anyone pushing and shoving near that sink, because someone's going to spill water on the floor and slippery floors cause accidents.'

General question   'How can we make sure everyone gets a fair chance to do well in their exams next summer?'

Specific question   'What would happen if nobody in the school had name tags on their clothes?'

Case law   'Haven't you started yet?' 'I don't understand what we're supposed to do.' 'Well, if you're not clear about something you should put your hand up, instead of just sitting there waiting, and I'll come over and explain it to you.'

Negotiation   'I've allowed you to talk to each other while you're doing your projects, but it's getting far too noisy, so let's just discuss for a minute what we can do about it.'

This activity is designed to involve pupils in looking at certain aspects of their own behaviour in a mature way. From primary school right up to the end of secondary education many boys do less well than girls at school, especially in language-type activities and in terms of behaviour. Four or five times as many boys as girls are excluded from school for poor behaviour. Boys are also more likely to jeer at their fellows who appear to work hard in class, using terms like 'boff', 'boffin' or 'keano'. This activity is suitable for the younger pupils in a secondary school, older pupils need a modified approach. It should be completed at the beginning of the year, but it may be done later. Students or inexperienced teachers should only do this in close collaboration with someone more experienced. The form and wording will need to be modified according to the age, ability and background of the pupils.

1   Explain to the class that, as you will be working together in future, you all need to be clear about behaviour.
2   Ask orally, or in writing, for 'Reasons why we come to school', and then discuss these. Most children will give replies like, 'To learn to read and write' or, 'To help us get a job', but other answers like, 'Because we have to' are worth discussing.
3   Ask pupils to suggest or write down some simple rules of behaviour and procedure which will help everyone learn better. This will often produce suggestions like, 'Don't interfere with others who are working', or, 'Don't mess about.' Related matters can then be raised, like, 'What about when we're discussing something?' (no calling out, listen to others) or, 'What about when we're working in groups?' (share things, wait your turn, don't ridicule the efforts of others).
4   Ask if there are any differences between the ways that boys and girls behave in class. Discuss, in as sensitive a manner as possible, the common finding that in many schools girls are doing better academically than boys.
5   Get everyone to make a special effort to establish a climate that helps people learn and work harmoniously together.

Self-monitoring   'You'll have to make a lot of decisions yourself when you're older, so let's see how well you can manage your own work, without me having to tell you what to do all the time.'

Relationships

Rules and relationships can be closely connected. Much of what has been covered in this unit so far is not just a matter of rules but also of personal relationships. The following observation notes from contrasting events in lessons make this clear. Both concern pupils who were not working when they should have been, but the first is more benign in its exposition and enforcement than the second and creates a positive relationship, while the second achieves the opposite effect.

A A girl has not started her work in a maths lesson. 'Don't you understand what I want?' the teacher asks. 'Oh yes. I understand what you want, but I don't see why,' she replies. The teacher stands by her and explains fully and carefully that it is an exercise in relationships and shapes, one with another. He has noticed that some people were making mistakes, did not know what to emphasise, or were not looking carefully. The girl listens attentively and, apparently quite satisfied, goes on with her work, looking very carefully.

B The teacher is talking to the whole class in her science lesson when two boys begin to talk to each other. The teacher swings round rapidly, points and glares at one of the offending lads and barks out in a very loud and frightening voice, 'Did I ask you to talk?' He pauses for two seconds in the ensuing silence and stares. 'Well, don't then.' The boys stop talking and the observer notes that the rest of the class appears shocked. There had been a considerable change in the teacher's voice, strength and tempo.

Personal relationships between teacher and pupils can be shaped in many locations and contexts. Consider just some examples of these, both positive and negative in their effect.

Academic	Explaining patiently to pupil who does not understand a new concept.
	Making a sarcastic remark to someone who doesn't understand a new concept.
Managerial	Smiling at and thanking someone who has helped clear away.
	Blaming someone for mess, choosing the wrong pupil.
Social	Chatting to pupils as they enter classroom about what they did at the weekend.
	Belittling someone's hobby or family/cultural interest.
Expectation	Looking for positive qualities and achievements in children.
	Having low expectations or always focusing on the negative side of pupils' work or behaviour.
Home/school/ community	Talking positively with parents and members of children's communities.
	Showing no interest in children's origins and values.
Individual	Taking a personal interest in children as individuals.
	Seeing class entirely as a group without individual identities.

Personal relationships between pupil and pupil are just as important as those between teacher and pupil. Teachers can play a significant part in the establishment of such relationships. One of the techniques we frequently use in our research is the identification of events that happen in classrooms and that seem to be indicative of the styles, preferences and effects of various teachers. Several hundred such critical events have been collected and analysed. In each case the observer records what led up to the event, what happened and what appeared to be the outcome. After the lesson, the teacher, and sometimes the pupils, were interviewed to elicit their view of what had transpired. One of the aspects of teaching highlighted in this way is how teachers set about establishing relationships between themselves and their pupils.

Use the 'critical events' approach to help you analyse the relationships in a classroom.

1   Find a fellow teacher or student who is willing to be observed. It is a useful paired activity, in which two students, or teachers, or a teacher and a student can observe each other's lessons.
2   During the lesson, look for something that happens that illustrates relationships between (a) teacher and pupil(s) and (b) pupil(s) and pupil(s). The events do not have to be spectacular: indeed, in most cases they will be ordinary everyday happenings, including, perhaps, a few words, a smile, a telling-off, some movement or some humour.
3   Fill in a pro-forma like the one given here.
4   After the lesson, interview the teacher about the event, using a neutral opening like, 'Towards the beginning of the lesson you spoke to Rachel about her conversation with Alice. Can you tell me a bit about what happened?' You can then probe further with 'Why' questions or 'What do you think the effect was?' Avoid starting off with leading or tendentious questions such as, 'Why on earth did (or didn't) you …?' or 'Why were you so soft on Rachel and Alice …?'
5   Interview pupils only if the teacher concerned and the head of the school agree. Talking to children about their classroom relationships with each other and/or their teacher is a sensitive matter, which must be handled in a thoroughly professional way. Student or inexperienced teachers should certainly ensure that they receive proper supervision for such an exercise.
6   See what generalisations and what specific points emerge from your classroom scrutiny. For example, it might seem, as a general conclusion, that the teacher has good relationships with the girls in the class, but less happy ones with the boys, or the other way round. A specific conclusion might be that the way a teacher handled a particular confrontation with a child who had misbehaved had been positive or negative.
7   Does anything need to be done to make relationships in this particular classroom better? What inferences, if any, can you draw about your own teaching?

Observation sheet – Personal relationships

A   What led up to the event?

B   What happened and who was involved?

C   What was the outcome?

D   Interview with teacher

E   Interview with pupil(s) (if agreed)

F   Conclusions

Consider the following account of science teacher Mr B in his second lesson with a class of newly inducted 11-year-olds, after a somewhat stern first lesson. He went on to establish a very positive relationship with the class and is generally liked and respected in the school with the reputation of being firm but fair. His pupils achieved good results in examinations. Note how he uses a skilful mixture of humour, self-deprecation, as well as a reminder that he too has a family, to change the mood to a more friendly, though still purposeful one.

> I've got a son your age, and so when my wife and I were invited out to dinner the other night we tossed up to see who would stay at home babysitting, and of course I lost. I decided to watch football on television with my boy and the commentator began to use some very funny language – 'a square ball', 'the referee blew up', 'he left his foot behind' [laughter]. Well, we have some special language that we use in science that you will need to learn.

Rewards and punishments

Since teachers must act as a responsible parent does, society has to give them certain powers to exercise control or discharge the 'duty of care' which the law requires. Forms of punishment in particular in a school must be approved by the governors. This is to avoid, for example, children being kept in detention after school if this meant that they would miss their bus home to a remote rural area, or to a dangerous part of a city. Punishments are in fact governed by the law, which decrees that they must be 'reasonable', defined by one judge as

- moderate
- not dictated by bad motives
- such as is usual in the school
- such as the parent of the child might expect it to receive if it had done wrong.

This certainly rules out racks and thumbscrews, and the 1986 Education Act made corporal punishment illegal in maintained schools. This ban applies not just to forms of corporal punishment, such as caning and hitting with a ruler, slipper or the hand, but also to a 'clip round the ear', which in any case was a potentially dangerous punishment.

Rewards are one of two principal kinds:

extrinsic   getting a star, a badge, a trophy, a prize, a privilege, something external, often visible, bestowed on behalf of the school or by the teacher.

intrinsic   satisfying one's curiosity, a glow of pride from a job well done, something coming more from within the individual.

Rewards and punishments can too readily be stereotyped as 'good' or 'bad'. For example, it would be easy to assume that rewards themselves are invariably positive and punishments are always negative. Yet a reward out of all proportion to whatever deed earned it, or a minor punishment that was fair and timely and, in retrospect, appreciated by the recipient as having had a positive effect, can soon reverse these simple labels. Similarly, it might be assumed that extrinsic rewards are crude bribes and that intrinsic rewards are the only things worth striving for,

Look at the use of rewards and punishments in your school, remembering some of the more subtle ones like smiles, nods, using pupils' ideas, withholding attention or recognition, displaying children's work. Record some of these at both school and classroom level in the grid below. If you see more than one teacher, look for similarities and differences.

Rewards	*Punishments*
At school level	
Public signs of reward – what does the school value? Pupils' work on display? Children made monitors? Academic success rewarded?	What is the school policy on punishment? What is permitted? Detention? Extra work? What is regarded as mild misbehaviour and what as more serious?
At classroom level	
Look at teachers' use of rewards. Note the public ones but also smiles, nods, use of praise, encouragement.	Make notes about any punishments you see, either formal or less obvious. Look for sanctions such as loss of privilege, change of seat, sending out of class or to head, reprimands.

but some people need external recognition so that they can set their own standards for themselves. What is often much more important is the effect of rewards and punishments on the children concerned, whether the punishment was unfair, something greatly resented by children, or whether they had earned the reward for their own efforts.

Most rewards and punishments are unspectacular, often short-lived and taken for granted. This does not mean that they are of no importance. The two incidents below only occupied a few seconds, but they demonstrate that even a fleeting exchange can have a significant influence. The first shows a girl receiving praise for coping with her own embarrassment, the second describes a public shaming.

The class has been making lists of the characteristics of the animals in *Animal Farm*. The teacher selects one person to read out her list. Amidst giggling, the girl complies. She appears embarrassed at having to stand up. When she has finished reading the teacher says, 'Well done, that was very good.' She smiles encouragement at the pupil who smiles back and sits down.

The teacher states that she will not tolerate pupils talking when she is explaining something in her science lessons. She sees a girl talking as she says this, so she moves quickly over to her, puts her hands on the bench and stares into her face from close range. 'I will not tolerate [pause] talking at the same time.' At the teacher's speed of movement and shortening of the distance between her and the pupil the girl reddens and the class falls silent.

References

Bantock, G. H. (1965) *Freedom and Authority in Education*, London: Faber and Faber.
Glasser, W. (1969) *Schools without Failure*, New York: Harper and Row.
Rogers, C. R. and Freiberg, H. J. (1994) *Freedom to Learn*, New York: Macmillan.

CHAPTER 6

LEARNING AND TEACHING STYLES

Susan Bentham

Introduction

When investigating issues regarding learning and teaching styles it is easy to become overwhelmed by the variety of terminology used and the quagmire of inventories and indexes available which claim to measure some aspect of your *learning style*. In regard to terminology, there are learning styles, cognitive styles, learning strategies, teaching styles and instructional strategies. It is hoped that by the end of this chapter the differences in terms of what these concepts mean will be apparent. This chapter will attempt to make sense of some theories of learning style, and address the limitations of measurement devices as well as exploring how learning and teaching styles can lead to an improvement in learning effectiveness.

Definitions

What is a learning style? Bennett (1990) stated that learning style is a

> consistent pattern of behaviour and performance by which an individual approaches educational experiences. It is the composite of characteristic cognitive, affective, and physiological behaviours that serve as relatively stable indicators of how a learner perceives, interacts with, and responds to the learning environment.
>
> (Bennett, 1990, p. 140)

Dunn *et al.* (1985) identified twenty-two elements relating to learning style. These elements are related to dimensions as follows:

- *Environmental*: preferences regarding bright versus dim light; sound present or absent; cool versus warm temperature; and formal or informal classroom design.
- *Emotional*: individuals will differ on levels of persistence and motivation, and on issues such as degree of responsibility versus non-conformity.
- *Sociological*: preferences in relation to who to work with, that is, alone, in groups or in pairs.
- *Physical*: refers to perceptual strengths such as whether the individual is an auditory, visual or tactile learner. This measure would also include time-of-day preferences, that is, whether the individual prefers to learn in the morning or evening.
- *Psychological*: refers to such dimensions as whether the individual is impulsive or reflective (Griggs, 1991).

Just to complicate issues, Riding and Cheema (1991) note the distinction between cognitive styles and learning styles, although they comment that many theorists will use these terms interchangeably. They would see cognitive style as underlying learning style and involving theoretical academic descriptions of processes involved, while learning style is more immediately apparent and of interest to trainers and educators.

Structure or process

Riding and Cheema (1991) further comment that learning style has been perceived in three ways:

1 *Structure* (content): learning style is seen to reflect a presumed stable structure which remains constant over time; therefore it is the task of an educator to determine what an individual's learning style is for that environment and to match or adapt the method of instruction to the learning style.
2 *Process*: learning style is seen as being in a state of continuous change, and therefore the focus should be on discovering how it changes and how an instructor can foster that change.
3 *Structure and process*: this view would see learning style as being relatively stable but at the same time being modified by events.

Curry's Onion Model

Curry's Onion Model of Learning Styles (Curry, 1983) attempts to explain how learning style can be viewed as both a structure and a process, both relatively stable and at the same time open to modification. Curry's model argues that all learning-style measures may be placed into three groups or 'strata resembling layers of an onion':

1 *Outermost layer of the onion*: Curry refers to this as *instructional preference*, and of all measures of learning styles this is the most unstable. Learning environment and individual and teacher expectations can influence instructional preferences. An example of a learning-style measure at this level would be the 'Learning Preference Inventory' (Rezler and Rezmovic, 1981).
2 *Middle layer of the onion*: Curry refers to this as the *informational processing style*. This learning style reflects the individual's intellectual approach to integrating or assimilating information. This type of learning style is more stable than instructional preferences but may still be influenced by learning strategies. An example of a learning-style measure at this level would be the 'Learning Style Inventory' (Kolb, 1976).
3 *Innermost layer of the onion*: Curry refers to this as *cognitive personality style*, which is defined as the individual's approach to assimilating and adapting information. This dimension does not interact with the environment, although this dimension fundamentally controls all learning behaviour. An example of a learning-style measure at this level would be the Myers-Briggs Type Indicator (Myers, 1962).

Of interest in this model is the implication that learning strategies can influence certain learning styles. A learning style is a fairly fixed and stable characteristic of an individual, whereas a learning strategy outlines a way to approach a situation, task or problem and may be learned and developed over time. Over the course of a lifetime an individual might learn many learning strategies, but their learning style will remain fairly constant (Riding and Cheema, 1991).

Teaching style and instructional strategy

To add to this collection of definitions we also have the distinction between teaching style and instructional strategy. Bennett (1990) described a teacher's method or instructional strategy as their preference for lecture, small group work or oral reports, whereas 'teaching style refers to the teacher's pervasive personal behaviour and media used during interaction with learners. It is the teacher's characteristic approach whatever the method used' (Bennett, 1990, p. 161). One example of a teaching style is a formal or an informal approach. A formal teaching style would focus on the subject to be taught and the responsibility of the teacher to impart this knowledge. An informal teaching style would emphasise the individual's specific learning needs and the teacher's responsibility to create the appropriate learning experiences.

Progress exercise 6.1

Match the following terms to the following definitions:
teaching style   learning styles   cognitive styles   learning strategy

1   Differences in perceptual strengths (visual or auditory learners) or differences in preferences regarding time to learn (morning vs evening) are examples of _____.
2   _____ are academic descriptions of processes involved in learning which underlie learning styles.
3   A learning style is a fairly fixed and stable characteristic of an individual, whereas a way of remembering the following sequence ICIIBMCIAFBI by grouping the sequence into meaningful chunks such as ICI-IBM-CIA-FBI is an example of a _____, which can be learned.
4   _____ is described as a teacher's characteristic approach regardless of instructional strategy used.

(Answers can be found on p. 84)

Theories

There are many theories of or approaches to measuring learning styles. In this section we will concentrate on three theories.

Myers-Briggs Type Indicator (MBTI)

This theory would classify individuals' learning style according to four dimensions or scales. These scales were derived from Jung's theory of psychological types. The scales are shown in Table 6.1.

Table 6.1 Myers-Briggs Type Indicator

Extroverts	vs	*Introverts*
Focus on outer world		Focus on inner world
Sensors	vs	*Intuitors*
Emphasis on facts and procedures		Emphasis on meanings and possibilities
Thinkers	vs	*Feelers*
Decisions are made on the basis of logic and rules		Decisions are made on the basis of personal considerations
Judgers	vs	*Perceivers*
Set and strictly follow agendas		Can change with circumstances

According to this model, individual scores on these scales, in combination, form a total of sixteen different learning styles. For example, an individual could be an extrovert, sensor, thinker and judger (Felder, 1996).

Kolb's learning-style inventory

Kolb (1976) saw the learning process as being separated into two distinct components: perception (how the information is taken in) and processing (how the information is internalised).

In terms of perception (how the information is taken in), an individual would either have a preference for

Concrete experience: participating in specific situations. Relating to people with an emphasis on feeling.

or *Abstract conceptualisation*: an emphasis on analysing, thinking and planning, rather than feeling.

In terms of processing (how the information is internalised), an individual would either have a preference for

Active experimentation: preference for doing something with the information, emphasising risk taking and being involved in practical applications that influence people.

or *Reflective observation*: preference for thinking about the information rather than doing, with an emphasis on understanding, searching for a meaning, and seeing the situation from different perspectives.

These two dimensions of perceiving and processing information result in four types of learners:

Type 1: (*concrete experience + reflective observation*)
Type 2: (*abstract conceptualisation + reflective observation*)
Type 3: (*abstract conceptualisation + active experimentation*)
Type 4: (*concrete experience + active experimentation*)

(Felder, 1996; FEDA, 1995)

The Honey and Mumford learning styles

Honey and Mumford adapted Kolb's theories and formulated a learning-style questionnaire. Honey and Mumford (1986) defined four learning styles:

Activist	Functions in immediate present, prefers hands-on activities, loves challenges, gets bored with implementation, does not necessarily recognise problems.
Reflector	Prefers to stand back and observe. Likes to think and analyse. Tends to be cautious.
Theorist	Is rational, logical and analytic. Likes theories, models and order.
Pragmatist	Likes new ideas. Excels at lateral thinking. Is keen to see if new ideas work in practice.

Progress exercise 6.2

For each of the following students' comments, state what type of learning style you think the student has.

1   When I go into a lesson, I like to be involved. I like to jump right in and do something.
2   I like stimulating input! I love it when I hear a really interesting and thought-provoking lecture I need time to digest and think about what I have heard I don't like to be personally involved in the lesson and I don't like answering questions.
3   I like structure and order. When I go into a lesson I want to know what we are going to do, when we are going to do it and why we are going to do it.
4   I like activities in a lesson but there must be a reason for the activity, there must be a purpose to the activity.

(Answers on p. 84)

Measurement of learning styles

Many indexes of learning styles are formulated on the basis of questionnaires. Learning-style inventories are an example of a psychometric test and consequently will have certain advantages and limitations.

Concerns regarding measurement of learning styles

- *Reliability*: there are issues regarding reliability or consistency in regard to scores on learning-style questionnaires. Test scores should not fluctuate with such factors as mood or time of day when the test was taken.
- *Validity*: the test should be valid, that is, it should measure what it sets out to measure, not other factors. Consideration needs to be given to question design. For example, if a questionnaire had asked for a response to the statement 'Do you like watching TV?', what would a response to that statement really tell us about an individual's learning style? Some questions on some learning-style questionnaires will call for a *yes* or a *no* answer, but do *yes* or *no* answers really reflect how we feel regarding an issue?
- *Response bias*: do we answer the way we feel we should answer?
- *Are we aware of how we learn*? Are some individuals more aware of how they learn than others? Honey and Mumford (1992) felt that although individuals

prefer different ways of learning most individuals were not aware of these preferences. Would degree of self-awareness affect the validity of a learning-style inventory?

- *Tendency to place individuals in discrete categories*: there is a danger of type-casting. Is it true that once an activist always an activist? Kolb (1984) states that the aim in identifying preferred learning styles should be to lead to greater choices, decisions and possibilities. Perhaps knowledge of personal learning styles (including strengths and limitations) and knowledge of other learning styles (including strengths and limitations) will encourage the individual to experiment with alternative learning styles.
- *How do the numerous indexes of learning styles relate to each other?* Learning-style inventories measure a range of variables. An individual could find out their learning styles in regard to room temperature, or time-of-learning prefer-ence, as well as to what degree they were an activist or a reflector. The ques-tion is: how does all this information fit together? Lewis states that many theorists seem 'determined to pursue their own pet distinctions in cheerful disregard of each other' (1976, p. 304).
- *What is the relationship between learning styles and specific instructional styles?* Reiff (1992) states that although many learning styles have been identi-fied, the usefulness of such information has yet to be established. Clear links between learning styles, specific educational environments and specific instructional approaches need to be set out.

Advantages of learning-style indexes

If learning styles can be ascertained, then instructional strategies can be geared to learning style, resulting in improvement in learning effectiveness. The next section in this chapter will look at studies that have tried to make links between learning styles, instructional strategies and improved performance.

Alternative methods of measuring learning style

As stated earlier, learning style is often measured by questionnaires, but are there other ways? If there is a match between learning styles and instructional strategies, then perhaps we only have to determine preferred instructional strategy to infer learning style. It would be possible to systematically present a number of instruc-tional strategies to an individual and measure their performance on each, to determine what instructional strategy resulted in maximum performance.

Progress exercise 6.3

The MADEUP learning-style inventory to differentiate between visual and auditory learners
(To each of the following, answer *yes* or *no*)

1 I always prefer reading rather than listening to the radio.
2 I would prefer that my teacher just talked rather than wrote information on the board.
3 When driving somewhere new do you make a tape-recording outlining step-by-step instructions of how to get there, and then listen to the tape when driving?

4   Reading makes my eyes sore.
5   I like writing notes in class.
6   I find the notes on the OHP particularly helpful.
7   I prefer to tape-record what happens in class.

Scoring
If you answered yes to nos, 1, 5 and 6 you are a visual learner.
If you answered yes to nos, 2, 3, 4 and 7 you are an auditory learner.

Questions
1   How would you evaluate the MADEUP learning-style inventory?
2   Evaluate another learning-style inventory that you have used.

Individual differences in learning styles

In this section, we will look at differential learning styles in relation to gender and ethnic minority groups. We will also look at possible individual differences in learning style in relation to autism. The studies mentioned are attempting to make links between learning style, instructional strategies and learning effectiveness. Of course, it is important to remember that although trends do emerge, they can and do obscure differences that exist within groups.

Gender

Boaler (1997) carried out a study which supported the view that boys and girls have preferences for different ways of 'knowing'. Boaler (1997) studied and tracked a group of Year 9 students in two different schools in regard to mathematical achievement for three years. The schools chosen were in similar areas and the students had similar scores on cognitive ability tests at the commencement of Year 9. The only difference between the two groups was the way in which maths was taught. In the first school, the approach was traditional, content-led and textbook based. The second school had an approach that was open and project-based with an emphasis on process. After three years, differences in achievement were found between the two schools. Girls achieved less when taught with a traditional approach; this was most noticeable within the top sets. Interviews with students suggested a female preference for learning tasks that were open-ended, project-based, related to real situations and which gave time for thinking and discussion. Males, though preferring discussion, were more willing and better at adapting to traditional approaches which required memorising abstract facts and rules. Arnot *et al.* (1998) on evaluating this study note that generalisations based on such a small study would be dangerous; however the hypothesis of gender differences in learning styles deserves further testing.

Autism

Edelson (2000) writes regarding the learning styles of students with autism, specifically their preference for visual (learning through seeing), auditory (learning through hearing) or kinaesthetic (learning by touching) modes. Edelson and colleagues believe that many autistic individuals rely on only one style of learning; therefore a careful assessment of preferred learning styles could lead to more appropriate teaching interventions. Edelson states that one common problem cited by teachers involves difficulties with autistic students running around the classroom in disregard of teacher instruction. Edelson comments that perhaps such a student is not an auditory learner and teacher instruction should be based on another modality or learning style. Perhaps a kinaesthetic approach (placing a hand on the child's shoulders and guiding the child to his chair) or a visual approach (showing the child a picture of a chair and gesturing to him to sit on it) would be more effective. If in doubt regarding preferred learning style then it is advisable to teach concepts using all modalities.

Ethnic minority groups

Griggs and Dunn (1996) write on the learning styles of various ethnic minorities, with specific reference to Hispanic American students. Learning style was looked at from five dimensions and the following differences were noted:

1   *Environmental learning style*: It was noted that Mexican-American elementary and middle school pupils preferred a cool temperature and a formal classroom design.
2   *Emotional learning style*: This learning style referred to responsibility, structure, persistence and motivation. It would seem that Mexican-Americans require a higher degree of structure than other groups.
3   *Sociological learning style*: More Caucasian students preferred working alone than either Mexican-American children or African-American children, with African-American children expressing the greatest preference for group work (Dunn and Dunn, 1992; Sims, 1988).
4   *Physiological learning style*: Puerto-Rican college students exhibited a strong preference for learning in the late morning onwards. Sims (1988) found that Caucasian students preferred eating and drinking while studying significantly more than Mexican-Americans. Caucasians and African-Americans were significantly more auditory and visual in their learning style than Mexican-Americans. Latinos were rated as kinaesthetic learners (Yong and Ewing 1992; Dunn et al., 1993).

Griggs and Dunn (1996) state that it is important to be aware of the limitations of such research and to appreciate that individual learning style will be affected by many variables, ethnic background being just one. Learning style will also be influenced by socio-economic status, region, religion, family structure, etc. However, noting the limitations of such research, Hispanic students on the whole prefer a cool environment, peer-orientated learning, and kinaesthetic instructional resources, and have energy peaks in the late morning and afternoon.

Improving learning effectiveness and study skills

There are various strategies that claim to raise achievement. These strategies themselves could be categorised as follows:

•   Strategies that attempt to match learning styles with instructional approaches.
•   Teaching of specific study skills such as time management and note-taking skills, and steps involved in researching and improving reading techniques.
•   Meta-cognitive approaches: teaching learners how to learn. This would include thinking skills programmes such as Feuerstein's Instrumental Enrichment and Process Based Instruction.

From learning styles to instructional approaches

Given that we have identified an individual's learning style, what should happen next? If a teacher realises that they are not teaching to the individual's preferred learning style, should they change or adapt the material? What if the demands of the curriculum necessitate whole group teaching? What if each student in the class has a different learning style? One way of getting around this issue would be to use various instructional strategies which aim to teach some of the students' preferred learning styles at least some of the time. This approach would also work if you didn't know what the students' learning styles were. Taking a different viewpoint, Felder (1996) argues that if a teacher teaches exclusively to the student's preferred learning style then the student 'may not develop the mental dexterity they need to reach their potential for achievement in school and professions, where they will need to be flexible in their approach to learning' (Felder, 1996, p. 18).

4-MAT system

McCarthy (1990) took Kolb's learning-style descriptions and modified them to create the '4-MAT system', which is used in designing and developing classroom lesson plans for students ranging from 5 to 17. From Kolb's model, McCarthy outlined four types of learners and eight aspects of lesson design (as outlined in Table 6.2).

McCarthy argues that each learning style has its own strengths and weaknesses and that this method of lesson presentation allows each student to experience their preferred way of learning as well as working through other ways of learning. This method of lesson planning would give all students valuable experience in all learning styles. But what does this system look like in practice? At this point it is helpful to look at a specific example.

Example of the 4-MAT approach to lesson planning

Aim of the lesson: to teach learning styles to a class of learning support assistants.

Motivation
1   *Create the experience*: Students are asked to design what they consider to be the perfect lesson plan for the topic 'The truth behind UFOs'.
2   *Reflect on the experience*: Students are asked to get into groups and to compare their ideas on what they consider to be the perfect lesson plan.

Concept development
3   *Integrate reflection into concepts*: A general discussion is held to compare and contrast lesson plans. The theme that would be developed, through discussion, would make connections between differences in ideal lesson plans and individual preferred learning styles.
4   *Present and develop theories and concepts*: A handout of learning styles includes Kolb's, Honey and Mumford's and McCarthy's theories. The handout is discussed.

Practice
5   *Practise and reinforce new information*: The students are required to complete Honey and Mumford's learning-style inventory.
6   *Personalise the experience*: The students are requested to get into groups and discuss what they have found out in regard to their unique learning style.

Table 6.2 4-MAT system

Kolb's model	McCarthy's type of learner	Aspect of lesson plan
Concrete experience	Innovative/imaginative The student perceives information by feeling and sensing. These individuals need to reflect on their experiences.	Motivation This aspect of the lesson is geared to those students who need to be actively involved. These students need to know why the information is relevant and how it is related to their existing experiences. The motivation aspect of the lesson would be divided into • create the experience; • reflect on the experience.
Reflective observation	Analytic The individual student processes information by watching and thinking and then proceeds to develop theories.	Concept development This aspect of the lesson is geared to those students who like to have information presented to them in the form of what the experts say, or what the text states. The concept development part of the lesson would be divided into • integrate reflections into concepts; • present and develop theories and concepts.
Abstract conceptualisation	Common sense The individual first formulates and develops theories, then needs to know whether they work in practice.	Practice This aspect of the lesson allows the students to understand the information presented in the previous stage through practical exercises and activities. This aspect of the lesson is divided into • practise and reinforce new information; • personalise the experience.
Active experimentation	Dynamic The individual student learns by feeling and sensing and then by experimenting with ways in which they can use this information.	Application This aspect of the lesson would have students exploring ways in which information learned can be applied to new situations. This aspect of the lesson is divided into • develop a plan for applying new concepts; • do it and share it with others.

Application

7   *Develop a plan for applying new concepts*: Students are told to get into small groups and in their groups to develop a lesson plan for the topic 'The truth behind UFOs', using the 4-MAT system.

8   *Do it and share it with others*: A member of each group presents their lesson plan to the class. The class discusses issues such as whether it will work and whether it will work with all students.

Evaluation of the 4-MAT system

Bowers (1987) investigated the effect of a 4-MAT system on fifty-four gifted Year 6 students. The students were randomly assigned to either a 4-MAT group or a Restricted-Textbook group. Both groups were taught a unit on Newton's First Law of Motion. A test was given at the end of the unit. Significant differences were found on overall scores and critical thinking scores in favour of the 4-MAT system.

Sangster and Shulman (1988) studied a pilot programme involving the implementation and evaluation of the 4-MAT curriculum in secondary schools. Some 31 teachers and 572 students were involved. Questionnaires and interviews revealed that both students and teachers perceived the system favourably.

Study skills

There has been a wealth of information regarding how to study more effectively. These include tips for organising your time, improving your reading technique, how to take notes in class, how to write essays and how to revise for exams. In terms of time management, Johnson *et al.* (1982) recommend the following:

•   Set aside times and places for work.
•   Set priorities and follow them.
•   Break larger tasks into smaller ones.
•   Do not overwhelm yourself with tasks; be reasonable in regard to how many tasks you can do in a day.
•   Work on one thing at a time.
•   Check your progress often.

Robinson (1970) developed the SQ3R method of effective reading.

1   *Survey*: before you start to read a chapter, try to get an overview of what information the chapter is presenting. Read chapter outlines. Look at the various headings.
2   *Question*: for every heading presented in the chapter, convert it into a question. Asking questions will help you to become more involved in your reading.
3   *Read*: read one specific section at a time. Read the section with the aim of answering the question you have just formulated.
4   *Recite*: recite the answer to the question out loud (if possible) and in your own words. You might want to make notes at this point. Keep repeating steps 2–4 until you have finished reading the chapter.
5   *Review*: when you have finished the chapter, go back over key points and questions.

Evaluation of study skills programmes

Leland-Jones (1997) investigated the use of a study skills programme in raising academic achievement in Year 6 students. A unit of study skills emphasising the use of resource material, interpreting data and creating chapter outlines was incorporated into individual chapters on a social studies course. The programme resulted in increased knowledge of study skills and higher achievement scores.

Brown and Forristall (1983) investigated the use of a 'Computer-Assisted Study Skills Improvement Program'. The computer program provided interactive instruction on topics such as time management, improving memory, taking lecture notes and reading textbooks. Students completing the program showed significant improvement in study skill and academic abilities.

One scheme that aims to encourage study skills is called 'Playing for Success'. This scheme targets underachieving young people in Key Stages 2 and 3 within inner city areas, and establishes the study support centres in English Premiership and First Division football clubs. Using the environment of football, the centres focus on skills in literacy and numeracy. The centres also provide opportunities for pupils to develop ICT and study skills and to complete their homework. Evaluation indicates that as many girls as boys participate and that both boys and girls benefit equally in terms of attitudes and improved reading and maths abilities (Sharp *et al.*, 1999).

Meta-cognitive approaches

Meta-cognition involves our personal awareness of factors that influence our own thinking, learning and problem-solving abilities. It is argued that the more we know about the process of learning, the more we can incorporate this knowledge into our own learning, thus becoming more independent and efficient. This view stresses the role of the learner as being actively involved in the learning process. There are a number approaches in this area such as Feuerstein's Instrumental Enrichment and Process Based Instruction.

Feuerstein's Instrumental Enrichment

Key to this programme are the concepts of 'structured cognitive modifiability' and 'mediated learning experiences'. This programme places an emphasis on both the emotional and cognitive factors underlying learning. A central role within the programme is that of the teacher who places themselves between the child and the environment in order to control and interpret incoming stimuli to promote a greater understanding of the environment. This process is described as mediated learning experiences, with the teacher as the mediator (Feuerstein *et al.*, 1980). Successful mediation requires the teacher to ensure that students

- understand what they are supposed to do;
- understand why they are doing the task;
- appreciate that the task has value or applications beyond the here and now of the classroom;
- develop an appreciation of what they can realistically do, an awareness of when they need help and the skills necessary to ask for help;
- through the above goals, are encouraged in skills of self-reflection and awareness of inner thoughts and feelings.

It is through these mediated learning experiences that the underlying cognitive structures are modified or changed.

Table 6.3 Four components of Process Based Instruction

Component	Skills taught
Cueing	Where to start and how to start.
Acting	The sequences of actions needed.
Monitoring	How to review whether the plan is working as expected.
Verifying	How to determine whether the task has been completed correctly or whether to go back and try again.

Process Based Instruction

This programme (Ashman and Conway, 1993) aims to teach students how to learn and solve problems through the development of meta-cognitive strategies. The programme focuses on four components, which aim to promote skills such as self-questioning, decision making and evaluation (see Table 6.3).

Doran and Cameron (1995) state that these skills should be taught, commencing in reception classrooms.

Progress exercise 6.4

A Year 7 student has been given an assignment of writing two pages on a famous scientist. Using the Process Based Instruction approach, what advice would you give a student who just doesn't know what to do regarding this assignment?

Summary

In this chapter we have looked at various definitions including: learning styles, cognitive styles, learning strategies, teaching styles and instructional strategies. We have looked at three theories regarding learning styles: Kolb's, Honey and Mumford's and the MBTI. As learning styles are often measured by an individual completing a questionnaire, various points of concern were raised. Some research concerned with revealing differential learning styles in relation to gender and ethnic minority groups was discussed. What has emerged from this short introduction to the field of teaching and learning styles is not only the potential benefits of matching learning styles to instructional strategies, but also the real need for further research in this area.

Review exercise

1 What does the research say in regard to improving learning effectiveness?
2 There are an incredible number of learning-style inventories or indexes available. Your task is to find and complete as many as possible. The internet is a good place to search. After completing as many inventories as possible, what have you found out about yourself?

Answers to progress exercises

6.1 Missing phrases: 1 learning styles, 2 cognitive styles, 3 learning strategy, 4 teaching style.
6.2 1 activist, 2 reflector, 3 theorist, 4 pragmatist.

Further reading

Further Education Development Agency (1995) *Learning Styles*. This short booklet looks at Honey and Mumford's model of learning styles in considerable depth. The advantage of this booklet is that it has a copy of the learning-style questionnaire, adapted for 16–19 year olds, in the appendix.

The National Foundation for Educational Research (Nfer) is a valuable source for information regarding current projects. The Nfer has a very useful internet site with many publications available. This is one of my favourite sites: http://www.nfer.ac.uk/

An interesting site for those interested in more information regarding study skills is: http://www.utexas.edu/student/lsc/ststr.html

References

Arnot, M., Gray, J., James, M. and Rudduck, J. (1998) *A Review of Recent Research on Gender and Educational Performance*, OFSTED Research Series, London: The Stationery Office.

Ashman, A. and Conway, R. (1993) Using cognitive methods in the Classroom, London, Routledge.

Bennett, S. I. (1990) *Comprehensive Multicultural Education, Theory and Practice*, Boston: Allyn & Bacon.

Boaler, J. (1997) *Experiencing School Mathematics: Teaching Styles, Sex and Setting*, Milton Keynes: Open University Press.

Bowers, P. (1987) *The Effect of the 4MAT System on Achievement and Attitudes in Science*, ERIC No: ED292660.

Brown, W. F. and Forristall, D. A. (1983) *Computer-Assisted Study Skills Improvement Program*, ERIC No: ED234295.

Curry, L. (1983) An organization of learning styles theory and constructs, *ERIC Document*, 235, 185.

Doran, C. and Cameron, R. J. (1995) Learning about learning: meta-cognitive approaches in the classroom, *Educational Psychology in Practice*, 11(2), 15–23.

Dunn, R. and Dunn, K. (1992) *Teaching Elementary Students through their Individual Learning Styles: Practical Approaches for Grades 3–6*, Boston, MA: Allyn & Bacon.

Dunn, R., Dunn, K. and Price, G. (1985) *Manual: Learning Style Inventory*, Lawrence, KS: Price Systems.

Dunn, R., Griggs, S. and Price, G. (1993) Learning styles of Mexican-American and Anglo-American elementary-school students, *Journal of Multicultural Counselling and Development*, 21(4), 237–247, EJ470183.

Edelson, S.M. (2000) *Learning Style and Autism*, Centre for study of Autism, Salem, OR. Online, available HTTP: http://www.autism.org/styles.html (17 April 2000).

FEDA (1995) Learning Styles, London: Meridan House.

Felder, R. M. (1996) Matter of Style, *ASEE Prism*, 6(4), 18–23.

Feuerstein, R., Rand, Y., Hoffman, F. and Miller, R. (1980) *Instrumental Enrichment*, Baltimore, MD: Baltimore University Press.

Griggs, S. A. (1991) *Learning Styles Counselling*, ERIC Digest.

Griggs, S. and Dunn, R. (1996) *Hispanic-American Students and Learning Style*, ERIC Digest.

Honey, P. and Mumford, A. (1986) Using your Learning Styles, Maidenhead: Peter Honey.

Honey, P. and Mumford, A. (1992) *The Manual of Learning Styles*, Maidenhead: Peter Honey.

Johnson, M. K., Springer, S. P. and Sternglanz, S. H. (1982) *How to Succeed in College*, Los Altos, CA: William Kaufman.

Kolb, D. A. (1976) *The Learning Styles Inventory: Technical Manual*, Boston, MA: McBer & Company.

Kolb, D. A. (1984) *Experiential Learning: Experience as the Source of Learning and Development*, Englewod Cliffs, NJ: Prentice-Hall.

Leland-Jones, P. J. (1997) *Improving the Acquisition of Sixth-Grade Social Studies Concepts through the Implementation of a Study Skills Unit*, ERIC No: ED424154.

Lewis, B. N. (1976) Avoidance of aptitude-treatment trivialities, in S. Messick (ed.) Individuality in Learning, San Francisco, CA: Jossey-Bass.

McCarthy, B. (1990) *Using the 4 MAT System to Bring Learning Styles to Schools*, ERIC No: EJ416429.

Myers, I. B. (1962) *The Myers-Briggs Type Indicator Manual*, Princeton, NJ: Educational Testing Service.

Reiff, J. C. (1992) *Learning Styles*, Washington, DC: National Education Association.

Rezler, A. G. and Rezmovic, V. (1981) The learning preference inventory, *Journal of Applied Health*, 10, 28–34.

Riding, R. and Cheema, I. (1991) Cognitive styles – an overview and integration, *Educational Psychology*, 11(3–4), 193–215.

Robinson, H. B. (1970) *Effective Study*, 4th edn, New York: Harper and Row.

Sangster, S. and Shulman, R. (1988) *The Impact of the 4 MAT System as a Curriculum Delivery Model*, Research Report, ERIC No: ED316567.

Sharp, C., Osgood, J. and Flanagan, N. (1999) *The Benefits of Study Support, a Review of Opinion and Research* (DfEE Research Report 110), Sheffield: DfEE.

Sims, J. (1988) *Learning Styles of Black-American, Mexican-American, and White American Third and Fourth Grade Students in Traditional Public Schools*, doctoral dissertation, University of Santa Barbara, Santa Barbara, CA.

Yong, F. and Ewing, N. (1992) A comparative study of the learning style preferences among gifted African-American, Mexican-American and American born Chinese middle-grade students, *Roeper Review*, 14(3), 120–123.

PART III

TEACHING THE WIDER CURRICULUM

How we consider the generic notion of 'curriculum' is determined by our own definition of the term. For some it is simply a list of ten or so subjects on the school timetable. For others it is much broader, encompassing the whole of what happens inside and outside the classroom, including what are sometimes called the 'hidden curriculum' and 'extracurricular' activities, even though these may link closely with what is on the published timetable.

In addition to the vitally important traditional single school subjects, children also become proficient about combining them. They should learn to use their imagination, for example. Another challenge is to communicate intelligently, and not only in their English lessons, for language has to be applied in a context, perhaps in a field like history, where specialist terms must be learned and applied. This section considers such wider aspects as the intricate link between language and a subject like science, learning how to think, and moral education.

Alan Peacock, in Chapter 7, shows how a literacy strategy need not be seen as entirely separate from the teaching of a science curriculum. He analyses one commonly used approach to the teaching of the topic 'electricity' and points out some of the difficulties that children will encounter when trying to understand a textbook portrayal of the concept of an electrical current. The word 'energy' is used four times, but not explained, as it is, rightly or wrongly, taken for granted that pupils will understand it. Grappling successfully with key language issues can help children understand quite complex scientific principles.

The question of whether schools should offer a specific thinking skills programme, rather than rely solely on developing children's thinking incidentally, via the various subjects they study, has been raised over many years. Gerald Smith, in Chapter 8, discusses whether general thinking skills can be learned and applied that will help pupil with the challenges they will face as children and adults. In the last part of his essay he brings out one of the most important matters to be considered, which is that there is only a point to teaching thinking skills explicitly if teachers make the effort to help children transfer their newly acquired skills to real life. Without such a transfer the programme would have been an arid desk exercise.

Gary Fenstermacher brings a philosopher's perspective to the topic of moral development. 'Personal', 'social', 'moral', 'health' are all terms that are used, individually or in combination, when the education of the whole person is discussed. In Chapter 9, the author looks at the notion of 'manner', by which he means the teacher's role in nurturing children's moral and intellectual development, in contrast to the more usual focus on 'method'. He gives an intriguing account of how different teachers play out this role. This can involve short-term measures, like having a private conversation at the appropriate moment, or calling out to pupils who transgress the agreed code, as well as longer-term strategies like working hard to construct a caring community in the classroom and school.

CHAPTER 7

THE POTENTIAL IMPACT OF THE 'LITERACY HOUR' ON THE TEACHING OF SCIENCE FROM TEXT MATERIAL

Alan Peacock

The literacy demands of science text

An earlier review of research into the use of science text material (Peacock, 1995b) indicates that such text makes many demands on primary school children. These demands can be characterized as intrinsic (the difficulty of the ideas and concepts being taught), linguistic (having to do with the words, sentences and paragraphs used), visual (images in the form of pictures, diagrams, charts and symbols), formatic (having to do with the way the page is designed and how words and images are related), and sociological (the implied voice and message of the text). The cognitive load of such non-fiction illustrated texts in science is, thus, determined not only by the language and structure of the written text, but by a combination of all these factors (Sweller, 1994). European research in the field has tended to focus on the cognitive aspects (de Jong and van Hout-Wolters, 1994).

The evidence from this research is that, when using a science text, learners have to process text, image and intrinsic concepts simultaneously. Thus, the level of interactivity (Sweller, 1994) between the different kinds of demand is crucial if readers are going to succeed in processing the information. Research on multimodal text suggests that an integrative approach, that is, to see the page as a whole, is necessary to making sense of text. Work on visual literacy in science text makes clear that meaning is as much in the images as in the words:

> Language has here been displaced by the visual as decisively as on the front page of *The Sun* or in a Bruna book:[1] instead of [being] the major medium of information, with the visual as 'illustration', it has become a medium for comment, with the visual as the main source of information.
>
> (Kress and van Leeuwen, 1996, p. 30)

Thus, in science texts, visual elements do not merely support the written text, they often carry the meaning and information. Children, therefore, need to be taught the different structures of science text. Teaching readers to process visual images effectively improves their comprehension of the intrinsic ideas embodied in the text (Gyselinck and Tardieu, 1994). All of this research starts from the importance of the mental models that learners generate, and how the different structures of science textual representations contribute holistically to development of these models.

The use of text in science is powerfully influenced by teachers' culturally embedded pedagogic strategies for science teaching, as indicated by research in Zimbabwe (Cleghorn, 1992; Ryf and Cleghorn, 1997), France (Gyselinck and Tardieu, 1994), South Africa (Macdonald, 1990; Langhan, 1993), Finland (Mikkila and Olkinuora, 1994), Australia (Unsworth, 1991; O'Toole, 1996) and the USA (Beck *et al.*, 1997; Glynn and Takahashi, 1998; Musheno and Lawson, 1999). This influence compounds the specific difficulties encountered by second-language text users, as indicated by research in Mozambique (Hyltenstam and Stroud, 1993) and in South Africa (van Rooyen, 1990). Williams (1994, p. vii), who reviewed UK science schemes for the Schools' Curriculum and Assessment Authority, has also written about the dangers of 'alienating pupils by pursuing an obsession with objective language':

> I sometimes wonder whether today's [science] textbooks should be renamed picture books. Text seems to have gone out of fashion. There are sound educational reasons for this – children understand more when illustrations are used . . . .

Text use for science is, thus, different from the use of text for literacy purposes. This is clearly apparent when science text contains, as it often does, instructions to follow or diagrams and charts to interpret. And, apart from the fact that visual elements of science text carry some of the intrinsic science meaning, they differ from narrative (and from most other non-fiction) texts in that they often prescribe or suggest activities for pupils to undertake. Dowling (1996) has analysed such texts from a sociological standpoint, in terms of the textual strategies by which they (re)produce activities, concluding that they often create a 'myth of participation', proposing activities which are not feasible in the eyes of the teachers and pupils who use the text. This analysis relates to the earlier seminal work of Bernstein (1990, pp. 23, 28–32) which established the concepts of voice and message. *Voice*, in essence, refers to the way in which what is communicated is legitimated; the voice, in effect, indicates who is speaking in the text, and with what authority. The *message*, on the other hand, is the consequence of the voice's interactional practice within a context, such as that of science learning, and indicates, for example, what it is that the reader has to do or learn. Dowling's analysis shows that, when the message (for example, the method of use of a page of text) is not made explicit in the text itself, 'what to do' has to be made clear by either the reader or the (classroom) setting, and this usually means that effective learning from the text is dependent on the co-presence of a teacher or other mediator who understands, and whose voice is able to over-ride or explicate the messages in the text.

This conclusion is supported by evidence from evaluations of innovative science materials in South Africa (Perold and Bahr, 1993; Handspring Trust, 1994; Peacock and Perold, 1995) which showed that, where the teachers and trainers implementing the new materials possessed a limited repertoire of teaching strategies, the materials were not used as intended, and the participation intended by the text did not take place. Thus, pupils often experience conflicting expectations, because the text possesses one implicit pedagogical stance and epistemological map (what Dowling (1996) refers to as the 'assumed transparency' of the task demand), while pupils try to make sense of it by reference to another and very different web of meaning determined by their own culturally determined life-world knowledge, that is, what they expect to have to do in a science lesson (Koulaidis and Tsatsaroni, 1996).

In this chapter, I relate these known problems associated with children's use of science text to the demands of science learning implicit in science books and schemes for primary children currently available in the UK. I analyse the extent to which the current interpretation of literacy advocated by the UK government's National Literacy Strategy[2] (Department for Education and Employment (DfEE), 1998a) encompasses the skill and knowledge demands of learning from existing science texts, and examine some of the areas in which there are discrepancies. I conclude by addressing the implications of these findings for initial teacher training in relation to the effective use of science text in primary teaching.

The representation of science knowledge in texts: analysis of an example and its potential use

The analysis of the use of examples of specific text materials with children has been discussed elsewhere (Peacock, 1997). One example only is provided here, using a double-page spread from the pupils' book on electricity and magnetism from the Nuffield Primary Science (NPS) (1993b, pp. 2–3) scheme. The teachers' handbook for this scheme (NPS, 1993a) emphasizes that pupils' books are supplementary, not a substitute for practical work and discussion. It is recommended that they be used flexibly as an aid for learning in organization of work that children can do on their own or in small groups. The double-page spread is reproduced as Figure 7.1.

The key concept to be learned in this extract is that of 'current'. The teachers' guide (NPS, 1993a) refers to the concept of current in several places. For example, it is mentioned as new vocabulary to be introduced and as a concept with which the children may have difficulty. Under 'background science', the guide provides a technical explanation to the teacher of its meaning in terms of movement of electrical charge. None of this is directly accessible to pupils. They may, however,

Figure 7.1 'Currents' (NPS, 1993b, pp. 2–3)

have carried out the activities on constructing circuits described in the teachers' guide.

To decide when and how to use the section on currents in the pupils' book during a science lesson the teacher must carry out the following:

- assess the language level of the text and compare it to that of the pupil(s) using the text;
- decide on the way the lesson is going to be managed in more general terms, and assess the match between the teacher's intention and what the text demands;
- consider the difficulties and demands that the graphics, illustrations and conventions (such as boxed text) might make in terms of possible ambiguities and contradictions;
- examine the way text and graphics relate to each other;
- consider the message of the text, the transparency of the tasks demanded (if pupils are to use it independently), and the extent to which active participation is required by the voice speaking in the text; and
- identify the concepts covered (current, energy, etc.), where they are explained, and the implied conceptual development, matching this to the level of development of the pupil(s).

Even a superficial analysis in these terms is quite demanding on the teacher. It also reveals that the text is likely to present problems or ambiguities which would not be covered by work focused only on the words on the page. For example, the sequence in Figure 7.1 in which the reader moves from words to graphics and back, and changes (sometimes across the double-page spread, sometimes down) without this being made explicit. The word 'energy' appears four times in four different parts of Figure 7.1, but it is not explained, nor does it appear in either the index or the glossary at the end of the book. Although the diagrams of the mixer and the bulb connected to the battery are intended to illustrate flow of current ('through a lightbulb'), they could be read as showing wires entering through the glass of the mixer and bulb, respectively. Nor is there, for the mixer, apparently, a complete circuit, which pupils have probably learned about from their practical work on electricity. Finally, questions are posed inviting participation ('Can you think of some other ways that the energy of an electrical current is used?'), but the message about how to answer is not transparent: Does this question expect an oral or written response? or neither?

The teacher would need to anticipate these difficulties and assist the pupil to surmount them, if the demands of the text are to be dealt with. Yet, many of these demands are outside the definition of literacy used in the UK government's *Framework* for literacy teaching (DfEE, 1998a).

The meaning of 'literacy' within the 'Framework for Teaching'

Prior to the arrival of the *Framework for Teaching* (DfEE, 1998a), most commentators and publishers, if not researchers, were using a working definition of 'literacy' almost synonymous with 'reading'. For example, Oxford University Press advertise their 'Reading Tree' series[3] as the key to successful planning and teaching in the Literacy Hour. The new titles advertised in the Cambridge Reading series are called 'Passports to Literacy'.[4] Judd (1998) explained that the Literacy Hour was to be seen as hour-by-hour instructions on how to teach reading, and quoted Anne

Barnes, General Secretary of the UK National Association of Teachers of English, as saying that 'the point of reading is to enjoy a good story'.

Few teachers would see reading simply as the de-coding and understanding of words and sentences. But, in the *Framework* (DfEE, 1998a), it is clear that reading skills are seen as being entirely word-related, because there is virtually no reference, even at text level, to visual literacy. For example, in thirteen pages, section 1 of the *Framework* makes only one reference which might be about non-verbal literacy, stating that 'graphic knowledge . . . should also have a teaching focus . . .' (p. 11). However, the 18-page glossary does not define 'graphic' or 'graphic knowledge' in this context, while the sections on 'word level work' for Years 1 and 2 children (ages 5–7) indicate that graphic knowledge is actually concerned with word-recognition and spelling.

Section 2 (DfEE, 1998a), in its detailed term-by-term prescriptions for non-fiction reading comprehension, has the following seven statements relevant to non-verbal literacy:

- to locate parts of text that give particular information, including labelled diagrams and charts . . . (Year 1, term 3, p. 25);
- to read flow charts and cyclical diagrams that explain a process (Year 2, term 2, p. 29);
- to skim-read . . . illustrations . . . to speculate what a book might be about (Year 2, term 3, p. 31);
- how written instructions are organized, for example, lists, numbered points, diagrams with arrows . . . (Year 3, term 2, p. 35);
- to identify key features of explanatory texts: . . . presentation, use of diagrams, other illustrations (Year 4, term 2, p. 41);
- how statistics, graphs, etc. can be used to support arguments . . . (Year 4, term 3, p. 43); and
- to identify . . . supporting illustrations (Year 5, term 1, p. 45).

The emphasis given to non-verbal literacy can be put in context by comparing these seven statements to the emphasis on other selected aspects of non-fiction text, as shown in Table 7.1. Table 7.1 indicates the number of references (points) to various aspects of text within the *Framework* (DfEE, 1998a) in each year of

Table 7.1 Comparison of references to aspects of text work in Section 2 of *Framework* (DfEE, 1998a)

Year of literacy course[a]	Total points mentioned	References to visual literacy	References to contents/index/ glossary	References to ICT[b] text	References fact/fiction
Year 1	10	1	2	—	1
Year 2	12	2	4	—	1
Year 3	13	1	2	2	2
Year 4	26	2	1	2	2
Year 5	28	1	1	1	—
Year 6	26	—	—	—	1

Notes:
a Year 1 is the first year of primary/elementary school (age 5+).
b Information and communications technology.

the primary school course. The number of references to comprehension of non-verbal aspects of text (visual literacy) indicates that this is given no more priority than such aspects as the distinction between fact and fiction and the use of on-screen text, while it is given less attention than references to contents pages, index and glossary. The actual references quoted indicate that locating and identifying such visual elements as graphs are emphasised more than reading and comprehending them. Several of the references also imply that the function of visual elements is to support the written text, a point returned to later. Nor does the *Framework*'s extensive lists of points relating to objectives (pp. 3, 8) and independent work (p. 12) make any reference whatsoever to 'reading' pictures, diagrams, symbols, charts or even things like the Literacy Hour's own clock (p. 9). Detailed objectives are about words, sentences, phonics, grammar, spelling, vocabulary and punctuation.

Nor does the accompanying pack entitled 'reading and writing for information' (Module 6: *Teachers' Notes*) (DfEE, 1998a) deal with the visual aspects of text. For example, in the section on 'interacting with texts', which deals with an active approach to comprehension, the notes stress the strategies of text marking and text restructuring (p. 12). In the Guide, the teacher is then given a handout with a passage of ~200 words, with no illustrations or graphics, on which to carry out specific tasks of text marking and restructuring (p. 12). This could be taken to imply that acquiring information from non-fiction text is only concerned with words. Indeed, nowhere in the teachers' notes on 'reading and writing for information' is there any reference to the reading of illustrated non-fiction text.

In the *Framework* (DfEE, 1998a, p. 35) there are only the following three references to instructional texts:

- to identify the purposes of instructional texts (e.g. recipes, route-finders, timetables, instructions, plans, rules);
- to discuss the merits and limitations of particular instructional texts, including IT [information technology] and other media texts . . . ; and
- how written instructions are organized, for example, lists, numbered points, diagrams with arrows, bullet points, keys.

Thus, in the *Framework*, non-fiction text is treated as being either predominantly explanatory, that is, conveying information, ideas and opinions, or specifically instructional, like a recipe book or a route-finder. However, most currently available science text material for primary schools is a mixture of exposition, comment, explanation, instruction and question, each of which comes in both verbal and visual form, usually in a complex and varying format.

So, how will children learn to read a science text? This is a serious issue because it is also clear that, during the prescribed sessions of the Literacy Hour, concept learning of a specifically science nature is to be ignored. The *Framework* (DfEE, 1998a) explicitly states that pupils might be searching and retrieving from information texts used in science during the Literacy Hour. Yet, in the following sentence (p. 13), readers are left in no doubt about priorities:

Nevertheless, the focus of teaching must be on the literacy objectives from the *Framework* and pupils must be working on texts. In other words, while links with the rest of the curriculum are fundamental to effective literacy teaching, other subjects should be treated as vehicles for literacy work and not displace it from its primary focus. . . .

Many people will no doubt agree with this, arguing that, at least in their teaching of younger children, teachers should not be deflected from their prime literacy concern, namely to enable all children to read and write confidently and fluently. However, the argument compels a reconsideration of literacy across the curriculum, inviting questions about what kind of literacy is valued across other curricular areas within the primary phase of schooling, because the separation of literacy from concept learning has serious implications for the learning of science.

Bruce and Davidson-Wasser (1996) have explored different theoretical models for relating literacy to wider curricular issues, namely via 'skills models', 'instrumental models' and 'inquiry models'. Theoretically, instrumental models or inquiry models would seem best suited to science learning, because they are based on the same constructivist principles as most science learning. They, thus, take account of prior knowledge, and are embedded in practices that go beyond reading itself. Instrumental models place reading at the centre of the curriculum. Inquiry models make activities the springboard for learning from text. Yet, in both cases, the approach as described is confined to verbal literacy, which is too limiting where the use of science text is concerned. Bruce and Davidson-Wasser (1996, p. 298) acknowledge this in concluding that 'it may be time to question the privileging of literacy – reading and writing instruction – over all other instructional goals'.

The issue of relating literacy to science has been raised in the current UK context by Russell (1998, p. 30) who is concerned that

> [educators] confirm literacy not as ruler but as servant. Basics are at the bottom – the building is constructed upon them. Indeed, the basics are hidden once they are in place. I, for one, do not want to have a hand in putting up a building which stops at the foundations.

The *Framework* (DfEE, 1998a, pp. 2–3) 'sets out teaching objectives . . . to enable pupils to become fully literate'. Under the heading 'What is literacy?', it points out that 'literacy unites the important skills of reading and writing'. In the same paragraph, it then makes clear that

> It is also relevant to teaching across the whole of the National Curriculum. Skills, especially those that focus on reading and writing non-fiction texts, should be linked and applied in every subject.

Science books, in the Literacy Hour, are, thus, a vehicle for literacy (reading and writing) work. Comprehension of the concepts and content in science books is the business of science lessons, to which the work of the Literacy Hour should be linked, presumably by the primary school teacher who (in most cases in the UK) is the same person in both lessons. Yet, if this is taken literally by teachers in relation to science text, there may be contradictory and, thus, confusing messages for children, especially where the teacher is struggling to understand the concepts in the science text. The implicit message is that, in the Literacy Hour each morning, children must learn how to read the science book, while, during the one afternoon of science each week, the children must then tackle the concepts and skills that the same text is trying to teach. There are serious practical consequences of this separation of the teaching of a text's functions from its content, which are discussed next.

New materials for teaching non-fiction science text in the 'Literacy Hour'

Commercial publishers have tackled the idea of using science books in the Literacy Hour in a variety of ways. For example, NPS (1998) has turned its pupil books, originally intended for individual use, into 'big books' for whole-class use, with detailed specifications for how to use them during the Literacy Hour. However, this use is explicitly focused on literacy rather than science objectives, and the manual *Science and Literacy: A Guide for Primary Teachers* (Nuffield Foundation, 1998), which explains the use of such text during the Literacy Hour, almost entirely ignores the visual images in the text. The *Guide*'s definition of 'the literacy of science' (on p. 8) is as follows:

> Science has its own literacy, which we might call the literacy of science. By this we mean its vocabulary and its own forms of oral and written discourse. For example, we would write up an experiment in a very different way from writing a story. Science also shares many styles of writing with other subjects, including using letters, poems and narrative stories as alternatives to formal reports of investigations.

This is quite different from notions emanating from the scientific community or the National Curriculum in England and Wales, both of which see science as a distinct way of knowing, with its own ideas, concepts, methods and structures, and see scientific literacy as an induction into an understanding of these. In the above-mentioned definition, the pre-occupation is with writing, rather than with science, and with production rather than comprehension.

A further example of a new science scheme specifically for the Literacy Hour is the Discovery World Literacy Lesson Books (e.g. Hughes and Hughes, 1997), large flip-charts which set out to teach children how to get information from non-fiction books. These do address aspects of the visual elements as well as the written text. But, the science concepts are rarely addressed, and the representations may lead to confusion. For example, one page (Hughes and Hughes, 1997, p. 21) distinguishes fiction ('has illustrations drawn by an artist') from non-fiction ('has photographs taken by a photographer') only to be followed by a page from a science book with both photographs and illustrations. This same page names the parts of a hornet's body (mouth, antennae, wings, legs, etc.) but nowhere does it emphasize the importance of understanding what these mean. In fact, the illustration is conceptually misleading as it labels the head as part of the body. This may not appear to be important during the Literacy Hour, as long as children can read the words and understand the idea of labelling. But, it is certainly important to children's science learning, and it, therefore, seems dangerous to separate the two aspects of learning in the manner prescribed by the *Framework*.

The page on the hornet is followed immediately by pages on dinosaurs, amphibians and machines, in that order (Hughes and Hughes, 1997). This sequence is intended to be followed during the Literacy Hour and has a coherence in relation to the book's literacy objectives. Yet, it would be impossible for a science scheme to follow this sequence, which, within the terms of science, has no logical structure or conceptual development. The page on amphibians, which is largely made up of a complex cross-sectional diagram illustrating the life cycle of a frog, is entitled 'Reading and using a dictionary' and is used as a vehicle for finding words. The teacher's instructions on the reverse of the flip-chart begin with the following words to say to the pupils: 'let's pretend [*sic*] we want to know what the word "amphibian" means' (Hughes and Hughes, 1997, p. 23). This, unfortunately, implies that children only have to pretend to want to understand the science. The message is that concepts contained in the diagram are not part of literacy: conceptual science learning goes on elsewhere.

However, a key part of the National Literacy Strategy for England and Wales is that literacy teaching should take up 1 hour per day, which implies five lessons of literacy for every one of science. Teachers' priorities in science will be with the knowledge and investigative skills they must cover in order to fulfil National Curriculum requirements and to remain within the school's programme of science topics. Many now follow the Qualifications and Curriculum Authority's (QCA) (1998) own recommended science scheme. But, before the next science lesson comes round, the teacher might have done literacy sessions on 'making your own jewellery', 'one green apple' and 'electricity', which are the substantive focus of three subsequent literacy activities proposed by the Nuffield Foundation (1998) in their guide to using science texts in the Literacy Hour. It would be impossible for a teacher to develop the science concepts in all these in the subsequent week, especially as they do not match any aspect of the QCA scheme. And, even if the teacher had unlimited time to follow up the text activities in science, rather than the 1 hour per week which is now typical, it would not be appropriate to jump from jewellery to categorizing fruit to electricity. Yet, the developmental scheme of the Literacy Hour makes no concessions whatsoever to what might be an appropriate conceptual development sequence in science.

The British primary science community has begun to express concern about this potentially negative impact on children's science learning of the Literacy Hour. For example, Russell (1998, p. 30), a Science Adviser from London, has talked in terms of the 'serious danger in this dismembered curriculum' as a result of the 'centralization of content and method' and of 'resentment' at the way its aims are to be achieved. He 'totally rejects this prescriptive model being applied to science teaching'.

Potential barriers to the development of textual literacy during science lessons

The 'amphibians' page referred to earlier has many important features of science text on it that could be the basis of valuable work to help children comprehend non-fiction text during science lessons. For example, it uses symbolic conventions such as arrows, notoriously misleading to young readers of science texts (Francis, 1996) and a cross-sectional drawing. Sectional drawings have long been known to present difficulties to learners (Reid and Beveridge, 1986; Constable *et al.*, 1988). But, none of these problems is referred to in the teacher's notes. This failure of Literacy Hour materials to address concepts, symbols and visual images in science text is likely to be a particular problem for children for whom English is an additional language, because they rely more on visual clues and explanation of concepts that may not exist in their mother tongue, and on mediation by bilingual support staff (Peacock, 1995b). For such children, however, it may not be possible for these aspects to be consolidated in the science lesson (which normally takes place now in the afternoon in most primary schools in England and Wales), because, in many inner-city multilingual schools, the language assistant who understands their mother tongue is almost certainly a part-time employee, and, therefore, only likely to be available during the (morning) Literacy Hour. Their language, but not their science learning, is, thus, being supported.

A further barrier may be presented by the difficulty of mediating individual reading in large classes. Much of the science text material produced commercially, such as the example in Figure 7.1, is intended for reference use by pupils working individually. Recent research (Peacock and Gates, 2000) has indicated that this is one way in which young teachers use science text with older children. Yet, because the Literacy Hour does not address the science concepts, a teacher has to address them when they arise for particular individuals or groups. The *Framework* (DfEE, 1998a, p. 4) emphasizes that support should come from structured use of appropriate texts, stating that 'in the early stages, pupils should have a carefully balanced programme of guided reading from books of graded difficulty, matched to their independent reading levels'.

Yet, research in South Africa has shown that, despite having been taught to read in exactly this way, many pupils could not comprehend science books. This is because when children first encountered science books, up to 60 per cent of the vocabulary, and much of the grammar and connectives as well as graphic and symbolic conventions, had never been encountered in their reading schemes, which were based largely on narrative text (van Rooyen, 1990). Where this is the case, teachers will have to spend large amounts of time mediating children's reading individually to help them grasp science concepts. Yet, these aspects of science-textual literacy may not be dealt with during science lessons, given teachers' known lack of confidence in science (Wragg *et al.*, 1991) and their lack of time to use existing text material (Peacock, 1995a). Science concepts have long been regarded as difficult to teach. They are now in danger of being relegated in importance, behind such matters as note-making, reviewing, spelling, investigations, text-marking and handwriting practice.

Clearly, no such programme of guided reading from books of graded difficulty as recommended for the Literacy Hour could ever be matched completely to the needs of all curriculum subjects in terms of vocabulary. But, it might have helped if the British National Literacy Strategy had required that the visual and symbolic conventions and complex text formats that children are going to meet in science, and other subjects such as geography, were presented to them and used systematically in the Literacy Hour. In this way, children may be more likely to make effective use of expository text material, particularly important as many children, on entering secondary schools, will be confronted with a set text in science of considerable complexity in these respects.

However, Literacy Hour materials oversimplify the idea of text types where science is concerned. For example, the *Science and Literacy Guide* (Nuffield Foundation, 1998) uses the classification from the Exeter Extending Literacy and Interaction with Text Projects (Wray and Lewis, 1995) to categorize texts. But this research did not take account of the range of complex science text formats available, so that when the *Guide* applies them to actual science texts, it is clearly a question of square pegs and round holes. In the section on 'text interaction strategies', ideas are provided for 'accessing other science text types' (p. 90). Yet, little practical help is offered. For example, when it comes to 'structure and mechanism texts', these are said to be 'similar to "Explanation" and "Recount" texts', and are 'very sophisticated . . . usually accompanied by, and referenced to, diagrams . . .' (p. 92). However, no example of such a text is given or analysed.

It seems unlikely, therefore, that the addressing of science concepts occuring in complex multi-modal texts will happen in a sufficiently systematic and comprehensive way within the tight prescription of the Literacy Hour. Yet it is not long since the UK's Chief Inspector of Schools (Alexander *et al.*, 1992, p. 1) bemoaned the fact that 'the progress of primary pupils has been hampered by the influence of highly questionable dogmas which have led to excessively complex classroom practices, and devalued the place of subjects in the curriculum'.

The current shift of emphasis in the UK towards literacy and numeracy and away from other subjects leaves science, still technically a core subject and formally assessed by national standard tests, in an ambiguous position. Hence, there is a need for guidance to teacher educators and student teachers concerning the use of science text material in the science curriculum, especially in a primary school system where there has never been prescribed use of text in science and where recent evidence suggests that use of such text is still given inadequate attention during training (Peacock and Gates, 2000).

Training primary teachers in the use of science text with children

The preparation of primary teachers to use science text effectively would, thus, benefit from being based on the research evidence alluded to above regarding such matters as the cognitive load of non-fiction illustrated texts (Sweller, 1994), pupils' mental modelling (Gyselinck and Tardieu, 1994), teachers' culturally embedded pedagogic strategies for science teaching (Handspring Trust, 1994; Koulaidis and Tsatsaroni, 1996; O'Toole, 1996; Ryf and Cleghorn, 1997), and the specific difficulties encountered by second-language text users (Peacock, 1995b). The role of text is clearly diverse in terms of the intentions of authors and publishers. Yet, the messages about role and use embedded in these texts are often not transparent, or run counter to teachers' accepted practices.

There are many issues here which UK teacher education needs to consider. For example, one implication of the Literacy Hour's deliberate separation of the use of science text from science lesson use is the need for greater collaboration in the training of primary teachers between teacher educators responsible for curriculum science programmes and those responsible for language and literacy training. Teachers, particularly during initial training, may need more help than they currently receive with how to make best use of existing text, particularly in terms of analysing text demand, as illustrated earlier, and mediating science text material in use during science lessons (Peacock and Gates, 2000). It is likely that such help will also need to be text- and context-specific, in terms of the books or schemes available and mandated, age, level and language background of pupils, and pedagogical styles used in schools.

Research and development relating to the extent, nature and efficacy of such training is urgently needed. It is important because text material of the kind available in recently published schemes in the UK is multi-modal, uses a range of media, and is not only concerned to communicate information (to tell children about science ideas) but also to ask questions, to set tasks, to present data for interpretation, and to involve children in investigations. As demonstrated earlier, texts may have flaws and present difficulties in the way they deal with these requirements. Nevertheless, it is arguably better for an inexperienced teacher to be able to interpret and use even an imperfect text for these purposes than not to engage learners with science concepts and investigations at all.

Evidence for this comes from South Africa where research indicates that teachers' own adaptations of texts, carried out in order to simplify or adapt them for pupils, often make them conceptually more confusing (MacDonald, 1990). In the UK, evidence from schools and teacher education institutions (Peacock and Gates,

2000) suggests that, as in the US, student teachers are not taught or encouraged to use existing text material in science. Rather, for many years, they have been encouraged to develop and use worksheets of their own construction in order to match work to the needs of individual children, as originally proposed following research by Harlen (1982) and Bennett *et al.* (1984). However, the quality of many recent UK science schemes such as NPS itself is high, being based on extensive research into children's conceptual learning, teachers' science knowledge and effective ways of representing science concepts to children.

The National Curriculum for Teacher Training in England and Wales (DfEE, 1998b, p. 75) is of interest in this respect. It requires student teachers to be taught the following:

> how to use science resources effectively, including knowledge of the range of available textbooks, science schemes, resource books, worksheets . . . ; and deciding whether the use of a particular resource will support the achievement of identified teaching objectives.

Thus, during initial teacher education, students will in future need to examine existing schemes, be analytic about their purposes, strengths and weaknesses, and carry out tasks in which they build into their planning the appropriate use of such material. This will need to be incorporated into college-based training programmes. But, it also needs to be incorporated into student teachers' work during the Literacy Hour as part of their school experience; and, more importantly, activities evaluating text use in science lessons with the help of peers, teachers, mentors and tutors will need to be included in their science activities. To do this effectively, there will need to be collaboration between language tutors and instructors, science tutors and instructors, and the mentors in the partnership schools used for student teachers' school experience.

Conclusion: teaching the use of science text material in different contexts

A paradox exists in relation to the use of science texts in countries such as the USA and UK where science teaching in primary schools has been fostered for several decades. On the one hand, recent international surveys such as the Third International Mathematics and Science Survey (TIMSS) indicate that science text materials are still seen as central to the process of teaching and learning science in most parts of the world (Valverde, 1999). Such evidence, for example, about the sheer size of US elementary science texts, reconfirms Shulman's (1987) finding that most teaching is initiated by some form of text. On the other hand, the American Association for the Advancement of Science (1989) found evidence that texts rarely contribute to effective learning, and Ball and Feiman-Nemser (1988) demonstrated that teachers in training in the USA, as in the UK, were discouraged from using the available and mandated texts, being instead encouraged to develop their own materials.

This lack of formal emphasis on text use seems to persist. There is currently international concern about school science curricula because young people are seemingly choosing science less and less as their preferred field of study. Ideas for remedying this have been put forward in various countries, for example, by Millar and Osborne (1998) in the UK. These concerns have been aired in recent issues of *Journal of Curriculum Studies*; thus Atkin (1998), reviewing the Organization for

Economic Co-operation and Development study of innovations in science, stresses that the crucial point at which curricular innovations succeed or fail is in the classroom interactions between teachers and students. Solomon (1999) points out that some major innovations, such as the US science curricula of the Sputnik era, failed because they attempted to bypass teachers: content, she explains, depends strongly on 'joint teacher and student perceptions of importance and situation' (p. 9).

Curricular innovation is largely communicated to teachers and students via text. For example, Millar and Osborne (1998) propose the notion of 'explanatory stories' as a way of popularising science culture. Yet, despite the TIMSS evidence for the apparently important role text plays in the teacher–student learning relationship in science, none of the authors cited refer to the role that text might play in representing new ideas or in communicating innovation to teachers and students, despite the millions of dollars spent annually on science texts throughout the world.

To use text effectively, then, teachers must have experience of a range of different types of published science text material and of analysing science text in terms of the whole cognitive demand made on children in the ways discussed earlier, rather than merely in terms of the linguistic demands. They need a repertoire of skills for choosing and using text, and an understanding of when it is and is not effective in science learning. They need to apply notions of voice and message to the science texts available or preferred, and consider how conflicts between the text message and their teaching style can lead to mythical participation by students.

As indicated by the research reviewed here, ineffective use of science text and inadequate emphasis on text use by pupils in science has been noted in many culturally distinct contexts. It may, thus, have come about as a result of many varying contextual factors. However, for the majority of primary teachers worldwide, who lack a background in science, it is still probably the case that a good science scheme and a selection of science information books is the teachers' best resource for representing science ideas to pupils. This situation will persist until such time as equivalent CD-ROM and internet facilities become widely available in classrooms. And, even then, the same skills of comprehending verbal and visual information reproduced in complex formats on the screen will be as important as it is now – hence the importance of teacher education in effective use of science text.

The prospect of having a set text or a set scheme of work for science in British primary schools may fill some teachers with horror. Equally, it may be seen by others as a blessing and a simplification of their complex planning and assessment tasks. Moves towards a set text have already taken place in the UK through national circulation of the (optional) science assessment units and the subsequent science scheme (QCA, 1997, 1998). These units set out, topic by topic in textbook form, how to organize and carry out the science teaching activities required by the National Curriculum and how to assess them. Although expensive and widely available science schemes have been purchased by many UK schools in recent years, they have never been used in practice to the extent that schemes and books have in other subjects such as English and mathematics. As yet, this phenomenon has not been adequately investigated. Such research is a prerequisite of any attempt to revise materials, write new texts or rethink teaching approaches. It requires, as both Atkin (1998) and Solomon (1999) have suggested, that researchers look much more closely at the individual teacher, and at his or her perception of the role of text in teaching and learning science in the primary phase, as the introduction of the Literacy Hour works its way through.

Notes

1   Dick Bruna is a widely read author and illustrator of children's books (e.g. Bruna, n.d.).
2   The UK National Literacy Strategy (1998) sets out teaching objectives for pre-Year 1 to Year 6 children (ages 4+ to 10+), and gives structured guidance for the conduct of the daily 'Literacy Hour', in which this teaching takes place.
3   The Oxford University Press (Educational Division) 'Reading Tree' series currently includes 346 story books, 64 poetry books, 60 information and 127 'big books'. Nineteen new titles were added in 1999.
4   Cambridge University Press 'Passports to Literacy' series includes separate books for Word, Sentence and Text level work, together with student readers (e.g. Hallworth, 1998).

References

Alexander, R., Rose, J. and Woodhead, C. (1992) *Curriculum Organisation and Classroom Practice in Primary Schools: A Discussion Paper* (London: Department of Education and Science).
American Association for the Advancement of Science (AAAS) (1989) *Science for All Americans: A Project 2061 Report on Literacy Goals in Science, Mathematics, and Technology* (Washington, DC: American Association for the Advancement of Science).
Atkin, J. M. (1998) The OECD study of innovations in science, mathematics and technology education. *Journal of Curriculum Studies*, 30 (6), 647–660.
Ball, D. L. and Feiman-Nemser, S. (1988) Using textbooks and teachers' guides: a dilemma for beginning teachers and teacher educators. *Curriculum Inquiry*, 18 (4), 401–423.
Beck, I. L., McKeown, M. G., Hamilton, R. L. and Kucan, L. (1997) *Questioning the Author: An Approach for Enhancing Student Engagement with Text* (Newark, DE: International Reading Association).
Bennett, N., Desforges, C., Cockburn, A. and Wilkinson, B. (1984) *The Quality of Pupil Learning Experiences* (London: Erlbaum).
Bernstein, B. (1990) *Structuring of Pedagogic Discourse: Volume IV: Class, Codes and Control* (London: Routledge).
Bruce, B. and Davidson-Wasser, J. (1996) An inquiry model for literacy across the curriculum. *Journal of Curriculum Studies*, 28 (3), 281–300.
Bruna, D. (n.d.) *The Christmas Book* (London: Methuen).
Cleghorn, A. (1992) Primary level science in Kenya: constructing meaning through English and indigenous languages. *International Journal of Qualitative Studies in Education*, 5 (4), 311–323.
Constable, H., Campbell, B. and Brown, R. (1988) Sectional drawings from science textbooks: an experimental investigation into pupils' understanding. *British Journal of Educational Psychology*, 58 (1), 89–102.
de Jong, F. P. C. M. and van Hout-Wolters, B. H. A. M. (eds) (1994) *Process-Oriented Instruction and Learning from Text* (Amsterdam, The Netherlands: VU [Vreij Universitet] University Press).
DfEE (1998a) *The National Literacy Strategy: Framework for Teaching* (London: DfEE).
DfEE (1998b) *Teaching: High Status, High Standards: Requirements for Courses of Initial Teacher Training* Circular 4/98 (London: DfEE).
Dowling, P. (1996) A sociological analysis of school mathematics texts. *Educational Studies in Mathematics*, 31 (4), 389–415.
Francis, V. (1996) Personal communication.
Glynn, S. M. and Takahashi, T. (1998) Learning from analogy-enhanced science text. *Journal of Research in Science Teaching*, 35 (10), 1129–1149.
Gyselinck, V. and Tardieu, H. (1994) The role of text illustrations in the construction of non-spatial mental models. In F. P. C. M de Jong and B. H. A. M. van Hout-Wolters (eds), *Process-Oriented Instruction and Learning from Text* (Amsterdam: VU [Vreij Universitet] University Press), 175–181.
Hallworth, G. (1998) *Carnival* (Cambridge: Cambridge University Press).
Handspring Trust (1994) How do teachers use innovative primary science materials? Report on an Evaluation of 'Spider's Place' [A series of 13 TV programmes produced by the South African Broadcasting System]. Handspring Trust, Johannesburg, South Africa.

Harlen, W. (1982) Matching. In C. Richards (ed.), *New Directions in Primary Education* (Lewes, UK: Falmer), 179–191.

Hughes, P. and Hughes, M. (1997) *Discovery World: Literacy Lesson Book 2* (London: Heinemann).

Hyltenstam, K. and Stroud, C. (1993) Final report and recommendations from the evaluation of teaching materials for lower primary in Mozambique: (II) language issues. Stockholm Institute of Education, Stockholm, Sweden.

Judd, J. (1998) Tough words to test our children. *The Independent*, 21 March.

Koulaidis, V. and Tsatsaroni, A. (1996) A pedagogical analysis of science textbooks: how can we proceed? *Research in Science Education*, 26 (1), 55–71.

Kress, G. and van Leeuwen, T. (1996) *Reading Images: The Grammar of Visual Design* (London: Routledge).

Langhan, D. (1993) The textbook as a source of difficulty in teaching and learning. A Final Report of the Threshold 2 Project. Human Sciences Research Council, Pretoria, South Africa.

MacDonald, C. A. (1990) Standard 3 general science research 1987–88. A Final Report of the Threshold Project. Human Sciences Research Council, Pretoria, South Africa.

Mikkila, M. and Olkinuora, E. (1994) Problems of current textbooks and workbooks: do they promote high quality learning? In F. P. C. M de Jong and B. H. A. M. van Hout-Wolters (eds), *Process-Oriented Instruction and Learning from Text* (Amsterdam, The Netherlands: VU [Vreij Universitet] University Press), 151–164.

Millar, R. and Osborne, J. (1998) Beyond 2000: science education for the future. School of Education, Kings' College, University of London, UK.

Musheno, B. V. and Lawson, A. E. (1999) Effects of learning cycle and traditional text on comprehension of science concepts by students at differing reasoning levels. *Journal of Research in Science Teaching*, 36 (1), 23–37.

Nuffield Foundation (1998) *Science and Literacy: A Guide for Primary Teachers* (London: Collins Educational).

Nuffield Primary Science (NPS) (1993a) *Nuffield Primary Science Scheme* (London: Collins Educational).

Nuffield Primary Science (NPS) (1993b) *Electricity and Magnetism*. Pupils' Book for Ages 7–11, Nuffield Primary Science Scheme (London: Collins Educational).

Nuffield Primary Science (NPS) (1998) Pupils' 'Big Books' [series] (London: Collins Educational).

O'Toole, M. (1996) Science, schools, children and books: exploring the classroom interface between science and language. *Studies in Science Education*, 28, 113–143.

Peacock, A. (1995a) The use of primary science schemes with second language learners. *Primary Science Review*, 38, 14–16.

Peacock, A. (1995b) An agenda for research on text material in primary science for second language learners of English in developing countries. *Journal of Multilingual and Multicultural Development*, 16 (5), 389–401.

Peacock, A. (1997) *Opportunities for Science in the Primary School* (Stoke on Trent: Trentham Books), 95–114.

Peacock, A. and Perold, H. (1995) Helping primary teachers develop new approaches to science teaching: a strategy for the evaluation of 'Spider's place'. Paper presented at the annual meeting of the Southern African Association for Research into Mathematics and Science Education, Cape Town, South Africa (School of Education, University of Exeter, UK).

Peacock, A. and Gates, S. M. G. (2000) Newly-qualified teachers' perceptions of the role of text in science learning. *Research in Science and Technological Education*, 18 (2), 155–171.

Perold, H. and Bahr, M. A. (1993) National Science Education Project dealing with preconceptions and problem-solving strategies in primary science: Report on the evaluation of the materials comprising the pilot programme. Handspring Trust, Johannesburg, South Africa.

Qualifications and Curriculum Authority (QCA) (1997) *Science Assessment Units 1–5* (London: Qualifications and Curriculum Authority).

Qualifications and Curriculum Authority (QCA) (1998) *Science: A Scheme of Work for Key Stages 1 and 2* (London: Qualifications and Curriculum Authority).

Reid, D. J. and Beveridge, M. (1986) Effects of text illustration on children's learning of a school science topic. *British Journal of Educational Psychology*, 56 (3), 294–303.

Russell, A. (1998) The uses and abuses of literacy. *Primary Science Review*, 53, 30.

Ryf, A. and Cleghorn, A. (1997) The language of science: text talk and teacher talk in second language settings. In M. Sanders (ed.), *Proceedings of the Annual Conference of the Southern African Association for Research in Mathematics and Science Education* (Johannesburg, South Africa: SAARMSE), 437–441.

Shulman, L. S. (1987) Knowledge and teaching: foundations of the new reform. *Harvard Educational Review*, 57 (1), 1–22.

Solomon, J. (1999) Meta-scientific criticisms, curriculum innovation and the propagation of scientific culture. *Journal of Curriculum Studies*, 31 (1), 1–15.

Sweller, J. (1994) Cognitive load theory, learning difficulty, and instructional design. *Learning and Instruction*, 4 (4), 295–312.

Unsworth, L. (1991) Linguistic form and the construction of knowledge in factual texts for primary school children. *Educational Review*, 43 (2), 201–212.

Valverde, G. A. (1999) Using the TIMSS curriculum study to understand the role of textbooks in conforming structures of educational opportunities across the world. Paper presented at the Comparative and International Education Society Conference, Toronto, Ontario (State University of New York, Albany, USA).

van Rooyen, H. (1990) The disparity between English as a subject and English as the medium of learning. Final Report of the Threshold Project, Human Sciences Research Council, Pretoria, South Africa.

Williams, J. (1994) Come in from the cold. *Times Educational Supplement: Extra Science*, 4096, 30 December, vii.

Wragg, E. C., Bennett, S. N. and Carre, C. G. (1991) Primary teachers and the national curriculum. *Research Papers in Education*, 4 (3), 17–45.

Wray, D. and Lewis, M. (1995) Extending interactions with non-fiction texts: an EXIT into understanding. *Reading*, 29 (1), 2–9.

CHAPTER 8

THINKING SKILLS
The question of generality
Gerald F. Smith

The decades-old quest to teach people how to think has engendered an equally aged controversy over thinking-skills instruction and the critical thinking (CT) movement. On one hand, CT proponents such as Ennis (1989, 1991) assert that there are important general thinking skills (GTSs) that apply across domains or fields of practice. Such skills can presumably be taught most effectively in general education courses where they will not be overshadowed by discipline-specific content. The contrary position, championed by McPeck (1981, 1990b), maintains that the only useful thinking skills are domain specific. Students should be taught how to think by taking courses associated with traditional academic disciplines.

McPeck (1981) offers two salient arguments against GTSs. The first, his 'content' argument, claims that thinking is always about something, and that the content of thought strongly shapes the nature of thinking. Consequently, GTSs are logical impossibilities. McPeck's (1990a, p. 12) second objection, the 'triviality' argument, alleges that purported GTSs are 'trivially obvious' and have no practical cognitive value. This is the case, he suggests, because the usefulness of a skill necessarily diminishes as its generality increases. The content argument has been rebutted (Miller, 1986; Siegel, 1988; Ennis, 1989; Andrews, 1990; Brel, 1990), although apparently not to McPeck's satisfaction. GTS proponents have also responded to the triviality argument by citing thinking skills – evaluating sources, for instance (Blair, 1992) – that seem to be both general and substantive. McPeck and his supporters ignore these counter-examples, focusing instead on purported GTSs – for instance, pinpointing the problem (Johnson and Gardner, 1999) – that are clearly deficient. In large part, the two sides of this debate talk past each other.

The GTS controversy has other dimensions as well. It is part of a broader debate over the effectiveness of CT programmes. McPeck and other scholars (e.g. Walters, 1992) assert that CT is an overly narrow and, for that reason, seriously inadequate approach to the improvement of thinking. While CT proponents almost invariably favour the GTS position, some GTS supporters (e.g. Norris and Ennis, 1989) admit that traditional CT instruction does not sufficiently consider creativity, problem solving, and other important parts of what is involved in being an effective thinker.

Another issue concerns the extent to which effective thinking is a matter of skill. Increasingly, scholars recognize that thinking effectiveness derives from various kinds of knowledge – of concepts, principles, standards and heuristics, among others (e.g. Bailin *et al.*, 1999a,b). Moreover, not only knowledge but also values and mental habits or dispositions influence thinking performance. Thus, the development of mental skills, general or domain specific, is only part, and perhaps not the most important part, of becoming a capable thinker.

The sometimes-forgotten pedagogical bottomline for this debate is simple: *by what means should educators teach people how to think?* More pointedly, is there a substantial body of important material (concepts, principles, skills and so forth) that is general (broadly applicable to practical affairs and various disciplinary domains) which could be taught, for instance, in general education courses in such a way that students would be able to transfer and apply their knowledge in other relevant contexts?

A simple resolution of the GTS controversy is to regard thinking-skill generality as a matter of degree, different skills occupying different positions along a continuum. Although this moderate position makes sense, it is not satisfying. Educators would like to have a deeper understanding of these issues, and a more principled resolution of the debate. In this chapter, I respond to this need by developing a more complete understanding of the nature of thinking skills and their potential for generality.

In the next section, I analyse the concepts of 'skill' and 'thinking skill', identifying ways in which the latter has been misapplied. I then consider the generality–power tradeoff, finding that it has been misunderstood, and that thinking skills usually lack power for want of operationality and specificity. A discussion of domains of thought suggests that they are not so discrete as GTS opponents have assumed. A 'domain of practical affairs' is identified as well as 'generic thinking tasks', the bases for many important GTSs. In the concluding section, I explore the implications of these findings for educational theory and practice.

Skill basics

The notion of skill has become controversial in educational circles (Hart, 1978), largely because of how the concept of 'thinking skill' has been applied. Disagreements ultimately derive from the fact that 'skill' is a family resemblance concept (Wittgenstein, 1953): it is defined by a cluster of properties, none of which is a necessary or sufficient condition for the concept's application. As such, 'skill' is a graded rather than a discrete classification, certain instances being central or prototypical, while others are marginal members of the class.

Skills

A skill is a capacity, usually acquired through training and experience, to do something well, to perform competently certain tasks. Skills are differentiated by the tasks they address. The skill of riding a bicycle is different from that of solving crossword puzzles. Ability is the nearest synonym for skill, although the latter term often connotes a higher level of training, experience and proficiency. The skill–ability relationship suggests that 'skill' has two distinct connotations. Some skills refer to an acquired ability or capacity; others imply highly competent performance. A toddler acquires the skill of walking, but a skilled driver can do more than just operate motor vehicles. Thus, 'skill' can be used to mean either 'mere ability' or 'special capacity'. As Griffiths (1987) points out, skill is also associated with procedural knowledge, what Ryle (1963) termed 'knowing how'. Although declarative knowledge, 'knowing that', can be involved, skills centre on knowing how to do something.

This core meaning of skill can be extended in several ways. As procedural knowledge, skills are sets of activities that can be 'schematized or purposively sequenced' (Smith, 1984, p. 227) in varying degrees. Skills are exercised by choice (Johnson and Gardner, 1999); their initiation and operation are largely subject to conscious control. Skills are repeatable and transferable (Smith, 1984), within limits: a skill applies to a certain kind of task, but task kinds do not always have clear boundaries. In these respects, skills have much in common with strategies, methods and techniques, more overt forms of procedural knowledge. Indeed, skills typically consist, in part, of strategies and methods that have been internalized, seamlessly incorporated into a performance routine. One's skill at playing tennis reflects learned strategies and methods for serving, volleying and other tennis-related activities.

Like methods and techniques, skills have a scope. A broad skill encompasses more activities than a narrow skill. Indeed, broad skills typically include narrow skills as their constituents. This characteristic of skills has created confusion about the concept's applicability. If I admit only very narrow abilities as skills, I will be defining the concept's most common referents out of existence, replacing them with 'micro-abilities' that rarely appear in everyday discourse: carrying and borrowing will supplant adding and subtracting in skill talk. On the other hand, by defining broad skills that are simply aggregations of narrower skills, I create instances of the concept which lack the structured procedural quality that is one of its defining characteristics. Objections to the notion of 'critical thinking skill' (Barrow, 1987; McPeck, 1990b) are well founded because there is no broad CT procedure that one could be skilled at. This apparent dilemma can be resolved if I only apply the skill concept to performances whose constituent activities are sequenced or otherwise structured into a coherent whole. On this view, ice-skating is a skill but playing hockey is not; performing brain surgery is a skill but being a physician is not. Problem solving is a skill insofar as its performance can be adequately represented by stage or functional models; otherwise it is not. I can speak of individuals as being skilled thinkers or as having strong CT skills, but I should not speak of 'critical thinking skill' *per se*.

Skills are evidenced through task performance. In most cases, the possession of relevant skills is neither necessary nor sufficient for successful performance. Luck can intervene (an incompetent baseball player gets a hit) and countervailing factors can override skill (a crafty pitcher strikes out the league's leading hitter). Skill is but one of many individual characteristics that bear on performance, there being numerous extra-individual influences as well. Over multiple performance instances, however, skill correlates positively with task achievement. In cases (e.g. walking, adding) where skill has a 'mere ability' connotation, skilled performance is the norm. When the concept's 'special capacity' connotation is in effect, the possession of skill implies that one's performance exceeds general standards. For this to happen, skilled activities must extend beyond or be better than is normal. Skills of this kind (e.g. communication skills) are not demonstrated by the exercise of natural performance capabilities.

Thinking skills

Thinking skills share characteristics that apply to skills in general, while also having attributes that are more distinctive. Like other skills, a thinking skill has procedural knowledge at its core; one knows how to perform certain mental activities. Although it is difficult to make crisp distinctions between thinking skills and other forms of knowledge (Nickerson *et al.*, 1985; Bailin *et al.*, 1999a), having a thinking skill entails more than just having declarative knowledge, say, of the fallacy of bifurcation. The mental activities comprising a thinking skill are sequenced or otherwise structured in some way. Being exercised by choice, thinking skills are high-level, consciously controlled, mental activities. The scope of a thinking skill – the set of mental activities it encompasses – can be broad or narrow. However, broad thinking skills are not simply collections of mental activities; their constituent parts must be organized into a coherent whole.

The intense educational interest in thinking skills has several implications for the concept. First, thinking skills must be teachable. Although this follows from the fact that they are relatively structured mental activities subject to conscious control, it deserves to be stated as an explicit criterion for the concept. The efforts of the vast thinking-skills movement in education should only be concerned with teachable, learnable mental activities. Second, thinking skills are 'special capacities', extending beyond the 'mere ability' to think. Most people are able to think with some base level of competence. The possession of thinking skills implies that one exceeds this baseline in certain ways. Thinking skills must be developed, typically through education.

Finally, although thinking skills are structured activities like other skills, they are not fully proceduralized. The notion of thinking, hence that of thinking skill, implies the exercise of discretion, the use of judgement and understanding, a sensitivity to context. This, in turn, implies that thinking skills cannot be fully proceduralized. They are not algorithms. Having a thinking skill is not like having a recipe, a complete set of instructions that can be applied by rote in any situation. Rather, one who possesses a thinking skill has procedural knowledge of how to perform certain thinking tasks. This knowledge is more or less detailed, but it is inevitably incomplete in the face of context-specific task demands. Mental tasks that have been fully proceduralized, reduced to algorithms, are no longer viewed as thinking tasks. They are given task-specific names (e.g. 'computation of return-on-investment') and turned over to computers. Some thinking skills are more judgement-dependent and context-sensitive than others. However, the notion of thinking skill implies a measure of mental discretion. Several scholars (Hart, 1978; Barrow, 1987) emphasize the role of judgement and understanding in thinking, without incorporating them into the notion of thinking skill.

Thus, thinking skills lie between two extremes. On the one hand, they must be sufficiently structured to be teachable, consciously controlled mental activities that can be exercised at their possessor's volition. On the other hand, they must not be so highly proceduralized as to lack thinking *per se*. Thinking skills lie between intuition and algorithms.

The foregoing analysis sheds light on the nature of thinking skills and provides a more principled basis for the concept's application. A thinking skill is a teachable, partially proceduralized, mental activity that reaches beyond normal cognitive capacities and can be exercised at will. Assessed against this definition, many current uses of the concept can be seen as inappropriate. Complaints that the notion of thinking skill has been too profligately applied (Hart, 1978; McPeck, 1981; Barrow, 1987) have considerable merit. The following misapplications are most common.

- *Collections of mental activities*: This mistake may derive from the 'naming fallacy' (Johnson and Gardner, 1999), in which the existence of a general label (e.g. problem solving) is taken to imply the existence of a general skill.

However, skills have a degree of procedural structure that mere collections of mental activities invariably lack. For this reason, it is a mistake, as suggested earlier, to regard CT as a skill.

- *Mental capacities that lack procedural content*: During the course of their cognitive development, people acquire mental capacities that enable certain kinds of performances. However, these capacities – intuition is an example – cannot be acquired through direct instruction, nor are they procedures that one can activate at will. Thus, they should not be viewed as thinking skills. For instance, reading comprehension and understanding are better regarded as mental capacities than as thinking skills (Smith, 1984; Woodhouse, 1991).

- *Mental activities that lack procedural structure*: Many purported GTSs, such as the ability to determine relevant facts, fall under this heading. These activities lack the procedural content required of a thinking skill. Conceivably such content could be developed, although perhaps only in particular domains – for instance, knowledge of generic criminal motives might point one towards relevant facts. However, without this kind of elaboration such 'skills' must be regarded as empty constructs expressing more hope than substance.

- *Applications of declarative knowledge*: A fixation on the skill side of the skill–content dichotomy has led educational theorists to excesses in couching other forms of knowledge as skills. Knowing a fallacy becomes the skill of detecting or avoiding it; understanding the notions of necessary and sufficient conditions becomes the skill of applying these concepts. This practice is justified when considerable procedural knowledge is involved, over and beyond the knowledge being applied, so there is more to having the skill than just knowing related facts. All too often, however, this condition is not met, and purported skills are created out of simple content knowledge.

- *Mental activities that are part of our normal cognitive repertoire*: Because the realm of normal is not well defined, one can rarely establish definitively that a purported thinking skill merely expresses normal human capabilities. However, some skills clearly offer less 'value-added' than others, raising the question of whether they should be regarded as skills. Some of de Bono's (1982) prescriptions are vulnerable to this criticism. Most people have an inclination and ability to evaluate alternatives before making a choice. Telling them to 'do a PMI', explicitly considering the pluses (P), minuses (M) and interesting (I) aspects of each option, may be beneficial, but it is unlikely to extend one's thinking ability to a considerable degree.

- *Simple mental habits*: Much of de Bono's work falls under this heading as well, being prompts to perform mental activities that effective thinkers undertake as a matter of habit. Unlike true thinking skills, these mental habits lack procedural depth: there is no real 'how to' to be learned, so there is no real skill to be acquired. The challenge lies not in knowing how to do the activity, but in remembering to do it. Purported thinking skills are just reminders or, as de Bono (1982) calls them, 'attention directors'. Rather than being a GTS, as suggested by Perkins (1985), asking 'Why not?' is a good mental habit. People can be helped to develop such habits, and related reminders should be included in programmes that teach people how to think. However, they should not be regarded as thinking skills.

Many supposed 'thinking skills' fall into these categories, failing to satisfy appropriate standards for the concept's application. At the same time, however, many legitimate thinking skills remain. Deductive reasoning, causal diagnosis, argument construction and conceptual analysis are examples. Of course, having thinking skills is only part of what is involved in being an effective thinker. Much of the knowledge that has been denied the 'thinking skill' designation is important and deserves to be included in instructional programmes. However, the debate over whether there are GTSs must be grounded in an adequate account of the 'thinking skill' concept. Having developed such a conceptualization, I now turn to the GTS debate.

The generality of thinking skills

Are there GTSs? This question lies at the heart of the thinking skills controversy because of its implications for how thinking should be taught. The generality of a thinking skill is its applicability across subject-matter domains and contexts; a GTS is procedural knowledge that can be applied to different kinds of content. The notion of thinking skill seems to imply some degree of generality, because thinking, as noted earlier, involves judgement, understanding and other context-sensitive activities. Even the most domain-specific thinking skill could not be a one-size-fits-all procedure. Beyond this base level, however, thinking-skill generality is likely to be a matter of degree, some thinking skills being more general than others (Baron, 1985). It is important to distinguish between a thinking-skill's generality and its scope, the latter concept referring to the breadth of mental activities a skill encompasses. McPeck (1990a), for one, is confused on this point. Counting and adding are skills of very narrow scope – they do not involve many different activities – but because they can be employed with virtually any content, they are, contra McPeck, extremely general.

However, matters are more complicated than what this section's simple opening question suggests. For one thing, the fact that a thinking skill is general – capable, in principle, of being applied in multiple domains – does not establish that it is generalizable – that thinkers will be able and likely to apply it in different fields, a point raised by both McPeck (1990b) and Johnson (1992). This, of course, is the issue of *transfer*, an empirical psychological question that will be examined later. My immediate concern – thinking-skill generality – faces an even more serious challenge from GTS opponents. Even if there are GTSs, they contend, such skills are inevitably weak and ineffectual, not worth the effort of learning. This is due to the generality–power tradeoff, a supposed 'iron law' that prevents general skills, methods, strategies and other procedural knowledge from being powerful means of performing tasks. To be general is inevitably to be weak, a charge that McPeck (1990a,b, 1992) makes repeatedly. Ennis (1990) responded by claiming that supposedly trivial GTSs (e.g. not contradicting oneself and not believing everything one hears) are still worth teaching because the mistakes are made so commonly. Whatever its merits, this rebuttal does not challenge the generality–power tradeoff, nor does it allay a concern that GTSs might not have much cognitive substance.

The real question to be examined is this: are there useful (reasonably powerful) thinking skills that are general (applicable in multiple domains) and that could be taught in thinking courses/programmes that are not discipline specific in a way that plausibly enable knowledge transfer to various fields of practice?

The generality–power tradeoff

Any skill, method, strategy, heuristic or other form of procedural knowledge can be characterized in terms of its generality and power. As Newell (1969) explains, the generality of a problem-solving method is a measure of the size of the method's domain, the set of problems to which it applies. A general method or skill can be used on more occasions, in more situations, than its less general counterparts. Power is the method's ability to deliver solutions, its effectiveness. Powerful methods reliably produce high-quality solutions for problems in their domains. Correspondingly, a GTS is one that can be used on many different occasions and situations encountered in multiple fields of knowledge and practice. A powerful thinking skill enables one to be consistently successful in performing the thinking tasks for which it is employed.

To be powerful, a method or skill must exploit opportunities created by characteristics of certain kinds of situations. Newell (1969) describes how linear programming, a powerful mathematical modelling technique, makes use of the linear constraints and objective functions of certain kinds of resource-allocation problems. However, its sources of power, at the same time, restrict the method's generality because relatively few situations possess these key characteristics. Thus, the generality–power tradeoff: General methods can only address generic problem characteristics that provide little problem-solving support. As a result, they lack power. Likewise, a GTS that is applied to many kinds of tasks and situations would not be powerful enough to be effective in any. This, it is argued, is the fate of GTSs like not contradicting oneself, not believing everything one hears (McPeck, 1990a), looking for tautologies, and making sure the conclusion follows (McPeck, 1990b).

Here the thinking-skills movement's want of conceptual discipline has got it into trouble. For the supposed GTSs denigrated by McPeck are not thinking skills at all, being better regarded as reminders (e.g. 'Don't believe everything you hear!'). Other purported GTSs that have been criticized – for instance, selecting and using evidence (Johnson and Gardner, 1999) – lack the procedural specificity to be true skills. The fault lies not with GTS opponents, but with GTS supporters, who have been much readier to propose GTSs than they have been to develop them.

On the other hand, GTS opponents can be faulted for not assessing thinking skills that GTS supporters claim are both general and useful. Reasoning by analogy (Weddle, 1984), experimentation (Swartz, 1987; Schunn and Anderson, 1999), and the evaluation of sources (Blair, 1992) have all been proposed as GTSs. Means–ends analysis, causal reasoning, mnemonics, argument analysis, design by top-down refinement and cost–benefit analysis could also be cited. Each is applicable to multiple domains and has the procedural content and other characteristics required of thinking skills. Perhaps GTS opponents have assumed that, because of the generality–power tradeoff, such skills must inevitably be weak. Yet, they certainly seem to be useful activities. How, in light of the generality–power tradeoff, can this be?

This conundrum is resolved when one realizes that the generality–power tradeoff is irrelevant to the GTS debate. The tradeoff has been misinterpreted and misapplied by McPeck and other GTS opponents. To understand this, one must recognize a distinction between generalizing over *tasks* and generalizing over *domains*. As explained earlier, skills and methods lose power when they generalize over tasks. In trying to do too much, they sacrifice the power achieved by exploiting characteristics of particular situations. However, the GTS debate is concerned with whether thinking skills apply in multiple domains of knowledge and practice. A skill focused on a particular task would be general if that task was addressed in more than one domain, and the skill would not lose power on account of being general in this way. Figure 8.1 graphically depicts the different kinds of generality. GTS proponents do not claim that a purported GTS addresses a broad array of

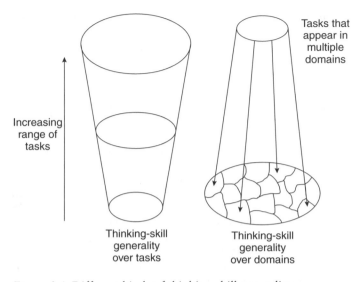

Figure 8.1 Different kinds of thinking-skill generality

thinking tasks, as shown on the left side of Figure 8.1. Rather, their claim is that the particular tasks addressed by a GTS appear in multiple domains of practice, as depicted on the right side of Figure 8.1. Thinking skills that are general over domains lose no power; they can be sufficiently well specified to be effective in diverse practical applications because they perform the same basic task in each.

Consider, for instance, the evaluation of sources, which Blair (1992) identified as a GTS. Because people in virtually every field use information collected from other sources, the need to evaluate source credibility is widespread. Thus, the target thinking task is general across domains. Moreover, this task can be nicely operationalized in terms of various characteristics of sources to consider in assessing their credibility. For instance, credible sources have relevant background and experience, they have no apparent conflicts of interest, and they use appropriate procedures in gathering information (Ennis, 1996a). Although domain knowledge might help one make related assessments within a domain, useful evaluations can be made without this specialized knowledge. There is considerable value in being aware of these general characteristics. Accordingly, the evaluation of sources is a reasonably powerful thinking skill that is highly general across domains.

Operationality and specificity

Although McPeck and other GTS opponents have misused the generality–power tradeoff, their allegation that many GTSs lack power is correct. It is important to understand why. The problem is not, as McPeck (1990b) claims, that GTSs are designed to apply too broadly to address so many kinds of tasks that they lose power. Rather, the problem is that such skills have not been developed or elaborated with the procedural specificity needed to make them powerful. Reasoning by analogy is a GTS because it encompasses enough domain-independent content (e.g. about mapping and types of analogies) to be a useful piece of procedural knowledge. The purported GTS of determining relevant facts, on the other hand, lacks this level of development, and probably could never attain it.

For a thinking skill to be powerful, two conditions – operationality and effectiveness – must be satisfied. First, the skill must be operational; it must be specified through instructions that individual thinkers can reliably perform. Second, the skill must consist of activities that constitute an effective way of performing the target thinking task. A key to operationality is specificity: the more specific the instructions and advice constituting the skill, the more likely it is that thinkers will be able to perform related activities. Unless the operationality condition is satisfied, the skill cannot even be assessed in terms of the effectiveness condition.

The trouble with most thinking skills, general and otherwise, is that they are underspecified. They are empty prescriptions, shells, rather than operational forms of procedural knowledge. Thinkers are not told what to do with their minds in order to actualize the skill. 'Generate creative alternatives': How? 'Synthesize': Tell me more! Virtually every criticism of alleged GTSs (McPeck, 1990a,b, 1992; Johnson and Gardner, 1999) focuses on their lack of specificity and consequent lack of power, even though generality is supposedly what is at issue. As suggested earlier, the notion of thinking skill implies a degree of proceduralization. Many purported thinking skills fail to satisfy minimal requirements in this regard.

Thinking skills become more powerful as a result of being made more specific and operational. With a GTS, the question is whether this can be done in a way that is independent of domain content. Figure 8.2 illustrates the concern. Its horizontal axis designates different degrees of thinking-skill specificity, while the vertical axis indicates whether the skill is general or domain specific. While some GTSs (e.g. cost–benefit analysis) fall in quadrant 4 in Figure 8.2, most are in quadrant 1, indeed on its left side, making it questionable whether they are thinking skills at all. To make such 'skills' more useful and legitimate, they must be specified more fully, developed in greater detail. This can be done by adding general or domain-specific knowledge, moving the skill to quadrant 4 or 3, respectively, in Figure 8.2. If the latter, the skill has gained power by losing generality, so it is now a more useful, but domain-specific, thinking skill.

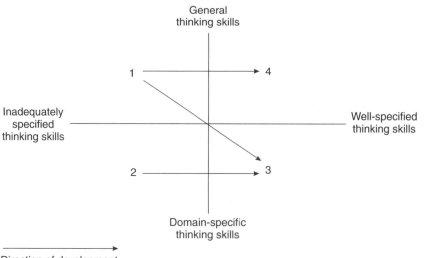

Figure 8.2 Thinking-skill generality and specificity

For instance, the purported GTS of 'identifying assumptions' involves recognizing the assumptions in an argument that, taken together with stated premises, render plausible the argument's conclusion. Although general, this advice provides scant procedural content and specificity for the crucial activity of recognizing assumptions. 'Identifying assumptions' could conceivably be developed into a GTS, but doing so would entail providing more detailed instructions for identifying assumptions in arguments from any field. More plausibly, one might be able to specify heuristics and other instructions for identifying assumptions in legal arguments, historical arguments, or reports of scientific research. Doing so would convert 'identifying assumptions' into one or more domain-specific thinking skills. Schunn and Anderson (1999) show how the general skill of experimental design is further operationalized and specified within a particular domain of practice (e.g. cognitive psychology). In that case, GTSs – experimentation, experimental design – coexist with more elaborate, domain-specific offspring. Even skills in quadrant 4 in Figure 8.2 must be implemented in context-sensitive ways, but this is true of all procedural knowledge: applications are always contextualized. What makes these skills general is the fact that they encompass significant amounts of knowledge that apply across domains and specific contexts of application. Acquiring the general skill is a valuable step towards learning its domain-specific variations.

Ultimately, the existence of GTSs hinges on the existence of generic thinking tasks, important mental jobs whose near-variants appear in multiple domains of practice. If these generic tasks have enough domain-independent content, then GTSs, targeted on those tasks, can be developed and taught. This issue is considered in the next section.

Domains of thought

The previous section rebutted arguments that GTSs are inevitably weak, by showing how the generality–power tradeoff has been misapplied. It also identified several useful and important GTSs, claiming that they are general because they address significant thinking tasks, each of which occurs in multiple domains of thought. This claim challenges a core assumption of GTS opponents: the belief that domains of thought are discrete and highly individuated, having little or no overlap of content, so that thinking in each domain is *sui generis*. This assumption and topics relating to it will now be considered in greater depth.

McPeck's content argument

In *Critical Thinking and Education*, McPeck (1981, pp. 3–5) used the observation that 'thinking is always thinking *about* something' as the basis for an argument leading to the conclusion that 'it makes no sense to talk about critical thinking as a distinct subject and that it therefore cannot profitably be taught as such'. This 'content argument' was repeated in his later book, *Teaching Critical Thinking* (1990b, p. 20) which expressed a key premise more explicitly: 'there are almost as many ways of thinking as there are things to think about'. Add in another premise that McPeck left unstated – the content of thought strongly shapes the process – and you have the following argument: thinking is always about some content. Contents vary significantly and strongly shape the thought process. Accordingly, ways of thinking vary with content, being different in different domains of thought. Thus, there are few, if any, general ways of thinking, or GTSs.

Although several scholars (Barrow, 1987, 1991; Rogers, 1990) have endorsed McPeck's position, the content argument has aroused considerable opposition (Weddle, 1984; Miller, 1986). McPeck (1990b) considered objections by Norris, Siegel and Paul but did not find them to be persuasive. An extensive challenge by Ennis (1989) led McPeck (1990a, p. 12) to allow that there are 'some very limited general thinking skills', but that these are vitiated by the generality–power tradeoff and the difficulty of applying them in specific contexts. Other criticisms (e.g. Andrews, 1990; Brel, 1990; Adler, 1991; Ennis, 1992), more recent and forceful, have gone unanswered.

The claim that thinking is always about something is, as Adler (1991) points out, trivially true. Thinking is the processing of mental representations that necessarily have content. It must also be granted that there is considerable variation in possible contents or objects of thought. However, to move from these premises to McPeck's intended conclusion – that there are no useful GTSs – requires the further assumption that thinking is strongly shaped by its content. Lacking this assumption, there is no reason to believe that 'there are almost as many ways of thinking as there are things to think about' (McPeck, 1990b, p. 20). Indeed, this claim seems ludicrous on its face: do yellow and green Volkswagens require different ways of thinking? What about cars and trucks? Vehicles and furniture? Where does one draw lines that separate different kinds of things, for thinking purposes, while satisfying the related challenge of designating a distinct kind of thinking for each specified kind of thing? His rhetorical excesses notwithstanding, McPeck wants to draw such lines to coincide with traditional domains of thought – academic disciplines, professional fields, and so forth. However, as Andrews (1990) and Ennis (1989, 1992) contend, these domains do not have clear boundaries.

What if domains could be clearly demarcated on some principled basis? No matter what boundaries were used, it would be easy to demonstrate the existence of significant content differences, for thinking purposes, within domains, so that new domains would have to be defined more narrowly. It would also be easy to demonstrate the existence of significant content commonalities, for thinking purposes, across domains, so new domains would have to be defined more broadly. Indeed, there is no way of parcelling up potential contents of thought into discrete packages, each of which requires a distinct way of thinking that has nothing significant in common with any other way of thinking required for any other package. However, this is exactly what the content argument proposes in claiming that there are no GTSs. Although McPeck and other GTS opponents can pick domains that have salient dissimilarities – for instance, physics and history (Rogers, 1990) – they have not begun to specify all the different 'ways of thinking' that the content argument postulates. Nor have they acknowledged the important commonalities of subject matter and thought possessed by seemingly dissimilar domains (e.g. history and geology, both of which deal with the past). These commonalities allow for the existence of GTSs.

Differentiating domains

McPeck's content argument reflects a very distinctive notion of academic disciplines, fields of practice, or, more generally, domains of thought. It regards domains as discrete entities having little or no overlapping of content or method. Each domain is its own world with its own subject matter and way of thinking. Because no thinking practices are held in common, there are no GTSs.

Epistemic holists, people who believe in the unity of knowledge, lie at the opposite extreme. During the twentieth century, this position was endorsed by positivists who asserted that all science could be grounded in physics and that logic and mathematics were the universally applicable foundations of scientific method. General systems theory, which emerged in the 1950s, is another version of holism. It proposed that systems concepts and techniques constitute a universal language and methodology for explaining reality.

This is an old debate, sometimes described as pitting 'lumpers' against 'splitters'. It is concerned with the value of making distinctions in a world in which any two things have both differences and commonalities. Holistically inclined lumpers ignore differences while emphasizing commonalities. This keeps them from making useful distinctions and risks leaving them in an undifferentiated conceptual morass, what Hegel termed 'the night in which all cows are black'. Splitters, on the other hand, fail to recognize useful commonalities. This reduces the value of their knowledge because it cannot often be applied. Moreover, it leaves them with the problem of determining when to stop making distinctions. McPeck's (1990b) claim that almost anything one can think about requires its own way of thinking illustrates the extremes to which this approach can be taken. Obviously, there are points beyond which lumping and splitting both have diminishing returns.

With regard to the task of differentiating domains of thought, it must be remembered that there are many characteristics in terms of which domains can be defined and many of these characteristics are graded rather than discrete. For instance, the difference between the individual and the social that demarcates psychology from sociology cannot be sharply drawn, hence the existence of social psychology. The boundaries of domains of thought are inherently vague, this vagueness being transmitted to the concept (Ennis, 1989; Sternberg, 1989).

Fortunately, there is a way out of the dilemma, an approach that does not require sharp domain boundaries to be drawn. It resolves the lumper–splitter debate by doing both, although at different levels of abstraction. Thus, the approach is hierarchical; it views knowledge as existing on multiple levels. At the lowest level, there are many domains of thought, each addressing a more-or-less distinct subject matter. While most of the concepts and methods employed at this level are domain specific, abstract notions that apply across multiple domains play important roles (e.g. conservation principles in the physical sciences, motivational notions in the human sciences, and experimental methods in both). Thus, domain differences at low levels coexist with commonalities at higher levels of abstraction. This hierarchical view of knowledge is reflected in the typical university structure, which groups specialists from fields and sub-disciplines into departments, and closely related departments into colleges or faculties.

The fact that general concepts are used in multiple domains having diverse subject matters is strong evidence of high-level commonalities across domains. Terms like 'feedback', 'equilibrium', and 'inflection point' have useful applications in many different fields. Notions of development and causality possess an almost universal relevance. Although GTS opponents acknowledge these commonalities (Johnson and Gardner, 1999), they do not admit the almost certain upshot: that some thinking tasks and practices (e.g. causal reasoning) must apply in multiple domains as well.

The trouble lies not in the identification of multiple domains of thought, but rather in the insistence, by McPeck and others, that each domain has distinctive ways or modes of thinking and its own epistemological standards. Unfortunately, there has been little or no demonstration of these multifarious ways of thinking. Weinstein (1990) cited some epistemological differences, but these are between very remote fields (e.g. literature and chemistry) and do not suggest anything like the degree of low-level domain differentiation that the argument against GTSs requires. As Siegel (1992) pointed out, although there are differences in criteria of reasons assessment across fields, these exist under a unitary epistemology. McPeck and his supporters have been as promiscuous in their use of terms like 'way of thinking' and 'epistemology' as others have been with the notion of thinking skill.

The domain of practical affairs

Despite the tendency towards excess in the differentiation of domains of thought, a very important domain, highly consequential for educational purposes, has gone unnamed, if not unnoticed. Nickerson (1994, p. 437) refers to 'the kinds of thinking and problem-solving challenges that people face in everyday life'; Weddle (1984) differentiated 'Field Dependent Life' from 'The Rest', suggesting that the latter was dominant in quantity and importance of thought. This is the field denoted here as 'the domain of practical affairs'. It encompasses the knowledge people use and the thinking they do in everyday life, both in their personal affairs and in the non-disciplinary aspects of their work. Professionals (e.g. accountants and engineers) use this knowledge when addressing interpersonal and organizational issues in the workplace. They, and everyone else, also use it in their homes, community organizations, and during recreational, shopping and other personal activities. The domain of practical affairs encompasses a huge variety of thinking tasks – designing gardens, diagnosing cars that will not start, negotiating with merchants, predicting the outcomes of football games, planning vacations, generating career options, and deciding which apartment to rent, among others. As will be seen, there is considerable overlap between these thinking tasks and those encountered in other domains of thought. Because the domain of practical affairs is intrinsically interesting and relevant to students, it offers a highly motivating context for the teaching of thinking.

It might be argued that one learns how to think about practical affairs through training in the disciplines included in a traditional liberal education. McPeck (1990a, p. 11) claims that 'the whole point of school-subject knowledge is to enlighten people about our everyday world for this everyday life', and that 'the disciplines had their origins in the human condition and are substantively about the human condition' (McPeck, 1990b, p. 30). Certainly, knowledge acquired from a liberal education provides a wealth of understanding that helps students navigate their ways through the domain of practical affairs. McPeck's (1990b) suggestion to teach explicitly the structure and philosophy of each discipline would increase this value to students. Nonetheless, the key thinking tasks that are encountered in practical affairs – diagnosis, design, planning, negotiation, prediction, evaluation, and so forth – are not often explicitly addressed by the disciplines, nor are related skills explicitly taught. Moreover, when these tasks and skills are covered, instructors quite naturally focus on discipline-specific applications. In light of what is known about transfer (Perkins and Salomon, 1989; Salomon and Perkins, 1989; McKeough *et al.*, 1995), it is unlikely that, under such conditions, students will carry their disciplinary knowledge over to the domain of practical affairs. Generalizable thinking skills must be taught *explicitly*, and the teaching must include direct applications to practical affairs for transfer to occur (Ennis, 1989).

It is naïve to expect instructors in the disciplines to do this, given their inevitable pre-occupation with discipline-specific content.

Thinking is, as McPeck asserts, always about something, and thinking can only be taught with some subject matter as its content. Owing to its interest and relevance to students, and to the range of thinking skills that are involved, the domain of practical affairs provides the natural content to use in thinking-skills instruction.

Generic thinking tasks

Recognition of the domain of practical affairs provides further evidence of the existence of generic thinking tasks, alluded to earlier. These are the ultimate basis for the existence of GTSs: thinking skills like argument-construction and means–ends analysis are general because they address thinking tasks that appear in multiple domains. Such tasks exist because people in many fields of endeavour routinely encounter certain fundamental challenges. Creative alternatives must be generated by artists, people who work for advertising agencies, and parents trying to come up with novel birthday gifts for jaded pre-teens. Predictions must be made by weather forecasters, securities analysts and farmers deciding which crops to plant. Managers evaluate their employees' performance just as teachers evaluate student essays and consumers evaluate product alternatives.

Admittedly, domain-specific knowledge is essential for performing such tasks in any particular field. However, there is also a considerable amount of general task-related knowledge that applies over multiple domains. Consider the task of diagnosis, determining the cause(s) of a problem, or other state of affairs. This task appears most saliently in medicine and equipment troubleshooting, but it also occurs in everyday affairs (e.g. 'Why can't I lose weight?') and in many other domains of thought (e.g. 'Why didn't that sales promotion work?'). Diagnosis-related knowledge from medicine and other diagnostic disciplines can be applied in other fields (Smith, 1998). For instance, the distinction between causes and conditions – active initiating factors vs passive enablements – is universally relevant. Physicians are taught to start with general causal categories (e.g. respiratory infection) and gradually narrow down to specific causal candidates, a strategy that applies as well with auto-repair. Troubleshooters look for patterns in the occurrence of a problem – certain times, places, or other conditions that are commonly problematic – another generalizable mental practice. There is much that students can learn about diagnosis that can be applied in their personal lives and in other disciplines in which they learn and practice.

Although the thinking-skills movement has recognized some generic thinking tasks (e.g. evaluating sources), many have not been addressed. This is due to the movement's traditionally narrow focus on CT. Adopting a broader view of effective thinking provides a more complete appreciation of the basic mental challenges people routinely encounter in their personal and professional lives (Smith, 2002). The domain of practical affairs offers a natural context for teaching task-related concepts, skills and heuristics in a way that will encourage knowledge transfer to other domains.

Conclusions

These findings have several important implications. First, educators and scholars must be far more restrained in their use of the term 'thinking skill(s)'.

Over-application of this concept has led to confusion, controversy and the misdirection of educational efforts. Legitimate thinking skills that are identified must be fully specified and developed. For instance, the skill should be defined, positioned within an overall repertoire of mental activities, and its component activities identified. A review of relevant literature should disclose how the skill is employed by expert practitioners and the ways in which it is typically taught. Domain-specific applications of the skill should be analysed, looking for differences and similarities that suggest general aspects of the skill. Recommendations for general and domain-specific teaching of the skill should be proposed, along with suggestions for research to develop skill-related knowledge. By setting higher standards for 'skill-talk', educators will eliminate current excesses and insure that future contributions have more practical and intellectual value.

A starting point for the identification of GTSs is an understanding of generic thinking tasks. Appearing in many different fields – design, for instance, is prominent in architecture, engineering, computer programming and the development of business products and processes – generic thinking tasks have spawned substantial research literatures, techniques, teaching methods and practical heuristic knowledge. This knowledge can be exploited to develop pedagogical materials for teaching task-related GTSs to appropriate populations of students.

The existence of generic thinking tasks indicates a need to expand the notion of effective thinking well beyond 'critical thinking', as traditionally understood and taught. Good thinking involves much more than reasoning and argumentation, the central foci of the CT movement. Among other things, students should be taught how to identify, define and analyse problems; how to think creatively when generating alternatives; how to make plans and design artifacts; and how to resolve conflicts through negotiation. Assuredly, many scholars and educators are reaching beyond traditional CT content. It is possible that CT can be broadened conceptually to encompass the needed array of knowledge (e.g. Bailin *et al.*, 1999b). Or it may be necessary for the thinking-skills movement to adopt a new conceptualization and label for its product (Smith, 2002). However, those who teach thinking must have a more expansive understanding of this endeavour than has historically been the case.

This expansion must occur on another dimension as well: the teaching of thinking must be viewed as more than the teaching of skills. Effective thinking requires knowledge of concepts, principles, standards and other forms of declarative knowledge, and of heuristics that are less proceduralized than skills. It also reflects values and dispositions that can be inculcated through education. Scholars have recognized this need and have proposed additions of content for the teaching of thinking (Ennis, 1996b; Bailin *et al.*, 1999b). However, it is not clear that these new contents have been adequately developed and effectively integrated into instructional programmes.

Recognition of the domain of practical affairs offers an opportunity to remedy another inadequacy of current instructional programmes: excessive use of puzzles and 'toy problems'. Insofar as problem solving has been taught as part of thinking-skills instruction, it has too often been taught through tasks like 'Towers of Hanoi' and 'Cannibals and missionaries'. Whatever their value for research purposes, these tasks are too structured and content-lean to have ecological validity for students or to develop practical thinking skills. Researchers should study the domain of practical affairs and identify the kinds of problems, situations and issues that people think about in their daily lives. This knowledge can be used to develop realistic instructional material that will capture student attention. It will also help scholars refine their understanding of the concepts, skills and other content to be included in GTS programmes.

Finally, despite concerns raised about illegitimate 'thinking skills' and unduly narrow conceptions of thinking, my findings strongly support the practice of teaching thinking apart from domain-specific content. The question raised in its opening section – is there a substantial body of important material (concepts, principles, skills and so forth) that is general (broadly applicable to practical affairs and various disciplinary domains) which could be taught, for instance, in general education courses in such a way that students would be able to transfer and apply their knowledge in other relevant contexts? – can be answered in the affirmative. There is ample knowledge – of concepts, heuristics, skills, and dispositions – that is both general and useful, to justify a dedicated course in both high school and college curricula. GTSs instruction should be reinforced by instruction in the disciplines, but the latter is no substitute for the former. Everything known about transfer (Perkins and Salomon, 1989; Salomon and Perkins, 1989; McKeough *et al.*, 1995) indicates that knowledge of thinking will only transfer if it is taught explicitly and with transfer firmly in mind. As Ennis (1989) noted, students taught to think through 'immersion' in domain-specific courses are unlikely to transfer their knowledge to practical affairs or any other field. In light of my argument that there are valuable GTSs that can be taught, it is essential that students acquire these skills in a way that encourages their greatest possible application.

References

Adler, J. E. (1991) Critical thinking, a deflated defense: a critical study of John E. McPeck's *Teaching Critical Thinking: Dialogue and Dialectic. Informal Logic*, 13 (2), 61–78.

Andrews, J. N. (1990) General thinking skills: are there such things? *Journal of Philosophy of Education*, 24 (1), 71–79.

Bailin, S., Case, R., Coombs, J. R. and Daniels, L. B. (1999a) Common misconceptions of critical thinking. *Journal of Curriculum Studies*, 31 (3), 269–283.

Bailin, S., Case, R., Coombs, J. R. and Daniels, L. B. (1999b) Conceptualizing critical thinking. *Journal of Curriculum Studies*, 31 (3), 285–302.

Baron, J. (1985) *Rationality and Intelligence* (Cambridge: Cambridge University Press).

Barrow, R. (1987) Skill talk. *Journal of Philosophy of Education*, 21 (2), 187–195.

Barrow, R. (1991) The generic fallacy. *Educational Philosophy and Theory*, 23 (1), 7–17.

Blair, J. A. (1992) The generalizability of critical thinking: the evaluation of sources. In S. P. Norris (ed.), *The Generalizability of Critical Thinking: Multiple Perspectives on an Educational Ideal* (New York: Teachers College Press), 125–137.

Brel, C. D. (1990) Critical thinking as transfer: the reconstructive integration of otherwise discrete interpretations of experience. *Educational Theory*, 40 (1), 53–68.

De Bono, E. (1982) *de Bono's Thinking Course* (New York: Facts on File).

Ennis, R. H. (1989) Critical thinking and subject specificity: clarification and needed research. *Educational Researcher*, 18 (3), 4–10.

Ennis, R. H. (1990) The extent to which critical thinking is subject-specific: further clarification. *Educational Researcher*, 19 (4), 13–16.

Ennis, R. H. (1991) Critical thinking: a streamlined conception. *Teaching Philosophy*, 14 (1), 5–24.

Ennis, R. H. (1992) The degree to which critical thinking is subject specific: clarification and needed research. In S. P. Norris (ed.), *The Generalizability of Critical Thinking: Multiple Perspectives on an Educational Ideal* (New York: Teachers College Press), 21–37.

Ennis, R. H. (1996a) *Critical Thinking* (Upper Saddle River, NJ: Prentice-Hall).

Ennis, R. H. (1996b) Critical thinking dispositions: their nature and assessability. *Informal Logic*, 18 (2 & 3), 165–182.

Griffiths, M. (1987) The teaching of skills and the skills of teaching: a reply to Robin Barrow. *Journal of Philosophy of Education*, 21 (2), 203–214.

Hart, W. A. (1978) Against skills. *Oxford Review of Education*, 4 (2), 205–216.

Johnson, R. H. (1992) The problem of defining critical thinking. In S. P. Norris (ed.), *The Generalizability of Critical Thinking: Multiple Perspectives on an Educational Ideal* (New York: Teachers College Press), 38–53.

Johnson, S. and Gardner, P. (1999) Some Achilles' heels of thinking skills: a response to Higgins and Baumfield. *Journal of Philosophy of Education*, 33 (3), 435–449.

McKeough, A., Lupart, J. and Marini, A. (eds) (1995) *Teaching for Transfer: Fostering Generalization in Learning* (Mahwah, NJ: Erlbaum).

McPeck, J. E. (1981) *Critical Thinking and Education* (New York: St Martin's Press).

McPeck, J. E. (1990a) Critical thinking and subject specificity: a reply to Ennis. *Educational Researcher*, 19 (4), 10–12.

McPeck, J. E. (1990b) *Teaching Critical Thinking: Dialogue and Dialectic* (New York: Routledge).

McPeck, J. E. (1992) Thoughts on subject specificity. In S. P. Norris (ed.), *The Generalizability of Critical Thinking: Multiple Perspectives on an Educational Ideal* (New York: Teachers College Press), 198–205.

Miller, R. B. (1986) Toward an empirical definition of the thinking skills. *Informal Logic*, 8 (3), 113–124.

Newell, A. (1969) Heuristic programming: ill-structured problems. In J. Aronofsky (ed.), *Progress in Operations Research, Vol. III: A Relationship Between Operations Research and the Computer* (New York: John Wiley), 361–414.

Nickerson, R. S. (1994) The teaching of thinking and problem solving. In R. J. Sternberg (ed.), *Thinking and Problem Solving* (New York: Academic Press), 409–449.

Nickerson, R. S., Perkins, D. N. and Smith, E. E. (1985) *The Teaching of Thinking* (Hillsdale, NJ: Erlbaum).

Norris, S. P. and Ennis, R. H. (1989) *Evaluating Critical Thinking* (Pacific Grove, CA: Midwest Publications Critical Thinking Press).

Perkins, D. N. (1985) General cognitive skills: why not? In S. F. Chipman, J. W. Segal and R. Glaser (eds), *Thinking and Learning Skills, Vol. 2: Research and Open Questions* (Hillsdale, NJ: Erlbaum), 339–363.

Perkins, D. N. and Salomon, G. (1989) Are cognitive skills context-bound? *Educational Researcher*, 18 (1), 16–25.

Rogers, P. (1990) 'Discovery', learning, critical thinking, and the nature of knowledge. *British Journal of Educational Studies*, 38 (1), 3–14.

Ryle, G. (1963) *The Concept of Mind* (London: Penguin).

Salomon, G. and Perkins, D. N. (1989) Rocky roads to transfer: rethinking mechanisms of a neglected phenomenon. *Educational Psychologist*, 24 (2), 113–142.

Schunn, C. D. and Anderson, J. R. (1999) The generality/specificity of expertise in scientific reasoning. *Cognitive Science*, 23 (3), 337–370.

Siegel, H. (1988) *Educating Reason: Rationality, Critical Thinking, and Education* (New York: Routledge).

Siegel, H. (1992) The generalizability of critical thinking skills, dispositions, and epistemology. In P. Norris (ed.), *The Generalizability of Critical Thinking: Multiple Perspectives on an Educational Ideal* (New York: Teachers College Press), 97–108.

Smith, G. F. (1998) Determining the cause of quality problems: lessons from diagnostic disciplines. *Quality Management Journal*, 5 (2), 24–41.

Smith, G. F. (2002) Towards a comprehensive account of effective thinking. *Interchange*, 32 (4), 349–374.

Smith, M. J. E. (1984) Mental skills: some critical reflections. *Journal of Curriculum Studies*, 16 (3), 225–232.

Sternberg, R. J. (1989) Domain-generality versus domain-specificity: the life and impending death of a false dichotomy. *Merrill-Palmer Quarterly*, 35 (1), 115–130.

Swartz, R. J. (1987) Critical thinking, the curriculum, and the problem of transfer. In D. N. Perkins, J. Lochhead and J. Bishop (eds), *Thinking: The Second International Conference* (Hillsdale, NJ: Erlbaum), 261–284.

Walters, K. S. (1992) Critical thinking, logicism, and the eclipse of imagining. *Journal of Creative Behavior*, 26 (2), 130–144.

Weddle, P. (1984) McPeck's *Critical Thinking and Education. Informal Logic*, 6 (2), 23–25.
Weinstein, M. (1990) Towards a research agenda for informal logic and critical thinking. *Informal Logic*, 12 (3), 121–143.
Wittgenstein, L. (1953) *Philosophical Investigations* (London: Blackwell).
Woodhouse, H. (1991) Is critical thinking just a generic skill? *Interchange*, 22 (4), 108–114.

CHAPTER 9

ON THE CONCEPT OF MANNER AND ITS VISIBILITY IN TEACHING PRACTICE

Gary D. Fenstermacher

What is manner in teaching?

What is manner in teaching, and how do you know it when you see it? Twenty years ago, when I began writing about the concept of manner,[1] I thought I knew the answers to these questions. Not to any level of certainty, of course, but with the reasonable assurance of one who believes he is arguing a worthwhile position, and doing so in a proper way. Now, after nearly two years of intense investigation of the concept in both philosophical and empirical contexts, my early assurance no longer seems justified. In this chapter, I explore grounds for my growing wonder towards the notion of manner, and look more carefully at its nuances in practice. The work reported here is part of a larger three-year research effort (1997–2000) to learn more about how teachers foster or impede the development of moral and intellectual virtues in their students.

A bit of near history sets the stage for the current analysis. Thirty years ago, many studies of classroom teaching were prompted by a desire to understand the relationship between how a teacher behaved in the classroom and what students learned from that teacher. The studies employed a distinctly behaviourist conception of teaching and learning, using highly quantitative designs and methodologies to search out compelling correlations between teacher behaviour and student learning. Several concerned critics of this genre of research worried that it was leading educators and policy makers to form excessively simple ideas of both the purposes and practices of teaching. These simple ideas implied a conception of teaching method that was centred almost exclusively on what teacher behaviours most likely lead students to acquire prescribed subject-matter knowledge.

As one of the concerned critics, I wondered how research might account for some of the more elusive, yet highly significant, aspects of teaching, such as the cultivation of highly regarded intellectual traits (e.g. critical thinking, regard for truth and respect for evidence), as well as the development of moral virtue (e.g. fairness, courage, caring). The guiding question for this inquiry was whether it was possible to develop a more robust conception of teaching by introducing a term that would serve as a contrast to 'method', at least to method as it was being interpreted by behavioural psychologists and learning theorists working at mid-century and the decades following. Enter the notion of 'manner'. My intention at the time was to use the concept of manner to direct attention to the teacher's role in fostering the moral and intellectual development of the young. Other scholars were at work on similar objectives, although with different approaches. These different approaches are summarized in excellent reviews by Valli (1990), Strike (1996) and Hansen (2001).

As the members of our small Manner in Teaching Project (MTP)[2] research team examined the data collected in the course of studying the work of eleven teachers in two very different schools (a predominantly White middle-class school in a small Midwestern city and an African-centred K-8 school in a large metropolitan area), it appears that my initial desire to draw attention away from method, directing it instead to manner, led to a far too rigid division between the two. It now appears that method is an extremely important means for fostering manner in students. However, I am getting ahead of the story. A bit more stage setting is in order if the connection between manner and method is to be developed in any convincing way.

An Aristotelian view of manner

My initial efforts to expound on manner were grounded in what I regarded as highly appealing moral theory. From Plato's *Meno* to Ryle's *The Concept of Mind* (1949), it has been generally accepted in Anglo-American philosophy that virtue cannot be taught, at least not as one teaches table manners or arithmetic. Instead, virtue is acquired or 'picked up' by association with people who are themselves virtuous. In compliance with this generally accepted view, I incorporated into my own analysis of manner the notion that virtue is not conveyed in the way academic content is conveyed, but rather is acquired as a result of being around virtuous people. The conclusion to this reasoning follows quite readily: teachers must themselves be virtuous persons if they are to foster virtues in their students.

Viewed in this way, the manner of the teacher is paramount if the teacher is to be successful in cultivating the moral and intellectual virtues of the students. In this case, manner is defined as conduct expressive of dispositions or traits of character that fall into a category of moral goods known as virtues. Amongst the virtues are honesty, compassion, truthfulness, fairness, courage, moderation and generosity. (I leave open here the very important issue of why these particular traits are to be regarded as virtues, doing so with the philosophically lame, but empirically compelling, claim that the literature, customs and norms of the vast majority of world cultures hold these traits in high regard.) Viewing manner in this way, students will acquire virtuous dispositions from a teacher *only if* that teacher is himself or herself a virtuous person. This rather straightforward view has long been honoured in its contrary form, as when it was believed to be a grave error to place students with teachers who were not virtuous, because students might thereby be led to conclude that non-virtuous conduct was tolerable, perhaps even acceptable.

This view of virtue in teaching borrows heavily from the work of the British philosophers of education, Dearden *et al.* (1972), as well as from Harvard philosopher, Scheffler (1985). It is, moreover, a highly Aristotelian or aretaic view of morality. There are other theoretical options for characterizing the moral conduct of teachers, such as consequentialism, or a Kantian deontological ethics, or an ethic of care, but at the time I opted for an aretaic ethics with little consideration for the alternatives.[3] Aristotelian ethics seemed to fit the context of teaching and learning with hardly any tinkering or adaptation required, thus giving it special appeal for the purpose of contrasting it to method. Method, given the spin I was seeking to place upon it, is the means used to impart knowledge and understanding of the various subject-matters of the school curriculum, whereas manner is the means used to convey virtuous conduct. This rather rigid bifurcation seemed to work, at least so long as no one asked to be shown a case of teacher manner. If someone were to insist on being shown, the task would become one of making manner visible.[4] How might that be done?

One might think it is a relatively easy task to make manner visible. After all, people readily recognize acts of generosity, or caring, or fair-mindedness, at least in their more common manifestations. One needs simply to look for these acts, isolate them, and one would then have a case of manner. Indeed, that does work. But what, if anything, do such acts have to do with fostering virtue in students? A person of the same mind as Socrates and Ryle would answer quite a bit. Our studies of teachers in classrooms lead us to a different response. Acting virtuously (also often referred to as modelling virtuous conduct) is but one of a number of means that teachers have for fostering virtue in students. What is more, it might not be the most powerful or compelling means that teachers have at their disposal. Our analysis of the data collected to date indicates that teachers employ several different ways to foster virtuous conduct in their students. Even more surprising to us is the extent that teachers use these various approaches, not only as a way to convey virtue, but to construct classroom settings that function optimally for the participants (Richardson and Fallona, 2001).

The upshot of discovering the importance of method in cultivating virtue is that the visibility of manner is no longer quite the interesting challenge it once seemed. So long as we thought that virtuous conduct in students was fostered exclusively by virtuous conduct in teachers, we tried to observe this conduct in order to learn more about it. However, the more we focused on the manner of the teacher, the more difficult it seemed to us to attend to what was being conveyed to students. To look only at whether or not the teacher's conduct is itself virtuous is to miss much of what the teacher is doing to foster virtuous conduct in students. As difficult as it was for me to back away from notions of manner as the central factor in cultivating virtue in students, the data before us demanded a different sense of how teachers sought to foster the moral and intellectual development of their students.

Six methods for fostering moral conduct

The analysis is best pursued by describing the various methods we found teachers using, as they attempted to advance the moral and intellectual capacities of their students. We have, thus far, encountered six methods used by most or all of the eleven teachers in our study to foster improved intellectual dispositions and enhanced moral relationships (for reasons explored later in this chapter, we exclude virtuous conduct by the teacher, which is often categorized as modelling). The six methods are: construction of the classroom community; didactic instruction; design and execution of academic task-structures; calling out for conduct of a particular kind; private conversations; and showcasing specific students. Each of these is briefly described here.

Constructing classroom communities

All teachers in our study have a vivid conception of the kind of place they want their classrooms to be.[5] Mutual respect, sharing, tolerance, orderliness and productive work are the notions most often mentioned by the teachers when describing their aspirations for their classrooms. To accomplish these aspirations, the teachers set rules and expectations for student conduct in their classrooms. These rules and expectations create a classroom that is a normative community, a community that imposes rules and duties upon its members, presumably for their mutual benefit.

All the teachers in our study were adept at the creation of classroom communities, although the teachers at Highlands Academy, the African-centred school, jointly subscribed to the view that their classrooms are sites of what Green (1984, 1999) calls 'strong normation'. As such, they have no difficulty with the notion that their classrooms clearly reflect the strong, personal and professional beliefs they hold as teachers about the importance of education and the role their classrooms and their school plays in the lives of their students. Moreover, there is little grace shown for infractions of the rules and expectations; there is a pervasive attitude that is perhaps best captured by the expression, 'shape up or ship out'.

The teachers at Jordan Elementary School are no less desirous of having classrooms that reflect a just and caring community, but their methods of attaining this end differ from those employed at Highlands Academy. At Jordan Elementary, the teachers are more likely to find the authority for constructing community in their personal relationships with each student, in contrast to the strong ideological commitment to the importance of community that characterizes both the mission of Highlands Academy and the personal philosophies of its teachers. That is, the teachers at Jordan Elementary are more likely to imply to their students that they need to behave in a particular way if they are to have a successful relationship to the teacher, or a successful experience in this teacher's classroom. The Highlands Academy teachers, in contrast, are more likely to insist that learning cannot go on unless students behave in a certain way. Thus, the rules and norms of classroom conduct are defended on the basis of the point or purpose of the school as a social unit (an offshoot of this difference is that while the Highlands Academy teachers may be quite sensitive to what the students think of them, they give the impression that it is not about whether students like or enjoy a teacher so much as it is about whether you learn from the teacher).[6]

These observations about constructing community are further expanded in two papers in *Journal of Curriculum Studies* 33(b). Sanger (2001), in his study of two teachers' views of morality, shows how the meaning of and grounding for the construction of community differs depending on the moral starting points of the teacher. Chow-Hoy (2001) examines the school-level constructs that may lead to teachers at the two schools to frame different views about the nature of community. Chow-Hoy describes how both schools have mission statements and principles that stress a wide range of moral and intellectual virtues. Given the missions and principles of the two schools studied, it should not surprise the reader that the eleven teachers in the study were quite conversant with talk about fostering virtue and the importance of becoming a morally good person.[7]

Constructing community turns out to involve more than laying down rules and building norms, as became apparent to us when noting the physical differences between the two schools. How the teacher sets up the furniture and arranges for student access to supplies and materials in the classroom also signals appropriate and inappropriate conduct. At Highlands Academy, the African-centred academy, for example, it is somewhat unusual to see small groups of students working independently. Whole-class instruction, with all eyes on the teacher, is the more characteristic mode of instruction – even in the primary grades. At Jordan Elementary, by contrast, student desks are arranged in groups of two, four or six, and small-group or one-on-one teaching is more common than whole-class, teacher-centred instruction. These room designs bear prominently on how the teachers construct community, for the whole-group setting in Highlands Academy is in some sense made possible by the strong ideological orientation to the need for community, whereas the small-group settings at Jordan Elementary are managed by the teacher's tendency to 'ground' the rules and norms in the relationship established between teacher and student. In addition, how a room is arranged affects the use of other methods for conveying the virtues, as noted later.

Didactic instruction

Didactic instruction, in the context of this study, is instruction that has, as one of its primary purposes, the direct presentation to the student of what is morally or intellectually desired by the teacher. Perhaps the most obvious example of this method in our study is the life-skills curriculum used at Jordan Elementary School. This curriculum is a direct, specific effort to gain student allegiance to and compliance with seventeen life-skills that constitute this curriculum, including integrity, initiative, humour, patience, friendship, pride, courage, and common sense. Jordan Elementary teachers in the study regularly discuss these life-skills as part of the programme of classroom instruction, and frequently refer to them in the course of teaching other subjects (e.g. a lesson on sustaining a healthy ecosystem, grounded primarily in general science, is an occasion for calling on students to see the importance of sharing the earth's resources, and of acting justly with respect to the development and distribution of these resources).

Highlands Academy has a different, but no less direct and didactic approach to the attainment of moral goods. The African-centred curriculum at Highlands Academy places extensive emphasis on such African-derived values as unity (*Umoja*), collective work and responsibility (*Ujima*), co-operative economics (*Ujamaa*), creativity (*Kuumba*) and faith (*Imani*). In the classrooms of many Highlands Academy teachers participating in the study, these values are cultivated quite directly, through the frequent telling of stories, through choral recitations of memorized songs and slogans, and through frequent references to these values when commenting on student conduct.

Teachers at both schools may be found providing lessons to the whole class on these ideals. These lessons are frequently grounded in recent actions by students or the teacher, and also are extended to how the students will behave later in life. At Highlands Academy, in particular, one finds teachers frequently discussing, as a planned lesson for the whole class, the futures of the students, referencing both scholastic attainment and careers, and moral goodness. These didactic lessons appear to be undertaken quite seriously by the teachers and the students at both schools, and their effectiveness shows up with remarkable clarity in the interviews we had with the students at each school.

Design and execution of academic task structures

Teachers have a broad range of choices in how they engage their students in the work required to gain mastery of a concept, topic or lesson. This choice becomes manifest in how they set up the tasks students engage in as they progress through their academic work. Doyle (1983, 1986, 1991) refers to these demands on students as 'academic task structures', and has written incisively on the power of such tasks. Many teachers in our study construct these tasks so that they can analyse and assess the students' work in ways that extend the students' ability to think more deeply or more imaginatively about the work, thereby fostering an enhanced range of intellectual virtue. Indeed, some teachers proved to be particularly adept at designing tasks so that they could gain ready access to the student's work, and offer extensive commentary on that work.

For example, Cheryl teaches a grade 7 English class at Highlands Academy. For a lesson on punctuation, she writes a number of unpunctuated sentences on the chalkboard, and then asks various students to go to the board to insert the correct punctuation. After Sheila inserts a semicolon in a particular sentence, Cheryl says to the class, 'Sheila put a semicolon in that sentence. I would like to know who agrees with her?' After a show of hands, Cheryl asks, 'Now who disagrees with her?' Another show of hands, this time far fewer, and Cheryl says that it is not enough to just agree or disagree, you have to have reasons to support your position. Then she turns to Mindy and asks her to go to the board to insert her correction. Mindy does so, substituting a colon for the semicolon. Cheryl asks her why, and Mindy is able only to say it seems right. Cheryl turns to Jamal and asks him if he can explain the difference between a colon and semicolon, and offer a good reason why one is better in this sentence than the other. Jamal offers an explanation, and Cheryl's speech brightens as she says, 'You're absolutely correct!'

The lesson to be gained here is difficult to miss: Cheryl's interest is in the explanation or argument for the decision about punctuation; Mindy inserted the correct punctuation, but went unpraised by Cheryl for her inability to provide a justifying rationale. What Cheryl does so often and so well is to set up academic task structures that engage the full class in the activity. She is then able to comment publicly on performance, frequently signalling to the entire class what kind of thinking she is seeking and the form she wants it to take as students respond to her questions. An observer has the sense that tasks are structured to permit an increase in the time provided for didactic instruction, as well as for what we have labelled 'call-outs'. Task structuring of this kind is in marked contrast to providing assessment in private asides with students or in the grading of individual student assignments.

Calling out for conduct of a particular kind

One of the most frequently observed techniques for cultivating student conduct was what we refer to as the call-out. It is simply the teacher saying something to the student that indicates to the student and all others within earshot how the student ought to behave. Call-outs typically consist of friendly reminders about deportment or outright censure for inappropriate conduct. Margaret, a Jordan Elementary teacher, has students working independently and in small groups. She is assisting a student who has been working alone when, upon looking up and over the full class, she calls out across the room, 'Soosun, how does what you are doing now help your team to complete it's work?' The question is rhetorical, for the student is aware that he is being disruptive, and refocuses on the task at hand. This call-out signals the expectation for non-disruptive, co-operative effort, and is, of course, heard by many other students in the class.

In a different Jordan Elementary classroom, Hannah convenes her class in the form of a circle, with many students sitting on the floor. The topic of discussion is caring for the environment. As she is preparing the ground for soliciting their views on issues explored in a prior assignment, one student loudly exclaims his view. Hannah says: 'Goodness, Jason, you're anxious to participate today. But isn't it polite to wait until the person speaking is finished, then raise your hand?' Jason nods, and sits back on his heels. Hannah follows with, 'It's also a fair way to bring others into the conversation, isn't it?' This comment is addressed not so much to

Jason as to the group as a whole (Jason does not acknowledge this second comment, and the teacher does not appear to expect him to do so). The message of this call-out to Jason is that people do not get heard by being the quickest or the loudest, but by taking turns; taking turns is the fair way to have a conversation. A great deal of moral freight seems to be carried by so modest a move.

Call-outs are frequently reminders to students of the rules and expectations for good deportment in the classroom. They are teacher-to-student communications, done within view and earshot of most or all of the class. They serve not only to call the non-obedient student to account, but to refresh everyone else's memory of what is desired in this setting. We found call-outs to be one of the most obvious and frequently used ways teachers signal their expectations for student conduct, particularly in moral domains involving co-operation, fairness and regard for others.

An interesting aspect of call-outs is that we almost missed them on our first pass through the data. There is a tendency to see them as demands for order, or quiet, or mere compliance to what some might regard as arbitrary rules. And indeed there are call-outs of this kind. However, there are also call-outs directed quite specifically to the cultivation and encouragement of virtuous conduct. At least in the case of the teachers participating in our study, the call-outs were, in the main, far from simple demands for compliance or order, but rather the expression of a very genuine interest in helping the student to become a good person. (This observation is based, in part, on listening to the comments the teachers made as they viewed videotape of their own teaching and shared their reactions with us.)

Private conversations

Didactic instruction and call-outs are public, visible means of cultivating the moral and intellectual dispositions of students. Private conversations are another method of doing so. They typically occur when a teacher takes a student aside for a 'chat', but may also occur as students enter the room at the beginning of the day, or at other times when the chance arises for a teacher to direct his or her attention to a single student. And, although many private conversations are intended to be corrective (i.e. the teacher is seeking to correct conduct that is harmful to the student or to the group or both), many are highly affirmative and nurturing.

For example, Darlene greets many students personally as they enter her classroom in the morning, seeking to have a private talk with as many of them as possible. Her purpose, she says, is to help the students make the transition from home to school, particularly in the case of students for whom the home experience is troubling at this time in their lives. Darlene indicates that these exchanges with students are rooted in a profound concern for the welfare of her students; she is especially concerned that her students are mentally ready for life in the classroom that day, setting aside worries they may have about matters beyond the school.

Letti, a teacher at Jordan Elementary, is often engaged in private conversations with students throughout the school day. The frequency of private conversations in the classroom may be related to the fact that it adjoins a special-education classroom, and students from both rooms frequently intermingle as a means of ensuring inclusion of the special students. As a result, Letti is not always able to manage her class as a single large group, nor is it clear that she would prefer to do so even if the opportunity were more available, for she is a person who makes deep, personal connections to her students. As such, she handles initial flare-ups with call-outs, but quickly shifts to private conversation if the matter is not soon resolved. Taking students aside, she tries to reflect their conduct back to them, in an apparent effort to make them aware of just what it is they are doing, and how it is affecting other class members and the teacher. In almost all instances of such private conversations that we observed, Letti's conversations focused on being co-operative, on respecting the needs of other students, and effecting moderation in one's behaviour.

It is clear that teachers have many different kinds of private conversations with their students. Of interest in the context of manner are those directed at altering a student's conduct to make it more closely conform to a moral ideal, either by censure of unacceptable behaviour or extended praise for appropriate conduct, or to elicit a deeper intellectual engagement in the topics of instruction. We witnessed a fair amount of this kind of private conferencing at Jordan Elementary, particularly in the classrooms with a higher concentration of special-education students. The ways that Jordan Elementary teachers design the physical environment makes it more conducive to private conferencing, because the other students have independent tasks or small-group work to keep them engaged whilst the teacher is having a private conference. We observed fewer private conferences at Highlands Academy, at least during regularly scheduled class periods. That there are fewer such conferences at Highlands Academy may be due to the more extensive use of teacher-led, whole-class instruction, and the greater likelihood that Highlands Academy teachers will discipline, reprimand or reward their students in a more public way (e.g. using a call-out). Moreover, it is difficult to have a private conversation during class time, because the classrooms are generally too small to permit teacher and student to separate themselves physically from the other students. On the other hand, private conversations are not uncommon before classes begin for the day, at change-of-class times, and at day's end.

Showcasing specific students

From a philosophical point of view, showcasing may be amongst the most interesting techniques used by classroom teachers. It is interesting because the teacher is not featuring his or her own virtues, but those of the student. In a sense, the teacher is not modelling virtuous conduct for the students, but placing students in the role of modelling such conduct for their peers. A Jordan Elementary teacher asks a question about whether the group liked a lesson being taught by a student teacher. One of the students shakes her head from side to side, and the teacher asks why. The student explains, and the teacher says:

> I like how Corinne is being honest. She's giving me an honest answer to my question, even though it may hurt a little bit. Thanks for being honest, Corinne.

The full group heard this praise for Corinne, and the message it contained about honesty. What we believe is taking place here is that the teacher is calling other students' attention to a virtue being displayed by one student, signalling the value of this virtue by showcasing this student. Of course, there is the element of reinforcement for the virtue of honesty that Corinne displays, and that is certainly a means for the teacher to encourage honesty in Corinne. Yet, we detect in our conversations with the teachers that they have more in mind when praising the good conduct of their students. The teacher is shifting the role modelling from himself or herself to a student, saying to other students something like: See, you don't have to be grown up like me to be able to act this way; here's one of your fellow students who is doing it quite well.

We know from our own experiences in school that there are risks here, for a teacher who praises a student may succeed in having that student identified as a teacher's pet or favourite, thereby reducing the student's impact as a model for other students. Yet, we found that the teachers we observed navigated these potential problems with considerable facility. They may indeed have favourite students, but the technique of showcasing is distributed with apparent even-handedness in the classrooms we observed. For example, Nandi, teaching an English lesson to grade 8 Highlands Academy students, directs a question at Alfred, whom she knows to be a marginal student. This time Alfred has the right answer. The teacher follows up with another question, and Alfred gets it right again. Nandi becomes effusive in her praise for Alfred, and encourages the class to commend his strong performance. They whistle and clap, and Alfred smiles broadly while holding his hands aloft with the victory sign on each hand. When this incident was explored with Nandi, she indicated that Alfred had a difficult time with this material, and she wanted him to feel proud of the progress he was making with it. She also wanted his classmates to honour his accomplishment, a trait she signalled as an important one by showcasing Alfred as she did.

Teachers appear to have multiple reasons for showcasing, ranging from reinforcement to a positive object lesson for all who are in view or earshot. Whatever the reason, showcasing seems a prominent method for signalling praiseworthy conduct, and for informing the group that it is within their grasp to exhibit similar conduct.

Some problems with modelling

Earlier in this chapter I mentioned modelling, and noted that members of the research team are unsure of its status as a means of fostering virtuous conduct in students. As such, it was excluded from the list of six methods just described. It cannot, however, be ignored in any discussion of how moral and intellectual goods are conveyed to students by their teachers.

There is a sense in which modelling *is* manner. That is too restrictive a claim, but it is not far off the mark. Manner, for the purposes of this chapter (and the larger MTP study we are engaged in), is conduct that expresses highly regarded moral and intellectual traits. Thus, when we speak of a person as fair-minded, caring, thoughtful, generous, honest, brave, and so on, we are describing the manner of that person. A person's manner could be morally unacceptable, too, as when he or she is described as mean, unfair, cowardly, lying, and so forth. However, in the context of our work, we have used the term 'manner' only to pick out conduct that evidences the various virtues. Hence, for us, manner picks out what is good, moral, sound and defensible about persons, rather than what is bad, immoral, silly or stupid about them. Yet, in a frame larger than ours, manner could point to conduct that is good, bad or both.

The manner of a teacher takes on particular importance, insofar as it serves as a model for the students. That is, the manner of the teacher would probably not concern us if it were not for its serving as a model, as something the student will see and believe proper, or imitate, or accept as a standard for how things should be. Yet, it is not quite so clear when manner is being modelled. For example, is a teacher modelling some virtue only when he or she intends that it be observed or imitated? Or, does modelling occur whenever the teacher displays a virtue, whether or not she intends to have it observed or noted by another? If modelling falls into the former category, it might be a kind of method. If it falls into the latter category, it appears to be the case that the teacher is acting without instructional intent or purpose. If there is no intent to have the manner observed with a measure of regard by the student, then it seems a stretch to think of modelling as a method employed by the teacher.

There is more at issue here than the teacher's instructional purpose or intent. One can try to model, but fail, in the sense that persons nearby pay no attention to person modelling. If no one pays attention, is the teacher modelling? (A variation on the common riddle, if a tree falls in the woods with no one near, is there any sound?) Does one need an attentive listener or viewer in order properly to be said to be modelling? What if the viewer is attentive, but fails to pick up properly on what is being modelled; did the person then model for the viewer? These modest conundrums can be resolved with precise, stipulative definitions, but their existence reveals some of the challenges to clear deployment of the concept of modelling.

Because of this confusion, we think it is wise to give modelling separate standing in the repertoire of ways to cultivate the moral and intellectual virtues in students. We find ourselves undecided on just how tightly linked manner and modelling are, and under what circumstances modelling may be said to be amongst the methods a teacher might use to foster virtue. We know that modelling takes place, and that most teachers, school administrators and parents place considerable stock in it, but our excursions through our data lead us to wonder about its precise status. Consider the intriguing possibility, as we are in the midst of doing, that a teacher whose manner could be viewed as somewhat deficient could employ the six methods described here with remarkable finesse. Entertaining this possibility leads us to wonder about the possibility that teachers may adopt personae on entering their classrooms, and that these personae may perform in roles more morally and intellectually powerful than is the case for the teacher as a person outside the classroom. In other words, whom are we looking at when we look at teachers: are we looking at a person who possesses a manner, which is somehow made manifest in the practice of teaching; or are we seeing someone in a role, who may perform with remarkable moral and intellectual acuity in that role – perhaps because the role demands acuity of this kind – but is something less a paragon on virtue when the teaching mask is off?

Nothing in our experience with the eleven teachers with whom we are working prompts us to ask these questions. That is to say, we have not found some of our teachers to be less moral or less intellectually sophisticated outside their classrooms than they are inside them, thus leading us to wonder whether the role of teacher alters the moral and intellectual character of the one teaching. Rather, this puzzlement about persona and role arises from seeking to frame the analysis of our data in the context of the intriguing philosophical questions about moral agency and moral development. Moral agency is that quality possessed by a person to act morally. Moral development is the bringing about in others of moral agency. Breaking these concepts apart permits us to ask some vexing – but exciting – questions about how fully developed a moral agent must be in order to be good at moral development. Put another way: how much manner is required to engage effectively in methods for moral development?

Returning to the nexus of manner and method

The preceding question sets us upon a conceptually slippery surface, inasmuch as it prompts us to ask how morally good a person need be in order to be good at cultivating moral goodness in students. Some of our evidence to date suggests that having a well-wrought moral point of view, and well-developed intellectual capacities, makes a considerable difference in how the six methods described here are deployed. Indeed, as Richardson and Fallona (2001) suggest, one's facility with the methods of moral development may be intimately connected to the depth and sophistication of one's moral agency.

Yet, there are other possibilities. In strong normative communities (such as the African-centred Highlands Academy), it is possible that teachers may experience more success in fostering moral development in others, without having to depend so extensively on their own moral agency to do so. Their success in moral development is more a matter of carefully and thoughtfully employing the methods described in this chapter. Of course, it may indeed be the case that such methods for moral development cannot be well deployed by those who are morally deficient in their own agency. There certainly seems to be some sort of requirement for moral agency on the teacher's part in order to be well and effectively engaged in the moral development of students. But, how much of a requirement? As high as I once thought, with my early notions of manner? It seems not. On the other hand, we have only begun to ponder these questions.

In the meantime, our progress to date indicates that a quagmire awaits those who draw too strong a distinction between the manner and methods of teachers (as I once did), especially if the point of such a distinction is to restrict manner to matters moral and method to matters epistemic. In addition, if one does succeed in making manner visible, particularly in the form of modelling, its place in fostering moral and intellectual virtue in the young may not be quite so substantial as earlier supposed. There are several methods teachers use to cultivate the moral and intellectual capabilities of their students, and these methods appear to have considerable force for the moral and intellectual development of students. In isolating and analysing these methods, and deliberating upon them in relation to modelling, moral agency, and moral development, we find ourselves peering across conceptual vistas unimagined just one year ago. In exploring these vistas, we, MTP researchers and participating teachers, hope to add just a bit more understanding to how moral education and development take place in teachers' classrooms.

Acknowledgements

An earlier version of this chapter was presented at the Annual Meeting of the American Educational Research Association, 19 April 1999, in Montréal, Canada. The work leading to the development of the ideas reported in this paper would not have been possible without the generous support of the Spencer Foundation. The author also gratefully acknowledges the contributions of the MTP research team, including the eleven classroom teachers participating in the study.

Notes

1   My writing on manner began with an AERA paper in 1980 (Fenstermacher 1980). I again picked up the topic in the third edition of the *Handbook of Research on Teaching* (Fenstermacher 1986). A more extensive discussion of the concept appeared in 1992, in a volume edited by Oser *et al.* (Fenstermacher 1992).
2   General details of MTP are provided in Richardson and Fenstermacher (2001). See also Chow-Hoy (2001), Richardson and Fallona (2001) and Sanger (2001).
3   Even though I was conscious at the time of adopting a particular ethical theory as the basis for the concept of manner, this move became quite blurred over time. My thanks to

Matthew Sanger for reminding me, in the form of a compelling second-year paper for his doctorate, that there are several theoretical alternatives for the ethical grounding of teacher manner.

4   The expression 'making manner visible' was first heard amongst our MTP staff when voiced by Fallona (1998), who, in the course of preparing her doctoral dissertation on manner in teaching, was faced with determining how to observe the manner of teachers. In struggling with this problem, she asked how she might make manner visible. When it became clear that there was no easy answer to this question, the question became one of the most important undertakings for the research project.

5   Perhaps the sole exception here is the physical education teacher at Highlands Academy, who has many fewer degrees of freedom for what takes place in his gymnasium, which is sometimes a site for physical education, but at other times serves as the cafeteria, the overflow area for school-wide events, and the main assembly point for all students entering or departing the building at the beginning and end of the school day.

6   On this point about the teacher's sensitivities to the views of the students, an incident at Highlands Academy offers a revealing insight. Because of a confused communication between the school and the research team, some members of the Highlands Academy staff who are not participating in the study were surprised to learn that members of the MTP research team were interviewing students, asking the students for their impressions of their teachers. Despite the fact that the interview protocol had been jointly constructed with and approved by the teachers participating in MTP, some Highlands Academy staff members expressed consternation at asking students what they thought about their teachers and classrooms; the sense was that students really are not in a position to answer such questions, and that asking them sends the wrong message about what they (the students) are in school to do. Students are not to judge teachers or the school; teachers and school judge the students.

7   We did not set out to select schools that had mission statements or building principles that placed such emphasis on moral ideals. Jordan Elementary became a candidate as a result of an acquaintance between an MTP staff member and the building principal. Highlands Academy became a site on the urging of one of the MTP graduate students who thought it important to include within the study a minority school in an inner-city setting. It was only later that we realized we had two schools that placed strong emphasis on moral development, but in quite different ways.

References

Chow-Hoy, T. K. (2001) An inquiry into school context and the teaching of the virtues. *Journal of Curriculum Studies*, 33 (6), 655–682.

Dearden, R. F., Hirst, P. H. and Peters, R. S. (eds) (1972) *Education and the Development of Reason* (London: Routledge & Kegan Paul).

Doyle, W. (1983) Academic work. *Review of Educational Research*, 53 (2), 159–199.

Doyle, W. (1986) Classroom organization and management. In M. C. Wittrock (ed.), *Handbook of Research on Teaching*, 3rd edn (New York: Macmillan), 392–431.

Doyle, W. (1991) Classroom tasks: the core of learning from teaching. In M. S. Knapp and P. M. Shields (eds), *Better Schooling for the Children of Poverty: Alternatives to Conventional Wisdom* (Berkeley, CA: McCutchan), 235–255.

Fallona, C. (1998) Manner in teaching: a study of moral virtue. Doctoral dissertation, University of Arizona, Tucson, AZ.

Fenstermacher, G. D. (1980) The value of research on teaching for teaching skill and teaching manner. Paper presented at the annual meeting of the American Educational Research Association, Boston, MA.

Fenstermacher, G. D. (1986) Philosophy of research on teaching: three aspects. In M. C. Wittrock (ed.), *Handbook of Research on Teaching*, 3rd edn (New York: Macmillan), 37–49.

Fenstermacher, G. D. (1992) The concepts of method and manner in teaching. In F. K. Oser, A. Dick and J.-L. Patry (eds), *Effective and Responsible Teaching* (San Francisco, CA: Jossey-Bass), 95–108.

Green, T. F. (1984) *The Formation of Conscience in an Age of Technology*. The 1984 John Dewey Lecture (Syracuse, NY: Syracuse University, School of Education).

Green, T. F. (1999) *Voices: The Educational Formation of Conscience* (Notre Dame, IN: Notre Dame University Press).

Hansen, D. T. (2001) Teaching as a moral activity. In V. Richardson (ed.), *Handbook of Research on Teaching*, 4th edn (Washington, DC: American Educational Research Association), 826–857.

Richardson, V. and Fallona, C. (2001) Classroom management as method and manner. *Journal of Curriculum Studies*, 33 (6), 705–728.

Richardson, V. and Fenstermacher, G. D. (2001) Manner in teaching: the study in four parts. *Journal of Curriculum Studies*, 33 (6), 631–637.

Ryle, G. (1949) *The Concept of Mind* (New York: Barnes & Noble).

Sanger, M. (2001) Talking to teachers and looking at practice in understanding the moral dimensions of teaching. *Journal of Curriculum Studies*, 33 (6), 683–704.

Scheffler, I. (1985) *Of Human Potential: An Essay in the Philosophy of Education* (New York: Routledge & Kegan Paul).

Strike, K. (1996) The moral responsibilities of educators. In J. Sikula, T. J. Buttery and E. Guyton (eds), *Handbook of Research on Teacher Education*, 2nd edn (New York: Simon and Schuster Macmillan), 869–892.

Valli, L. (1990) Moral approaches to reflective practice. In R. T. Clift, W. R. Houston and M. C. Pugach (eds), *Encouraging Reflective Practice in Education: An Analysis of Issues and Programs* (New York: Teachers College Press), 39–56.

PART IV

EDUCATION FOR ALL

One of the biggest questions in education worldwide is that of equity. Who gains access to teaching and who is denied? Which individuals and groups in society have been dealt an unfair hand of cards? Do girls, or boys, have an advantage? Is someone's religion, ethnicity, disability a barrier, and if so, what can be done to change the situation and give everyone their fundamental human right to learn?

The story can even change within a very short time. In the 1970s many talented girls left school at the minimum school leaving age, even though they were perfectly capable of studying to a high level. In the twenty-first century there is concern about the relatively low performance of boys, who now lag behind girls in almost every society, when both are offered the same educational programmes. Despite these improvements in achievement, however, there are still problems with the education of girls, who are less likely than boys to study subjects like mathematics, physics and engineering to a high level.

The three chapters in this part all address important aspects of access and equity. Diane Reay, in Chapter 10, draws a graphic picture of Shaun, a diligent white working-class boy, who is trying to balance his desire to study against the pressures from his mates, his peer group in an inner city boys' comprehensive school. It is a common phenomenon. Shaun is torn between his mother's desire that he should work hard and stay out of trouble, and the obligation he feels to support his peers, join them in fights, assert himself in the traditional macho way of his age and social group. It is a clash of cultures: the virtues and modes valued by school, versus the image of masculinity cultivated by adolescent boys. The author argues that solutions go beyond the usual suggestion that he should join a programme for the gifted and talented, for how would his mates react?

Gender issues apply to parents as well as pupils, and Curt Dudley-Marling, in Chapter 11, highlights the difficulties faced by the mothers of children who get into trouble at school, since they are often in the front line, rather than the fathers. He describes graphically the sense of despair and guilt that can consume mothers when they see their children in difficulties at school. Some are even blamed by their husbands, who assume that it is the mother who should be responsible for behaviour and learning. 'What are you doing? How come you didn't help him read?', one father accuses his wife, in the presence of the writer. As tension spills across from school to home emotions begin to boil over.

The assumption by many is that heads and teachers must be responsible for improving teaching and learning and that pupils have little or no role to play. Jean Rudduck and Julia Flutter refute this by looking specifically at children's rights and showing how they can participate in decision making. They argue that having a stake in their school is an important part of becoming an adult citizen, and that teachers need to listen to what children have to say about the conditions of learning, since they are the principal experiencers. The authors' extensive interviews with pupils in primary and secondary school reveal that they are often eager to participate, rather than be passive recipients.

CHAPTER 10

SHAUN'S STORY
Troubling discourses of white working-class masculinities

Diane Reay

Introduction

There is an extensive recent literature in the USA, Australia and the UK which examines how schooling interacts with wider social processes in the shaping of subjectivities (Wexler, 1992; Mac an Ghaill, 1994; Hey, 1997; Mcleod, 2000; Walkerdine *et al.*, 2001), while a growing body of work focuses specifically on the problem of white working-class masculinities in the schooling context (Skelton, 1997; Connolly, 1998). Less attention has been paid to the discrepancies; those instances of classed and gendered subjectivity that work against normative under-standings of the relationship between social class, gender and schooling, although there have been a few notable exceptions, for example, Stanley (1989) and Brown (1987) in the UK, Mehan *et al.* (1996) in the USA, and Connell *et al.* (1982) in Australia. This chapter concentrates on one such discrepant case. It tells the story of a hard-working, well-behaved, poor, white, working-class boy trying to achieve academically in a 'sink' inner-city boys' comprehensive school, whilst simultane-ously trying to maintain his standing within the male peer group culture. It also raises questions about the possibilities of bringing together white working-class masculinities with educational success in inner-city working-class schooling. I argue, through Shaun's case study, that to combine the two generates heavy psy-chic costs,[1] involving young men not only in an enormous amount of academic labour but also an intolerable burden of psychic reparative work if they are to avoid what Bourdieu terms 'the duality of the self' (Bourdieu, 1999, p. 511).

Shaun's story resonates with many earlier stories of white working-class boys struggling to achieve academically. There are similarities with Colin Lacey's Cready, 'a working class boy from a large family, making good' (Lacey, 1968) and Philip Brown's 'ordinary kids' (Brown, 1987). However, neither text provides suf-ficient information about either the boys' reputations and behaviour out of the classroom or their emotional responses to their positioning within schooling for the reader to gauge the psychological costs of their academic endeavours. In con-trast, in this chapter I am concerned to make links between children's and young people's inner emotional worlds and external social and structural processes. To this end, Bourdieu's theoretical framework is combined with psychoanalytic theo-ries in order to keep both internal and external processes continually in the frame.

I never expected to be engaged in recuperating white working-class masculini-ties, although the ways in which they have been homogenised in academic accounts and made to bear the weight of white racism and male sexism (Weis, 1993) has not been borne out by my experience of either teaching working-class children in the inner city or interaction with the middle classes in professional settings. Over thirty years of living in a working-class inner-city area has provided me with many examples of very different working-class masculinities to those inscribed in my memories of growing up. My own childhood and adolescent experience of white working-class masculinities was one scarred by violence, both physical and verbal abuse, plus the more symbolic, but equally damaging, violence of deeply entrenched sexism and racism within the male-dominated, coal mining community I used to be part of. However, of all the hundreds of children that I have interviewed over the past ten years, Shaun's story resonated most powerfully, apparently independently of my female and feminist subjectivity.

I have often felt a powerful empathy and strong identification listening to, in particular, working-class girls and women; a finding of myself in them that I have written about before (Reay, 1996, 1999). I have not been able to find myself in Shaun's narrative, at least not in any obvious way, nor does he offer the fascination of an 'exotic other'; those middle classes I am still trying to make sense of. Instead, to some extent, he reflects the uncomfortable image of the familiar oppressor. His story, then, is compelling in its own right and has written itself in spite, as much as because, of me as the author. Twice on returning tapes of Shaun's interviews my transcriber said that his words made her weep. I did not weep but his story did leave me with an overwhelming sense of anger at the way things are for boys like him. This chapter, then, is my attempt to do justice to his narrative, one that speaks to the complexities, the struggles, pains and possibilities, of white working-class masculinities at the beginning of the twenty-first century.

Shaun was part of a sample of 454 children interviewed as part of a large Economic and Social Research Council (ESRC) project on primary–secondary school transitions in two London boroughs. All the children were interviewed in focus groups, then a smaller sample of 45, including Shaun, was interviewed individually in Year 6, then three times over the course of their first year in secondary school. However, my contact with Shaun both pre-dated and post-dated the research project. He was part of a small pilot study conducted with Year 5 pupils and was also one of five children I stayed in contact with after the ESRC project finished. I have eight interviews with Shaun conducted over a four-year period from September 1997 to September 2001, four before the move to secondary school and four afterwards. As a consequence, this is primarily a tale of before and after, of anticipation and realisation, and the ways in which secondary school transfer can operate as a process of class sifting and sorting despite the egalitarian mythologising surrounding comprehensive education. This class process has changed little since Measor and Woods's (1984) and Delamont and Galton's (1986) seminal work over fifteen years ago, despite enormous changes within the educational field. But this chapter is also more than that; it is a case study of how psychic and social processes intertwine in convoluted and contradictory ways to fashion white working-class masculinities which are far more complex, nuanced and fragile than any of the stereotypical representations in dominant discourses.

Subjectivity and schooling

Julie McLeod (2000) argues for the need to address the dynamic between subjectivity and schooling, and this chapter attempts to make such links through an analysis of Shaun's struggles to belong to a good place within schooling. Bourdieu writes that 'when habitus encounters a social world of which it is the product, it finds itself "as a fish in water," it does not feel the weight of the world and takes the world about it for granted' (Bourdieu and Wacquant, 1992, p. 127). Following Bourdieu, we would expect Shaun, a poor, working-class, Irish boy to feel at home in the poor, inner-city, working-class, ethnically mixed comprehensive he ends up in. However, Shaun's tale is one of ducking and diving, not swimming; of being weighted down rather than being weightless. His words reveal both striving and struggling against the educational context he finds himself in.

Wexler (1992) writes about 'the class divided self' in his discussion of white working-class students in an urban American high school. Similarly, Shaun's tale is an example of contradiction and tension between the social order and psychological processes rather than the 'homology, redundancy and reinforcement between the two systems' that Bourdieu (1999, p. 512) asserts is normative. In contrast to the norm, Shaun's experience generates a habitus divided against itself; an experience Bourdieu (1999, p. 511) describes as 'doomed to duplication, to a double perception of self'. He is positioned in an untenable space on the boundaries of two irreconcilable ways of being and has to produce an enormous body of psychic, intellectual and interactive work in order to maintain his contradictory ways of being, his dual perception of self. There are resonances with the dilemma that the young men Edley and Wetherall (1999) interviewed found themselves in. They, too, were caught between two contradictory subject positions. However, there the similarities end. Edley and Wetherall's samples were all middle class and privately educated. Shaun, living on an inner-city, sink council estate in a lone mother family surviving on state benefits, belongs to a section of the working classes that has routinely been stigmatised within dominant discourses (Skeggs, 1997; Reay, 1998).

Shaun's narrative reveals how centrally class as well as gender is implicated in psychic processes and the fashioning of contemporary subjectivities. It provides an example of how processes behind class advantage and disadvantage work through the individual (Savage, 2000), but also of the continuing importance of material and social positioning within the educational field. Recent scholarship on masculinities has emphasised the shifting, fluid nature of identities. However, Connell cautions against too great an emphasis on fluidity, arguing that 'fluidity may be a great deal less fluid when examined in the institutional contexts of everyday life . . . It might indeed, be helpful to think about the "fixing" mechanisms that limit the fluidity of identities' (Connell, 2001, p. 8). Class operates as one such 'fixing mechanism', chaining Shaun to a place where his self-fashionings have limited efficacy (Bourdieu, 1999). The institutional constraints of inner-city schooling are a continual theme throughout Shaun's narrative, as when he tells me, 'we've never had a French teacher that has stayed for more than two weeks'; 'the kids that muck about all of the time, mostly they do it because they can't do the work very well. They need someone to help them but there isn't anyone', and 'I'm not so good at science cos we've had three teachers so far this year'. Sutton Boys', Shaun's third choice of secondary school, and the school he ends up in, serves an area of extreme social deprivation. Over 50 per cent of the pupils are eligible for free school meals, and over 70 per cent have very low or below average verbal ability on joining the school. Forty per cent of the boys speak English as an additional language. In 1995 the school was made subject to special measures on the grounds that it was failing to give its pupils an acceptable standard of education.

Bourdieu argues that 'narrative about the most "personal" difficulties, the apparently most strictly subjective tensions and contradictions, frequently articulates the deepest structures of the social world and their contradictions' (p. 511).

Bourdieu's words speak to what is probably the most difficult problem for theoretical understandings of the construction of gendered subjectivities – 'the extent to which individuals are constrained by their structural contexts and how far they can build alternative identities despite their stigma' (Heward, 1996, p. 41). Shaun's text is riven by such tensions. There is a continual movement between the material and psychological consequences of poverty, which implicate both school and home, and an optimism of the will that, although at times deflated and at others fragile, Shaun manages to sustain despite the odds. And the odds are enormous, involving Shaun in the immense amount of psychic and intellectual work necessary to keep both his and his mother's hopes alive. It is the very anomalies in Shaun's situation, the discrepancies between his social practices and those normative for 'boys like him' that make his narrative so rich and vivid, full of imagery and reflection. Shaun's contradictory situation has given him access to what Bourdieu terms 'socio-analysis' (Bourdieu, 1990, p. 116). Bourdieu, in writing about lay people's access to forms of socio-analysis, argues that 'practical analysts' are those individuals situated at the point where the contradictions of social structures are most apparent, chiefly for the ways in which they 'work over' such individuals, who in order to survive such 'working over' practise a kind of self analysis. Shaun, like Bourdieu's 'practical analysts', displays an awareness both of the objective conditions that have him in their grasp and of the objective structures expressed in and by these contradictions.

Shaun's story

In 1998, when Shaun was in Year 5, he was very clear not only about the secondary school he wanted to attend but also about the schools that he considered unacceptable:

> I'm gonna go to Westbury because my mate Mark's going there and my girlfriend.
> Sutton Boys' is like one of the worst schools around here, only tramps go there.

However, by the middle of the first term of his final year in primary school, Shaun's certainties were dissolving. Confronted with the headteacher's advice that Westbury would be far too risky a choice as he lived on the edge of its catchment area, and having been warned that other popular schools in the borough were even more remote possibilities, Shaun and his mother resigned themselves to applying to Sutton Boys':

> I might not get into Westbury cos it's siblings and how far away you live and I haven't got any siblings there and I live a little way out so I might have to go on a waiting list . . . I might go to Sutton Boys' instead cos all my mates are going there.
> I could have wept at the thought of him going to Sutton but what choice did we have cos Mrs Whitticker said we didn't have any.
>
> (Maura, Shaun's mother)

By the time I next interviewed Shaun in the last term of Year 6 his narrative displayed a continual ambivalence between optimism of the soul and a negative realism:

> It's a good school for me because I know some of the teachers there. David's brother Dean goes there, my cousin Paul and this kid, John, all these kids I know from off my estate, they all go there.

and:

> It's good to go somewhere where you've got lots of older kids looking out for you and that's what I'll have at Sutton Boys'.

But in constant tension with his positive anticipations were far more negative expectations:

> I've heard it might get closed down because it's no good or something . . . my friend used to go but he don't go any more. He's only 15 and he don't go to school any more because all the teachers used to bully him, always pick on him so he won't go any more.

and:

> I dunno anyone who's done well there, everyone does badly there, oh yeah, I do, my cousin done well there but that was before he was excluded.

Even at this stage, Shaun's efforts to retain a degree of optimism require a great deal of psychic work. He is not going 'to get dragged down'. Instead, he is determined 'to work much harder because like it's secondary and the most important school days of your life because that's when you're coming up to your GCSEs [General Certificate of Secondary Education]'. But this positive outlook must be maintained in the face of deeply demoralising information, including knowledge of how local educational markets operate:

> My mum and I think the standards might be too low because people just bunk and everything at Sutton.
> There's a bit of a problem with Sutton Boys' having low standards because it might get closed down.

Shaun has even begun to reflect on how Sutton Boys' could be improved – 'it would be a much better school if it allowed girls to attend' – whilst arguing that this is not a realistic proposition because 'it's not a safe place for girls because of all the people that go to that school, there's Triads and everything that go to that school. And there's all the people who think they are gangsters and come with knives and stuff'. He has also started to prepare in advance for his time there:

> I know that sometimes people sit and ask for 10p in Sutton Boys', because I've been finding out quite a lot about Sutton Boys' because I am going there. So I am going to try and find out as much as I can about it, because if I don't and I go into school and people go – have you seen something or so and so? And then they are going to pull you into the toilets and beat you up. So if I find out all about it I'll know how to protect myself from the rough kids.

Both Shaun and his mother told me that they had had 'lots of serious discussions' about how Shaun could still do well at Sutton Boys' despite its poor reputation: 'Like I need to change my attitude, change the way I behave, like no fights, no cheeking in the classroom because I don't want to let my mum down, let myself down just cos no one else is getting on with it'. Maura, his mother, said, 'we've had some real heart to hearts. He's putting a brave face on it but I can see how worried he is. I've said you just have to work twice as hard to do well if you go to a school like that rather than somewhere like Westbury where the kids expect to get on with their work instead of mucking about all the time'. However, even at this stage a major tension between Shaun and his mother is the peer group, or more specifically, Shaun's friendship with a number of boys with reputations for 'messing about' and 'getting into fights'.

Before the move to secondary school, Shaun's main rationale for accepting that Sutton Boys' might be a reasonable school for him was that lots of his friends were also going there. However, at the end of his first term in the school the main change that he identifies is 'my friendship with some people'. He asserts that he can no longer be friends with David, his best friend from primary school, because whereas before:

> Whenever David was in trouble with a fight I was always there to help him. We always helped each other or if someone needed us for a fight. But here now I'm not really into fighting. Fighting ain't nothing but trouble so I try and keep out of it . . . Fighting is for the kids who don't want to learn and don't want to do well at school and I don't want to be like that.

This new 'non-violent' Shaun is a recent, precarious self-invention. Shaun, who has twice been suspended from his primary school for fighting, has a local reputation for being 'tough', which he sees as vital to sustain if he is to survive in Sutton Boys':

> I'm not going to get into any fights myself but like everybody said, yeah, that me and David, we've been classed as the hardest in Year 7 and we've agreed, yeah, that if kids that can't fight are getting beaten up us two are going to jump in and help them. It's just like, you can't let someone that don't know how to fight, who is little get it all the time, you can't let them get picked on or hit . . . so I'm not fighting I'm helping.

When I query how he is going to reconcile being tough in the playground with being hardworking and achieving in the classroom he replies, 'I am just different in the class to what I am out in the playground. I'm just different'. This duality of being is something Shaun returns to time and again in his secondary school interviews: 'You see, when I get outside I go back to being cool and bad but not when I'm in class'. Shaun constructs himself as neither a 'lad' nor an 'ear'ole' (Willis, 1977) but a self-consciously crafted concoction of the two. Yet, this double perception of the self, tough in the playground and scholarly in the classroom, as becomes evident later, is riven with contradictions and requires almost superhuman efforts to maintain.

Foucault sees self-fashioning practices as 'patterns that the individual finds in his culture and which are proposed, suggested and imposed on him by his culture, his society and his social' (Foucault, 1987, p. 122). But Shaun's practices are quite clearly not supported by the social milieu he is part of and he is, in Bourdieuian terms, resisting the imposition of cultural necessity. In the context of the secondary classroom all his energy is expended in desperately trying to set himself apart from the rest of his peer group; 'all the other kids were spitting spit balls out of paper at the teacher and I just sat down and tried to take no notice'. But this contriving to be apart must avoid aloofness. Rather, he is attempting to carve out a space for academic success in a peer group context where, at least nominally, it is despised and where he still retains very strong desires to belong. The only other two boys 'to keep their heads down and try and get on with their work' are outsiders to the local male working-class peer group culture. One is American and in Shaun's words 'dead clever'. The other is Portuguese and has parents who are actively looking to place him in another school. Even in Martino's (1999) private mixed-sex school the scholarly displays that Shaun has begun to invest in, such as reading books and spending lots of time on homework, were pathologised among the male peer group. It is not surprising, then, that in Shaun's predominantly working-class boys' comprehensive such practices conflict with appropriate male behaviour for 'boys like us' and he has to constantly guard against being reclassified as 'a geek'. While existing research suggests that middle-class boys can continue to occupy positions of hegemonic masculinity by combining coolness with the seamless production of academic success (Mac an Ghaill, 1994; Martino, 1999), this is not a subject position available to Shaun. In contrast, Shaun has to continually negotiate peer group pressure to prove he is still really 'a lad':

> Like a kid will call you in the classroom and the others go 'Oh Shaun are you gonna take that? Are you gonna take that? Knock him out. Knock him out, he was dubbing your dad' and all that. I don't care about my dad but then they try and stir it and try and change what he said to get you to fight.

As is evident in the excerpt below, one of many Shaun recounted, the classroom context in Sutton Boys' is rarely conducive to academic learning:

> Some boys, yeah, in English yeah, some of the kids never shut up, never, ever shut up. Like, today, we were supposed to get out for lunch at ten past one, because all the bigger kids push in front of us, but because everyone was shouting and everything and I am the one that always goes – shut up. So whenever I tell them to shut up they are scared of me and they shut up, but then this boy Ryan, he always comes back and says something, so we have to stay in. He always pushes it. They all show off. Because Jay, yeah, this year, I think he's had more fights than he did out of all the time at Beckwith, so far, because like, today, yeah, that boy Ryan picked up a chair and Jay stood on the table and flying kicked the chair into the kid's face and then punched him and he fell back on the floor. And like David is encouraging him. He was going, go on Jay, go over there and punch him in his face. And when they were fighting and everyone was going, go on Jay, go on Jay. They can't just sit down and ignore it or try and break it up.

Against this constant backdrop of classroom disruption and intermittent eruptions of violence, Shaun is endeavouring to get on with his studies despite the peer groups' disapprobation:

> When I do my work the others think 'he's a fool, look he does his work. It's stupid working, he's a goody two shoes and all that'.

Yet, despite the negative reaction from 'all my mates', those boys in the class whose friendship and approval he values, Shaun refuses to conform to the localised regime of normalising practices through which boys come to adopt certain practices of masculinity and display themselves as particular kinds of boys (Martino, 1999). However, this constitutes a considerable loss of face which Shaun has to recuperate in other contexts in order to be accepted. As a consequence, in contradistinction to his displays of nonconformity to prevailing peer group values in the classroom, in the playground and on the estate, he resurrects his old self, reclaiming a very different identity as 'tough' and 'a skilful footballer' which redeems, most of the time, his 'geekiness' in the classroom. However, this brings Shaun into conflict with his mother:

> My mum said she don't want me mixing with the wrong people because, like the people I hang about with, like, they are all troublemakers, David, Jay and all that. My mum says she don't want me to hang around with them, but if I don't hang around with them I aint got no one to hang about with.

It is worth reiterating the tenuousness of Shaun's positioning. He is caught between two untenable positions, continually engaged in a balancing act that requires superhuman effort; on the one hand ensuring his masculinity is kept intact and on the other hand endeavouring to maintain his academic success. Sutton Boys' is a school where success is in short supply and, as a consequence, it is resented and undermined in those who have it. By the end of the first year at secondary school the two conflicting selves that Shaun has put so much effort into reconciling are beginning to come apart:

> It's getting harder because like some boys, yeah, like a couple of my friends, yeah, they go 'Oh, you are teacher's pet' and all that. Right? What? Am I teacher's pet because I do my work and tell you lot to shut up when you are talking and miss is trying to talk? And they go, 'yeah so you're still a teacher's pet'. Well, if you don't like it go away, innit.

That the effort has taken its toll is evident in Shaun's longing to be a baby again:

> I want to stay younger, like I wish I was younger now. So I wouldn't have to move, just sleep in my cot and have no responsibility. But you've got to get older. You can't just stay the same age.

Shaun's ambitions are created under and against conditions of adversity. Reputation in Sutton Boys' comes not through academic achievement but is the outcome of a jockeying for position among a male peer group culture, in which boys are 'routinely reproducing versions of themselves and their peers as valued because of their hardness, appearance, or capacity to subvert schooling' (Phoenix and Frosh, 2001). As O'Donnell and Sharpe (2000) point out, schools like Sutton Boys' are engaged in a losing battle to counterbalance the collective influence of the male peer group.

How can Shaun both set himself apart from and remain part of the wider working-class male collectivity? That is the task he has set himself and the dilemma it raises lies at the very heart of class differentials in attainment within education. However, I also want to argue that we need to look outside the school and into what at first sight could be viewed as 'the unpromising spaces' of his family life on one of New Labour's socially excluded sink council estates (Social Exclusion Unit, 1998) in order to understand sustenance and support for Shaun's resolve.

I want to try to unpick what keeps Shaun going despite the unpromising conditions of his schooling and locality, the constant turnover of teaching staff and the continual negative barrage from his fellow pupils. First, Shaun's desires to do well are very clearly not rooted in any intrinsic regard for school-based knowledge.

Rather, he shares with many of his peers a sense that the knowledge being offered in school is not really relevant to boys like him:

> I'd prefer to have more stuff that really prepares you for the future and you don't get that. Like some subjects I don't even know why they make us do it because it doesn't make sense for the future.

However, unlike most of them, he does have both a positive rapport and empathy with his teachers, and particularly with his female teachers. He had an especially good relationship with Claudette, his head of year. Every time I interviewed him he told me that she was brilliant. Later, when I interviewed her, the first thing she said about Shaun was 'he's just brilliant'. However, his understanding, sympathetic attitude extended to all his teachers:

> There was a time at the beginning of the term when the class was really good and then they started to go downhill and also the teachers can't really spend a lot of time with the kids because they're always having to sort out fights, sort out arguments. They can't really help because they haven't got enough time to look after the good kids.
>
> I feel really sorry for my French teacher . . . when Miss tell them to be quiet in French, yeah, our teacher, she always usually loses her voice. She goes, can you be quiet please? And she shouted so much she lost her voice. And I yell, oi, shut up, Miss wants everyone to be quiet. I went, Miss, shall I tell them to shut up and sit down? She goes, go on then. And I said, sit down and shut up. And everyone just sat down and shut up. And then as soon as Miss started talking they all started talking and when they don't listen to the teachers it makes me feel sorry for them.

Shaun is caught up in Bourdieu's 'paradox of the dominated'. Bourdieu, writing of the paradoxical consequences of compliance with the educational system, rejects the dichotomy between submission and resistance inherent in accounts of working-class schooling such as Paul Willis's *Learning to Labour*. Rather, he argues that 'resistance may be alienating and submission may be liberating' (Bourdieu, 1990, p. 155). Certainly, there have been tangible academic benefits in Shaun's compliance. He has received a certificate for outstanding achievement in his year and his mother recounted regular examples of letters home praising his performance and attainment in a range of subject areas. However, I want to argue that it is not just the academic rewards that motivate Shaun to veer off on his lonely path across a bleak inner-city educational landscape. Stephen Frosh and colleagues (2002) argue that many boys and young men struggle with ways of constructing masculine identities that are socially 'acceptable', particularly with regard to the values embodied in their peer group culture, whilst striving to hold on to their felt need for intimacy and emotional contact. It is such a reconciliation between the two that Shaun is struggling to achieve. His commitment to learning and his positive identification with his teachers are rooted in his relationship with his mother; a relationship which raises another paradox because, seen through the discursive lens of healthy male development, the closeness and continuing connectivity between Shaun and his mother are viewed as pathological rather than normative. I try and grapple with this contradiction in the next section of the chapter.

'Mummy's boy': reworking the pathologised as privileged

Although schooling is salient in the construction of subjectivities, family is the first site in which masculinities are fashioned. It is impossible to write about Shaun's subjectivity without writing about his relationship with his family, in particular his mother. Unlike the other children that I interviewed, Shaun regularly referred to his mother and family life throughout the interviews without any prompting from me. As a consequence, while most of the interviews lasted forty-five minutes to an hour, those with Shaun were always longer, one hour and fifteen minutes to an hour and a half. However, in April 2000, when he turned up in the deputy head's office, he was not his usual smiling equanimous self and proceeded to talk about his mother's illness and consequent hospitalisation. We talked for 40 minutes off tape about his mother and family life before reverting to our usual pattern of discussing school-based issues. Shaun lives in a lone parent family with his mother and two sisters. The family have a third floor flat in a large council estate and are currently surviving on income support. His love, concern and strong desire to please his mother shine through all the interviews. His father, though absent for most of the three years of the research project, remains a looming terror. When I first interviewed Shaun in Year 5, his father had returned to Ireland and was the ultimate sanction in Shaun's life for bad behaviour: 'My mum says if I get into any more trouble she'll send me to my dad in Ireland and no way do I want to have to go and live with him'. However, halfway through Shaun's first year at secondary school, his father re-emerged in the locality and became a much more tangible threat, subjecting the family to harassment and minor acts of violence, at one point killing and cutting up Shaun's younger sister's pet rabbits, until Shaun's mother was finally forced to get a restraining order.

Shaun's Year 6 teacher told me:

> Someone like Shaun will come up to me, 'I just want to get away from the other boys for a little while, all of us are dragging each other down'. You know, he takes equal responsibility for it. Because of all the boys he's the one most in touch with his feminine side, believe it or not. I do think he's more in touch with his feminine side but then he lives with three women, his mum, who he idolises, his elder sister, who he idolises, and his baby sister, who he idolises, so his feminine side is very much to the fore. Also, he loves his girl-friends. I do think Shaun sees them as quite a calming effect but then he's very much in touch with that.

While Ms Keithly inscribes both Shaun's close relationship with his mother and his feminine qualities positively, that is not how they would be represented within traditional conceptions of normative masculine development. I want to push against the boundaries of conventional orthodoxies in order to understand Shaun's familial relationships as far more enhancing than mainstream psychological texts allow. In *Masculinities* (1995), Connell writes about a group of 'new' men who have attempted to reform their masculinity in a process 'that was directed at undoing the effects of Oedipal masculinization'. He goes on to argue that 'it seems likely that this project was supported by emotional currents from pre-Oedipal relationships: centrally, the primal relationship with the mother' (1995, p. 135).

Psychological theorising has traditionally focused on 'oppositional categories of masculinity or femininity, fathers or mothers, identification or rejection' (Heward,

1996, p. 37). As Heward points out, such binary categorisation does not allow for the rejection of fathers by sons except as a deviant, pathological response. The normative Oedipal model for 'healthy' male identity formation is based on identifying with the father and rejecting the mother (Edley and Wetherall, 1995). And this has been translated into populist discourses which view normal male development as 'leaving the mother and "the feminine" behind and moving on towards a real masculine identity with the father' (Elium and Elium, 1992). Yet, for boys like Shaun, mothering has a potency and positive efficacy that is actively denied in conventional accounts of normative masculine development which implicitly pathologise lone mothering. However, there are other accounts, and it is those we need to turn to, to make positive sense of Shaun's relationship with his mother. In *Anti-Oedipus* (1984), Deleuze and Guattari argue that Freud's Oedipal complex is a key structure of capitalism which represses libido and desire, internalising a patriarchal family structure at an unconscious level. They assert that conventional psychological theories collude with capitalism and its repression of sexuality by accepting the familial constellation. However, their thesis also lends itself to interpretations which position psychological orthodoxies regarding normative development as implicitly misogynistic and mother blaming. As Jan Campbell argues, modifying the sexualised mother of Oedipal accounts with a tender mother 'is a move from cathecting her narcissitically to an interaction with her in terms of social and symbolic institutions' (Campbell, 2000, pp. 237–238). This permits a conceptual move beyond the derogation of the mother and the destructiveness of only privileging the father. Instead of denigrating the pre-Oedipal stage of connection with the mother as infantile, Deleuze and Guattari's theoretical framework opens up a space for more positive interpretations of relationships between adolescent sons and mothers in lone mother families. Such interpretations work towards addressing 'the vital need' Christine Heward identifies, for a theory of masculinities, 'in relation with fathers and mothers, identifying and rejecting features of both within a historical and social context' (1996, p. 38).

I am not arguing for a view of Shaun's relationship with his mother as uniformly positive; clearly, there are also negative aspects. Rather, I am arguing against the normative models which represent such relationships as pathological in a construction which implicitly blames the mother. Shaun's relationship with his mother, like that of all other working-class boys in lone mother families, and here class both intensifies and expands the process of pathologisation, is far too complex and multifaceted to be explained by the simplistic evoking of the Oedipal relationship. It also has a positive efficacy which merits recognition. Shaun, unlike a majority of boys his age, has not banished the feminine to the realms of 'the other' and has none of the usual adolescent male contempt for women and girls such splitting generates. Rather, he is more comfortable with the feminine both in himself as well as in others than is normative for his male peer group, although this is not to imply that there are not significant numbers of working-class boys who, like Shaun, have very close, mutually supportive relationships with their mothers. Existing research suggests that there are (Ball *et al.*, 2000). I would like to suggest that Shaun's acceptance and relative ease with the feminine in himself and others helps rather than hinders his relationship with education and remediates, whilst in no way removing, some of the class structural barriers to academic success. However, it is important to avoid conveying a sense that all is right for Shaun when patently it is not. He is left with ambivalent relationships to both femininity and masculinity. Both cause him a lot of conflict, one with authority, the other with his peer group. Rather than achieving a harmonious balance, he is caught up in a volatile state of fluctuating between acceptance and rejection of both.

Conclusion

Shaun's story troubles dominant versions of white working-class masculinities which for so long have been key repositories for all those unpleasant, uncomfortable feelings the middle classes don't want to take responsibility for – sexism, racism, homophobia, to just name a few. Shaun, who admires his mother 'more than anyone else in the world', thinks his black female teacher is just 'brilliant' and believes 'racism is the worst thing going on in the world', is just one illustration of how superficial and ill considered such discourses are. His narrative also suggests that the problem of 'failing boys' (Epstein *et al.*, 1998) cannot be solved through school-based initiatives. If part of 'normal' male development involves the expulsion of the feminine, which then becomes a target for contempt, learning, and in particular literacy-based subjects, which are encoded as feminine, will continue to be denigrated by the white working-class boys who are the main focus of concern within the 'failing boys' discourse. This is not the same as saying contempt of the 'feminine' is class-and race-specific. Rather, I would argue that it is a male trait which crosses both social class and ethnic boundaries. However, against the backdrop of contemporary economic changes and the hegemony of global capitalism, it is white working-class young men who have the strongest sense that their masculinities are under seige, and this has consequences for their defensive practices (Nayak, 2001). Until social processes of male gender socialisation move away from the imperative of privileging the masculine and allow boys to stay in touch with their feminine qualities, the problem of 'failing boys' will remain despite the best efforts of teachers and researchers.

It is not only dominant versions of white working-class masculinities that are unsettled by Shaun's story. His narrative allows us glimpses into the moral vacuum that stands for current 'common-sense' educational thinking. We can see in his account how educational processes help class processes to operate (Savage, 2000). Shaun's struggle against the educational context he finds himself in is yet one more instance of the myth of comprehensivisation and the sham of meritocracy. New Labour lashes out against 'bog standard comprehensives' (Cassidy, 2001), yet schools like Sutton Boys' do not have, and have never had, a comprehensive intake. As a previously 'failing' school which has just come out of 'special measures', both the school and its predominantly working-class, ethnic minority intake are demonised both locally and within the wider public imagination (Lucey and Reay, 2002; Reay and Lucey, 2003). Unlike the fantasies played out in New Labour policies, this is not an issue of school effectiveness and staff performance but a matter of class and race; of social structures and material resources.

Furthermore, despite the much vaunted National Curriculum, New Labour, no less than the 'Old Tories' have no interest in what counts as 'really useful knowledge' (Johnson, 1979) for working-class students. As Jackie Brine (2001) asserts, the continued failure to critically educate and to creatively stimulate working-class students is little short of criminal, and, at the very least, morally indefensible. Even Shaun, with his strong commitment to learning, finds most of what he is taught an irrelevance. His disaffected working-class peers in Sutton, as well as contemporaries in other inner-city schools, find little to engage them in the National Curriculum (Reay, 2001). Perhaps it is worth revisiting Bernstein's counsel of thirty years ago in order to radically rethink socially equitable education for all class groupings in society:

> We must ensure that the material conditions of the schools we offer, their values, social organisation, forms of control and pedagogy, the skills and sensitivities of the teachers are refracted through an understanding of the culture the children bring to the school. After all, we do no less for the middle-class child.
>
> (Bernstein, 1973, p. 175)

Finally, Shaun's situation highlights the irrelevance of the Excellence in Cities Initiative for working-class pupils. New Labour policy, through its Excellence in Cities initiative, might just result in a pupil like Shaun being included in a Gifted and Talented scheme, although, as a child who obtained level 4 in English, Mathematics and Science in his key stage 2 SATs (standard assessment tasks), his commitment, determination and hard work would probably not qualify him for inclusion. However, even if offered a place, taking it up would be extremely risky for Shaun, jeopardising the careful balancing act he has maintained between achievement and social acceptability. As I have tried briefly to sketch out in this conclusion, far more needs to change in inner-city schooling than extra provision for those deemed to be in 'the brightest 5–10 per cent'.

Note

1   Psychic work and psychic costs are apparent in the emotional labour such boys have to engage in when managing the tensions embodied in the 'duality of the self'. It became increasingly apparent over the course of the four years that I knew Shaun that he was both dealing with high levels of anxiety in relation to his 'split self' and having to mobilise an array of defence mechanisms (Klein, 1952; Winnicott, 1964) in order to protect and maintain a sense of coherent self.

References

Ball, S. J., Maguire, M. and Macrae, S. (2000) *Choices, Pathways and Transitions Post-16* (London, Routledge Falmer).

Bernstein, B. (1973) *Class, Codes and Control*, vol. 1 (St Albans, Paladin).

Bourdieu, P. (1990) *In Other Words: Essays Towards a Reflexive Sociology* (Cambridge, Polity Press).

Bourdieu, P. (1999) The contradictions of inheritance, in: P. Bourdieu *et al.* (1999) *The Weight of the World: Social Suffering in Contemporary Societies* (Cambridge, Polity Press).

Bourdieu, P. and Wacquant, L. (1992) *An Invitation to Reflexive Sociology* (Chicago, University of Chicago Press).

Brine, J. (2001) *Feet of class, relations of power and policy research, American Educations Research Association Conference*, Seattle, WA, April.

Brown, P. (1987) *Schooling Ordinary Kids* (London, Tavistock).

Campbell, J. (2000) *Arguing with the Phallus: Feminist, Queer and Postcolonial Theory* (London, Zed Books).

Cassidy, S. (2001) Are you a bog-standard secondary? *Times Educational Supplement*, 16 February, pp. 4–5.

Connell, R. W. (1995) *Masculinities* (Cambridge, Polity Press).

Connell, R. W. (2001) Introduction and overview, *Feminism and Psychology: Special Issue: Men and Masculinities: Discursive Approaches*, 11, pp. 5–9.

Connell, R. W., Ashenden, D. J., Kessler, S. and Dowsett, G. W. (1982) *Making the Difference* (Sydney, George Allen and Unwin).

Connolly, P. (1998) *Racism, Gender Identities and Young Children: Social Relations in a Multi-Ethnic, Inner-City Primary School* (London, Routledge).

Delamont, S. and Galton, M. (1986) *Inside the Secondary Classroom* (London, Routledge).

Deleuze, G. and Guattari, F. (1984) *Anti-Oedipus: Capitalism and Schizophrenia* (London, Athlone Press).

Edley, N. and Wetherall, M. (1995) *Men in Perspective: Practice, Power and Identity* (Hemel Hempstead, Harvester Wheatsheaf).

Edley, N. and Wetherall, M. (1999) Imagined futures: young men's talk about fatherhood and domestic life, *Journal of Social Psychology*, 38, pp. 181–194.

Elium, D. and Elium, J. (1992) *Raising a Son: Parenting and The Making of a Healthy Man* (Stroud, Hawthorn Press).

Epstein, D., Elwood, J., Hey, V. and Maw, J. (eds) (1998) *Failing Boys? Issues in Gender and Achievement* (Buckingham, Open University Press).

Foucault, M. (1987) The ethic of care for the self as a practice of freedom, *Philosophy and Social Criticism*, 12, pp. 113–131.

Frosh, S., Phoenix, A. and Pattman, R. (2002) *Young Masculinities* (New York, Palgrave).

Heward, C. (1996) Masculinities and families, in: M. Mac an Ghaill (ed.) *Understanding Masculinities*, pp. 50–60 (Buckingham, Open University Press).

Hey, V. (1997) *The Company She Keeps* (Buckingham, Open University Press).

Johnson, R. (1979) Really useful knowledge: radical education and working-class culture 1790–1948, in: J. Clarke, C. Critcher and R. Johnson (eds) *Working Class Culture: Studies in History and Theory* (New York, St Martin's Press).

Klein, M. (1952) *Developments in Psycho-analysis* (London, Hogarth Press).

Lacey, C. (1968) *Hightown Grammar* (Manchester, Manchester University Press).

Lucey, H. and Reay, D. (2002) A market of waste: pyschic and structural dimensions of school-choice in the UK and children's narratives on 'demonised' schools, *Discourse: Studies in the Cultural Politics of Education*, 23(3), pp. 253–266.

Mac an Ghaill, M. (1994) *The Making of Men: Masculinities, Sexualities and Schooling* (Buckingham, Open University Press).

Mcleod, J. (2000) Subjectivity and schooling in a longitudinal study of secondary students, *British Journal of Sociology of Education*, 21, pp. 501–521.

Martino, W. (1999) 'Cool boys', 'party animals', 'squids' and 'poofters': interrogating the dynamics and politics of adolescent masculinities in *school, British Journal of Sociology of Education*, 20, pp. 239–264.

Measor, L. and Woods, P. (1984) *Changing Schools: Pupils' Perspectives on the Transfer to a Comprehensive* (Buckingham, Open University Press).

Mehan, H., Okamoto, D. and Adams, J. (1996) *Constructing School Success: Consequences of Untracking Low Achieving Students* (Cambridge, Cambridge University Press).

Nayak, A. (2001) Ivory lives: race, ethnicity and the practice of whiteness in a northeast youth community, paper presented at the *Economic and Social Research Council Research Seminar Series: Interdisciplinary Youth Research: New Approaches*, Birmingham University, 18 May.

O'Donnell, M. and Sharpe, S. (2000) *Uncertain Masculinities: Youth, Ethnicity and Class in Contemporary Britain* (London, Routledge).

Phoenix, A. and Frosh, S. (2001) Positioned by 'hegemonic' masculinities: a study of London boys' narratives of identity, *Australian Psychologist*, 36, pp. 1–18.

Reay, D. (1996) Insider perspectives or stealing the words out of women's mouths: interpretation in the research process, *Feminist Review*, 53, pp. 55–71.

Reay, D. (1998) Rethinking social class: qualitative perspectives on gender and social class, *Sociology*, 32, pp. 259–275.

Reay, D. (1999) Children's urban landscapes: configurations of class and place, in: S. Munt (ed.) *Cultural Studies and the Working Class* (London, Cassell).

Reay, D. (2001) Finding or Losing Yourself?: working class relationships to education, *Journal of Education Policy*, 16(4), pp. 333–346.

Reay, D. and Lucey, H. (2003) The limits of choice: children and inner city schooling, *Sociology*, 37, pp. 121–142.

Savage, M. (2000) *Class Analysis and Social Transformation* (Buckingham, Open University Press).

Skeggs, B. (1997) *Formations of Class and Gender* (London, Sage).

Skelton, C. (1997) Primary boys and hegemonic masculinities, *British Journal of Sociology of Education*, 18, pp. 349–369.

Social Exclusion Unit (1998) *Bringing Britain Together: A National Strategy for Neighbourhood Renewal* (London, Social Exclusion Unit).

Stanley, J. (1989) *Marks on the Memory* (Buckingham, Open University Press).

Walkerdine, V., Lucey, H. and Melody, J. (2001) *Growing Up Girl: Gender and Class in the Twenty-First Century* (London, Macmillan).

Weis, L. (1993) At the intersections of silencing and voice: discursive constructions in school, *Educational Studies*, 24, pp. 1–22.

Wexler, P. (1992) *Becoming Somebody: Towards a Social Psychology of School* (London, Falmer Press).

Willis, P. (1977) *Learning to Labour* (Lanham, MD, Lexington Books).

Winnicott, D. W. (1964) *The Child, the Family, and the Outside World* (London, Penguin).

CHAPTER 11

SCHOOL TROUBLE
A mother's burden

Curt Dudley-Marling

There are few indications that, prior to the 1960s, teachers expected parents to take an active role in their children's schooling (Lareau, 1989). However, a taken-for-granted assumption underlying current versions of educational reform in Canada, the UK and the USA is that 'there should be a close and intimate relationship between families and education or between home and school in order to achieve effective . . . schooling' (David, 1993, p. 11). Federal legislation in the USA that aims 'to strengthen partnerships between parents and professionals in meeting the educational needs of children aged birth through 5 and the working relationship between home and school' (US Department of Education, 1998, on-line) is typical. The *partnerships* being advocated by educational policy-makers include the expectation that ' "parents" should be available both at home and in the school to work with their children in support of their education' (Standing, 1999, p. 57).

The desire to 'strengthen partnerships between parents and [school] professionals' is based on the conviction that children learn more when parents take an active role in their schooling. The Department of Education and Employment in the UK builds on this rationale to explain the need for home–school agreements specified in the School Standards and Framework Act (1998):

> Parents are a child's first and enduring teachers. They play a crucial role in helping their children learn. Children achieve more when schools and parents work together. Parents can help more effectively if they know what the school is trying to achieve and how they can help. Home–school agreements will provide a framework for the development of such a partnership. The processes involved in introducing and reviewing the agreement will clarify what the school is trying to achieve, and the agreement will set out the role of the school, parents and pupils in this vital partnership.
>
> (Department of Education and Employment, 1998, on-line)

In a climate of fiscal restraint, parent involvement is attractive to educational reformers and policy-makers seeking cost-effective ways to enhance learning time as a means of boosting student achievement (Keith, 1987; McAdams, 1994; Corno, 1996). Within the context of the 'new individualism', which emphasises 'each life being played out according to the person rather than the context' (David *et al.*, 1997, p. 399), the discourse of parent involvement also effectively shifts the 'blame' for lack of educational achievement onto parents (Smith, 1998), especially mothers (Standing, 1999), and off policy-makers and, to a less extent, practitioners. In the USA, the head of the Massachusetts Department of Education publicly blamed parents for the poor performance of many children on the state's educational achievement tests (Hart, 1999). Of course, since children attending schools in economically impoverished areas are far more likely to perform poorly on these tests than children living in wealthier neighbourhoods (Sacks, 1999), poor parents – often immigrants, single mothers, and people of colour – come in for the largest share of the blame. The doctrine of personal responsibility performs the neat trick of transforming the victims of poverty, discrimination and poor schooling (Kozol, 1992) into irresponsible parents who are solely responsible for their children's educational failures.

The significance of parent involvement is supported by a body of quantitative research that indicates a strong, positive relationship between parent involvement and higher levels of school achievement, particularly in reading (Stevenson and Baker, 1987; Lareau, 1989; Green, 1995). However, quantitative studies, with their emphasis on statistically constructed *average* parents, efface the meaning of parent involvement for individual mothers and fathers. Political and policy discourses on *parental involvement* also suffer from a fixation on normative families. Smith (1998), for example, observed that 'schools, school curriculum, and the professional training of teachers orient to the idealised middle-class family of two parents, one of whom (understood usually to be the mother) does not work in paid employment and is available to support the schools her children attend' (p. 23). In general, parental involvement has been presented as an 'unproblematic, ungendered concept, free from class and cultural associations' (Standing, 1999, p. 57). It is clear, however, that the implications of parent involvement are not the same for all parents.

It has been well established that the burdens of schooling do not fall evenly on fathers and mothers. As a policy goal, *parent involvement* includes the participation of both mothers and fathers in their children's schooling. In practice, as the domestic role of mothers has expanded to include responsibility for children's cognitive development and schooling (Baker and Stevenson, 1986), parent involvement refers more often to the work of women in support of their children's schooling (Smith, 1987; Griffith, 1996). The coordination and supervision of children's educational activities often demands a significant portion of mothers' waking hours, particularly in the case of mothers whose children do poorly in school (Lareau, 1989). This work typically includes monitoring children's school standing; communicating with teachers; helping children organise their time to do homework; helping children with homework itself; and, in the case of children who have difficulty in school, taking action to remedy the problem (Smith, 1987; Griffith and Smith, 1990). Mothers assume the main responsibility for their children's education at home, whether they are single or partnered, working or middle class, employed or stay-at-home mothers (David, 1998; Standing, 1999). The degree to which educational researchers have focused their attention on the relationship between factors like mothers' employment status and mothers' involvement in their children's schooling and the academic success of their children (e.g. Milne *et al.*, 1986; Grolnick *et al.*, 1997; Shumow, 1997) is a further indication that supporting children's schooling is generally taken to be 'women's work'.[1]

But even among mothers, there are profound differences in how parent involvement is experienced. All mothers do not, for example, have access to the same social, economic and cultural resources to support their children's schooling. They do not

> all live in the same area or in the same standard of housing, they do not all have the same levels of education, the same social networks, the same amount of income, the same position in the labour market, the same family structure and roles, the same race/ethnicity, the same physical and mental health and ability, and so on and so on.
>
> (David *et al.*, 1997, p. 401)

Of course, the presumption that all parents have the same access to time, knowledge, and various cultural and material resources is a necessary fiction if parents, particularly mothers, are to be held responsible for their children's school failure.

The meaning of *parent involvement* for mothers (and for fathers who take an active role in their children's schooling) is also affected by the degree to which children succeed in school. For example, parents are expected to pick up the slack when their children have difficulties in school (Smith, 1998). Children's school troubles often demand more contact with teachers and more time spent both 'monitoring' children's schoolwork and taking whatever steps are required to 'repair' the problem (Smith, 1987). Fewer demands may be placed on the parents of students who do well in school. Ironically, parents of children who do well in school may be *credited* with high levels of involvement in their children's schooling regardless of the degree of support they actually provide for their children's education. Parents of children who experience difficulties in school, however, may be accused of not being sufficiently involved in the education of their daughters and sons even though these parents tend to be more involved in their children's schooling (Lareau, 1989). Since there is a strong relationship between academic success and socio-economic status (e.g. Sacks, 1999), the pretence that 'parent involvement equals academic success' offers comfort to those who prefer to blame poverty on the poor themselves. Similar reasoning may be used by those who wish to attribute failing students living in households headed by single mothers to mothers' marital status.

Foucault observed 'that the most insightful way to understand society is to consider it from the perspective of the professions that have emerged to contain its failures' (Skrtic, 1991, p. 24). Dudley-Marling and Dippo (1995), for example, found that special education was a particularly good place from which to engage in a broader critique of schooling and society. Similarly, an examination of the impact of school failure on the lives of families may offer insights into the 'the consequences for family organisation of societal processes that "subcontract" educational responsibilities for homework and so forth to the family and in particular to the mother' (Smith, 1987, p. 21). The standards movement that is dominating the educational reform agenda in North America and the UK, because of the persistent demand that the success of a *few* be defined in terms of the failure of *many*, adds some urgency to the need to examine the effects of 'school troubles' on the lives of families in general and mothers in particular.

This chapter draws on data collected in an interview study examining the effects of schooling on parents whose children have experienced some level of academic failure. Of particular interest here is the finding that, among the parents interviewed for this study, the material and emotional burdens of school trouble fell most heavily upon mothers, depriving these mothers of many of the pleasures of parenthood (and personhood).

The study

To understand better the impact of school failure on the lives of families, twenty-three interviews were conducted with parents whose children struggled in school. These interviews ranged from 45 minutes to 1 hour 50 minutes in length, with the average interview lasting approximately 1 hour 15 minutes. The parents included married couples and single mothers, although, even in two-parent families, many fathers were unable or, in some cases, unwilling to be interviewed. Therefore, the findings favour the perspectives of mothers. In all, the interviewees included six single mothers, ten mothers from two-parent families and seven couples. All the parents lived in Ontario (Canada) or the Midwestern USA.

Families were identified with the help of school officials, a colleague who was active in the African-Canadian community, the director of a university-based reading clinic, and advertisements placed in school newsletters. Three families were known to me before I undertook this study. Since race, socio-economic status, culture and language affect how parents experience their children's schooling (Lareau, 1989; Purcell-Gates, 1995; Valdes, 1996), interviewees included parents from a range of racial, socio-economic, linguistic and cultural backgrounds. The sample included Asian (2), black (8), and white (13) parents. One family had immigrated to North America from Ireland, two families from Jamaica, and two from Taiwan. The Taiwanese parents were Mandarin speakers who did not speak English in their homes. The interviewees were a socio-economically diverse group, including upper-middle-, middle-, and working-class families. One single mother was receiving public assistance at the time of the interview. Less than half of the parents who were interviewed had completed college. Several parents indicated that they had not graduated from high school, including a mother who had completed only 6 years of schooling. Two of the parents had doctoral degrees.

The *struggling learners* discussed with parents included eight girls and fifteen boys ranging from 8 to 17 years of age. Most of these students attended publicly funded schools, although two were being home-schooled by their mothers and two others were enrolled in private schools. There were significant differences in the degree to which the children discussed with parents struggled in school. The majority of the children did poorly in most school subjects and a few exhibited serious behaviour problems in school. Eleven of the children had been identified as learning disabled (LD) and/or attention deficit disordered (ADD). One child was identified as language disordered, another as gifted. Two parents indicated that their children were not failing any school subjects, but were doing less well than they expected. What all the children had in common was their parents' perception that they were struggling in school.

During the interviews, I relied on open-ended questions to encourage parents to talk about the nature of their children's struggles in school and how school troubles had affected their lives and the lives of their families. Some parents talked without interruption after the initial question, 'Tell me about your child's struggles in school and how it has affected your family', was posed. When interviews bogged down, I referred to my interview guide (Weiss, 1995), which indicated the general areas I was interested in discussing with parents.

A number of themes emerged from a qualitative analysis of the interview data (Bogdan and Biklen, 1992; Weiss, 1995). One of these themes – the degree to which mothers assumed the material and emotional burdens of their children's struggles in school – is the focus of this chapter. The themes discussed in this chapter help explicate the nature of the material and emotional effects of school failure on mothers.

These emerged as core themes from mothers' accounts of their families' responses to school failure and not from any a priori categories or theoretical frame.

'We're on a strict routine'

Among the parents I interviewed, school troubles had a significant impact on the lives of both mothers and fathers. Mothers *and* fathers felt the pain of children who suffered through failure at school. Mothers *and* fathers made financial sacrifices to pay the cost of academic testing, tutoring and private schools. Mothers *and* fathers were affected by the loss of income when two of the mothers I interviewed left the workplace to home-school their children or, in the case of Edna Bunker,[2] postponed entry into the workplace so that she could devote herself to supporting her son's schooling. Nor did any parent escape the family tensions that always surrounded school trouble.

Some of the mothers and fathers I interviewed also shared the material burdens of school trouble; that is, helping children with their homework, talking with teachers, driving children to after-school tutoring, and so on. Martin Springs, John Mandell and Ralph Thorn were among the fathers who attended teacher conferences with their wives and John Cooper and Jeb Moore were among the fathers who said they 'did their best' to help their children with their homework – even if, as in Mr Moore's case, it frequently taxed his patience. Two fathers – David Thibault and George Connor – assumed nearly complete responsibility for their children's schooling. Still, with these notable exceptions, the married mothers in my sample indicated that they received little assistance from their husbands in support of children's schoolwork. Rosa Jones, for example, said that she received no help at all from her husband with their daughter's schoolwork. 'He ain't interested', she said. 'With homework and when it comes to the children, I feel single'. Janet Moore also felt that she was generally responsible for her son Archie's schoolwork: 'If you want testing or anything done, I'm the one who takes him [and if the teachers call] I'm the one who ends up talking to them for an hour or two'. And, although Janet's husband, Jeb, did sometimes help with homework, the ability of his son to, in his words, 'push his buttons' while they did homework meant that homework was usually Janet's responsibility. This was all said without any apparent resentment in the presence of Jeb Moore, who did not disagree. The description of Jeb Moore's contributions as 'helping' reinforced the sense that Mrs Moore was 'generally responsible' for their children's schoolwork. Similarly, it was Edna Bunker, not her husband, Sheldon, who monitored her son's homework, met with teachers, and gathered materials for his assignments. 'I guess we share', she offered, 'but I feel I do more of it than him'. When pressed, Mrs Bunker was unable to offer any concrete examples of her husband's 'help' with their children's schoolwork.

Arguably, Janet Moore, Edna Bunker and Rosa Jones are stay-at-home mothers who might be *expected* to assume the bulk of their family's domestic responsibilities. But the distribution of domestic responsibilities was not much different in families where mothers were involved in paid employment outside the home. Alice Mandel, for example, held a demanding job as the director of a social service agency, but, because she had a background in education, her husband assumed that she would take charge of their daughter's homework, meet with teachers, and so on. 'My husband says, "It's your field. You know what to do" ', Alice told me. But the expectation that *schoolwork is women's work* was no different for mothers working outside the home who were not expert about education. Michelle Phills was employed outside the home and had no background in education, but spent enormous amounts of her time searching for appropriate services for her daughter, Joy, and doing whatever she could to persuade school personnel to provide an education that met Joy's needs. Diane Riggs worked part-time in the family business, but volunteered regularly in her children's school, managed her children's homework, and organised tutoring for her son and daughter. 'It is very difficult to get out in the evening to do something for myself', Diane offered. Cybil Thorn met frequently with her sons' teachers, itinerant specialists, and the principal at her children's school. She was also an active member of the school council and the district association for students with learning disabilities. Cybil characterised this work in support of her sons' schooling as a 'second full-time job'. At the time I interviewed Marilyn Cooper, she was home-schooling her two children and working as a nurse (she left for work as soon as her husband returned home from his job). Arguably, Marilyn Cooper managed three full-time jobs: teacher, home-maker and nurse.

In two-parent families, there is at least the possibility that mothers will be able to share domestic chores – including supporting children's schoolwork – with their partners. No such relief was available to the single mothers I interviewed. Celine Street, for example, was nearly overwhelmed by the demands of providing for the needs of her son, Dennis, a difficult child who had been diagnosed as ADD. Here is how Celine responded to a question about finding time for her needs:

> No, I don't have time. My whole life is focused on Dennis. I have no other life. Absolutely none. If I do go somewhere, I have to think of something to do with Dennis. I have to think about where I am going because I am taking Dennis with me and the whole time that I am there . . . it's very tension filled. Because he doesn't listen, because he is running around.

Celine went on to describe her daily schedule as a means of supporting her assertion that she had almost 'no life' beyond Dennis:

> We're up at 5:30 in the morning. We're out of here by a quarter to seven. . . . It's come down to a routine. We get up at a certain hour . . . and there's no fooling around. . . . [Then] I take him to a sitter. The sitter is across from the school. At 8:30 he leaves and goes to school [and] I'm already at work. . . . I'm at work by 8:00. . . . I get home from the [commuter] train and I pick him up and I come home. So there's never any time when I'm without him. The only time I get a break is when I am at work and on the train, which is when I do my reading, because it's a half hour there and a half hour back. So that's my time. That's the only time I get to myself.

Celine also had to cope with telephone calls from Dennis's teachers, and there had been lots of calls from Dennis's teachers, even calling Celine at work to complain about his behaviour. Then there were conferences with teachers at Dennis's school, visits to the doctor's office, monitoring Dennis's medication, and on and on.

Celine Street was a good and caring mother who would not have characterised her son as a burden. Certainly, she would have liked some relief from the relentless demands of being a single mother of a son who required nearly constant vigilance and a firm hand. As she herself put it, 'Dennis wears people down' and his mother was one of those who Dennis had worn down. Still, the only thing unique about Celine Street's experience among the single mothers I interviewed was its intensity. All of the single mothers I spoke to described domestic routines nearly as demanding as Celine Street's. Betty Blake, for example, responded to my comment that 'being a single mother doesn't leave you a lot of time' by observing:

> Oh, no it doesn't. Oh, we're on a strict routine. We walk through that door at 6:00. He goes into the shower. While he's in the shower I'm getting [the evening meal] ready. When he comes out of the shower, he lotions his skin, puts on his [night clothes] and, if the table's not set, he sets the table. Or he starts his homework if he has homework and the dinner's not ready. Like, we're on a strict routine. That's right. So that eating and homework are finished by 8:30. The latest.

Betty Blake, like most of the parents I interviewed, believed that it was important for her son to have a life beyond school so she enrolled him in karate on Mondays and a Heritage Language Program on Saturdays and took him to church on Sunday – all of which made additional demands on her time.

Single mother Molly Reeves also described a family life that provided little time for her needs:

> I make them go to bed at 9. But when they go to bed, I got to get up and get all my cleaning and stuff done. Pick up this. Pick up that. And I go to bed. I can't watch the news [on television], you know. I can't sit up late. I get up at 5:00 and I can't, the latest I've sat up in I don't know how long is about 10:30.

When I interviewed Molly Reeves, she was attending school to work towards a high school equivalency certificate as a government-imposed requirement for receiving public assistance. She found, however, that the demands of organising the household and supporting her sons' school work left her little time for her own homework, as the following exchange illustrates.

> CDM: I get the impression that when the kids are home from school, you spend a good deal of your time on their homework.
> Molly: On homework and helping them read the little books [assigned by the university reading clinic].
> CDM: That doesn't give you much time to relax, even to do your work.
> Molly: No, because I'm supposed to do my homework, but yet I can't do it because I run out of time helping my son. And then by the time I get my share of stuff taken care of, because I get up at 5:00 like I said, then I'm ready to go to bed.

As indicated in the introduction to this chapter, the material demands on parents are increased when children experience problems at school (Smith, 1987; Lareau, 1989). Single mothers had to shoulder the additional burdens imposed by *school troubles* alone.[3] When Maria Scott's daughter Tiffany began to struggle in school, for example, Maria sought out alternatives, once waiting in line overnight in order to enrol her daughter in a magnet school.[4] When Tiffany's poor school performance continued, Maria struggled to find the time between her job at a daycare centre and taking classes at the local university to visit schools that might be more suitable for her daughter. Maria also had no one with whom she could share the responsibility of taking her daughter to weekly tutoring at a reading clinic, karate, or other after-school activities. When I offered that it must be very hard to meet these demands she agreed and explained, 'because I'm by myself . . . doing everything by myself'.

As hard as mothers worked to maintain households and support children's schooling, few mothers felt they ever did enough. 'You feel that you're not doing enough for your child' is how Rosa Jones put it. The degree to which mothers assumed the emotional burdens of school troubles is the subject of the next section.

'I've cried a thousand times'

Betty Springs had this to say about the emotional impact of her son's school struggles:

> I wasn't sleeping. It consumes you when you are afraid, when you are so afraid for your kid. It consumes you and you feel so useless and there's not anything you can do. Like we tried to do everything we could do. . . . I was angry. I was scared. I was terrified. I thought, 'What's going to happen?'

When I asked Betty, who was employed as a classroom teacher, about the degree to which these feelings dominated her life, she indicated that there was no time during the day when she was able to escape completely feelings of sadness, anger, frustration and anxiety:

> I couldn't focus. I was trying to write a paper [for a graduate course]. I couldn't focus on it. I couldn't maintain my attention. I know for a fact that the students I was working with this year didn't get all of me that I gave them 2 years before. It just didn't seem quite as important to me. I wasn't sleeping. I wasn't eating. I was worrying constantly.

Feelings of distress over school troubles were common among the mothers I interviewed. When I asked Maria Scott, for example, if worries over her daughter's struggles in school affected her job or her schoolwork, her response echoed themes raised by Betty Springs:

> It made it very hard. I didn't have time to study because I was thinking about her troubles in school. She's my first priority. . . . Sometimes I didn't want to get up and go in to work if I was worrying. I wasn't getting so much sleep. So it's like I didn't want to be there. . . . Especially when [the school] told me she might have an attention deficit disorder and she couldn't read. I thought: my child? It was hard. . . . I'd wake up maybe about 3:00 in the morning, wake up and stay up until around 4:00 and then I had to be at work at 6:00. It was hard for me just thinking about how her day was going. Am I going to get a call from the teacher? Is her report card going to be this way or that way? I would just worry about it. Like I said, you want your best for your child, you want your child to do well [in school]. And when they are not doing well, it's hard.

School troubles also intruded on Betty Blake's life at work:

> I lived in fear at work. I lived in fear and prayed when I got to work that I would not get a call from the school. That's how bad it was. I prayed every day for the school not to call. Every time I saw the light flashing on my phone, I was afraid it was the school calling.

Mothers were also haunted by worries about their children's future. Edna Bunker, for example, was anxious about how her son would fare in high school:

> I'm scared for high school. I'm just scared that he won't get the individual attention that he really needs. . . . It scares me. . . . I'm thinking that he won't do great in ninth grade. It's like I'm gearing myself up already. I'm gearing myself up for high school to sort of lower my expectations. It's a change of schools and he doesn't do well with changes, so if he can just get through the year, and I'm thinking that should be enough.

'Gearing up' for the future made for a very stressful present for many of the mothers I interviewed. But it was life in the present that was most troubling for mothers – particularly the effect school troubles were having on their children. Struggling in school often made their children miserable – 'miserable for $6\frac{1}{2}$ hours day' is how Janet Moore described her son's school experience – and no parent wants their child to suffer. Sheila McIsaac echoed a theme I heard frequently from mothers:

> It was terrible. It was a nightmare. . . . It's sad to see your child going [through that]. You love your child and you try to do everything you can for him . . . and he goes off in the morning and you know that he's gone all day, and you see him go off and he's so miserable – like a puppy with its tail between its legs. He just looked so forlorn and lost. And you think he is going to spend the whole day there like that. . . . It was terrible. It was a nightmare to see him go off and know he wasn't achieving anything, he wasn't getting anything positive out of the day . . . That was disturbing.

Given an educational system that is 'deeply dependent on the availability of women's unpaid work' (Smith, 1998, p. 25) and a 'discourse of mothering' that accord[s] mothers an indefinite responsibility for the well-being of their children and for their achievements at school (Smith, 1998, p. 22), it is not surprising that mothers were more likely than fathers to take responsibility for helping children with homework or meeting with teachers. But some fathers also helped with homework and met with teachers. Mothers were more likely than fathers to worry or lose sleep over their children's struggles in school, but some fathers also worried about school troubles. What clearly set mothers apart from fathers, however, was that the mothers I interviewed often felt personally responsible for their children's struggles at school. Mothers' guilt is the subject of the next section.

'I do feel like it was my fault . . .'

School trouble made Celine Street 'feel that I wasn't raising my child properly. It was *my* fault. It was something I did'. Single mother Elma Kinkead also took her daughter's struggles in school as evidence of her inadequacy as a parent:

> I wonder if [my daughter's] poor performance is a reflection of my poor performance as a mother because I'm not taking the time to do certain things because I am busy doing whatever it is that I have been doing. . . . I think that in between the yelling and screaming [other mothers] say wonderful things about their children to their friends but I don't say anything wonderful about my child. . . . *I don't think I'm a good mother.*

Carol Dumay was another mother who attributed her daughter's poor performance in school to her shortcomings as a parent:

> It was really frustrating for me. . . . I wanted her to do well like my other kids . . . and then she comes with Ds and Fs. That weighed on me kinda bad. Maybe I was trying to get her to do something she wasn't capable of. . . . Maybe I had some part in that. . . . But in your mind, you don't think you're doing wrong. You're just trying to get them to do the best that they can and I kept thinking that she could do better. But then maybe she couldn't. I don't know. I couldn't figure that. But that was frustrating to me. To be in that kind of a predicament, you know. It was stressful. . . . I do feel like it was my fault, in some way or that in bringing her up. . . . *I think that I failed somewhere.*

Carol Dumay felt guilty about what she had done in response to her daughter's struggles in school and guilty about what she felt she had not done. 'I truly believe that maybe I should have started doing something before second grade,' she told me. Michelle Phils attributed her daughter's school problems to 'weakness' during childbirth. 'If I'd been a stronger person [the doctors] wouldn't have had to do all those [medical interventions] and that may have made it all better'. Other mothers were plagued by the nagging worry that 'you're not doing enough for your child', as Rosa Jones put it. Still others may have identified with Edna Bunker, who told me, 'I guess I just feel guilty that I can't fix it'.

Some husbands also blamed their wives for their children's struggles in school. Rosa Jones said her husband accused her with the remark, 'What are you doing? How come you didn't help him read?' John Cooper (in his wife's presence) suggested that his wife's 'coddling' had been a factor in their son's school troubles. John Mandel shifted the responsibility for their daughter's learning problems to his wife with the remark, 'It's your field'. The closest any father came to blaming himself for his child's school trouble was Ralph Thorn's insight that his son's ADD might have had its roots in his own (genetic) learning problems when he was in school. This insight carried no apparent guilt, however.

Cultural norms indicate the range of *appropriate* gender roles for the members of any society. In a patriarchal society like ours, women, in their role as mothers, have been held to be responsible for all things domestic, including children's schooling, and men, in their role as fathers, have not. Certainly, gendered roles for parents can and have been challenged. Among the parents interviewed here, for example, there were fathers who assumed primary responsibility for their children's schooling. Still, it will always be difficult to resist dominant, socially constructed images of the 'good mother' or the 'good father', role expectations reinforced by schools (David *et al.*, 1997). Within the dominant patriarchal discourse, a child's success in school is proof of a woman's success as a mother while a child's problems in school demonstrate a mother's deficiencies (Smith, 1987, 1998). Mothers who are asked to do too much, but can never do enough for their children will almost certainly feel 'perennially guilty' (David *et al.*, 1997) about their mothering and even more so if their children's performance at school fails to affirm their status as *good mothers*. In this context, it is easy to understand Carol Dumay's assessment that it was 'her fault' her daughter struggled in school or Elma Kinkead's evaluation of herself as a 'poor mother'. Idealised, culturally determined models of the *good mother* make little space for mothers whose children fail in school, limiting the satisfaction these women are able to derive from their roles as mothers.

'There's always tension in this house'

Among the parents I interviewed, the presence of a child who struggled in school had a significant impact on family roles and relationships, adding to the emotional burdens of school troubles. The mothers who spent 'hours and hours' supporting their children's homework were denied time for themselves *and* the time to spend with other family members. Diane Riggs, for example, regretted that the time she spent helping her son, Roger, who struggled in school, often left little time for her to spend with her other children:

> What happens is [my younger son] Ben needs my help and [my older daughter] Esther needs my help as well. My husband is at work for long hours so I'm really by myself at night with them doing their homework. I don't give equal time to my children and it's Ben who is suffering because he seems to be able to pick it up very quickly. . . . Esther needs a lot more help in mathematics and I've let that slide.

The time mothers in two-parent families spent supporting the needs of children who struggled in school sometimes led to resentment by husbands, who felt abandoned by their wives. Carol Dumay's husband, for example, resented all the time Carol spent doing schoolwork with their daughter because it denied him time he wanted to spend with his wife. 'My husband blamed me', she said. ' "You shouldn't sit there so much", he'd say. "Let her alone. . . . Why do you sit there with her night after night and go through that?" So there was a lot of tension between us two.' When I asked Mrs Dumay why it bothered her husband when she worked with her daughter, she offered, 'Maybe it was taking a tantrum, I believe. I do believe that. But I told him, "She needs help" '.

According to the parents I interviewed, school troubles had an effect on all family relationships, but the mothers I spoke to were most disturbed by the effect school troubles had on their relationships with the child for whom school was a struggle. Sharon McIsaac, for example, talked generally about the effect homework had on her relationship with her son, Robert:

> School affected my relationship with Robert. . . . I think if I had kept him in school it would have caused a barrier between us. There was always homework. There were hours of homework. In the evening sitting at the kitchen table just it doing over and over and over again. So it was quite stressful. It did create quite a stress.

Maria Scott offered a more specific example of how her interactions with her daughter, Tiffany, about homework threatened their relationship:

> So I'll say to Tiffany, 'Ok let's read. I'll read one page and you read a page'. So I'd read a page and she'd listen to me read and then, when it's time for her to read, she'd get frustrated when she got stuck on a word. I don't know if it was because when I read I was going through with it and she wanted to go through the words exactly the same way or if she wanted to get through the story just as quickly as I got through it with that first page. And she just sat there and got so upset. And sometimes she would make me upset and I would say, 'Tiffany, you know this word. Start with the first letter and sound it out'. And she'd get upset so we're both sitting there trying to figure out this word. And

sometimes I would even say, 'Oh, just forget it!' Because, see, I didn't know what to do. I'd get so frustrated. If she sits there and gets mad at me because I won't tell her this word and I'm trying to help her sound the word out. . . . I would yell and say, 'We'll just go! Just leave me alone!' And she'd get upset and started to cry and all that.

Ms Scott believed that doing homework with Tiffany did neither of them much good: 'It damaged my daughter as well as our relationship', she said. 'Whenever we did homework we were fussin' and fighting and getting frustrated with each other.'

Single mother, Betty Blake, also told a tale of frustration and fighting:

I tend to yell a lot. I don't spank him, but I yell. I know that's not good for him because I know that it is probably doing a lot of harm to his self-esteem. I try not to yell, but I don't know what else to do because it's not like I can say, 'Speak to your father'. I have to try, I have to go to work, do what is going on with work, and hear the school calling me, then come home and try to talk to him and discipline him about whatever it is that he's done that's wrong and it's overwhelming for me. . . . I get so frustrated. I don't even know what to say any more. Even tonight, doing that math. It just drives me crazy because I'll spend half a day showing him how to do something and he'll know how to do it as long as I'm sitting here. But if I move and say do it on your own, all of a sudden it's like, 'What?' He always wants me to be there and I keep telling him that I'm not always going to be there. I'm not in the class with you. You have to do it on your own. . . . He gets very upset when I yell at him to the point where he cries. . . . I think the fact that I get frustrated, it might have affected our relationship. . . . [but] education is very important, [so] I have yelled and screamed until there was no tomorrow.

The tensions and frustrations over schoolwork also led some parents to (occasionally) resent their children for their part in their struggles in school. Edna Bunker told me that she sometimes resented:

all the time that [school work] takes. I resent that I seem to have to fight for him all the time. Going to teachers. [But] it's just what I have to accept. I resent it, but that's the way it is. There is nothing I can do about it so I just have to do it.

Carol Dumay talked about her frustrations with her daughter's 'attitude':

I have to find other avenues to get that pressure off of me. It does, it gets pretty bad sometimes when I see the attitude. 'Cause sometimes her attitude is like, 'I don't care'. That's what I think. But that may not be it. You know. It may not be . . . it's just that I feel that she don't care. She doesn't give it really that. . . . But I do some pushing. I have done a lot of pushing. I do have to push her a lot. But she has upset me a lot, where I felt I didn't like this child at all. Her attitude needs to be changed. . . . And I do have a feeling towards her like, maybe I shouldn't say I dislike her, but I just dislike her attitude. That's it, her attitude.

Stories of conflict and resentment over schoolwork were common among the mothers I interviewed. It is impossible to know if school troubles damaged long-term relationships between parents and their children. In the short term, however, school troubles interfered with parents' ability to derive pleasure from their relationships with their children – and since mothers assumed most of the burden for working with their daughters and sons, the impact of school troubles was greater for them. Most of the mothers I interviewed would probably have agreed with Janet Moore, who told me, 'I don't look forward to school starting [in the fall] because of the fighting and all that'.

Conclusion

The available evidence indicates that, in most households, domestic work, including responsibility for children's schoolwork, continues to be women's work (Bird, 1999). Therefore, if school troubles increase the domestic burdens of families, it is likely that those burdens will fall most heavily on mothers. This was certainly the case among the parents I interviewed. The material effects of children's struggles in school – doing homework with their children, meeting with teachers, searching for alternative programmes, and so on – fell most heavily on mothers. The demands of school troubles threatened to overwhelm single mothers although the situation was not much better for the mothers who lived with husbands who provided little or no help with their children's schoolwork.

The mothers I interviewed also bore the weight of the emotional burdens of school troubles. Fathers were not immune to the effects of school problems, but mothers, not fathers, talked about losing sleep worrying about their child's schooling. Mothers, not fathers, reported that worry over school troubles frequently intruded on their lives at work. It was also a mother, not a father, who told me that she worried so much about her son's struggles in school that she was not eating. Mothers were also more likely to indicate that 'fussin' and 'fighting' over schoolwork diminished the quality of their relationships with their children. It was, however, guilt that they were not doing enough to support their children's schooling that really set the mothers apart from the fathers among the parents I interviewed.

The burden of guilt was, among the parents I interviewed at least, a uniquely maternal response to school troubles. The mothers I interviewed had made extraordinary sacrifices for their children, whom they loved very deeply. Yet, in their eyes, they either had not done enough or they had done the wrong things. Perhaps, they compared themselves to ideal mothers who did not yell or scream, who did not expect too much or too little of their children, who would have been stronger during childbirth, who would always do just the right thing at just the right time. To the extent that this is true, the cultural imposition of an 'ideal mother' against whom mothers can compare their own actions is a set-up that will always make mothers feel less than adequate, even under the best of circumstances. Under less than ideal circumstances, when schooling goes wrong, for example, mothers' guilt can be painful and destructive, robbing mothers of some of the pleasures of parenthood and – to the degree that women's identities are constructed through their roles as mothers – their personhood.

The mothers interviewed for this study, all of whom had children who struggled in school, made it clear that the demands of schooling had diminished the quality of their lives by stealing from them many of the pleasures and personal satisfaction of being women and mothers. These mothers were all highly involved in their children's schooling, but the demand for ever higher levels of parent involvement requires even more of these mothers, further subordinating their 'unpaid labor to [their] children's schooling and to the professionals who have taken charge of [their] child[ren]' (Smith, 1998, p. 22). Parent involvement has been presented as an ideologically neutral policy for increasing student achievement. However, in a society where *schoolwork equals women's work*, parent involvement increases the material and emotional burdens on mothers who feel that they are already being asked to do too much (David *et al.*, 1997). Whatever the relationship of parent involvement to student achievement, politicians and educational policy-makers must at least consider the possibility that, for some parents, especially mothers of children who struggle in school, the costs of parent involvement may too high.

Notes

1   Surveys in the USA indicate that women continue to perform the majority of household labour and, although women work outside the home more than they once did, there has been no increase in the amount of housework performed by men over the last twenty years. Men whose wives work outside the home spend no more time, on average, doing housework than men whose wives are full-time homemakers (Bird, 1999).
2   Pseudonyms are used throughout this chapter to protect the privacy of participants.
3   I do not doubt that many single fathers shoulder the same burdens as single mothers. My sample did not, however, include any single fathers.
4   In the USA, magnet schools – conceived as a means of remedying racial segregation in school enrolment – are schools or education centres that offer a special curriculum (e.g. music, art, mathematics, science) capable of attracting substantial numbers of students of different racial backgrounds.

References

Baker, D. P. and Stevenson, D. L. (1986) Mother's strategies for children's school achievement, *Sociology of Education*, 59, pp. 156–166.

Bird, C. E. (1999) Gender, household labor, and psychological distress: the impact of the amount and division of housework, *Journal of Health and Social Behavior*, 40, pp. 32–45.

Bogdan, R. C. and Biklen, S. K. (1992) Qualitative research for education: an introduction to theory and methods (Boston, MA, Allyn and Bacon).

Corno, L. (1996) Homework is a complicated thing, *Educational Researcher*, 25(8), pp. 27–30.

David, M. E. (1993) Theories of family change, motherhood and education, in: M. Arnot and K. Weiler (eds) *Feminism and Social Justice in Education: International Perspectives*, pp. 10–31 (Washington, DC, Falmer Press).

David, M. E. (1998) Involvements and investments in education: mothers and schools, *Journal for a Just and Caring Education*, 4, pp. 30–46.

David, M., Davies, J., Edwards, R., Reay, D. and Standing, K. (1997) Choice within constraints: mothers and schooling, *Gender and Education*, 9, pp. 397–410.

Department for Education and Employment (1998) *Why Introduce Home–School Agreements?* On-line. Available at: http://www.dfee.gov.uk/hsa/why.htm

Dudley-Marling, C. and Dippo, D. (1995) What learning disability does: sustaining the ideology of schooling, *Journal of Learning Disabilities*, 28, pp. 408–414.

Green, R. (1995) High achievement, underachievement, and learning disabilities, in: B. A. Ryan, B. R. Adams, T. P. Gullotta, R. P. Weissberg and R. L. Hampton (eds) *The Family–School Connection: Theory, Research, Practice*, pp. 207–249 (Thousand Oaks, CA, Sage).

Griffith, A. I. (1996) A chorus of voices: mothers in schools, paper presented at the Popular Feminism Lectures, Center for Women's Studies in Education, University of Toronto, Toronto, Canada.

Griffith, A. I. and Smith, D. E. (1990) What did you do in school today? Mothering, schooling, and social class, *Perspectives on Social Problems*, 2, pp. 3–24.

168   *Curt Dudley-Marling*

Grolnick, W., Benjet, C., Kurowski, C. and Apostoleris, N. (1997) Predictors of parent involvement in children's schooling, *Journal of Educational Psychology*, 89, pp. 538–548.

Hart, J. (1999) Getting answers from the test: use results to gauge strengths and weaknesses, *Boston Globe*, 15 September, p. L1.

Keith, T. Z. (1987) Children and homework, in: A. Thomas and J. Grimes (eds) *Children's Needs: Psychological Perspectives* (Washington, DC, National Association of School Psychologists).

Kozol, J. (1992) *Savage Inequalities: Children in America's Schools* (New York, HarperPerennial).

Lareau, A. (1989) *Home Advantage: Social Class and Parental Intervention in Elementary Education* (New York, Falmer Press).

McAdams, R. P. (1994) Improving America's schools: lessons from abroad, *Principal*, 74(2), pp. 34–35.

Milne, A. M., Myers, D. E., Rosenthal, A. S. and Ginsberg, A. (1986) Single parents, working mothers, and the educational achievement of school children, *Sociology of Education*, 59, pp. 125–139.

Purcell-Gates, V. (1995) *Other People's Words: The Cycle of Low Literacy* (Cambridge, MA, Harvard University Press).

Sacks, P. (1999) *Standardized Minds: The High Price of America's Testing Culture and What We Can Do to Change it* (Cambridge, MA, Perseus).

Shumow, L. (1997) Daily experiences and adjustments of gifted low-income urban children at home and school, *Roeper Report*, 20, pp. 35–38.

Skrtic, T. M. (1991) *Behind Special Education: A Critical Analysis of Professional Culture and School Organization* (Denver, CO, Love Publishing).

Smith, D. (1987) *The Everyday World as Problematic: A Feminist Sociology* (Boston, MA, Northeastern University Press).

Smith, D. (1998) The underside of schooling: restructuring, privatization, and women's unpaid work, *Journal for a Just and Caring Education*, 4, pp. 11–29.

Standing, K. (1999) Lone mothers' involvement in their children's schooling: towards a new typology of maternal involvement, *Gender and Education*, 11, pp. 57–73.

Stevenson, D. L. and Baker, D. P. (1987) The family–school relation and the child's school performance, *Child Development*, 58, pp. 1348–1357.

US Department of Education (1998) Goals 2000: Educate America Act. On-line. Available at: http://www.ed.gov/legislation/GOALS2000/TheAct/sec401.html

Valdes, G. (1996) *Con respeto: Bridging the Distance between Culturally Diverse Families and Schools – An Ethnographic Portrait* (New York, Teachers College Press).

Weiss, R. S. (1995) *Learning from Strangers: The Art and Method of Qualitative Interview Studies* (New York, Free Press).

CHAPTER 12

PUPIL PARTICIPATION AND PUPIL PERSPECTIVE

'Carving a new order of experience'*

Jean Rudduck and Julia Flutter

Introduction

This chapter explores four related observations that stem from our work on pupil participation and perspective.

- In a climate that respects the market and the consumer it is strange that pupils in school have not been seen as consumers worth consulting. We need to understand more about why we haven't taken account of the views of pupils and why the situation is now beginning to change.
- In our efforts at 'school improvement' we need to tune in to what pupils can tell us about their experiences and what they think will make a difference to their commitment to learning and, in turn, to their progress and achievement. We should recognise, however, that there are difficulties in directly eliciting pupils' views of some aspects of schooling; for instance, their views of 'the curriculum'. Pupils are often ready to comment directly on 'bits and pieces' of the curriculum – content that does or does not engage them, for instance – but they have no basis for comparing the present with any earlier version of 'the curriculum' nor, usually, any systematic sense of curriculum possibilities. They may say that they would like more group work or more opportunities to use their own ideas, but for the most part pupils have little overall sense of how differently learning *might* be structured and handled and what different values alternative approaches might represent. However, there is a lot in what they say *incidentally* about particular lessons that we can recognise, and use, as a commentary on the curriculum and on the assumptions that underpin it.
- In our experience pupils do not have much to say about the curriculum as Young (1999, p. 463) defines it: 'the way knowledge is selected and organised into subjects and fields for educational purposes'. Rather, they talk about forms of teaching and learning that they find challenging or limiting and, importantly, about what we have called (Rudduck *et al.*, 1996) the *conditions of learning* in school; how regimes and relationships shape their sense of status as individual learners and as members of the community, and consequently, affect their sense of commitment to learning in school.
- We could do more to help pupils develop a language for talking about learning and about themselves as learners so that they feel that it is legitimate for

them to contribute actively to discussions about schoolwork with teachers and with each other.

Pupil perspective and pupil participation

Children's rights

In order to understand attitudes to pupil participation and pupil voice we have to look briefly at the progress of the children's rights movement. Children's rights have mainly, but not exclusively, been argued for by adults on behalf of pupils whereas 'pupil participation and perspective' suggests a stronger input by pupils themselves and a readiness among adults to hear and to take seriously what they have to say. We also need to see in what arenas – social and welfare and/or education – the debates have been pursued.

The children's rights movement has 'a rich and substantial heritage' (Franklin and Franklin, 1996, p. 96). Activity has been high profile at different times and for different reasons but because, Proteus-like, the movement has changed its concerns and its constituencies, its impact has not been cumulative. The movement has been most at risk from those who hold traditional views of the place of the child in school and in society.

The first formal Declaration of the Rights of the Child in 1924 focused on support for children who lost families and homes in the 1914–1918 war; the next Declaration came thirty-five years later. The main concerns of such initiatives were conditions *outside* school but there have been some attempts to focus directly on young people's experiences *in school*. In the early 1970s there were two initiatives worth mentioning in this brief sketch, one taken by young people themselves. In autumn 1972 the outcome of a national conference for the National Union of School Students (NUSS, a group formed, for a short time only, within the NUS) was a policy statement which, according to Wagg (1996, p. 14) 'must rank as one of the most uncompromising and idealistic statements of liberation philosophy ever seen in British educational politics'. What is interesting, as we suggested earlier, is that pupils themselves focus more on aspects of school organisation than they do on curriculum. The document called for the following:

> The speedy abolition of corporal punishment and the prefect system, and . . . an increase of student responsibility and self discipline in schools.
>   All forms of discipline to be under the control of a school committee and all school rules to be published.
>   . . . the abolition of compulsory uniform . . . , students having the right to determine their own appearance at school.
>   . . . free movement in and out of the school grounds and buildings during break, lunch time and free periods.
>   . . . school students of all ages to have a 'Common Room' and to have facilities of relaxation similar to those enjoyed by teachers and sixth-formers.
>   (Wagg, 1996, pp. 14–15; there were 27 items in all)

It is interesting to see which proposals have been acted on and which still reflected the concerns of pupils in the 1990s.

Three years later Lawrence Stenhouse, director of the controversial Humanities Curriculum Project, drew up a statement of the 'demands' that pupils should be able to make of the school and the expectations that they could justifiably hold of it. The work was commissioned by the then Schools Council, but the Council refused to give the principles its imprimatur and it was published not by the Council but by the author some years later (Stenhouse, 1983). These are some of the items that Stenhouse thought would make a difference to young people's experience of school; they are similar in focus and spirit to those of the NUSS document:

Pupils have a right to demand

- that the school shall treat them impartially and with respect as persons;
- that the school's aims and purposes shall be communicated to them openly, and discussed with them as the need arises;
- that the procedures and organisational arrangements of the school should be capable of rational justification and that the grounds of them should be available to them.

Pupils have a right to expect

- that the school will offer them impartial counsel on academic matters, and if they desire it, with respect to personal problems;
- that the school will make unabated efforts to provide them with the basic skills necessary for living an autonomous life in our society;
- that the school will do its best to make available to them the major public traditions in knowledge, arts, crafts and sports, which form the basis of a rich life in an advanced society;
- that the school will enable them to achieve some understanding of our society as it stands and that it will equip them to criticise social policy and contribute to the improvement of society.

The activities of the early 1970s, characterised by Franklin and Franklin (1996, p. 96) as the struggle for 'libertarian participation rights', took schools as the arena for action and the discourse was essentially about empowering students. The International Year of the Child in 1979, according to Franklin and Franklin, re-centred the children's rights movement on child protection and relocated it in the social and welfare arena. It was the United Nations Convention on the Rights of the Child in 1989 that brought the issues of protection and participation together: the right of young people to talk about their experiences and be heard, and to express a view about actions that might be taken in relation to them, was seen as a basis for protection. According to Freeman (1996, p. 36) this was 'the first convention to state that children have a right to "have a say" in processes affecting their lives'. It proposed that 'the child who is capable of forming his or her own views' should be able to 'express those views freely' in all matters affecting him or her, 'the views of the child being given due weight in accordance with their age and maturity' (see Freeman, 1996, p. 36). Freeman comments:

The right enunciated here is significant not only for what it says, but because it recognises the child as a full human being with integrity and personality and the ability to participate freely in society. . . . The views of children are to count (in relation to) decisions ranging from education to environment, from social security to secure accommodation, from transport to television.

(1996, p. 37)

Winter and Connolly (1996, p. 40) remained sceptical, saying that the right to express an opinion was 'largely confined to social services intervention' and could be overthrown by appeal to adult judgement on the grounds of 'acting in the best interests of the child'. And Lansdown (1994, p. 37) commented, wryly, that despite the national rhetoric of pupil voice there was no attempt to elicit the views of pupils 'about testing and the National Curriculum . . . and how schools are run'.

Franklin and Franklin summed up the situation in the mid 1990s in this way:

> The UN Convention . . . has offered a rallying point. . . . it also offers a pro-gramme of proposals designed to empower children and young people. The future of children's rights . . . is uncertain in the current political climate with its emphasis on retreating from any progressive policy. But the hope must surely be that in . . . the next phase, children will be the key political actors, seeking to establish their rights to protection but also their rights to participate in a range of settings which extend beyond the social and welfare arenas. . . . The future is open.
>
> (1996, p. 111)

We shall see if their optimism is well founded.

Constraints on the development of pupil participation and perspective

Progressivism and politics

The children's rights movement has been criticised for being tarred with the brush of progressivism – as offering young people rights without responsibility; part of the weaponry was the perceived contribution of progressive and child-centred practices to the lowering of educational standards. Hodgkin confirms the force of this perspective: ' . . . the phrase "child-centred" has negative connotations. It has become associated with *laissez-faire* forms of education which . . . (it is said) failed children, neither equipping them with the basic skills nor giving them a confident approach to learning' (Hodgkin, 1998, p. 11). Offering children a voice was seen, according to Wagg (1996, p. 17), as part of the leftist agenda that promoted such things as 'anti-racism, anti-sexism and "peace studies" ', while traditional values and images of children were being sidelined.

It seems that governments have not seen children's rights as a vote winner. The caution of central policy makers is evidenced by Franklin and Franklin (1996, p. 103) who claim that 'when the Polish government initially suggested a Convention on Children's Rights in 1979, the British Government suggested that it was unnecessary'. And ten years later, according to Lansdown (1994, p. 37), the government was slow to endorse the recommendations of the Convention, with the then Department of Education and Science (DES) claiming that it already 'fully complied with the Convention and that there was therefore no action required to achieve compliance'. The terms of the Convention were in fact ratified in 1991, but as Franklin and Franklin (1996, p. 103) observe, 'the word should not be mistaken for the deed' for the principles were to some extent in conflict with the image of the supremacy of the family that the Tory party, then in power, was pro-jecting: the 'emphasis on children's rights does, by default, begin to undermine the traditional familial relationship between parent and child' (Winter and Connolly, 1996, p. 36).

Ideologies of childhood

There is a legacy of public perceptions of childhood that has made it difficult, until recently, for people to take seriously the idea of encouraging young people to contribute to debates about things that affect them, both in and out of school. Even the 1989 Convention elicited familiar counter arguments: according to Lansdown (1994, p. 42), children were portrayed as 'lacking morality, as being out of control and lacking the experience on which to draw for effective participation'.

Freeman (1983, p. 8) reminds us that 'childhood' is a social construct. In the tenth century, he says, 'artists were unable to depict a child except as a man (*sic*) on a smaller scale' and the concept was 'invented' as a distinct period in about the seventeenth century by the upper classes 'who alone had the time and money' to support it; later, the trend 'diffused downwards through society' (Prout and James, 1997, p. 17). When 'young people' were given a form of attire that marked them out as children and that set them apart from adults, childhood became associated with ideas of innocence or natural waywardness and, consequently, with the need for formalised induction and discipline.

The most enduring assumption, and one that has shaped policy and practice in many aspects of life, has been that childhood is about dependency; what Gerald Grace (1995, p. 202) calls 'the ideology of immaturity'. Hart (1992, p. 8; cited by Holden and Clough, 1998, p. 27) saw children as 'the most photographed and the least listened to members of society'; a character in an Anthony Powell novel (quoted in Silver and Silver, 1997, p. 5) described pupils as 'uneasy, stranded beings'. And Oakley (1994, p. 23), following the sociologist Ronald Frankenburg, comments on 'the derogatory tone' of the term 'adolescence' which perpetuates the idea that teenagers, rather than being actors in their own right, are still 'people who are *becoming* adults'.

Outside school, as James and Prout (1997, p. xiv) have said, 'the conception of children as . . . inadequately socialised future adults, still retains a powerful hold on the social, political, cultural and economic agenda'. Morrow and others have demonstrated the selective visibility of young people in relation, for instance, to surveys of domestic labour where 'children (are rarely mentioned) as sources of assistance in their homes . . . except to a minimal extent in the literature on (girls') socialisation where such work is seen entirely as role rehearsal for future adulthood and not intrinsically useful or valuable in any way' (Morrow, 1994, p. 134). James and Prout (1997, p. xv) offer further evidence: they mention six problems concerning the visibility of children which were highlighted in a document presented to the UN World Summit on Social Development by The Save the Children Fund:

> . . . a failure to collect child specific information; lack of recognition of children's productive contribution; no participation of children in decision-making; the use of an inappropriate 'standard model of childhood'; the pursuit of adult interests in ways which render children passive; and lack of attention to gender and generational relationships.

In the 1980s Freeman, professor of English Law, offered a swingeing critique of the status of children in our society, pointing to the anomalies and inconsistencies that the system has constructed:

> Children have not been accorded either dignity or respect. They have been reified, denied the status of participants in the social system, labelled as a problem population . . . .
>
> (Freeman, 1987, quoted in Davie, 1993, p. 253)

It is time to review our notions of childhood and take account of recent work in sociology which argues that 'childhood should be regarded as a part of society and culture rather than a precursor to it; and that children should be seen as already social actors not beings in the process of becoming such' (James and Prout, 1997, p. ix). In such a framework, the idea of pupil participation and pupil perspective may be more acceptable than it has been in the past.

Pupil participation and pupil voice: its legitimacy in the 1990s

Although bruised by association with 'progressivism' and in tension with traditional notions of the child as dependent on the family and the school for socialisation into adulthood, the issue of pupil participation survives. What is giving it legitimacy at the moment?

The closely observed school studies published by Hargreaves (1967) and Lacey (1970), at a time when pupil participation issues were highly controversial, 'gave a powerful impetus to interest in children's views of their everyday life' (Prout and James, 1997, p. 19). Since then there has been a succession of studies which have attempted to highlight the importance of seeing school from the pupils' perspective. Such studies have helped to keep the issue alive. And although the force of the United Nations Convention has been relatively slight in mainstream education, it is there to be invoked as an additional source of legitimacy.

However, it is the school improvement movement that has provided the most striking opportunity for teachers, researchers and policy makers to work on a common agenda of concern and it is in this context that the issue of pupil participation and voice is being most obviously addressed.

The school improvement movement

Lateral security is provided by trends in other countries where researchers, over the last decade, have been asking some pointed questions. In the USA, Erickson and Schultz (1992, p. 476, quoted by Levin, 1995, p. 17) point out that 'virtually no research has been done that places student experience at the centre of attention'. In Canada, Fullan (1991, p. 170) has asked, in relation to school reform: 'What would happen if we treated the student as someone whose opinion mattered . . . ?'. In Sweden, Andersson (1995, p. 5) has said that 'politicians who decide about school reforms and the teachers who run the classrooms seldom ask how the students themselves perceive their school'. Levin (1995, p. 17), from Canada, notes that while the literature on school-based management 'advocates more important roles for teachers and parents . . . students are usually omitted from the discussion'. And Nieto (1994, pp. 395–396), from the USA, brings the issue of pupil perspective firmly into the school improvement frame:

> One way to begin the process of changing school policies is to listen to students' views about them; however, research that focuses on student voice is relatively recent and scarce.

She points out that pupils' perspectives have, for the most part, been missing 'in discussions concerning strategies for confronting educational problems' and she also says, importantly, that 'the voices of students are rarely heard in the debates about school failure and success' (p. 396). This view is echoed by Suzanne Soo

Hoo (1993, p. 392) who says: 'Traditionally, students have been overlooked as valuable resources in the restructuring of schools'. Nieto adds a cautionary note, explaining that a focus on students 'is not meant to suggest that their ideas should be the final and conclusive word in how schools need to change'; to accept their words as the sole guide in school improvement is 'to accept a romantic view of students that is just as partial and condescending as excluding them completely from the discussions' (Nieto, 1994, p. 398).

Patricia Phelan *et al.* (1992, p. 696), also from North America, argue that it is important to give attention to students' views of things that affect their learning, not so much factors outside school but those in school that teachers and policy makers have some power to change. And in the UK we, along with other researchers, have argued that pupils are our *'expert witnesses'* in the process of school improvement (Rudduck, 1999a). This position, especially since it is commanding so much support from teachers, seems to be one that does not offer the kind of threat that derailed the movement in earlier years.

Pupils *are* observant and have a rich but often untapped understanding of processes and events; ironically, they often use their insights to devise strategies for avoiding learning, a practice which, over time, can be destructive of their progress. We need to find ways of harnessing pupils' insight in support of their learning. Pupils' accounts of their experiences of being a learner in school can lead to changes that enable pupils to feel a stronger sense of commitment to the school and to the task of learning; and commitment can lead to enhanced effort and enhanced levels of attainment. But what is our motivation? Are we 'using' pupils to serve the narrow ends of a grades-obsessed society rather than 'empowering' them by offering them greater agency in their schools?

Citizenship education

Young argues (1999, p. 463) that the curriculum is 'a way of asking questions about how ideas about knowledge and learning are linked to particular educational purposes and more broadly to ideas about society and the kind of citizens and parents we want our young people to become'. His observations are timely given the resurgence of interest in citizenship education and its potential for endorsing the idea of pupil participation and pupil perspective in school.

The recent Report of the Government's Advisory Group, *Education for Citizenship and the Teaching of Democracy in Schools*, argues the need for citizenship education to be part of the formal curriculum:

> We unanimously advise the Secretary of State that citizenship and the teaching of democracy . . . is so important both for schools and the life of the nation that there must be a statutory requirement for schools to ensure that it is part of the entitlement of all pupils.
>
> (1998, p. 7)

The most challenging, and easily glossed over, dimension is the need for pupils to learn about citizenship in a structure that offers them *experience* of the principles of citizenship. The benefits of citizenship education, the Report says, will be to empower pupils to participate effectively 'in *society*' and 'in *the state*' as active, informed, critical and responsible citizens' (p. 9; emphasis added), but it doesn't say '*and in the school*'. Harold Dent (1930, p. 15), about seventy years ago, believed that every school could offer young people 'a developed and sane comprehension of how the affairs of a community are managed'; but, he said, 'pupils will learn not by talking about civics – a futile process – but by living civics' (see Rudduck, 1999b). This view is echoed in the nineties by Hodgkin (1998, p. 11): 'Democracy . . . is not something which is "taught", it is something which is practised'.

The next step is to build more opportunities for pupil participation and pupil voice into the fabric of the school's structure. But it takes time and very careful preparation to build a climate in which both teachers and pupils feel comfortable working together on a constructive review of aspects of teaching, learning and schooling. Many schools may rely on their school council but we know that these only work well if they are the centre – and symbol of – school-wide democratic practice. If the school is not ready for pupil participation then a school council can become a way of formalising and channelling students' criticisms; an exercise in damage limitation rather than an opportunity for constructive consultation. And the agenda of schools councils often do not roam far outside the charmed circle of lockers, dinners and uniform.

We should not fudge the issue by taking pupil performance in tests and examinations as proxy for school improvement but accept the simple logic that school improvement may, after all, be about *improving schools*, their organisational structures, regimes and relationships; in short, 'the conditions of learning'. This, after all, is what the pupils tell us. The changes we are talking about 'will not happen by accident, good will or establishing *ad hoc* projects. They require new structures, new activities, and a rethinking of the internal workings of each institution . . . ' (Watson and Fullan, 1992, p. 219, quoted by Fullan, 1993, p. 96).

Pupils and the curriculum

As far as pupils are concerned, it is not evident that we have learned the lessons of the curriculum development movement of the 1970s. Two things became clear (see Rudduck, 1991). First, the concept of 'relevance' was invoked to persuade us that the content of the curriculum would appeal to pupils but it was often an adult view rather than a pupil view of what was meaningful for young people. Second, there was little attempt to discuss with pupils why changes to content and pedagogy were being made. Teachers went on training courses that justified and helped them to cope with the break from traditional ways of working; pupils had no such support and they could respond by using their collective power as a class to resist or subvert the innovation. An alternative to imposed change through the authority of the teacher is to explore the need for change with the pupils themselves – what Ted Aoki (1984) called 'a communal venturing forth'; the discussion of purpose, he said, was a precondition of working effectively together. In the same spirit, Stenhouse saw 'standards' not as benchmarks imposed from 'outside and up there', but as criteria developed and shared by the working group for judging what counts as quality in their work together (see Stenhouse, 1967; Rudduck, 1997).

Aoki and Stenhouse were writing about opportunities for consultation on aspects of curriculum work in the 1960–1980s. But what about in the 1990s? Meighan (1988, pp. 36–38) has argued that even within the framework of a National Curriculum there *are* spaces for pupils to have an input. He distinguishes between a 'consultative curriculum', a 'negotiated curriculum' and a 'democratic curriculum'. A consultative curriculum, he says, is based on an imposed programme, but regular opportunities for learners to be consulted are built in. Feedback is reflected upon by the teacher and modifications may be proposed. In the negotiated curriculum, 'the degree of power sharing increases': what emerges 'is an agreed contract . . . as to the nature of the course of study to be undertaken'. The negotiation 'constitutes an attempt to link the concerns and consciousness of the learners with the world of systematic knowledge and learning'. Finally, there is the democratic curriculum, 'where a group of learners write, implement and review their own curriculum, starting out with a blank piece of paper'. The challenge is to identify opportunities for participation, at the consultative level at least, within the framework of the National Curriculum.

What lies behind Meighan's categorisation is an awareness that what matters to pupils is that they feel that they have a stake in school and are respected enough to be consulted. Teachers can often construct choices for pupils within most courses of study, but listening to what pupils have to say about the *'conditions of learning'* in school is also important (see Rudduck *et al.*, 1996). Our recent interviews with pupils in primary and secondary schools across the country (see Flutter *et al.*, 1998; Rudduck and Flutter, 1998) confirm that pupils are interested in changing structures that cast them in a marginal role and limit their agency. Pupils of all ages ask for more autonomy, they want school to be fair and they want pupils, as individuals and as an institutional group, to be important members of the school community. Policy makers may think about school primarily in terms of lessons and formal learning, but for pupils school is a holistic experience: it is about lessons, it is about what happens between lesson and it is about the regimes that define who and what matter to the school.

From our interview data we were able to construct a model of the things that affect pupils' commitment to learning and their identity as learners (Figure 12.1). The regimes of school, which embody values operating through structures and relationships, shape pupils' attitudes to learning and their view of themselves as learners. The more that the regimes are changed to reflect the values that pupils call for (intellectual challenge, fairness, etc.), the stronger pupils' commitment to learning in school is likely to be.

When talking *directly about learning in the classroom*, as opposed to these overarching concerns, pupils also have a lot to tell us that is worth hearing. They can, for instance, explain which of their classmates they work well with in different subjects and which they don't like working with (and yet teachers rarely elicit

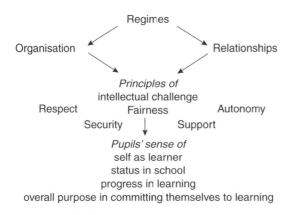

Figure 12.1 The conditions of learning in school

and use this information). They are capable of working on the problem of noise in the classroom (pupils in a primary school came up with a set of voice levels for different situations, each colour coded for easy memorisation; they ranged from pale blue, for the quietest whisper to the teacher when others are working, to red, the playground voice). Pupils affirm the excitement of problem-solving tasks and tasks that allow them to use their own ideas. They can often explain what levels of difficulty they find productive in different kinds of task.

We interviewed boys who were judged to be underperforming and they had a lot to say about changes that would help them. They told us that they *do* read but that the kind of reading that they like (technical journals, often using highly specialised vocabularies) is not valued in school. They said that they like to learn skills that can be used in everyday situations (such as map reading for family outings). Boys said that they prefer small challenges that can build up to something large (an essay, for instance, that is structured around a series of short, well-defined sections). They told us that they like to be active in class and that they like team work and work where oral contributions count and not just writing (see Rudduck and Flutter, 1998).

The pupils we interviewed seemed to be, although using very different words, as concerned as Young is about the curriculum as a product of the way in which knowledge is socially stratified. Their comments confirm Young's view that the curriculum is characterised by

- the superiority of subject-based knowledge;
- the under-valuing of practical knowledge;
- the priority given to written as opposed to oral forms of presenting knowledge; and
- the superiority of knowledge acquired by individuals over that developed by groups of students working together (Young, 1999, p. 468).

Conclusion

Teachers are very aware of the difficulties of engaging all pupils in learning and know that schools have changed less in their deep structures in the last twenty or thirty years than young people have changed. As Nieto (1994, pp. 395–396) says: 'Educating students today is a far different and more complex proposition than it has been in the past'. We need to recognise the implications of this change. Out of school, many young people find themselves involved in complex relationships and situations, whether within the family or the peer group. Many carry tough responsibilities, balancing multiple roles and often finding themselves dealing with conflicting loyalties. In contrast, the structures of secondary schooling offer, on the whole, less responsibility and autonomy than many young people are accustomed to in their lives outside school, and less opportunity for learning-related tensions to be opened up and explored. This traditional exclusion of young people from the consultative process, this bracketing out of their voice, is founded upon an outdated view of childhood which fails to acknowledge children's capacity to reflect on issues affecting their lives.

We should recognise pupils' social maturity and experience by giving them responsibilities and opportunities to share in decision making. Hodgkin (1998, p. 11) recalls the lessons from industry where productivity went up as a consequence of worker participation schemes: good ideas were used, workers felt that they mattered and they understood more about the enterprise as a whole and their part in it. She concludes

> The fact is that pupils themselves have a huge potential contribution to make, not as passive objects but as active players in the education system. Any (policy) concerning school standards will be seriously weakened if it fails to recognise the importance of that contribution.
>
> (Hodgkin, 1998, p. 11)

Policy makers are beginning to see the wisdom, or prudence, of taking account of pupils' experiences of learning (the QCA has recently commissioned work on pupil perspectives on assessment, on different curriculum subjects and on the National Curriculum; the Department for Education and Employment has emphasised the importance of the pupil perspective in many of the research projects that it is funding). Teachers up and down the country are finding ways of tuning in to pupils' accounts of learning in school, and they say that they find pupils insightful, measured and constructive. Consulting pupils need not be threatening, provided that teachers and policy makers genuinely see 'the pupils' world as worth becoming engaged with' (Sleeter and Grant, 1991, p. 67).

In conclusion, we cannot do much better than to urge readers to think about the two categories that Young offers us, Curriculum of the Past and Curriculum of the Future; Curriculum of the Future reflects the values of participation and perspective that feature so strongly in our own research on pupil voice. Young identifies the key features of the Curriculum of the Past as follows:

- it embodies a concept of knowledge and learning 'for its own sake';
- it is almost exclusively concerned with transmitting existing knowledge;
- it places a higher value on subject knowledge than on knowledge of the relationships between subjects;
- it assumes a hierarchy and a boundary between school and everyday knowledge, thereby creating the problem of the transferability of school knowledge to non-school contexts.

He invites us to contrast this with a Curriculum of the Future that expresses:

- a transformative concept of knowledge which emphasises its power to give learners a sense that they can act on the world;
- a focus on the creation of new knowledge as well as the transmission of existing knowledge;
- an emphasis on the interdependence of knowledge areas and on the relevance of school knowledge to everyday problems.

(Young, 1999, pp. 469–470)

Note

*   The quotation in the title is from the work of Maxine Greene (1995).

References

Andersson, B.-E. (1995) Why am I in school?, paper presented at the *European Conference on Educational Research*, University of Bath, 14–17 September 1995.

Aoki, T. (1984) Towards a reconceptualisation of curriculum implementation, in: D. Hopkins and M. Wideen (eds) *Alternative Perspectives on School Improvement*, pp. 107–139 (Lewes, Falmer Press).

Davie, R. (1993) Listen to the child: a time for change, *The Psychologist*, June, pp. 252–257.

Dent, H. (1930) The aim: an educated democracy, *The Nineteenth Century and After*, CVII, pp. 10–16.

Erickson, F. and Schultz, J. (1992) Students' experience of the curriculum, in: P. Jackson (ed.) *Handbook of Research on Curriculum*, pp. 465–485 (New York, Macmillan).

Flutter, J., Kershner, R. and Rudduck, J. (1998) *Thinking about Learning, Talking about Learning* (Cambridge, Homerton Research Unit for Cambridgeshire LEA).

Franklin, A. and Franklin, B. (1996) Growing pains: the developing children's rights movement in the UK, in: J. Pilcher and S. Wagg (eds) *Thatcher's Children? Politics, Childhood and Society in the 1980s and 1990s*, pp. 94–113 (London, Falmer Press).

Freeman, M. D. A. (1983) *The Rights and the Wrongs of Children* (London, Frances Pinter).

Freeman, M. D. A. (1987) Taking children's rights seriously, *Children and Society*, 1(4), pp. 299–319.

Freeman, M. D. A. (1996) Children's education: a test case for best interests and autonomy, in: R. Davie and D. Galloway (eds) *Listening to Children in Education* (London, David Fulton).

Fullan, M. (1991) *The New Meaning of Educational Change* (New York, NY, Teachers' College Press).

Fullan, M. (1993) *Change Forces* (London, Falmer Press).

Grace, G. (1995) *School Leadership* (London, Falmer Press).

Greene, M. (1995) *Releasing the Imagination* (San Francisco, Jossey-Bass).

Hargreaves, D. (1967) *Social Relations in a Secondary School* (London, Routledge and Kegan Paul).

Hart, R. (1992) *Children's Participation: From Tokenism to Citizenship*, Innocenti Essays no. 4 (Florence, UNICEF International Child Development Centre).

Hodgkin, R. (1998) Partnership with pupils, *Children UK*, Summer.

Holden, C. and Clough, N. (1998) The child carried on the back does not know the length of the road, in: C. Holden and N. Clough (eds) *Children as Citizens: Education for Participation*, pp. 13–28 (London, Jessica Kingsley).

James, A. and Prout, A. (1997) Preface, in: A. James and A. Prout (eds) *Constructing and Reconstructing Childhood*, 2nd edn, pp. ix-xvii (London, Falmer Press).

Lacey, C. (1970) *Hightown Grammar: The School as a Social System* (Manchester, Manchester University Press).

Lansdown, G. (1994) Children's rights, in: B. Mayall (ed.) *Children's Childhoods: Observed and Experienced*, pp. 33–44 (London, Falmer Press).

Levin, B. (1995) Improving educational productivity through a focus on learners, *International Studies in Educational Administration*, 60, pp. 15–21.

Meighan, R. (1988) *Flexi-schooling. Education for tomorrow, starting yesterday* (Ticknall, Education Now Publishing Cooperative).

Morrow, V. (1994) Responsible children? Aspects of children's work and employment outside school in contemporary UK, in: B. Mayall (ed.) *Children's Childhoods: Observed and Experienced*, pp. 128–141 (London, Falmer Press).

Nieto, S. (1994) Lessons from students on creating a chance to dream, *Harvard Educational Review*, 64, pp. 392–426.

Oakley, A. (1994) Women and children first and last: parallels and differences between children's and women's studies, in: B. Mayall (ed.) *Children's Childhoods: Observed and Experienced*, pp. 13–32 (London, Falmer Press).

Phelan, P., Davidson, A. L. and Cao, H. (1992) Speaking up: students' perspectives on school, *Phi Delta Kappan*, 73, pp. 695–704.

Prout, A. and James, A. (1997) A new paradigm for the sociology of childhood? Provenance, promise and problems, in: A. James and A. Prout (eds), *Constructing and Reconstructing Childhood*, pp. 7–33 (London, Falmer Press).

Rudduck, J. (1991) *Innovation and Change* (Milton Keynes, Open University Press).

Rudduck, J. (1997) Lawrence Stenhouse's vision of the teacher, the student and learning, talk given at the University of the Basque Country, Vitoria, May 1997.

Rudduck, J. (1999a) Teacher practice and the student voice, in: M. Lang, J. Olson, H. Hansen and W. Bunder (eds) *Changing Schools/Changing Practices: Perspectives on Educational Reform and Teacher Professionalism*, pp. 41–54 (Louvain, Graant).

Rudduck, J. (1999b) 'Education for all', 'achievement for all' and pupils who are 'too good to drift' (the second Harold Dent memorial lecture), *Education Today*, 49(2), p. 3.

Rudduck, J. and Flutter, J. (1998) *The Dilemmas and Challenges of Year 8* (Cambridge, Homerton Research Unit for the Essex TEC).

Rudduck, J., Chaplain, R. and Wallace, G. (1996) *School Improvement: What can Pupils Tell Us?* (London, David Fulton).

Silver, H. and Silver, P. (1997) *Students – Changing Roles, Changing Lives* (Buckingham, SRHE and Open University Press).

Sleeter, C. E. and Grant, C. A. (1991) Mapping terrains of power: student cultural knowledge versus classroom knowledge, in: C. Sleeter (ed.) *Empowerment through Multicultural Education* (Albany, NY, State University of New York Press).

Soo Hoo, S. (1993) Students as partners in research and restructuring schools, *The Educational Forum*, 57, pp. 386–393.

Stenhouse, L. (1967) *Culture and Education* (London, Nelson).

Stenhouse, L. (1983) The aims of the secondary school, in: L. Stenhouse (ed.) *Authority, Education and Emancipation*, pp. 153–155 (London, Heinemann Educational Books).

Wagg, S. (1996) 'Don't try to understand them': politics, childhood and the new education market, in: J. Pilcher and S. Wagg (eds) *Thatcher's Children? Politics, Childhood and Society in the 1980s and 1990s*, pp. 8–28 (London, Falmer Press).

Watson, N. and Fullan, M. (1992) Beyond school–district–university partnerships, in: M. Fullan and A. Hargreaves (eds) *Teacher Development and Educational Change*, pp. 213–242 (Lewes, Falmer Press).

Winter, K. and Connolly, P. (1996) 'Keeping it in the family': Thatcherism and the Children Act 1989, in: J. Pilcher and S. Wagg (eds) *Thatcher's Children? Politics, Childhood and Society in the 1980s and 1990s*, pp. 29–42 (London, Falmer Press).

Young, M. (1999) Knowledge, learning and the curriculum of the future, *British Educational Research Journal*, 25, pp. 463–477.

PART V

MANAGING TEACHING AND LEARNING

Teaching and learning are complex activities, often involving hundreds of pupils in a single school, which has to employ teachers, classroom assistants and ancillary workers, and liaise with large numbers of parents, members of the community and various agencies and related professions. The intelligent management of this disparate set of activities, and the budget that goes with it, is a significant assignment for those involved.

Senior managers in schools have usually been recruited from the ranks of teachers, so they are assumed to have an understanding of what teaching and learning entail. In order to manage effectively, however, they usually need support from their middle ranking colleagues, and indeed co-operation from all teachers, for they cannot teach all the classes in the school themselves. They also have at their disposal incentives and sanctions, so that they can respond to teachers doing their job particularly well or badly.

One of the most controversial issues in management is the use of financial incentives, especially performance-related pay. Many teachers and their trade unions have opposed such schemes when they have been introduced, on the grounds that they are divisive, setting teachers against each other when they should be collaborating. In Chapter 13, Rosemary Chamberlin and her three fellow researchers review the literature on performance-related pay, not only in teaching, but also in other fields. One difficulty in a profession like teaching is the measurement of 'performance', a term that some teachers dislike. Many merit pay schemes have folded because they were too costly, or too vague in their criteria. Those that succeeded were often low profile, involving teachers in their construction and implementation, so they were not alienated.

Secondary schools are usually divided into subject departments, each with a head who is part of the middle management. Alma Harris, in Chapter 14, analyses what can be done to improve the effectiveness of such departments. She looks at what makes departments run well or badly and finds that changes in leadership style can lead to improvement, especially when the head of department takes steps to improve the learning environment, targets particular pupils, talks to people about what needs to be done and harnesses the enthusiasm of the teaching members. Even good departments can improve, for example, by judicious risk taking.

Finally Marianne Coleman reports her study of female headteachers, describing the nature of their leadership styles. Often female heads pride themselves on valuing individual differences, being caring, tolerant and creative. Some of the people surveyed reported resentment from male staff, unhappy with the concept of women as a boss. One describes how the secretary and caretaker threatened to resign when she was appointed. There were fears that women would not be able to handle difficult male pupils. Most women heads felt that they had to work hard to prove their worth as senior managers, yet nearly two-thirds reported that they had found it an advantage to be female, often because they were able to defuse macho aggression amongst males. The under-representation of females among headteachers remains a concern as a matter of equity.

CHAPTER 13

PERFORMANCE-RELATED PAY AND THE TEACHING PROFESSION

A review of the literature

Rosemary Chamberlin, E. C. Wragg, Gill Haynes
and Caroline Wragg

> I cannot promise the House that this system will be an economical one and I cannot promise that it will be an efficient one, but I can promise that it shall be one or the other. If it is not cheap it shall be efficient; if it is not efficient it shall be cheap.
>
> (Bourne and MacArthur, 1970, p. 20)

With these words, performance-related pay for teachers in England was introduced to the House of Commons in 1861. The plan, which, it was thought, would cut the growing cost of education if teachers did not succeed or raise standards if they did, was the idea of a commission into the state of popular education in England (The Newcastle Commission). It proposed: 'to institute a searching examination . . . of every child in every school . . . and to make the prospects and position of the teacher dependent, to a considerable extent, on the results of the examination' (Bourne and MacArthur, 1970, p. 20).

The notorious 'payment by results' system lasted for thirty years, during which time teachers taught to the test, were confined to a narrow, boring curriculum, attempted to arrange the school intake, cheated, ignored bright children and drilled and beat the slower ones until they could satisfy the all-powerful inspectors. Although this was over 100 years ago, the experience had a lasting effect on the British teaching profession's folk memory, colouring their views and prejudicing them against performance-related pay in any form. Until the current plans for Threshold Assessment and Performance Management were introduced, performance-related pay for classroom teachers in England had not been tried again, though it has been in operation for headteachers since 1991.

Performance-related pay: a definition

There are five different ways in which an organization can reward its employees according to its perception of their individual merit. Three of these, piecework and the distribution of Equity and Profit shares, are not relevant to a public sector profession such as teaching. The fourth – the allocation of one-off bonuses, often on the completion of a particular project or in recognition of a specific contribution – is not currently under discussion in England. The fifth is performance-related or merit pay which, once agreed, becomes a regular part of the employees' salary and is usually taken into account for pension purposes.[1]

According to Murlis (1992) this form of performance-related pay may be organized in four ways. First, arrangements may be made for those perceived to be performing well to proceed more quickly up an incremental scale. This often occurs in unionized organizations, as it is compatible with a negotiated uniform salary structure, but it has two main drawbacks – good performers get stuck on the top of the scale, and even the poor performers will get there eventually. This problem is partially addressed by the second arrangement whereby employees are paid between 80 per cent and 120 per cent of a midpoint, so that poor performers never reach the top – though there still comes a time when good performers have nowhere further to go. Under this arrangement, higher increases may be paid to those who perform well when relatively new to the job – on the grounds that people with more years of experience could be expected to perform well, whereas the new ones are still learning. The third form of performance-related pay which, again, often occurs in unionized work places, is performance-related increases in addition to a cost of living increase for everyone. Finally there is the arrangement of giving increases only for personal performance, often within the range of 0–20 per cent possibly at the discretion of the manager.

Rationale

Many advantages are claimed for performance-related pay, though its primary purpose in any organization is to recruit, retain and motivate the workforce. It is believed that high quality workers are attracted to an organization where they believe their ability will be rewarded, while the current workforce is given the message that good performers are valued and poor performers are not. The prospect of earning more money is assumed to motivate workers to work harder and/or more effectively.

There are additional aims, one of which is to make employees more aware of or more committed to certain organizational goals. When employees learn that certain skills or specific behaviour is rewarded in a performance-related pay system, they also learn what it is that their employer considers important. As Protsik (1996) says, the ways an organization pays, or as she puts it, 'compensates' its employees is strategic: 'Compensation . . . serves more than the simple purpose of paying people for their time and hard work. Compensation systems communicate organizational desires to employees' (p. 266).

Other objectives of performance-related pay identified by Kessler and Purcell (1991) are as given in the

- weakening the power of the unions by making individual rather than collective contracts;
- making managers responsible for taking decisions;
- giving better value for money;
- advertising the organization's core values; and
- changing the culture of the organization,

while the OECD's study of performance-related pay in the public sector (1993) also mentions the following:

- encouraging greater accountability;
- strengthening the relationship between individual job goals and organizational goals;

- giving managers greater flexibility;
- saving money by reducing automatic increments; and
- enhancing job satisfaction.

Evidence

There is a body of research into the effects of pay – performance-related or otherwise – on employees' behaviour. The findings are not conclusive, however, in supporting the belief that performance-related pay will improve motivation, recruitment and retention of high quality staff.

Motivation

Empirical studies of some non-teaching organizations which introduced performance-related pay do show that it has a motivational effect. Lazear (1999) studied a car windscreen fitter over the 19 months in which it changed its pay structure by switching to piece rates and increasing its output by 44 per cent, half of which was attributed to improved working by the existing staff and half to improved recruitment. Fernie and Metcalf (1996) found that jockeys performed better when paid according to results than when paid under a retainer system. Because of this, over time, the retainer scheme became less popular, though it is not explained how this success could be maintained. A horse race can have only one winner, and so once all jockeys are paid according to their performance, the success of performance-related pay in producing winners must diminish.

Murnane and Cohen (1986) claim that performance-related pay works best where there are clearly measurable outcomes, and, although this applies to fitting windscreens and racing horses, it is not true of teaching, unless pupil test results are the sole criterion of success. As Murlis (1992, p. 69) says:

> New systems need to match the culture and values of the organization. For those in education, this means that the pay and performance management systems operated in industry cannot be translated wholesale. They must be modified, adapted, even rethought, to match the special demands of schools and other educational institutions.

There are other public sector jobs with hard to measure outcomes, however, where performance-related pay has been introduced and its motivational effect observed. Marsden and Richardson (1994) studied the effects of the introduction of performance-related pay into the Inland Revenue and found that staff did not report that their motivation had improved. Asked if performance-related pay had led them to change in line with a range of objectives such as improve the quality or quantity of their work, work harder or give sustained high performance, a large majority replied negatively. Marsden and Richardson (1994, p. 253) concluded that 'The positive motivational effects of Performance Pay . . . were at most very modest. . . . Even worse, there is clear evidence of some demotivation' (p. 253).

Similarly, Marsden and French's study of performance-related pay in public services (1998) found that most staff did not believe it had raised their own motivation, though about a half of civil service and hospital line managers believed that it had raised productivity and, to a lesser extent, quality. Richardson (1999a), in his report commissioned by the NUT, considered studies into the introduction of performance-related pay in local government (Heery, 1996) and the NHS (Dowling and Richardson, 1997), which again rely on self-reported judgements about individual behaviour. While over half of the local government respondents said that performance-related pay had had an impact on their work behaviour, a large majority did not believe that they worked harder. Amongst the NHS workers, just under 30 per cent agreed that performance-related pay had improved their motivation, but it was still a small percentage (12 per cent) that agreed that they worked harder.

When considering the finding that workers did not believe performance-related pay had motivated them, however, it should be remembered that the admission that one works harder for extra money is not easy to make as it involves admitting that one could have worked harder previously but chose not to. Indeed, it may be especially difficult for those involved in public service rather than private industry. It also should be remembered that even if all employees do not work harder or more effectively, improving the performance of between 12 and 30 per cent may be considered worthwhile (as long, of course, as the other 70–88 per cent are not demotivated and working less effectively).

In the 1960s, a study of employee motivation (Herzberg, 1966) suggested that employees are influenced by two types of rewards which he calls 'motivators' and 'hygiene' factors. Motivators are intrinsic rewards such as recognition, responsibility, achievement and the actual work, while 'hygiene factors' are extrinsic. These make work less unpleasant than it otherwise would be – good working conditions and salary. Herzberg argued that hygiene factors have little effect on increasing effort because they do not promote psychological growth, and, from this, Jacobson (1992) deduces it would be more productive to try to improve the intrinsic rewards of teaching, such as recognition of the value of teachers' work and the time they are able to devote to the children in their classes.

Another 1960s model of employee motivation known as the Expectancy Theory was put forward by Vroom (1964). This states that prospective rewards will motivate employees only if they believe that they can improve thier performance by working harder, that if they do work harder there is a high probability they will be rewarded, and if they are attracted by the thought of having more money. Relating this theory to teaching, Jacobson (1992) claims that the relationship between teachers' efforts and performance or results is not straightforward and that the realization that certain conditions such as overcrowded classes and poor resources were preventing teachers from gaining their anticipated performance-related rewards might be demotivating. He also questions the extent to which teachers are motivated by money, whether in the form of performance-related pay or high salaries and additional payments suggesting that 'people should not be expected to work hard for rewards they do not find especially attractive' (p. 37).

The findings on the attraction of money for teachers are somewhat contradictory – or perhaps illustrative of the fact that teachers' motivations are not one-dimensional. Jacobson (1992) cites the work of Lortie (1975) which indicated that the financial rewards of teaching were not as attractive as the opportunity to work with children and do a worthwhile job. Yet Jacobson (1995) claims that teachers in the US do respond to financial incentives, and sometimes demand extra payment for activities such as attending school governors' meetings which other governors do voluntarily. This may be resented, and points, he considers, to a dilemma in that 'school systems turn to monetary incentives to motivate teachers, yet they really don't want teachers who are primarily motivated by money' (p. 30).

Recent research by Heneman and Milanowski (1999) into new performance-related pay plans in Kentucky and Charlotte-Mecklenburg found that teachers valued their bonuses. Given seventeen outcomes of the scheme, the $1,000 bonus scored well for desirability, but Heneman and Milanowski were less sure about whether it actually motivated teachers. It should also be remembered that the teachers were asked, however, to rate the various outcomes of the scheme according to desirability, and not asked about the desirability of the scheme itself.

Money, though motivating, is not the only reward teachers value. Jacobson (1995) notes that in Canada, where teachers have had the opportunity to take unpaid leave since the 1970s, many do so, even at financial cost to themselves, because they prefer increased leisure or educational opportunities to more money: 'Those who advocate the use of monetary incentives in education believe that teachers presently have plenty of free time, and therefore additional time and effort to be purchased. But . . . many teachers view time as a more attractive incentive than money' (p. 33).

Current suggestions that teachers in England may wish to take a salary cut or spread four years' salary over five years in order to have the fifth year off have been criticized as unlikely to be taken up widely. Time will tell whether many English teachers, like those in Canada, prefer time to money.

Recruitment

School districts in the US set their own wage rates, and teachers' salaries vary widely. This makes it possible to study the effect of differences in starting salaries, and even in the majority of districts which do not have performance-related pay the effect of monetary reward may be observed. Jacobson (1995) studied districts of New York with different starting salaries and found that those offering more money than neighbouring districts were better able to attract applicants of high quality, thus indicating that newly qualified teachers do respond to financial incentives.

Richardson (1999a) also argues that starting salaries are more important in recruiting newly qualified teachers than the prospect of performance-related pay:

> Some may be attracted by the (uncertain) prospect of accelerated increments but the effect on their career choice now of moving on to the proposed new pay spine in 5–9 years' time looks rather small. . . . It is probably starting salaries that have a disproportionate influence on young teachers' career choices.
>
> (p. 28)

Kyriacou and Coulthard's findings on that point (2000), however, cast some doubt on Richardson's claim. Asked to select various factors which might be important in the choice of career, their sample of students placed a good starting salary 18th out of 20 possible factors, with only 19 per cent of them saying that a good starting salary was 'very important' in their choice of career (and only 5 per cent thinking they would find it in teaching). The students were divided into three groups – those who already wanted to teach, those who definitely did not and those who had considered teaching and might be encouraged to choose it as their career. The factors the whole group identified as most likely to encourage them to teach were the long holidays, a wish to share their knowledge and the fact that they would not have to pay for a PGCE course. They were influenced against teaching by the media image of teachers and the belief that they would have to deal with disruptive pupils, perform bureaucratic tasks, face OFSTED inspections and work in underfunded schools. The undecided group was then asked about policies which might encourage them to take up teaching, and it was at this point that 64 per cent selected improved starting salaries. At the top of this list (selected by 68 per cent) were improved resources for schools and higher salaries generally (65 per cent), while down the bottom (considered as definitely encouraging by only 27 per cent) was performance-related pay. While it is clear that salary has an effect on recruitment, Kyriacou and Coulthard's findings suggest that it is not paramount in the choice of teaching as a career.

Retention

Murnane *et al.* (1991) found that in Michigan and North Carolina, where attempts were made to attract people to teaching and cut staff turnover, teachers who received $2,000 per annum more than the state average were half as likely to leave teaching after one year than those who received $2,000 less than average. This accords with the findings of Jacobson (1988) that those districts which gave attractive salaries to teachers in mid-career were those with the lowest rates of turnover. He notes that this applied also to women, thus challenging the commonly held assumption that salary is of less importance to women. Chapman and Hutcheson (1982) and Goodlad (1983) also found that although teachers might not expect large salaries early in their careers, eventually they became unhappy with their remuneration and this affected the decision of some not to remain in teaching.

The OECD (1993) examined many public service performance-related pay schemes but reported they provided little firm evidence about staff turnover. In the US, performance-related pay schemes were introduced in the '80s into several naval research laboratories on an experimental basis and these were then compared with similar laboratories without performance-related pay. Turnover among high performers at the demonstration laboratories was lower than at the controls, and average salaries were higher.

When investigating the possible effects of performance-related pay on retention in the teaching profession, Richardson (1999a) considered the possibility that the expected decrease in turnover of teachers who receive performance-related awards will be offset by increased turnover of disaffected teachers who do not receive the awards. He also speculated that the pay increases for some will be met, not by new money from the treasury, but by lower increases for other teachers, thereby risking that overall turnover will increase. As one of the usually stated aims of performance-related pay, however, is to encourage high performers to stay and poor performers to leave, this may be seen as a positive rather than negative outcome – though not, presumably, if it results in an overall shortage of teachers.

Kerchner and Elwell (2000) considered the US Department of Education's Baccalaureate and Beyond study which followed those who gained degrees in 1992–3. It found that 20 per cent of those who started teaching in 1993 left within three years. However, it was not evident that they left because of dissatisfaction with their salary. Lack of a proper teacher induction programme meant that new teachers were more than twice as likely to leave as others, as were those dissatisfied with their school's environment and student discipline.

Kerchner and Elwell argue that the career plans of today's US teachers may be very different from those of a previous generation, in a climate in which most of their contemporaries will change jobs several or even many times. Some evidence supporting this claim comes from Peske *et al.* (2000) who studied new teachers in Massachusetts and found that some of them were exploring whether they liked the job rather than anticipating dedicating themselves to it for life, others had taken up the job for altruistic motives, while others again were doing the job to subsidize the activities which were more important to them, such as music. Peske *et al.* say that whether the group they call 'explorers' stay in teaching depends on whether they find it interesting rather than the pay they receive.

Disadvantages of performance-related pay

Despite some evidence that performance-related pay motivates employees to work harder or more productively, attracts suitable recruits and helps retain high quality staff, there is also evidence of disadvantages and failures. Sometimes the problems are that the scheme does not produce the hoped for benefits and sometimes that it has some of the unacceptable and undesirable side effects described in this section.

Neglect of unrewarded tasks

By rewarding particular aspects of a job, performance-related pay sends out messages about what is valued and the sort of behaviour that is desired. This is recognized as being an objective of performance-related pay but it may also be counter-productive as one of the main criticisms of performance-related pay is that employees become so firmly fixed on hitting their measurable targets that other important elements of their jobs are ignored. According to Kessler and Purcell (1991) the most commonly cited difficulty is that individuals tend to focus on specified objectives as a means of ensuring enhanced payment and to neglect other features of the job.

Examples of this problem abound. Asch (1990) studied a Navy recruitment scheme, which set targets of how many recruits were wanted, and rewarded recruiters if they reached their targets by specific dates. Asch records how, immediately before the critical date, the number of recruits rose and their quality fell, suggesting that recruiters became less discriminating in response to their expected reward.

Heery's study (1996) of Local Authority employees found that 14 per cent admitted to concentrating on the measurable aspects of their job, while 10 per cent said they were less prepared to take on tasks not covered in their appraisal. This is not a large proportion of the workforce, but still undesirable and potentially dysfunctional. Richardson (1999a, p. 29) notes that the proposed annual performance review for teachers set out in the Government's Green Paper is expected to concentrate on three objectives. He says:

> Unless some of these are set out in terms that are so general as to be vacuous there is a real danger that such a limit will mean that important parts of a teacher's normal duties will not be covered. If so it is very likely that some teachers will disregard some of their normal tasks.
>
> (Richardson, 1999a)

Murnane and Cohen (1986) identify what they call opportunistic behaviour among some recipients of performance-related pay. They argue that workers ironing shirts and being paid piece rates may neglect their machinery, while teachers may concentrate on raising pupils' test scores but neglect their emotional needs or wider curricular goals. In some industries it is possible to overcome this problem by employing other workers to concentrate on those neglected tasks (e.g. service the machinery), but it would not be easy to employ additional workers to instil into pupils a sense of responsibility or a distaste for taking drugs. Corbett and Wilson (1989) similarly express concern that teachers become over-concerned about test results and then: 'the end result is that the major emphasis in the school becomes to improve the next set of test scores rather than some longer-term more general goal of improving student learning' (p. 36).

Teachers might also concentrate their attention on the pupils most likely to improve their test scores, ignoring those who were already good enough or those who would need a great deal of time and attention and still might not attain the required standard. There is anecdotal evidence that this occurs in schools attempting to raise their proportion of pupils gaining GCSE A to C grades and it was one consequence of 'Payment by Results' in nineteenth-century England. Gramlich and Koshel (1975) found that it also happened in the US when some private firms were rewarded for teaching reading in state schools on the basis of pupils' test scores.

Disagreement about goals

The problem that teachers might concentrate on certain measurable tasks is further compounded by disagreement about the goals of education. For example, in Cincinnati, a new performance-related pay scheme which was agreed by a majority of the district's teachers was opposed strongly by teachers at the district's Montessori schools (Pilcher, 2000). Their philosophy of education and teaching methods differ from those in mainstream schools and there was concern that they might be judged according to goals they do not necessarily share. Johnson (1984) argues that without a clear consensus on what schools and teachers are aiming to do, merit pay, which rewards certain outcomes above others, is unsuitable: 'If schools do not define their goals, and if they pursue many goals simultaneously, expectations for teacher performance will be vague, muddled, or conflicting. No evaluation instrument, however carefully designed, can settle such issues' (p. 181).

She lists many of the things teachers are expected to teach – reading, computation, inferential reasoning and critical analysis, creative expression, handwriting, exposition, social adjustment, and more, and points out that for teachers, though not for manufacturers, 'The quality and consistency of the raw materials of teachers' work – the children whom they teach – are beyond their control. Teachers are expected to do the best with what they are given; discards are not permitted' (p. 182).

Lack of openness

Murnane and Cohen (1986) say that employees with performance-related pay will expect to have convincing reasons as to why some employees get more than others, and will want clear guidance as to how they too can earn more money. Teaching, they argue, is not easy to evaluate in such a clear-cut way and that one result may be that teachers are less willing to discuss problems with the headteacher, fearing, that once their coach has turned referee, these will be held against them. They also argue that because of the imprecise nature of teaching, supervisors cannot give a clear answer to the teacher who wants to know what s/he could do to earn the merit pay.

Without an unequivocal answer to this second question, teachers may have little incentive to change their behavior in pursuit of higher income. What is worse, teachers may learn that concealing their problems and playing up to evaluators is what the organization rewards – dramatically complicating managers' evaluation problem.

(Murnane and Cohen, 1986, p. 7)

Cost

Despite the assumption that performance-related pay schemes save money because money does not have to be spread so widely, there are significant costs. Not only is there the actual money paid to the employees who are thought to deserve it, but also the cost of administration including monitoring, appraisal and performance management. On the subject of administration, Lipsky and Bacharach (1983, p. 7) claim

> the single salary schedule reduces uncertainty and unpredictability of future salary costs. . . . In terms of administrative cost per se, the simplicity of the single salary schedule makes it quite inexpensive to implement. . . . In comparison with other schemes (such as merit pay), few administrative personnel are needed to maintain the system. Widespread adoption of some alternative pay plan would probably require districts to hire additional administrators and would no doubt lead to a substantial restructuring of roles within the administration and possibly within the teaching staff itself.

Studying US school districts which dropped their merit pay plans, Cordes (1983) found that 17 per cent blamed financial problems (wholly or partially). Heywood (1992) draws attention to the difference between funding performance-related pay schemes in the public and private sectors. He cites the scheme organized for Her Majesty's Inspectorate (HMI) which was resented because funds were limited and inspectors who had earned additional pay did not receive the full amount. He assumes that within teaching money will always be in short supply and the number of bonuses given will be limited. This is different from the situation in the private sector where costs can be passed on to customers, and it can cause resentment and rivalry. Hatry *et al.* (1994) studied eighteen US school districts from 1983 and found that few performance-related pay schemes were successful and lasting. They found that schemes are expensive if done well, but attempts to impose quotas on the number of teachers able to receive the awards, in order to limit costs, are destructive of teacher morale.

Protsik (1996) refers to the scheme in a district of Virginia US in which bonuses were awarded to teachers who were rated 'skilful' or 'exemplary', but after five years the plan was suspended because of budget cuts. She claims this is the common fate of performance-related pay plans in teaching, saying 'Most merit pay plans are discontinued within six years, largely due to problems of administration and personnel, collective bargaining, and budgetary shortfall' (p. 274).

The OECD (1993) report also refers to funding problems in the public sector generally, as it is not so easy to assess the cost–benefit of improved performance. Consequently, attention is focused on the cost of the scheme rather than the more nebulous benefits. There is also the likelihood that 'funding for performance pay schemes in the public sector may be vulnerable to budgetary cutbacks in times of economic constraint. This is a critical issue because the level and stability of funding for schemes are likely to have a major impact on the success of schemes' (p. 62).

It is also critical because teachers' acceptance or rejection of a scheme may depend on their beliefs about its fairness, reliability and longevity. Marsden (2000) found that 82 per cent of the teachers he asked agreed with the statement that 'many excellent teachers will not pass the Threshold because there is certain to be a quota on places available'. Teachers in England may not follow the progress of performance-related pay schemes in the US, but their scepticism about politicians' promises and their experience of funding problems makes them suspect that at some stage the money will not be available to fund the scheme fully or fairly.

The money needed is not simply for the additional salary for good performers. Evaluating performance requires meetings, lesson observations and a variety of administrative tasks. Performing these will have costs, either in paying supply teachers and additional administrative staff or the cost of other worthwhile activities left undone. As Murnane and Cohen (1986) observe 'Monitoring the output or actions of individual workers is costly'. Evaluating a complex activity such as teaching is not easy. Either it is done thoroughly, with a great deal of thought going into the assessment criteria and taking up the time of the headteacher and senior management team, or it is done perfunctorily in which case it will be resented and may result in dissatisfaction and demotivation.

Demotivation for the unrewarded

The theory behind the motivational effects of performance-related pay is that the unrewarded will get the message that their performance is unsatisfactory and either improve or leave – both satisfactory outcomes from the perspective of the employer. Like many theories, however, it is too simple for complex reality, and, in practice, many employees who are satisfactory or better may be demotivated by schemes which do not benefit them. In some schemes, in order to prevent spiralling costs or 'rating drift', quotas are set so that only a certain percentage of employees can receive bonuses or merit awards. The OECD (1993) reports that in a scheme in the UK civil service introduced in 1987, a 25 per cent quota was set, later raised to 35 per cent. Thus 65 per cent of the staff, the vast majority of whom were appraised as being 'fully satisfactory', received no benefit. Dissatisfaction with this aspect of the scheme led to it being replaced by a new scheme with no quota. The OECD (1993, p. 66) says:

> If the aim of the performance pay scheme . . . is to raise the performance of all managers then any assumptions regarding normal distributions of performance, and the resulting forced distributions of rewards, may be dysfunctional. Forced distributions and quotas create 'winners' and 'losers' with the latter suffering some loss of self-esteem and becoming demotivated.

If everyone benefits, however, the purpose of the scheme is undermined. The OECD cites examples of plans where the majority of managers were rated as superior or outstanding, which, if the comparison was internal, is not logically possible. This corroborates findings on teachers' appraisals also, whether or not linked to pay awards. For example, in Baltimore, Philadelphia, in 1983, 44.6 per cent of teachers were rated 'outstanding' (Digilio, 1984), and Bridges (1992) cites examples of teachers, diagnosed as extremely poor performers, who had been given good evaluations for many years in the hope of raising their esteem and encouraging them to live up to expectations.

Thus, if everyone is rewarded the scheme is undermined, but if quotas are maintained these may demotivate the majority of satisfactory or good performers and also lead to the possibility of competitive attitudes replacing co-operation.

Competition instead of co-operation

There are several studies of the effects of performance-related pay on the level of co-operation in public services. Marsden and Richardson (1994) found that 26 per cent of their sample of Inland Revenue staff reported that performance-related pay had made them less willing to assist colleagues. A follow-up study by Marsden and French (1998) found that, despite management attempts to deal with some of the earlier disadvantages of the scheme, this percentage had risen to 63 per cent. The same survey found that 67 per cent agreed with the sentiment that performance-related pay discourages team-working, while the percentage who thought that it had caused jealousies had risen from 62 to 86 per cent. Heery (1996) found that among employees from four Local Authorities, 18 per cent felt that co-operation and team-work had been damaged, while in a study of NHS managers, Dowling and Richardson (1997) found that although 14 per cent thought they co-operated less or much less with their colleagues, 9 per cent thought they co-operated more or much more, and 77 per cent reported no change in co-operative behaviour. Similar findings emerge from a study of the Employment Service (Marsden and French, 1998) in which 52 per cent of the sample said that staff were less willing to assist colleagues with their problems at work, and 78 per cent reported jealousies between staff.

Co-operation at work is required not only between equals but also between employees and their managers. Heery (1996) found that, of his sample of Local Authority employees, 16 per cent agreed that performance-related pay had eroded some of the trust between employee and manager, while Marsden and French (1998) found that 19 per cent of the NHS workers they surveyed admitted being less willing to co-operate with management. Marsden and French (1998) also looked at the problem from the perspective of NHS line managers and asked them about the attitudes of their subordinates, and 30 per cent reported that many members of staff were less willing to co-operate with management. It is interesting that a higher proportion of managers reported decreased co-operation between employees and management than did the employees themselves.

In his report for the NUT, Richardson (1999b, p. 30) concludes:

> Very many public sector workers see individual performance-related pay as leading to heightened tensions at work. It is seen to create jealousies amongst staff . . . a sense of unfairness and . . . to lead to a frequent loss of respect for management. . . . It strengthens a them-and-us attitude and reduces the sense of the team as a whole.

In an attempt to avoid the problems of competition, some performance-related pay schemes reward teams of employees rather than individuals. One such scheme is described in the following section on the experience of merit pay for teachers in the US.

Merit pay for teachers: the picture from the US

Although performance-related pay for teachers in England was discontinued over 100 years ago, in the US, where the idea of individual financial reward fits well with their market-orientated society, it has rarely been off the agenda. In 1918, 48 per cent of school districts operated some form of merit pay, but schemes were usually short-lived, 'merit' often turned out to mean being white and male, and by the end of the 1920s the percentage of districts with merit pay had fallen to 18 per cent. The reasons given for introducing merit pay were similar to those set out in the section 'Rationale', but were often prompted by events which promoted a perception of failing educational standards. As Johnson (1984, pp. 175–6) says

> In the 1920s and again in the 1960s, educators enthusiastically instituted merit pay plans throughout the country. Each time widespread public concern about the country's international standing, promoted in the first instance by World War 1 and in the second by the launching of Sputnik and the ensuing space race, fueled merit pay plans. Many citizens were convinced that if schools were to prepare students to meet international challenges, they would have to become more rigorous, businesslike places.

Later, in the 1980s, 'A Nation at Risk' (National Commission on Excellence in Education 1983) – a critical report of America's education standards – prompted debate about teachers' pay. President Reagan (1983) contributed the view that teachers should be 'paid and promoted on the basis of their merit and competence' if schools were to improve.

The 1950s to the present day

Postwar, enthusiasm for merit pay – from administrators and the public if not from teachers – has come and gone in waves since the mid-1950s, and there are now signs that it is on the increase again. Previously, although schemes varied across the country, there were some discernible trends, with earlier schemes favouring evaluations of teaching made by supervisors, either making subjective assessments or ticking lists of supposedly desirable teaching behaviour. These were widely criticized, for example by Darling-Hammond (1986) who claimed that ticklist evaluation 'exacerbates the tendency to think of teaching as an unvarying didactic exercise that is unresponsive to the characteristics of students or the nature of learning tasks' (p. 535). Johnson (1984), too, argued that merit pay, which may be easy to organize in certain industries, is unsuitable in education because of the difficulties of measuring teacher effectiveness.

By the early 1970s, the number of merit plans in existence had halved, down to 5.5 per cent of school districts, and most had not lasted long. According to Johnson (1984, p. 180), a survey of plans by the Education Research Service in 1978 found that they had been dropped:

> for a wide range of technical, organizational, and financial reasons: difficulties in evaluating personnel, failure to apply criteria fairly, teacher and union opposition, poor morale, staff dissension and jealousy, failure of the plans to distinguish between merit and favoritism, failure of the plans to meet their objectives, changes in the school systems' leadership or philosophy, collective bargaining, funding shortages, overall expense of the programs, and recognition that the merit pay bonuses did not provide sufficient incentives to teachers. The problems were legion.

Despite this, in the 1980s merit pay was once more on the agenda, due, according to Johnson (1984) to concern about the decline of productivity in the

US relative to Japan and other industrialized countries. This time, the financial incentives offered were often given for quantity rather than quality (Jacobson, 1992), with bonuses given for extra work or good attendance. The problem was that while subjective judgements were just that, liable to bias and open to accusations of favouritism, supposedly objective judgements measured what was measurable and not necessarily what was important. Neither form of evaluation was based on the outcomes of good teaching – pupil progress.

Despite criticism and problems, the interest in merit pay for teachers never dies away in the US, especially in the poorer, southern states, and in the 1990s it was being discussed once again. Johnson (2000) believes that new and prospective teachers have different expectations of their career from those trained in the 1960s and may be more enthusiastic about a pay system which rewards their performance. A variety of new schemes are being introduced.

In Cincinnati, for example, a plan has been agreed whereby different standards will be expected of teachers at different stages of their careers and they will be able to progress through five levels from apprentice to accomplished teacher. Their progress through the levels (and up the salary scale) will depend on evaluation of their performance in sixteen standards in four areas: planning and preparation; creating a learning environment; teaching for learning; and professionalism, and time limits will be set as to how long they can remain on the lower levels. Teachers in shortage subjects may progress more swiftly – an arrangement which prompts difficult questions about equity. Under a new scheme in Philadelphia, teachers will receive a bonus simply for agreeing to take part, but rewards will then be conditional on evaluations of their teaching ability. Most of these plans do not tie teachers' pay explicitly to pupils test results, but in Denver a scheme is being piloted in which teachers will be rewarded if the majority of their students improve according to attainment tests (Janofsky, 1999). It will be interesting to see whether all or any of these schemes last longer than those of previous decades.

Group payment schemes

Attempting to overcome the problems of individual performance-related pay and to answer the criticism that it is divisive and unfair, some school districts have experimented with schemes which reward the whole staff if certain goals are met. For example, in a pilot scheme in Kentucky, schools are assessed according to 'accountability goals' and placed at one of five levels. Only those schools on the top level – the ones which exceeded their goals – receive a financial reward while those down in the bottom three categories have to produce 'transformation' plans, either on their own (category three) or with the help or under the control of a distinguished educator. To start with, the rewarded schools were given the money and staff voted whether to share it among themselves or spend it in some other way, and, unsurprisingly, this caused some dissension, with disagreements about whether non-teaching staff should share the bonuses. Kentucky has now joined some other states in rewarding the school with money to spend on extra equipment. Investigating the success of the scheme, Kelley (1998) found that teachers were motivated more by fear of the sanctions and negative publicity that accompanied being judged to be a school in crisis than they were by the expectation of money if they succeeded.

Protsik (1996) argues that group-based performance pay plans help to focus teacher's efforts on working together to improve student learning. The jury is still out, however, on the success of such group schemes. While group rewards are intended to promote a collaborative culture, they too have potential drawbacks. The extent to which merit pay can influence the content of lessons, for example, may be seen in reports of a school in North Carolina. A bonus of $1,500 was on offer for all teachers if students improved, but as one of the targets for improvement was Maths, teachers of all subjects focused on that subject. According to the New York Times (Steinberg, 2000, p. 20, col. 3):

> Several times a month, in preparation for a statewide math exam later this school year, the opening minutes of every 9th and 10th grade class . . . are devoted to math, no matter whether the class is Latin, history or physical education. The math teachers give the gym instructors problems about batting averages, and ask the social studies teachers to work through equations related to the population of Japan. High school teachers sometimes isolate themselves in their classrooms, but the instructors . . . in this suburb . . . have been brought together, at least in part, in pursuit of a common goal: money.

Many people may applaud such a cross-curricular effort, but the possibility exists that subjects such as P. E. or music might be downgraded in importance and that children may be short-changed and miss out on a broad curriculum as their teachers strive to secure the bonus that comes from good Maths scores. The morale of P. E. and music teachers might also be affected adversely.

Kelley (1998) analysed similarities between the Kentucky schools which achieved their goals and were rewarded, and her findings that might fuel the worries of those concerned about the loss of teachers' autonomy and the imposition of particular goals. Describing the successful schools (successful, that is in achieving the goals set by the district authority) she said:

> All of these schools aligned their curriculum to the assessment instrument and/or to the state curriculum guides. All incorporated test-taking strategies into their regular curriculum . . . they had direct contacts with the accountability program through professional teacher ties and current or past participation of teachers on state committees. As a result, these schools were more likely than others to know how to use and interpret the considerable amount of information issued by the state as a guide to help schools improve practice.
> (p. 309)

Fears of the return of 'teaching to the test' will not be allayed by Kelley's findings. One of the aims of performance-related pay is to alert employees to those elements of their jobs that employers wish to emphasize, and this is as true of group schemes as it is of individual ones. With all the discussion about the merits of merit pay, there has been little discussion about the ends of education. The worries of Cincinnati's Montessori teachers (Pilcher, 2000) are understandable if they are not involved in discussing the criteria according to which they will be judged.

Long-lasting merit pay schemes

As has been said, most schemes are short-lived, but in an attempt to find factors which enabled some districts to buck this trend, Murnane and Cohen (1986) surveyed those with long-lasting systems. They looked in vain for districts in urban or disadvantaged areas – the very places to find schools in most need of the high-quality, well-motivated teachers that performance-related pay should encourage – but found that they were mostly small districts with homogenous populations and that most gave bonuses too small to be motivational. Murnane and Cohen then selected six districts which did give larger differentials (up to $2,000 per annum in the 1980s) for closer scrutiny. These were all desirable neighbourhoods with above-average pay scales and good working conditions and they also had the following in common:

(1) They gave extra pay for extra work, often also requiring teachers to produce evidence and documentation to prove their suitability.
(2) They strove to make all their teachers feel special and did not force teachers to participate in the merit pay scheme.
(3) The schemes were low-profile.
(4) Teachers were involved in planning the schemes, so there was general acceptance of the criteria for the awards and a feeling of ownership.

Murnane and Cohen concluded that these schemes did not really address the problems or provide the benefits that merit pay is generally supposed to – motivation, recruitment, retention and improving educational standards – but that they had other benefits. They supported good teachers and gave them the choice of whether to opt for a higher workload or more free time, and they encouraged teachers to be involved in evaluation. In a country where local democratic involvement in education is high and often vociferous, they also helped to build community support for local schools and their teachers.

The way forward

Some of the most intractable problems surrounding performance-related pay for teachers have been associated with evaluating the work that they do. Either assessment is based on the subjective opinion of principals, or the objective judgements of the ticklist or the pupils' tests. In addition, according to Odden (2000), there have been problems caused by lack of funding and 'because merit pay is at odds with the team-based, collegial character of well-functioning schools' (p. 362). Despite past failures, however, he believes that the time is now right to introduce a new way of paying teachers, one that reinforces the elements that intrinsically motivate teachers, such as learning new teaching skills and being successful in helping pupils learn.

In order for performance-related pay schemes to work, Odden and Kelley (1997) argue that they need the following:

- involvement of all the key parties;
- adequate funding;
- training;
- no quotas; and
- persistence.

These criteria could have been met in the past, but the crucial difference now is the existence of fairer, broad-based evaluation instruments to assess what teachers know and can do. Odden (2000) cites, as examples, The Educational Testing Service (ETS) and the Council of Chief State School Officers (CCSSO) assessment instruments for use early in a teacher's career and the National Board for Professional Teaching Standards (NBPTS) standards for outstanding experienced teachers. For use at stages in between, Odden cites the criteria devised by Danielson (1996) to be used in mid-career. These cover four aspects of a teacher's role – planning and preparation, the classroom environment, instruction and professional responsibilities – which are similar to the criteria used in English teachers' Threshold Assessment.

This similarity is not simply coincidental. Odden has been consulted by the DfEE, and, according to Lewis (2000, p. 4) the British Government is now moving further and faster than that of the US. She says:

> None of the British reforms are unknown in this country. True, centralization makes the task of instituting them comparatively easier in Britain, but schools with top performance are free of most supervision – other than a national assessment system. The major contrast, other than a willingness to link teacher performance to teacher pay, is a sense of urgency about the reforms. Professional development in Britain, for example, is expected to produce improvement within months, not the years predicted in the U.S.

It is these 'months' which the Teachers Incentive Project is studying. There is evidence, however, from our national questionnaire survey of 1,000 headteachers and from our surveys of both 'successful' teachers and those who have been deemed to have 'not yet met' the standards required under the Threshold Assessment procedure, that there has been little impact on classroom performance as yet.

Note

1   Economists distinguish between the terms 'performance-related pay' and 'merit pay'. The former is used in situations where there are specific measurable outcomes, whereas 'merit pay' may be given for less easily measured behaviour. It follows, therefore, that performance-related pay is more common for manual workers and merit pay for non-manual and professional workers. That said, most writers do not distinguish between the terms and tend to use 'merit pay' if they are American and 'performance-related pay' if they are British.

References

Asch, B. (1990). 'Do incentives matter? The case of Navy recruiters', *Industrial Labour Relations Review*, 43, 89–107.

Bourne, R. and MacArthur, B. (1970). *The Struggle for Education 1870–1970*. London: Schoolmaster Publishing Co.

Bridges, E. M. (1992). *The Incompetent Teacher: Managerial Responses*. London: Falmer Press.

Chapman, D. and Hutcheson, S. (1982). 'Attrition from teaching careers: a discriminant analysis', *American Educational Research Journal*, 19, 1, 93–105.

Corbett, D. and Wilson, B. (1989). 'Raising the stakes in statewide mandatory minimum competency testing'. In Hannaway, J. and Crowson, R. (eds) *The Politics of Reforming School Administration*. Philadelphia, PA: Falmer Press.

Cordes, C. (1983). 'Research finds little merit in merit pay', *American Psychological Association Monitor*, 14, 9, 10.

Danielson, C. P. (1996). *Enhancing Professional Practice, A Framework for Teaching*. Alexandria, VA: Association for Supervision and Curriculum Development.

Darling-Hammond, L. (1986). 'A proposal for evaluation in the teaching profession', *Elementary School Journal*, 86, 531–51.

Digilio, A. (1984). 'When Tenure is tyranny', *The Washington Post Review*, 12 August, 12–14.

Dowling, B. and Richardson, R. (1997). 'Evaluating performance-related pay for managers in the NHS', *International Journal of Human Resource Management*, 8, 3, 348–66.

Fernie, S. and Metcalf, D. (1996). 'It's not what you pay it's the way that you pay it: Jockeys' pay and performance', *CentrePiece Magazine*, 2 June.

Goodlad, J. (1983). *A Place Called School*. New York: McGraw-Hill.

Gramlich, E. and Koshel, P. (1975). *Educational performance contracting*. Washington, DC: Brookings Institution.

Hannaway, J. and Crowson, R. (eds) (1989). *The Politics of Reforming School Administration*. Philadelphia, PA: Falmer Press.

Hatry, H. P., Greiner, J. M. and Ashford, B. G. (1994). *Issues and Case Studies in Teacher Incentive Plan*, second edn. Washington, DC: Urban Institute Press.

Heery, E. J. (1996). 'Performance-related pay in Local Government: a case study of the New Industrial Relations'. PhD Thesis, University of London.

Heneman, H. G. and Milanowski, A. T. (1999). 'Teachers' attitudes about teacher bonuses under school-based performance award programs', *Journal of Personnel Evaluation in Education*, 12, 4, 327–41.

Herzberg, F. (1966). *Work and the Nature of Man*. New York: Crowell Publications.

Heywood, J. (1992). 'School teacher appraisal'. In Tomlinson, H. (ed.) *Performance-Related Pay in Education*. London: Routledge.

Jacobson, S. (1988). 'The distribution of salary increments and its effect on teacher retention', *Educational Administration Quarterly*, 24, 178–99.

Jacobson, S. (1995). 'Monetary incentives and the reform of teacher compensation: a persistent organizational dilemma', *International Journal of Educational Reform*, 4, 1, 29–35.

Jacobson, S. L. (1992). 'Performance-related pay for teacher: the American experience'. In Tomlinson, H. (ed.) *Performance-Related Pay in Education*. London: Routledge.

Janofsky, M. (1999). 'For Denver teachers, a pay-for-performance plan', *New York Times*, 10 September.

Johnson, S. (1984). 'Merit pay for teachers: a poor prescription for reform', *Harvard Educational Review*, 54, 175–85.

Johnson, S. (2000). *'Teachers' Compensation and School Improvement: A Review of the Literature and a Proposal to Build Capacity'*, Paper prepared for the National Education Association.

Kelley, C. (1998). 'The Kentucky school-based performance award program: school-level effects', *Educational Policy*, 12, 3, 305–24.

Kerchner, C. T. and Elwell, C. L. (2000). *Paying Mindworkers: What is the Incentive to Teach?* Paper based on presentation to the Council for Greater Philadelphia, Teacher Accountability Conference, in Horsham, Pennsylvania, 16 May.

Kessler, I. and Purcell, J. (1991). *Performance-Related Pay: Theory and Practice*. Paper presented at the 10th Colloquium for the European Group of Organisation Studies, Vienna, July 1991. Oxford: Templeton College, The Oxford Centre for Management Studies.

Kyriacou, C. and Coulthard, M. (2000). 'Undergraduates' views of teaching as a career choice', *Journal of Education for Teaching*, 26, 2, 117–26.

Lazear, E. (1999). *Performance Pay and Productivity*. Stanford California: Stanford University Research Paper.

Lewis, A. C. (2000). 'Parochialism and performance pay for teachers', *Phi Delta Kappan*, 82, 1, 3–4.

Lipsky, D. and Bacharach, S. (1983). 'The single salary schedule vs. merit pay', *NEA Research Memo*. Washington, DC: National Education Association.

Lortie, D. (1975). *Schoolteacher: A Sociological Study*. Chicago: University of Chicago Press.

Marsden, D. (2000). *Teachers Before the Threshold*. LSE Discussion Paper 454. London: Centre for Economic Performance, London School of Economics.

Marsden, D. and French, S. (1998). *What a Performance?* London: Centre for Economic Performance, London School of Economics.

Marsden, D. and Richardson, R. (1994). 'Performing for pay? The effect of "merit pay" on motivation in a public service', *British Journal of Industrial Relations*, 32, 2, 243–62.

Murlis, H. (1992). 'Performance-related pay in the context of performance management'. In Tomlinson, H. (ed.) *Performance-Related Pay in Education*. London: Routledge.

Murnane, R. J. and Cohen, D. K. (1986). 'Merit pay and the evaluation problem: why most merit pay plans fail and a few survive', *Harvard Educational Review*, 56, 1, 1–17.

Murnane, R. J., Singer, J. D., Willet, J. B., Kemple, J. J. and Olsen, R. J. (1991). *Who Will Teach? Policies That Matter*. Cambridge, MA: Harvard University Press.

National commission on excellence in education (1983). *A Nation at Risk: The Imperative for Educational Reform*. Washington, DC: US Government Printing Office.

Odden, A. (2000). 'New and better forms of teacher compensation are possible', *Phi Delta Kappan*, 81, 5, 361–6.

Odden, A. and Kelley, C. (1997). *Paying Teachers for What They Know and Do*. Thousand Oaks, CA: Corwin Press.

Organisation for economic co-operation and development (OECD) (1993). *Private Pay for Public Work: Performance Related Pay for Public Sector Managers*. Paris: OECD.

Peske, H. G., Liu, E., Kardos, S. M., Kauffman, D. and Johnson, S. M. (2000). *Envisioning 'Something Different': New Teachers' Conceptions of a Career in Teaching*. Paper presented at the American Educational Research Association Annual Meeting. New Orleans: Harvard Graduate School of Education.

Pilcher, J. (2000). 'Educators will watch merit pay closely: teacher merit-pay plan first in U.S.', *Cincinnati Enquirer*, 17 September.

Protsik, J. (1996). 'History of teacher pay and incentive reforms', *Journal of School Leadership*, 6, 3, 265–89.

Reagan, R. (1983). Speech at Seton Hall University, South Orange, New Jersey, May.

Richardson, R. (1999a). *Performance-Related Pay in Schools: An Assessment of the Green Papers*. London: NUT.

Richardson, R. (1999b). *Performance-Related Pay in Schools: An Evaluation of the Government's Evidence to the School Teachers' Review Body*. London: NUT.

Steinberg, J. (2000). 'Academic gains pay off for teachers and students', *New York Times*, 1 October.

Vroom, V. (1964). *Work and Motivation*. New York: Wiley.

CHAPTER 14

EFFECTIVE LEADERSHIP AND DEPARTMENTAL IMPROVEMENT

Alma Harris

Introduction

During the past decade there has been an increasing momentum in England, as in many other educational systems, towards educational reform directed at raising school performance. This increase in expectations has been accompanied by a string of government policies aimed at generating the impetus for school improvement, including developmental planning, target setting and performance management (Fidler, 1999). One common response to the problem of underachievement in many Western countries has been to restructure and to mobilise change efforts at the level of the whole school (Fullan, 1991). This type of intervention is premised upon a view that the key to school improvement lies in management systems and administrative arrangements. It has been argued that this approach neglects the importance of the process of change in schools, and more importantly, underestimates the 'capacity of the school for development' (Hopkins et al., 1997, p. 3).

Research evidence concerning school improvement underlines the importance of building the capacity for change within the organisation by focusing change efforts at different levels within the organisation. (Creemers, 1992; Hopkins et al., 1994; 1996). The importance of school-level, department-level and classroom-level change has been shown to be essential in effective school improvement programmes (Hopkins et al., 1996; Hopkins and Harris, 1997; Stoll and Fink, 1997). Similarly, empirical evidence from the school effectiveness field has shown that a substantial proportion of the variation in effectiveness among schools is due to variation within schools, particularly at the subject department level (Creemers, 1992; Fitz-Gibbon, 1992; Scheerens, 1992; Sammons et al., 1997).

The work of UK researchers (such as Bennett, 1995; Harris et al., 1995, 1996a,b; Sammons et al., 1996a,b; Harris, 1998) suggests that heads of department within English secondary schools contribute to departmental performance in much the same way as headteachers contribute to overall school performance. This departmental sphere of influence has been termed the 'realm of knowledge' because of the importance of the subject boundary (Siskin, 1994). Furthermore, it has been suggested that at the department level there is both the opportunity and the possibility to influence whole-school development and performance (Huberman, 1990).

The head of department has a direct influence upon the quality of teaching and learning within a subject area. Research studies have shown that the head of department is an important factor in differential departmental effectiveness

(Harris *et al.*, 1995; Sammons *et al.*, 1997). The leadership approach adopted by the head of department does affect departmental performance. However, the different types of department found within a secondary school also makes leadership of a department particularly difficult and complex role to fulfil (Busher and Harris, 1999). This chapter examines the role of the head of department within school and departmental improvement. In summary, it

- explores the dimensions of the leadership role of the head of department;
- considers the impact upon the leadership potential of the head of department of different types of departments;
- outlines differential strategies for departmental improvement; and
- examines the relationship between departmental and school development.

The central argument of this chapter is that in order to survive in an increasingly turbulent and changing environment, issues of school development can no longer be seen as the exclusive preserve of senior staff. For strategy to be successfully implemented, staff at all levels in an organisation need to be involved in decision-making and policy formation. Heads of department are very much in the front line and, to be most effective, will need to be more involved in wider strategic planning for the organisation as a whole. However, in reality, levels of involvement vary according to the nature of the organisation, the management approach of senior staff and the culture of the organisation. Most importantly perhaps, levels of involvement are a function of the various dimensions of the leadership role expected of the head of department.

Leading from the middle

The role of the head of department essentially involves working with and through others in pursuit of particular goals (Blandford, 1997; Harris, 1999). Heads of department are agents who work on behalf of the whole staff in the interests of students, parents and other stakeholders. With schools becoming ever more accountable, an increasing challenge is placed on those in key roles in schools to perform at even higher levels. Inevitably, tensions arise for those in leadership positions as they are faced with competing demands. This raises a number of important issues about the leadership role of heads of department in schools and how they deal with the tensions between different functions of their role.

Drawing upon the work of Glover *et al.* (1998) and Busher and Harris (1999), it is possible to identify four dimensions of the head of department's work. The first dimension concerns the way in which heads of department translate the perspectives and policies of senior staff into the practices of individual classrooms. This *bridging or brokering* function remains a central responsibility. It implies a transactional leadership role for the subject leader. In this role, heads of department make use of power – usually 'power over' others (Blase and Anderson, 1995) – to attempt to secure working agreements with departmental colleagues about how to achieve school and departmental goals and practices. Part of this role is the managing and allocating of resources available to the department.

A second dimension focuses on how heads of department encourage a group of staff to cohere and develop a group identity. The area, or areas, of subject knowledge that the department shares usually defines the boundaries of the group. An important role for the head of department, therefore, is to foster *collegiality* within the group by shaping and establishing a shared vision. This necessarily implies a leadership style that empowers others and that involves subject leaders using 'power with' or 'power through' other people to generate such collaborative departmental cultures (Blase and Anderson, 1995). This style of leadership is people-oriented and requires a leadership approach that helps other people to transform their feelings, attitudes and beliefs. Transformational leaders not only manage structure but they purposefully impact upon the culture in order to change it. Hence, an important dimension of the head of department's work is to shape and manage departmental culture.

A third dimension concerns the *improvement of staff and student performances.* At one level this implies a transactional leadership role for the head of department in monitoring the attainment of school goals and meeting particular prescribed levels of curriculum performance. On the other hand, as Glover *et al.* (1998) note, it suggests an important mentoring or supervisory leadership role in supporting colleagues' development and the development of students academically and socially. This mode of leadership also draws on the expert knowledge of heads of department and that of their referent power as sources of power to bring about improvement in practice.

The fourth and final dimension of the head of department's work is a *liaison or representative* role. This requires the subject leader to be in touch with a variety of actors and sources of information in the external environment of the school and to negotiate, where necessary, on behalf of the other members of the department (Busher, 1992). One aspect of this dimension is in helping departmental colleagues keep in touch with the views of, for example, other professional workers in their subject area – perhaps through liaison with a professional association. Another aspect will be helping colleagues to stay in touch with the views and needs of colleagues in other departments within the school. Part of this dimension then, of a head of department's role, is representing the views of departmental colleagues to the senior staff and to other middle managers within the school.

These four dimensions of the leadership role of heads of department are both complementary and potentially competing in their demands. They reflect the complexity of a management role within the middle of a hierarchy and reveal the tensions facing leaders in a middle management position. However, for individual heads of department, this role is made even more challenging because of the different ways departments are configured and perform. Both these aspects directly affect the leadership capacity of heads of department.

The realm of the academic department in secondary schools presents a considerable range of organisational differentiation. Departments in secondary schools in England range from multidisciplinary departments (e.g. Design and Technology departments), to departments with many staff in them (e.g. English) to departments staffed by one or two and several part-time staff (e.g. a Music department or a History department). This diversity leads to two observations: first, that heads of department have widely differing arenas in which to exercise their power and face competing leadership demands; second, and most important, that the task of departmental improvement is primarily dependent upon the 'growth state' of the department and the 'type' of department in question.

Improving departmental performance

Much departmental improvement work assumes in practice that all departments are the same, that is, a strategy such as development planning will work as well in one department as in another. Yet the research on departmental effectiveness (see, e.g., Sammons *et al.*, 1997) demonstrates that departments are differentially effective. This would suggest that departments at different levels of effectiveness will require different improvement strategies. Put simply, departments at different stages of development and growth will require different strategies not only to enhance their capacity for development, but also to provide a more effective education for their students. Strategies for departmental development need to fit the 'growth-state' of the department, that is, the particular phase of development in which the department finds itself.

Research by the American Quality Foundation (1992), for example, suggests the need to recognise that different strategies are required at different phases of the performance development cycle. In 1992, the American Quality Foundation conducted an international study of 945 quality management strategies in 580 commercial and industrial organisations and found that only three quality management strategies had universal application across organisations at different points in their performance development cycle. Cuttance (1994) has summarised them as follows:

- a strategic focus on process improvement;
- strategic planning; and
- supplier certification programmes.

The most important finding from this research was that different quality management strategies were effective in different phases of the organisational performance development cycle. In the early part of the cycle, the strategies which were most effective in improving performance were

- building teams;
- empowering staff to solve problems;
- general and specific training; and
- a strong emphasis on monitoring performance.

Organisations in the middle of their performance development cycle benefited most from

- the use of teams, a continued emphasis on training;
- a focus on process improvement through its simplification;
- the implementation of staff development programmes;
- the use of quality assurance systems;
- tight control over strategic planning; and
- the monitoring of progress against targets.

Organisations approaching the top of the performance development cycle gained most advantage from

- empowering employees to interact directly with their customers;
- undertaking benchmarking studies;
- implementing process simplification; and
- making innovation and creativity the focus of quality assurance strategies.

The vital message from this research is that developmental strategies need to be differentiated and matched to the performance level of the organisation. So, in terms of school or departmental improvement, the strategies required for a highly performing school/department need to be different from those required to assist an underperforming school/department (Hopkins *et al.*, 1997). Yet, we know little about how different improvement strategies affect different departments. The research base on the effects of departmental development strategies is unfortunately very weak. At present, research is ongoing but some initial proposals based on the empirical data gathered to date are available (Harris, 1999). These ideas are presented as a tentative list of strategies that departments could use to improve their effectiveness.

In the following section, strategies for departments operating at different levels of performance and with different growth states are outlined. Drawing upon the work of Hopkins *et al.* (1994) that identified school 'type', three different 'types' of department are analysed. The first type of department is the ineffective department. By both academic outcome measures and value-added scores, this department is significantly underperforming. In terms of its growth state, it could be characterised as a *stuck* department. The second type of department is the underachieving department. By academic outcome measures, this department may be considered on the surface to be performing reasonably well. Yet, low value-added scores reveal that this department is underachieving and could be characterised as a *complacent* department. The third type of department is an ideal type of effective department that scores highly on both value-added scores and academic outcome measures. The combination of stability and balanced development characterises this department as a *moving* department (Rosenholtz, 1989).

The 'ineffective' department

Research concerning ineffective departments is not extensive but the work that does exist demonstrates that ineffective departments are 'stuck' departments in need of a high level of external support (Harris, 1998, 1999). Within these departments, a number of early interventions and changes need to be made which have a direct focus upon basic organisational issues. These include

- changes in leadership;
- immediate external support;
- data and diagnosis;
- early visible change;
- a focus on learning;
- staff development;
- building collaboration.

Changes in leadership. It is too sweeping to say that the heads of failing departments do not have the capacity to be effective department leaders. It is certain though that they do not have the capacity to resurrect that department and therefore are potentially a part of the problem. Research suggests that leadership is, to some extent, context related so failing departments need changes in leadership practices. Poor management and inappropriate leadership approaches are a consistent feature of ineffective departments (Harris, 1998). Consequently, the overall style of leadership needs to be changed in that particular context and new leadership opportunities will need to be created for different staff, using new models, to achieve new goals.

Immediate external support.   Departments in a failing situation are likely to be isolated and in a state of cultural stasis. They are unlikely to have the potential for constructive self-analysis or evaluation and will need support from outside to provide knowledge about department improvement strategies and models of ways of working. It is important, however, that the department has some ownership over the selection of the external support and should be able to choose from a range of providers considered to be most suited to their needs.

Data and diagnosis.   For improvement strategies to be most effective, the process of data collection and diagnosis is an important first step. Most ineffective departments will need to collect or analyse data to find out why they are unsuccessful and where to direct their efforts for greatest improvement. Data would need to be gathered at whole-school level, at departmental level and at classroom level in relation to individual students and groups of students. The purpose of this data collection exercise would be to locate existing good practice within the department to build upon it. This approach has the potential to give the department ownership of the improvement agenda and to locate the problem away from individuals to a whole department focus.

Early visible change.   Following a period of low morale, small, visible changes will demonstrate that things are to be different in the department. These changes should reflect the core values that the new leadership is articulating. Evidence would suggest that such early indicators of a climate change in the department are important in sustaining further improvement. They have a symbolic and real function, in so far as they show that change is taking place and that a new and different department culture is emerging.

A focus on learning.   Much of the evidence concerning the improvement of ineffective or failing departments points towards an emphasis upon managing learning behaviour rather than behaviour management (Harris, 1998). This means creating the conditions within which learners can learn most effectively. Strategies for managing learning behaviour would inevitably include a focus upon praise and positive reinforcement, rather than punishment and discipline, throughout the department.

Staff development.   Staff development in the ineffective department needs to be both context-specific and culturally related. There should be a preoccupation with effective teaching and learning throughout the department. Therefore, specific training and development opportunities should be made available to both teachers and students. In the first instance, the focus for staff development could be quite simple classroom management issues – for example, seating arrangements, classroom organisation, the phasing of lessons or active use of resources. Teachers could explore these issues in teams in order to create new partnerships and to build collaborative enquiry.

Building collaboration.   In the ineffective department, any restructuring or planning must be focused upon what happens in classrooms. Collaboration and planning should be about enhancing student achievement and about developing the potential of all staff. These areas need to be activated simultaneously as the core agenda for improvement. Time needs to be set aside for collaboration, for developmental work and for the sharing of ideas. Consequently, nothing is more important than timetabling staff together to engage in mutual learning and to plan curriculum and department improvement in a failing department. It is also the case that the gap cannot be allowed to become too large between the effective teams and the less effective teams – an intense improvement focus could produce that result. In this respect, the improvement process needs to be internally supported, with expertise and time being given to those less effective teams to ensure that the balance and momentum of change is maintained.

The 'underachieving' department

Research suggests that underachieving departments need to refine their developmental priorities and focus upon specific teaching and learning issues, and build capacity within the department to support this work. These strategies usually involve a certain level of external support, but it is theoretically possible for these departments to improve themselves. Developmental strategies for this type of department include

- change in leadership approaches;
- improve the environment;
- lengthen the lesson unit;
- target particular students;
- talk to students;
- harness the energy and optimism of staff new to the department;
- generate an ongoing dialogue about values.

Change in leadership approaches.   This change incorporates both leadership styles and range. Some restructuring will be necessary in order to diversify leadership opportunities. Department improvement task groups, multiple team leadership, task-related leadership are strategies which will unlock static structures and systems. Such changes will enable the process of management to become more dynamic and to be geared towards increasing the capacity for change.

Improve the environment.   Alterations in the department environment can have a dramatic effect on teaching and learning processes. For example, the creation of work areas, enhanced display of students' work, improved social space all indicate to students that the department values them and that they should value the department. The constant reinforcement that learning is valued will contribute to raise staff morale and can affect pupil achievement.

Lengthen the lesson unit.   Some curriculum restructuring will be needed in order to support the reskilling of teachers. Time will be needed to focus on a wider repertoire of teaching/learning styles and on the development of learning behaviours. The longer the time unit, the more time staff will have to plan together and to practise different teaching approaches. Different lesson lengths might be necessary to support teachers in the process and practice of reskilling.

Target particular students.   If achievement is to matter, then underachievement at all levels should be targeted. Data about performance will provide opportunities to generate dialogue with staff and with students – in groups and individually; by gender and by ability. Mentoring students is one effective strategy to offset potential underachievement. It is visible relationship-building and should ideally involve all staff.

Talk to students.   Departments are good at internally assessing pupil effort and achievement. They are less skilled at assessing potential and it is in this gap that the potential for improvement lies. The gap between achievement and potential is only meaningful in terms of pupil life and aspirations. Achievement has to mean something, so formal mechanisms of rewarding all types of pupil achievement are important and should be built in to any department restructuring programme.

Harness the energy and optimism of staff new to the department. Underachieving departments will tend to have staff who are disillusioned. Morale will be low but staff who have accepted jobs at the department within the last year or two will have done so with optimism, faith in the department and hope for what they might achieve. These staff can be used to re-energise others and can become a catalyst for change. It is important, therefore, that the new leadership's efforts to re-ignite the values of all staff focus initially upon staff comparatively new to the department. This will provide a basis for improvement upon which further allegiances can be formed.

Generate an ongoing dialogue about values. The values and beliefs, both of the profession and the department, need to be articulated and reaffirmed. All staff need to be helped to be clear about the value dimension of almost everything that is done in the department. For example, why do we have this assessment system? Why this homework policy? Why these rules or this code of conduct? Why did we deal with this incident in this way? All these decisions will have their roots in the values and beliefs of the department community – and they need to be shared and debated.

The 'good' or 'effective' department

There has been relatively little debate, or research undertaken, which has focused upon improving the good or effective department. Most attention has been located with improving poor or low-performing departments. Yet, it is imperative that those departments which are effective remain so. Consequently, in this last type of department there is a need for specific strategies to ensure the department remains a moving department which continues to enhance pupil performance. These strategies include

- reinforcing values;
- involve students;
- external support;
- risk taking;
- celebrate and share successes.

It is a department leader's role to articulate the department's values and to reinforce them at every opportunity. Research has shown that within highly effective departments these values are shared by all staff (Harris *et al.*, 1995). Consequently, departments need to be clear about the interpretation and articulation of values within their individual department context.

Reinforcing values. Effective departments should constantly strive to raise ever higher expectations (teacher, pupil and the wider community) regarding potential pupil achievement. This means departments need to be explicit, eloquent and prolific in their definition of achievement. They should then celebrate it, communicate it and develop a reward system which will eliminate the need for most sanctions. Such a process will ignite the enthusiasm of staff and generate motivation amongst students. It is additionally important to give students (and the wider community) ownership of the department's achievements and to involve them in organising and participating in regular celebrations of the department's success.

Involve students. Once systems, structures, processes, values and professional skills have been developed within the effective department and even when schemes of work and classroom management strategies have been refined, it is still the students who have to take responsibility for their own achievement. It is important that they feel involved and empowered in the process of learning. For example, students can contribute by offering an assessment of teaching and learning processes. By providing their views about how their learning can be improved in the individual classroom, and within the department, students are contributing to the improvement process via their constructive feedback.

External support.   Even the most effective department will eventually become inward-looking and atrophy if it becomes too self-sufficient. Isolation from external stimulus and support can be damaging to any department irrespective of its performance level. A department which is a learning department will seek out best practice elsewhere and will use outside support to develop the knowledge-base and to initiate networks. External expertise and support can also offer alternative teaching practices and new ways of teaching and learning. Teachers can become skilled in these new processes by working alongside others both within the classroom and in functional teams.

Risk taking.   Effective departments need to encourage experimentation and risk-taking. They should accept messiness and muddle rather than aim for efficiency. They should subscribe to the view that safe teaching is mundane teaching and aim high and take joy in the successes and talk about the failures. Indeed, real learning lies in understanding the failures rather than the successes.

Celebrate and share successes.   All departments at whatever stage in their development should take joy in every demonstration of success. They should aim to orchestrate optimism and celebration of teacher *and* student achievement. Everyday professional and social interactions of teachers and students should focus upon the positive rather than the negative, upon success rather than failure to ensure that this permeates the whole department and every classroom. Cynicism about students, the department, the profession needs to be eroded by making it totally unacceptable within the department.

These lists of strategies for developing departments at three stages of the development cycle are still in a rather early stage. Three characteristics of these lists are worth highlighting here. The first is that these strategies are not homogeneous but holistic and electic. The second is that this combination of strategies has a disparate focus: these strategies are at the same time directed at the structure/organisation of the department, the achievement of students, and the intangible 'culture of the department'. Third, these strategies represent a combination of external and internal strategies; the particular blend of strategies is modified to fit the 'context specificity' of the individual department.

Commentary

Departments are dynamic subcultures and this dynamism needs to be understood at a conceptual, contextual and empirical level before effective strategies for development can be devised. The notion of 'performance cycle' or 'growth state' rather than derisory labels such as 'failing' or 'ineffective' are useful here for they capture for us a more dynamic, realistic and optimistic view of department development. Conceptions of effectiveness and ineffectiveness need to be understood holistically rather than as is currently the case, atomistically.

While these ideas about the 'department's capacity for development' remain somewhat speculative, they are increasingly being grounded in research data (Harris,

1998, 1999). Despite this tentativeness, the issues raised in this chapter have the potential to offer a better grasp of the dynamics of the process of department development and its link to school restructuring. This means taking seriously individual department's performance or 'growth state' and securing differential strategies for department development. For it is this that holds the key to sustaining enhanced levels of student progress and achievement for all departments whatever their 'growth state' or their preferred strategies for change. Therein lies the real possibility and potential for school development.

Acknowledgement

This analysis is based upon the earlier work by Hopkins, D., Harris, A. and Jackson, D. (1997). Understanding the school's capacity for development: growth states and strategies. *School Leadership and Management*, 17, pp. 401–411.

References

American Quality Foundation (1992) *The International Quality Study Best Practices Report* (Cleveland, OH, American Quality Foundation and Ernst and Young).

Bennett, N. (1995) *Managing Professional Teachers: Middle Management in Primary and Secondary Schools* (London, Paul Chapman).

Blandford, S. (1997) *Middle Management in Schools: How to Harmonise Managing Teaching and Learning for Effective Schools* (London, Pitman Press).

Blase, J. and Anderson, G. L. (1995) *The Micropolitics of Educational Leadership: From Control to Empowerment* (London, Cassell).

Busher, H. (1992) Reducing role overload for a head of department: a rationale for fostering staff development, *School Organisation*, 8, pp. 99–108.

Busher, H. and Harris, A. (1999) Leadership of school subject areas: tensions and dilemmas of managing in the middle, *School Leadership and Management*, 19, pp. 305–317.

Creemers, B. (1992) School effectiveness and effective instruction: the need for a further relationship, in: J. Bashi and Z. Sass (ed.) *School Effectiveness and Improvement*, Conference Paper, pp. 37–48 (Hebrew University Press).

Cuttance, P. (1994) Quality systems for the performance development cycle of schools paper: presented at the *International Congress for Effectiveness and Improvement*, Melbourne, 3–4 January 1994.

Fidler, B. (1999) *Strategic Planning for School Improvement* (London, Pitman).

Fitz-Gibbon, C. T. (1992) School effects at A level: genesis of an information system? in: D. Reynolds and P. Cuttance (ed.) *School Effectiveness: Research, Policy and Practice* (London, Cassell).

Fullan, M. (1991) *The New Meaning of Educational Change* (London, Cassell).

Glover, D. C., Gleeson, D., Gough, G. and Johnson, M. (1998) The meaning of management: the development needs of middle managers in secondary schools, *Educational Management and Administration*, 26, pp. 279–292.

Harris, A. (1998) Improving the effective department: strategies for growth and development, *Educational Management and Administration*, 26, pp. 269–278.

Harris, A. (1999) *Effective Subject Leadership* (London, David Fulton).

Harris, A., Jamieson, I. M. and Russ, J. (1995) A study of 'effective' departments in secondary schools, *School Organisation*, 15, pp. 283–299.

Harris, A., Jamieson, I. M. and Russ, J. (1996a) What makes an effective department? *Management in Education*, 10, pp. 7–9.

Harris, A., Jamieson, I. M. and Russ, J. (1996b) How to be effective: what marks out departments where students achieve most, *Times Educational Supplement*, School Management Update, 10 November, p. 7.

Hopkins, D. and Harris, A. (1997) Improving the quality of education for all, *Support for Learning*, 12, pp. 147–151.

Hopkins, D., Ainscow, M. and West, M. (1994) *School Improvement in an Era of Change* (London, Cassell).

Hopkins, D., Ainscow, M. and West, M. (1996) Unraveling the complexities of school improvement: a case study of the Improving the Quality of Education for All (IQEA) Project, in: A. Harris, N. Bennett and M. Preddy (eds) *Organisational Effectiveness and Improvement* (Milton Keynes, Open University Press).

Hopkins, D., Harris, A. and Jackson, D. (1997) Understanding the school's capacity for development: growth states and strategies, *School Leadership and Management*, 17, pp. 401–411.

Huberman, M. (1990) *The Model of the Independent Artisan in Teachers' Professional Relations*, paper presented at the *American Educational Research Association Conference*, Boston.

Rozenholtz, S. (1989) *Teachers' Workplace: The Social Organisation of Schools* (New York, Longman).

Sammons, P., Thomas, S. and Mortimore, P. (1996a) *Improving School and Departmental Effectiveness*, paper given at the *British Educational Management and Administration Society Research Conference*, Robinson College, Cambridge, 25–27 March.

Sammons, P., Thomas, S. and Mortimore, P. (1996b) *Promoting School and Departmental Effectiveness, Management in Education*, 10, pp. 22–24.

Sammons, P., Thomas, S. and Mortimore, P. (1997) *Forging Links: Effective Schools and Effective Departments* (London, Paul Chapman).

Scheerens, J. (1992) *Effective Schooling Research, Theory and Practice* (London, Cassell).

Siskin, L. S. (1994) *Realms of Knowledge: Academic Departments in Secondary Schools* (London, Falmer Press).

Stoll, L. and Fink, D. (1997) *Changing Our Schools* (Buckingham, Open University Press).

CHAPTER 15

THE FEMALE SECONDARY HEADTEACHER IN ENGLAND AND WALES

Leadership and management styles

Marianne Coleman

Introduction

The study of women in leadership and management in education is relatively rare. Hall (1996), when researching female headteachers, makes the point that

> I found it difficult at first to avoid using men's behaviour as educational leaders as a yardstick for describing women in similar positions . . . Putting the picture straight by changing the subject from men to women does not involve saying women are different or better. My purpose is rather to explain how they are in this role (headship), in this context (schools), in this period of time (1990s).
>
> (p. 3)

Theories of leadership and management have often been based on assumptions derived from the male discourse (Blackmore, 1989; Shakeshaft, 1989), but in relatively recent years the female manager in education has been studied in her own right (Adler *et al.*, 1993; Ouston, 1993; Ozga, 1993). The disproportionate number of female secondary headteachers, only 24 per cent in 1996 (GB. DFE, 1997), also raises issues of equity. Evetts (1994) studied twenty secondary heads of whom ten are male and ten female, making gender an important variable in her study, and Grace (1995) included a chapter on women in educational leadership. Studies of individual headteachers have included a balance of male and female heads (Ribbins and Marland, 1994; Hustler *et al.*, 1995; Ribbins, 1997). The present author has conducted interviews with five women headteachers (Coleman, 1996) and, most notably, Hall (1996) has undertaken an in-depth study of six female headteachers of whom three are secondary and three primary. Elsewhere, Hall and Southworth (1997) point to the fact that research into headship is the weaker for largely ignoring the variable of gender:

> Using a gender perspective creates new possibilities for exploring the lives of men and women who teach, manage and lead in education. As researchers into headship we have both concluded that educational leadership is firmly

rooted in professional identity. Gender, in turn, is a crucial component of that identity. Future research into headship that fails to take this and the gendered nature of schools and colleges into account is likely to be incomplete.

(p. 167)

However, research on the management and leadership of women in education has tended to be qualitative in nature.

Survey of female headteachers in England and Wales

In summer 1996, the present author undertook a survey of all the 670 female secondary headteachers in England and Wales covering their leadership and management styles, and their career progress to headship. The response rate of 70 per cent, well above normal response rates, gives an objective measure of the interest that the headteachers had in the area. Comments included on the returned questionnaires and accompanying letters showed the measure of this interest and indicated the relative isolation that was felt by many of the respondents. Female headteachers have not previously been surveyed separately as a group, although gender as a variable was included in the survey research of Weindling and Earley (1987), Jones (1987) and Jirasinghe and Lyons (1996).

The survey data reported here are those relating to the management and leadership styles of the headteachers, including the values that they were promoting in their schools. In addition, this chapter covers aspects of their experience of management and leadership, including the ways in which they relate to their staff and their professional development. Finally, data relating to the perceived difficulties and the advantages of being a woman headteacher are reported.

Approximately half of the headteachers were aged between 40 and 49 and half between 50 and 59, with very few under 40 or over 60. More than two-thirds of the headteachers were married, with marriage more popular amongst the under 50s than the over 50s. Just over half of the heads had a child or children, but childlessness was more common amongst those under 50. Just over two-thirds of those responding were heads of co-educational schools, the remainder were heads of single sex schools. Of these, only three individuals were heads of boys' schools.

The management and leadership styles of female headteachers in England and Wales

In analysing management and leadership styles, there are certain qualities that are identified with a 'feminine' or a 'masculine' style of management. Both of these styles may be adopted by men or by women, although the expectation is that men might adopt a style that is predominantly masculine and women one that is predominantly feminine. The lists of qualities identified by Bem (1974) and by Gray (1989, 1993) are both attempts to identify such a paradigm or ideal type. In the survey, the headteachers were presented with the masculine and feminine qualities identified by Gray (1993) and asked to indicate which of the qualities they felt applied to them. These qualities are derived from work associated with the training of headteachers, and are not based on empirical research. Their use in this questionnaire was intended to provide a possible redefinition of the paradigms. The qualities were not identified in any way as 'male' or 'female' in the questionnaire.

Six of the adjectives and descriptions that are included in the feminine paradigm (see Table 15.1) were identified by 59 per cent or more of the headteachers. More

Table 15.1 Qualities identified by headteachers from the masculine and feminine paradigms of Gray (1993): percentages indicated are those which they felt they had the quality

Feminine paradigm	%	Masculine paradigm	%
Aware of individual differences	86.0	Evaluative	61.1
Caring	79.4	Disciplined	60.4
Intuitive	76.2	Competitive	50.6
Tolerant	68.7	Objective	50.6
Creative	63.0	Formal	14.9
Informal	59.4	Highly regulated	13.2
Non-competitive	21.5	Conformist	10.9
Subjective	13.8	Normative	4.0

Table 15.2 Qualities identified by 50 per cent or more of headteachers

Aware of individual differences	(f)	86.0
Caring	(f)	79.4
Intuitive	(f)	76.2
Tolerant	(f)	68.7
Creative	(f)	63.0
Evaluative	(m)	61.1
Disciplined	(m)	60.4
Informal	(f)	59.4
Competitive	(m)	50.6
Objective	(m)	50.6

Note:
(f) = feminine and (m) = masculine in Gray's (1993) paradigm.

than three-quarters of them judged themselves to be 'aware of individual differences', 'caring' and 'intuitive'. However, there were also four adjectives in the masculine paradigm which were identified by over half of the headteachers as applicable to them. Although the characteristics identified most often were from the feminine paradigm, those chosen by more than 50 per cent ranged across both paradigms (see Table 15.2). The qualities listed in Table 15.2 present an empirically based alternative to the feminine paradigm identified by Gray (ibid.).

Overall, it would appear that there is a strong identification with most of the feminine traits on the part of the headteachers, and a weak identification with most of the masculine traits. However, there are a number of masculine traits, specifically 'evaluative', 'disciplined', 'competitive' and 'objective', which are identified by 50 per cent or more of the respondents, and which therefore temper the picture of a pure feminine paradigm of management style amongst the female secondary headteachers of England and Wales and indicate a more androgynous style of management.

Key words to describe the headteachers' style of management

Open-ended questions included in the survey were intended to allow the headteachers to express their own perceptions of their style and of the values that they are trying to promote in the school. The headteachers were given the opportunity to list three separate words that describe their style of management. This question appeared in the survey before the question involving the list of masculine and feminine paradigms, so it is unlikely that these adjectives had any influence on the free choice of the three words. No guidance whatsoever was given, to allow them to provide unprompted responses. This led to there being a large range of adjectives offered. However, it was possible to group them, and establish some idea of the prevalent styles of management that the female headteachers considered that they adopted. The themes that were identified are listed here, with the percentage of the total number of adjectives in each group:

1 A collaborative style of management
   e.g. consultative, open   (38.5 per cent)
2 A people-oriented style of management
   e.g. team-related, supportive   (23.8 per cent)
3 An autocratic/directive style of management
   e.g. decisive, firm   (14.9 per cent)
4 An efficient style of management
   e.g. focused, planned   (11.7 per cent)
5 A values-driven style of management
   e.g. visionary, fair   (11.1 per cent).

There is a clear indication that the single most popular style of management was that termed 'collaborative'. However, it is notable that most of the headteachers use terms like 'consultative', 'open', 'collaborative' and 'participative' rather than 'collegial' or 'democratic'. It appears that the majority of the headteachers adopting this style of management reserve the right to make the final decision. The potentially overlapping 'people-oriented' style of management was also strongly indicated by the choice of adjectives grouped within that theme. The range of adjectives chosen is very wide, but the styles of management that are indicated in the majority of responses are consistent with the adjectives most often chosen from the female paradigm – 'aware of individual differences', 'caring', 'intuitive' and 'tolerant'.

Certainly, the identification of the collaborative and people-oriented style of management with the way that women manage is in accord with a range of earlier findings. Research on female headteachers and principals in the USA, the UK, Australia, New Zealand and Canada appears to indicate that female managers are likely to work in a cooperative style, empowering their colleagues and characteristically making use of teamwork (Blackmore, 1989; Adler, 1994; Hall, 1996; Jirasinghe and Lyons, 1996). This generalization is borne out by research findings from outside education (Ferrario, 1994).

The author's survey of all female secondary headteachers in England and Wales thus largely endorses earlier research, but although it is clear that the preferred management style of female headteachers is collaborative, there appears to be a minority of the heads for whom this is not true. Although the collaborative and people-oriented styles were endorsed by a majority, there were a considerable number of adjectives offered that were grouped as either 'autocratic/directive' or 'efficient'. This represents a proportion of headteachers who, through their choice of adjectives, identified their style of management as probably more akin to the masculine paradigm than the feminine. This style of management might be identified with some of the 'male' adjectives, such as 'disciplined', 'evaluative', 'formal' and 'competitive'.

In the given analysis, the adjectives were considered singly. When considering the adjectives in their groups of three, it was rare for all three to be grouped within the same theme. For example, 'efficient' adjectives might be combined with either 'people-oriented' or 'autocratic' adjectives. However, a dominant style was considered to be where at least two of the three adjectives came from either collaborative and people-oriented or from the autocratic/directive and efficient categories.

For those headteachers aged 49 or under, about 10 per cent chose at least two of their three words from the autocratic/directive style of management combined with the efficient style of management, but the proportion of those 50 or over doing so was just over 20 per cent. The tendency to be more collaborative may be linked with 'youth', and this appeared to be the case in earlier research with head-teachers (Weindling and Earley, 1987). Alternatively, a difference in style of the younger heads may be linked to a change in the expectations of what is required in headteachers in the last years of the twentieth century. Several of the heads interviewed by Hustler *et al.* (1995) indicated that their management style had moved towards being one of collaboration in keeping with 'a reformulated idea of the leading professional' (Thompson in ibid., p. 90). Hall (1996) comments on the need for a different style of headteacher to cope with the demands of the post-1988 reforms, and identifies that all six of the women heads she studied are different from their predecessors whether male or female. In addition, a more 'collegial' style of management is now generally considered to be normatively superior to other styles (Wallace, 1989; Bush, 1995), at least in Western cultures.

The final group of adjectives, termed 'values driven', represents a strand of thinking that is probably not separate from the others, but identifies the values that may well underpin the management style of many headteachers. The most common category of adjectives within this group referred to being 'visionary', the second to being 'fair' or 'honest'.

Overall, there appears to be a range of management styles indicated by the lists of adjectives provided, with one side of the spectrum occupied by the majority of the headteachers who adopt a 'collaborative' and 'people-oriented' style of management and the other side of the spectrum occupied by a minority of the headteachers operating an autocratic/directive style of management often linked to choice of the more 'efficient' adjectives. The 'values-driven' style may well underpin any or all of the other styles (see Figure 15.1).

Key values promoted in the school

The headteachers were also given an opportunity to indicate a free choice of the key values that they are trying to promote in the school. The respondents tended to

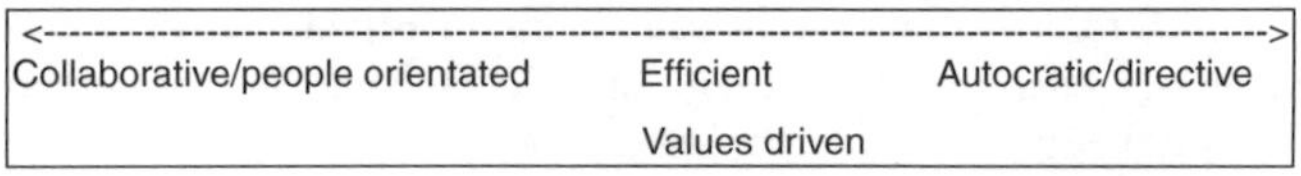

<--->		
Collaborative/people orientated	Efficient	Autocratic/directive
	Values driven	

Figure 15.1 Spectrum of styles of management

indicate phrases, rather than individual words. The sentiments that are included in the value statements can be divided into four areas.

1   *Academic excellence and educational achievement*   Many of the value statements mentioned academic achievement, sometimes in association with caring values:

'academic achievement in a caring community which develops all pupils for their own potential.'

'The pupils' learning is central.'

2   *The importance of every individual achieving their potential*   These statements are often linked to the importance of hard work:

'everyone committed to the success of each student.'

'everyone has the potential to achieve, but you must work hard to succeed.'

3   *Respect for self*   There was awareness of the need to promote:

'high self-esteem for all.'

'the importance of self-worth, and valuing others.'

4   *Respect and caring for others*   There was awareness in these statements of the need for: 'respect for individual differences; valuing others [pupils and staff]' and that: 'students should aim high, with compassion for those around them.'

The achievement of academic excellence could be considered an objective that is innate in the purpose of almost any school. This value is very much in accord with the key quality of strategic direction and development of the school outlined in the *National Standards for Headteachers* (TTA, 1998), in terms of the creation of an ethos and vision which will secure achievement by pupils. However, the remaining values identified are related to the qualities of caring and respect for individuals that the headteachers have already identified within the Gray (1993) paradigms, where the four most popular qualities – 'aware of individual differences', 'caring', 'intuitive' and 'tolerant' – were all drawn from the feminine paradigm.

The words listed in Table 15.3, are those that were mentioned most in all the statements about values from the headteachers. These words indicate the importance of both achievement and respect as key values – achievement sometimes, but not always, specifying learning, and respect including respect for self and for others, both individuals and the community.

Aspects of educational leadership can be seen very clearly in the key values that the headteachers in the survey were trying to promote in their schools, and these aspects also endorse the idea that women are particularly concerned with the teaching and learning aspects of their role in comparison with administrative or other responsibilities. There is no doubt that the two key value words used most frequently, 'achievement' and 'respect', are in keeping with the concept of educational leadership, and very much in line with existing research on the ways in which women in educational management operate (Gross and Trask, 1976; Shakeshaft, 1989, 1995; Hill and Ragland, 1995; Gold, 1996; Grogan, 1996; Kruger, 1996; Riehl and Lee, 1996). This research was concerned only with female secondary headteachers, and it may be that a survey of male colleagues would

Table 15.3 Words mentioned most often in
statements relating to key values
promoted in the school

Word	No. of times used
Achievement	126
Respect	123
Self	95
All	94
High/higher/highest	84
Care/caring	80
Value(s)/valued/valuing	80
Others	69
Learning	65
Individual(s)	56
Pupil(s)	52
Community	47

reveal that men too are moving towards a 'feminine' style of management and share many of the key values identified by the surveyed female headteachers.

Management in action

The headteachers were asked a limited range of questions relating to the practicalities of their style of management. In particular, they were asked about their availability to staff, and the amount of time they spent out of the office when in school. They were also asked about the ways in which they encouraged all teachers to develop their careers, and if there was any special way in which they tried to encourage the careers of female teachers.

The majority of headteachers seem to make themselves available to their staff whenever possible (see Table 15.4). The headteachers also appear to be visible in the school for quite a large proportion of their time (see Table 15.5). In answer to the question 'while you are in school, what proportion of your time do you spend out of your office?', approximately 80 per cent claimed that they spent between 10 and 50 per cent of their time in the school, but out of their office.

Most of the headteachers report that they spend a considerable proportion of their time out of their office. They were not asked how this time was spent, but presumably some of it would be in teaching and some would involve 'management by walking about'. When coupled with the information about the availability of the majority to talk to teachers, there would appear to be some evidence to support the dominant management style indicated by the majority of the headteachers. It seems that a large proportion of the headteachers consider that they operate in an open way and are highly involved with their staff and the operation of the school.

Encouragement of all teachers to develop their careers

Headteachers sought various ways to encourage teachers to develop their careers. Courses, appraisal and mentoring were the most often cited means, but 'other' ways were written in by 52.9 per cent of the respondents (see Table 15.6). Of those who indicated 'other', most stated that they were encouraging one-to-one meetings

Table 15.4 Opportunities for staff to talk to the
head (percentages)

Any time if not in meeting	84.3
Any time within specified limits	8.9
By appointment	6.8

Table 15.5 Time spent out of office

Under 10%	3.5
10–25%	32.0
26–50%	47.9
51–75%	16.6

Table 15.6 Means of encouraging
teachers to develop careers
(percentages)

Courses	87.2
Appraisal	69.6
Mentoring	65.7
Role play	3.0
Other	52.9

for all members of staff to discuss career planning. The meetings either took place with themselves as headteacher, with another member of the senior staff, the INSET coordinator, a consultant or an unspecified person. The general feeling was that it is 'very important to find time to have one-to-one conversations about individual strengths and needs.'

Other possibilities mentioned were career development opportunities inside and outside the school, and other, generally practical, means of encouragement such as practice interviews. The development opportunities included specific interventions: 'departmental monitoring, work shadowing, teacher placement.'

There was some indication of encouragement of development through means other than promotion such as: 'involvement in teams to develop projects'; 'opportunity for role rotation, being given support to lead initiatives (curriculum and pastoral).'

One headteacher specified the development opportunity that was available in a largely female school: 'taking on "acting" responsibilities during our frequent maternity absences.'

Since a minority of headteachers in England and Wales are women, they present important role models for other female teachers. The heads were asked if they particularly encouraged women teachers in their career progress. The largest single group responding to this question indicated that they did not treat women differently from men (see Table 15.7).

Some of the headteachers indicated more than one way in which they encouraged female teachers. The large proportion indicating 'No special ways' is actually greater than 46.6 per cent, since some of those commenting in the 'other' category reiterated that all staff were treated equally in their school (18.6 per cent)

Table 15.7 'How do you encourage female teachers in their career progress?' (percentages)

No special ways	46.6
Women-only courses	21.3
Mentoring	19.6
Other	37.2

or that staff were all treated according to the equal opportunities policy (4.2 per cent). A further 6.7 per cent stated that they pursued the same policies that they had indicated for the staff as a whole.

In addition, some of the headteachers of girls' schools commented in the 'other' comments that the question of treating female staff differently does not really arise for them, since the majority of their staff are women. Such comments accounted for about 10 per cent of those in the 'other' comments.

It is therefore likely that the majority of headteachers do not have any special policies with regard to the encouragement of female teachers. However, over 20 per cent do state that they encourage women through women-only courses and a similar proportion through mentoring. In addition, the largest proportion of comments written in as 'other' referred to specific encouragement of women. This encouragement often included the headteacher's own importance as a role model and, in some cases, referred to the doubts and lack of confidence evidenced by their women staff:

> 'Personal conversation: I always encouraged competent women, from being a scale 1 teacher onwards, making sure they see themselves as possible runners, and boosting their confidence.'

> 'Individual discussion, also with male staff, but I find many women, although very good, do not have confidence to put themselves forward for promotion. Three examples in my school spring to mind . . . '

The encouragement of women through being a role model was seen to be important, particularly in the context of the domestic role of women: 'I talk to them about the issues, making it clear I have children, etc. – i.e. trying to be a role model.' There was also awareness of the need to overcome stereotyping: 'There is a high percentage of female role models – SMT, heads of science and maths, etc.'

Finally, some of the encouragement specifically addressed to women was associated with issues such as the handling of maternity leave, and more radical suggestions to help women such as job-sharing:

> 'Being flexible about moves between part-time and full-time. Job shares (though not yet at present school).'

> 'Finding opportunities for responsibility in a variety of ways – particularly important for returners. Enhancing the role of positive women in whole-school issues.'

> 'Flexible return to work after maternity leave.'

Whilst there is a commitment to staff development as a whole, it would appear that a substantial minority of the headteachers are aware of a need to separately foster the career progress of women. However, it is only a small minority of the headteachers who have moved beyond courses and mentoring to actively encourage female staff in practical ways such as job-sharing and flexible work practices.

Male resentment of female leadership

Over half of the surveyed heads reported experiencing sexist attitudes from their male colleagues. This experience was reported more by those under 50, and those who were married and had children, in comparison with those who were single and childless. Similarly, the heads of girls' schools were less likely to report sexism from their peers than the heads of co-educational and boys' schools (see Table 15.8). These differences are statistically significant. It would appear that women who are married and who have children, particularly those working in co-educational schools, may be identified more strongly with a domestic stereotype and implicitly considered less able to lead and manage.

Once established as headteachers, they were strongly aware of the fact that men found difficulty in dealing with female leaders. Being patronized and feeling isolated were two common features of the experience of headship. The female heads also reported examples of stereotyping linked to their sex. Many comments express: 'difficulties with the concept of women as a boss'; some were more specific:

> 'I inherited a school with a good number of staff who didn't want a female head. The secretary and caretaker threatened to resign, some male teachers made it clear they didn't want a woman telling them what to do.'

Occasionally, the resentment is linked to disapproval of management style that is not seen as 'traditional': 'Some staff wanted as head a "big man who shouted" – I'm the opposite.' There was also expectation that females would manage in a certain way: 'The assumption was that you will be a female stereotype – keep changing one's mind, can't handle difficult male pupils, etc.'

Whilst the stereotype of the woman as a 'soft' manager predominates, there is evidence of a different range of stereotypes associated with women:

> 'the suggestion that career women are cold, hard and single-minded.'

> 'more a question of little bits of prejudice against single-woman role. Rumours seemed to vary: I'm assumed to be either a promiscuous heterosexual or a latent homosexual.'

The majority of the headteachers (62.7 per cent) stated that, as a woman, they had felt the need to 'prove their worth' in a management position. There was little difference in the proportion of women who felt this amongst those of differing age groups, but some differences between those of different marital status and those

Table 15.8 Percentage of heads stating they had experienced sexism from peers

Over 50	52.4	Children	57.7
Under 50	56.9	No children	51.1
Heads of		Married	55.7
girls' schools	47.7	Single	47.1
Heads of		Separated	35.7
other schools	57.7	Divorced	66.7

who headed girls-only schools, compared with the rest. The need to 'prove your worth' is felt more strongly by those with children, and less strongly by the single and heads of girls' schools. This difference may well be linked with the tendency to stereotype married women who are mothers with the domestic role, which was particularly evident in responses relating to discrimination linked to promotion. The largest category of responses to the question of the need to 'prove your worth' related to combating the range of stereotypes that are held about women in management.

Despite the range of stereotypes relating to female leadership, much of the resentment was linked to the softer, more participatory style of management of the female heads on the part of subordinate males who were used to a more decisive, autocratic style. The present research appears to replicate the findings from qualitative research in the UK (Hall, 1996) and quantitative work in the USA (Riehl and Lee, 1996) and Israel (Goldring and Chen, 1994), that there are considerable difficulties for some men in adjusting both to working for a woman and adapting to the preferred management style of most women.

The advantages in being a woman headteacher

The majority of the group surveyed have been successful in terms of a traditionally male career path, and some have adopted the norms associated with a career that takes little account of family life. Only 10 per cent identified 'being a woman' as a reason for success. By far the most frequent reason for success quoted was 'hard work', with support from others being the second most important reason. Both of these tend to indicate the difficulties that a woman may face in reaching a position of leadership, particularly when the leader is stereotypically expected to be a man. However, there are benefits in being a woman once head-ship has been achieved. Nearly two-thirds of the headteachers reported that they had found it an advantage to be a woman headteacher (see Table 15.9).

The most mentioned advantage was in terms of being able to defuse macho behaviour on the part of males: students, teachers and parents. In this case, the fact that men feel the need to be aggressive with other men, and that aggression is not associated with females, acts to their advantage. A number of the headteachers quite consciously acted up to the stereotype of femininity and played on the susceptibilities of males, such as governors or local authority personnel, who were likely to perceive them first and foremost as women.

Table 15.9 Advantages of being a woman headteacher

	% of total examples given
Able to defuse 'macho' behaviour	35.6
Being noticed	15.1
Not constrained by male stereotype	14.7
Approachable to women and girls	10.9
Using 'feminine guile'	7.7
Empathy and use of emotion	7.1
None	3.2
Head of girls' school	2.9
Other	2.9

Another advantage quoted by the headteachers was 'being noticed'. Since they were a relative rarity as a female, they tended to be offered opportunities, particularly by the local education authority. It is possible that a rise in the number of female headteachers, which would lead to a reduction in such opportunities, might therefore not be entirely welcomed by some of the heads.

The headteachers were positive about their gender in terms of their approachability. They felt that people, particularly girls, mothers and female members of staff, could approach them more freely than they might a man. In addition, they considered that they had the freedom to empathize with families and be sympathetic in a way that most men could not. Although the general assumption that the leader and manager is male may prove a handicap for the female manager, there is the other side of the coin, namely the freedom of the female manager to behave in a way that is not constrained by the normal stereotypes associated with leaders. It may be that being a woman in management allows some freedom (Hall, 1996) and gives the opportunity to the female headteacher to develop in fresh ways that are unencumbered by the perceptions of others. In addition, Grogan (1996) refers to the life experience of women, as wives and mothers, moulding them as administrators – the experience making them different from males in the same positions.

Conclusion

The survey of the entire population of female headteachers in England and Wales has contributed in a number of ways to the understanding of the management and leadership of women headteachers in the 1990s. The high response rate to the survey gives confidence in the validity of the findings and allows the possibility of some generalizations to complement existing and future qualitative research.

One of the major findings emerging from the research is the continuing discrimination that has been faced by women who are now senior managers in education. The experience of isolation and instances of sexism from peers, recounted by the headteachers, indicate that they are operating in a context which may be inimical to success unless women are prepared to adapt to the prevailing values. These might include opting for a single state, childlessness or working harder and longer than any competitors, male or female.

Many of the headteachers in the survey reported on their experience of resentment, on the part of males and some females, at being subject to female leadership. However, the majority also identify ways in which being a woman leader frees them from the stereotypes of male leadership. Both of these factors exemplify the differences in the context within which male and female headteachers operate, indicating the relevance of gender to the study of leadership and management.

The research strongly endorses the view that most women manage their schools in a way that can clearly be identified as consultative and people orientated. The majority of the headteachers, particularly those under 50, chose adjectives that identified them as collaborative and caring. The choices also endorsed the importance placed on teamwork and on 'power to' rather than 'power over'. However, they do not claim to be democratic, rather they say that the final responsibility for decisions rests with them. In reviewing effective management in schools, Bolam *et al.* (1993) commented that the headteacher of an effective school 'Has consultative "listening" style; is decisive and forceful but not dictatorial; is open to other people's ideas; and is easily accessible to staff' (p. 119).

The headteachers' choices of adjectives to describe their management style and values generally reflected and endorsed the findings of previous research. The predominant management style was collaborative and people centred. However, there is a small proportion of the heads for whom this is not true. About 15 per cent of the heads may be adopting, consciously or unconsciously, a style of management and leadership that may have more in common with elements of the more stereotypical 'masculine' style, which involves a more directive way of operating. The survey also endorses the tendency for women to be educational leaders, placing stress on the learning of their students rather than on the importance of administrative tasks. The values that the headteachers chose were indicative of the values of educational leaders, 'achievement and respect'.

Whilst the quality of leadership may best be judged within the context of the individual school, the majority of the surveyed heads operate in a manner that largely coincides with concepts of effective leadership in education. It was noted in the introduction that the under-representation of women in senior management in education constitutes an issue of equity. Since women tend to operate in a collaborative manner that is likely to empower others and endorse values of educational leadership, their under-representation also indicates a loss of potentially effective leadership in schools.

References

Adler, N. J. (1994). 'Competitive frontiers: women managing across borders', *Journal of Management Development*, **13**, 2, 24–41.

Adler, S., Laney, J. and Packer, M. (1993). *Managing Women: Feminism and Power in Educational Management*. Buckingham: Open University Press.

Bem, S. L. (1974). 'The measurement of psychological androgyny', *Journal of Consulting and Clinical Psychology*, **42**, 2, 155–62.

Blackmore, J. (1989). 'Educational leadership: a feminist critique and reconstruction.' In: Smyth, I. and John, W. (eds) *Critical Perspectives on Educational Leadership* (Deakin Studies in Education Series 2). Lewes: The Falmer Press.

Bolam, R., McMahon, A., Pocklington, K. and Weindling, D. (1993). *Effective Management in Schools: A Report for the Department for Education via the School Management Task Force Professional Working Party*. London: HMSO.

Bush, T. (1995). *Theories of Educational Management*. Second edn. London: Paul Chapman.

Coleman, M. (1996). 'The management style of female headteachers', *Educational Management and Administration*, **24**, 2, 163–74.

Evetts, J. (1994). *Becoming a Secondary Headteacher*. London: Cassell.

Ferrario, M. (1994). 'Women as managerial leaders.' In: Davidson, M. J. and Burke, R. J. (eds) *Women in Management: Current Research Issues*. London: Paul Chapman.

Gold, A. (1996). 'Women into educational management', *European Journal of Education*, **31**, 4, 419–33.

Goldring, E. and Chen, M. (1994). 'The feminization of the principalship in Israel: the trade-off between political power and cooperative leadership.' In: Marshall, C. (ed.) *The New Politics of Race and Gender*. London: The Falmer Press.

Grace, G. (1995). *School Leadership*. London: The Falmer Press.

Gray, H. L. (1989). 'Gender considerations in school management: masculine and feminine leadership styles.' In: Riches, C. and Morgan, C. (eds) *Human Resource Management in Education*. Milton Keynes: Open University Press.

Gray, H. L. (1993). 'Gender issues in management training.' In: Ozga, J. (ed.) *Women in Educational Management*. Buckingham: Open University Press.

Great Britain. Department for Education (1997). *Statistics of Education Teachers in England and Wales 1997*. London: Government Statistical Service.

Grogan, M. (1996). *Voices of Women Aspiring to the Superintendency*. Albany, NY: State University of New York Press.

Gross, N. and Trask, A. (1976). *The Sex Factor and the Management of Schools*. New York: John Wiley.

Hall, V. (1996). *Dancing on the Ceiling: A Study of Women Managers in Education*. London: Paul Chapman.

Hall, V. and Southworth, G. (1997). 'Headship', *School Leadership and Management*, **17**, 3, 151–70.

Hill, M. S. and Ragland, J. C. (1995). *Women as Educational Leaders: Opening Windows, Pushing Ceilings*. Thousand Oaks, CA: Corwin Press.

Hustler, D., Brighouse, T. and Ruddock, J. (eds) (1995). *Heeding Heads: Secondary Heads and Educational Commentators in Dialogue*. London: David Fulton.

Jirasinghe, D. and Lyons, G. (1996). *The Competent Head: A Job Analysis of Heads' Tasks and Personality Factors*. London: The Falmer Press.

Jones, A. (1987). *Leadership for Tomorrow's Schools*. Oxford: Blackwell.

Kruger, M. L. (1996). 'Gender issues in school headship: quality versus power?', *European Journal of Education*, **31**, 4, 447–61.

Ouston, J. (1993). *Women in Education Management*. Harlow: Longman.

Ozga, J. (ed.) (1993). *Women in Educational Management*. Buckingham: Open University Press.

Ribbins, P. (ed.) (1997). *Leaders and Leadership in the School, College and University*. London: Cassell.

Ribbins, P. and Marland, M. (1994). *Headship Matters*. Harlow: Longman.

Riehl, C. and Lee, V. E. (1996). 'Gender, organizations, and leadership.' In: Leithwood, K., Chapman, J., Corson, D., Hallinger, P. and Hart, A. (eds) *International Handbook of Educational Leadership and Administration*. Boston, MA: Kluwer Academic Publishers.

Shakeshaft, C. (1989). *Women in Educational Administration*. Newbury Park, CA: Sage.

Shakeshaft, C. (1995). 'Gender leadership style in educational organisations.' In: Limerick, B. and Lingard, B. (eds) *Gender and Changing Educational Management*. Rydalmere, NSW: Hodder Education.

Teacher Training Agency (TTA) (1998). *National Standards for Headteachers*. London: TTA.

Wallace, M. (1989). 'Towards a collegiate approach to curriculum management in primary and middle schools.' In: Preedy, M. (ed.) *Approaches to Curriculum Management*. Milton Keynes: Open University Press.

Weindling, D. and Earley, P. (1987). *Secondary Headship: The First Years*. Windsor: NFER-NELSON.

PART VI

TEACHING AND TEACHER EDUCATION

In this final part, a number of issues covered in earlier chapters recur. Teaching as a profession is demanding, its rapidly changing nature exerting considerable stresses on those who practise it. Sadly a number of teachers have been unable to cope with the heat and have left the profession or become ill. Some of these tensions are the result of normal pressures, which exist in any modern society, being magnified for those working in a caring profession.

The first chapter in this part, Chapter 16, is a good example of that, as it deals with attitudes towards race and racism. Any citizen can hold views about such a topic, but student and experienced teachers come under greater scrutiny, because they must actually work with people of all backgrounds and beliefs. Chris Wilkins looks at the personal values of trainee teachers as they confront the issue of race and racism during their training. Several students were confused or uncertain, though the majority were sympathetic to ethnic minorities, very few subscribing overtly to popular racial stereotypes. Nonetheless, there was a view that the training course spent too much time on issues such as racism, some students claiming they had switched off, or refused to attend certain sessions. The author concludes that most students want a fair and tolerant society, but feels that the restrictions imposed by national bodies that control the school and teacher training curriculum are a threat to anti-racist teaching.

Mentors play a vital role in the training of new teachers in schools, because their attitudes, values, beliefs and behaviour can influence the next generation for good or ill. In Chapter 17 in this section, Marion Jones describes how mentors in England and Germany see their roles. In both countries the mentors agreed that their role was more as adviser, rather than friend, or model. A significant difference, however, occurs in the case of assessment, because English mentors have to assess their students, whereas in Germany this is done by an external agency, thus welding mentor and student more closely together as fellow practitioners in the same school. German mentors say that they prefer the continuous type of assessment practised in England, because their own system involves an external assessor taking a snapshot, which they find less satisfactory way of appraising trainee teachers' classroom competence.

Whereas a few years ago teacher stress received relatively little attention, it has become a much more central topic since. Teaching became renowned as one of the more stressed occupations, when members of the profession began to retire early in large numbers, or fall victim to the many changes forced upon them by governments keen to improve standards of education. Chris Kyriacou has studied the topic for many years and in the final chapter in this collection he highlights the major sources of pressure. These include teaching the unmotivated, trying to keep order, time constraints and workload, rapid change, external evaluation and inspection, dealings with fellow teachers, low self-esteem and status, and poor working conditions. He concludes that schools can do a great deal to reduce stress through good communication, a strong sense of collegiality, consensus, positive feedback and praise, good resources and facilities, support with problems and reduced bureaucracy. All of these would aid teaching and learning in school, the central purpose of being a teacher in the first place.

CHAPTER 16

STUDENT TEACHERS AND ATTITUDES TOWARDS 'RACE'

The role of citizenship education in addressing racism through the curriculum

Chris Wilkins

Context

This research explores the attitudes of postgraduate student teachers in England to a broad range of issues relating to 'race' in the UK, the changing nature of racism in society and the role that education has to play in challenging racism. These findings emerge from a wider study looking at the students' notions of citizenship and the role of schooling in producing 'good citizens'. Those taking part in the study have mostly come to adulthood in the post-1979 era, in a climate of shifting social and political attitudes where collectivism has been largely portrayed as being discredited and the rhetoric of individualism – 'freedom, choice and opportunity' – dominates. For this generation, then, there appears to be a tension between growing up in a political culture which states that there 'is no such thing as society' and the expectation that they, as teachers, should promote civic virtues. The nature of living in a diverse multicultural society is clearly a significant issue explored within this study, and as such, many of the findings are of relevance for those directly concerned with 'race' and education.

The author is a teacher educator, teaching and researching in citizenship education, and is also a committed anti-racist educator adhering to a socially transformative model of education for citizenship. Naturally, therefore, the research is informed by this theoretical perspective. Researching in the social sciences is always a politically and socially embedded process (Epstein, 1993, pp. 6–7) and this study is no exception. Thus, it makes no spurious claim of 'objectivity', but argues from a standpoint of a political commitment to egalitarianism and social justice.

'Race' issues in citizenship education

For a decade or more, 'race' and other social justice issues have been viewed with caution by schools. In the UK, the Conservative Party's 'Back to Basics' agenda, which viewed education for equality as being incompatible with the pursuit of 'standards' and 'excellence', was enthusiastically endorsed by the Labour Party administration elected in 1997. Now, however, the climate has shifted. The Qualifications and Curriculum Authority (QCA), the statutory body responsible for the review of the National Curriculum, has endorsed the majority of the key recommendations of the Crick Report (Advisory Group on Education for Citizenship and the Teaching of Democracy in Schools [AGECTDS], 1998) into the teaching of citizenship in schools, and recommended that citizenship education should feature more prominently in schools (QCA, 1999). Citizenship education clearly has links with issues of social justice, and so it is significant that the guidelines have been released in the same year as the report of the MacPherson Inquiry into the racist murder of Stephen Lawrence, giving official credence to the presence of institutional racism in UK society (MacPherson, 1999).

The Crick Report, in accepting that citizenship and representative democracy occupy a contested space, goes much further than earlier National Curriculum guidance (National Curriculum Council [NCC], 1990). In outlining 'needs and aims', it sets out some of the tensions and conflicts within UK society, and acknowledges the 'democratic deficit', the widespread alienation of young from the civic sphere. This view is supported by numerous studies of social attitudes over the past decade (Wilkinson and Mulgan, 1995; Crewe, 1996; Jowell *et al.*, 1996). However, despite the shift in wider political discourse inspired by the MacPherson Report, the Crick Report is conspicuous in its avoidance of personal, institutional and structural racism. The reasons for this may well be strategic, tailored for the approval of a Secretary of State for Education keen to avoid conflict with educational conservatives. However, it is a trend consistent with the 'deracialisation' of educational policy, the subsuming of 'race' amidst a range of other social categories and reducing racism to the level of individual ignorance and prejudice (Gillborn, 1995, p. 33). As a result, whilst racism clearly remains a significant problem in UK society, there is no explicit encouragement for schools to challenge racist attitudes, and the issue of institutional racism raised by MacPherson is effectively sidestepped (Skinner and MacCullum, 2000, p. 150).

The Crick Report does make reference to the need for promoting tolerance and diversity, with an emphasis on combating personal prejudice, and aims 'to find or restore a sense of common citizenship, a national identity secure enough to find a place for the plurality of nations, culture, ethnic identities and religions long found in the United Kingdom' (AGECTDS, 1998, p. 17). However, the Report relies on some problematic assumptions, particularly that which sets out different citizenship priorities for different ethnic groups; whilst 'majorities' 'must respect, understand and tolerate minorities', 'minorities' 'must learn and respect the laws, codes and conventions as much as the majority' (1998, pp. 17–18). These statements not only distinguish, 'minority cultures' by their *difference* from a presumed majority (i.e. white, Anglo-Saxon), but also *problematise* them. The assumption is that there is a particular need to inculcate 'mainstream' social values, and that minorities are burdened by the need to learn the ways of the 'host culture'. Overall, the Crick Report suggests that racism is due to simple ignorance and prejudice, that through teaching about 'other cultures', the white majority will come to understand (and so respect and tolerate) minorities.

This view of the relationship between social values and schooling is cited in the particular political philosophy of liberalism. It has been argued that the central concept of liberal social ideology is that of *equality of opportunity*, emphasising 'the enhancement of *individual* life-chances not on the diminution of *group* inequalities' (Jeffcoate, 1984, p. 186). For Jeffcoate, the classroom is essentially a neutral arena in which tolerance can be fostered by understanding, and through the personal enlightenment that ensues, equality of opportunity can be achieved. The most striking example of this philosophy in practice has been that of multicultural education, which to a degree permeates the entire National Curriculum, and is embodied in the Crick Report and the QCA recommendations for the teaching of citizenship (AGECTDS, 1998; QCA, 1999). The background to the development of multicultural education practice has clear messages for those examining the role of citizenship education and its potential for challenging racism.

In the late 1970s and early 1980s, multicultural education emerged in the wake of mounting evidence of the failure of the education system to educate ethnic minority children as well as white indigenous ones (Stone, 1981). It marked a change of emphasis in establishment attitudes towards ethnic minorities; from one of *assimilation*, the expectation that immigrants should adopt the lifestyle of the indigenous population, to one of *integration*, where cultural pluralism would prevail in an atmosphere of mutual respect and understanding. In the classroom, the 'neutral chair' position of the teacher dominates this approach, and cultural study is based on a largely anthropological examination of the external features of 'other' cultures, frequently through the medium of religion (Parekh, 1986, pp. 26–27).

Multiculturalism, exemplified by the highly influential Swann Report (Department of Education and Science [DES], 1985), has been fiercely attacked from both left and right. The political right have focused on its cultural relativism (Scruton, 1986, p. 132), whilst anti-racist educators (Cole, 1989) employ a broadly Marxist perspective to argue that, like class and gender, 'race' operates structurally in a capitalist society. However, it should be stressed that this political and academic debate has scarcely made any inroads into the classroom; where schools give attention to issues of ethnicity and culture, multiculturalism still dominates.

Many commentators, citing the work of Barker (1981), have argued that the 1980s saw a reconceptualisation of racism. This 'new racism' shifted the emphasis from the 'biological racism' of negative stereotyping and prejudice to a 'cultural racism', motivated by a desire to maintain a perceived 'British identity' and exclude those whose culture is considered 'alien' (Short and Carrington, 1996, pp. 65–66).

Whilst acknowledging the complexity of the culture dimension of racism, viewed from an anti-racist perspective, racism is more than individual prejudices reproduced through institutions; it is cited in the structure of the capitalist state, and no amount of prejudice reduction will alter this (Cole, 1992, p. 250). Whereas for the multiculturalist, racism is synonymous with prejudice, for the anti-racist, racism is prejudice *plus* social power. Anti-racist educators have been frequently criticised for ignoring cultural racism at the expense of a class-based analysis of institutionalised biological racism (Mohood, 1992, p. 75). This is a debate that has been exhaustively explored elsewhere (see, for instance, Cole, 1997, 1998), and clearly remains a contested notion. The place of culture in anti-racist education is analysed at a theoretical level (see e.g. Cole, 1998, pp. 28–42), and in terms of practical policy application, both in schools and in teacher education (Hillcole Group, 1991, 1997; Hill *et al.*, 1997; Hill and Cole, 1998). In fact, possibly the most persuasive challenge to multicultural education has been based not on theoretical *structure*, but on *content*.

The 'cultural anthropology' approach, with its concentration on safe cultural sites – food, music and clothing (frequently satirised as 'The 3Ss – Steel bands, Saris and Samosas' [Bhavnani and Bhavnani, 1985, p. 203]) – is both patronising and ineffective. This 'cultural tourism' *reinforces* stereotypes instead of challenging them by its emphasis on that which is 'different' (Carrington and Short, 1996). This limitation of multiculturalism has been discussed widely in recent decades (Modgil *et al.*, 1986; Cole, 1992, 1998; Troyna, 1993). Unfortunately, this narrow vision persists in the Crick Report, which aspires to cultural homogeneity, emphasises the problematic nature of cultural diversity and focuses on young people's sense of alienation from the civic discourse rather than actually address the issues which *cause* this alienation.

The research

The first stage of research was a questionnaire survey sent to students beginning their one-year full-time Postgraduate Certificate in Education (PGCE) courses (both primary and secondary) at two of the largest teacher education institutions in England. The total completed questionnaires received was 418, a response rate of approximately 62.5 per cent. In this questionnaire, the students were questioned about their attitudes to a wide range of issues, such as political affiliation and action to welfare and wealth redistribution, class, 'race' and gender issues, environmentalism, etc.

One of the principal techniques used in analysing the questionnaire data is the use of attitude scales, where a range of items relating to particular topics is compounded to produce a 'scale score'. This approach to social attitudinal studies is a common one, and by combining scores from large sets of items (up to fifteen separate questions within a common theme), looks beyond context-specific responses to individual questions and identifies core values. A significant example of this approach to research is the British Social Attitudes research project, a large-scale annual research project now well into its second decade (Jowell *et al.*, 1996). Two sets of questions used by the BSA were used in this project, and others in a modified form, in order to provide comparison with this robust longitudinal research data. Altogether, eleven attitude scales were produced in order to provide a wide-ranging portrait of the students' individual world-view; the issues covered are as follows:

- *Authoritarianism–libertarianism* – a range of items examining general moral issues;
- *Left–Right* – attitudes towards redistribution and social justice;
- *Race relations and racism* – perceptions of levels and causes of racism;
- *Gender* – the role of women (at home and at work);
- *Environmentalism* – relationship between science and technology and environment;
- *Environmental lifestyle* – way in which own life is affected by environmental concerns;
- *Sexuality* – tolerance of homosexuality in a variety of public spheres;
- *Education issues* – range of education-related items (selection, religion in schools, etc.);
- *Life control* – factors affecting 'success in life';
- *Drug issues* – permissiveness towards legal and illegal drugs;
- *Abortion* – acceptability of abortion in range of circumstances.

The questionnaire data, having been analysed, were used to frame a series of semi-structured interviews with respondents. A small sample of twenty-six students were randomly selected from those returning the questionnaire, and these students were interviewed at two stages of their course; towards the end of the first term and after the completion of their PGCE year, that is at the end of the third term. The first set of interviews focused on the broader social attitudes and values identified through the questionnaire, and the students were invited to expand on the responses given. Respondents also discussed their motivation for entering teaching and how they saw the role of the teacher in relation to their social world-view. The second set of interviews focused more narrowly on the students' notions of citizenship education, their experience of dealing with the subject in their training institution and on school placements, and the extent to which they felt prepared to teach the subject in their future career. This chapter concentrates on the findings relating to 'race' and racism, discussing the responses to the questionnaire items which refer to this issue (see Tables 16.2–16.9) and the subsequent exploration of these in the semi-structured interviews. A report of the broader findings, particularly in relation to notions of citizenship, is published elsewhere (Wilkins, 1999).

The students

The demographic characteristics of the students responding to the questionnaire closely match the national picture for postgraduate student teachers, in terms of age, gender and ethnicity (Graduate Teacher Training Registry [GTTR], 1996). Approaching 70 per cent are women (the gender balance was close to 50–50 amongst secondary students), and as can be seen from Table 16.1, there were large numbers of mature students, reflecting the national trend in recent years of a relatively older intake. In analysis of the data collected, age was a significant variable affecting social attitudes across a broad range of issues, particularly in directly political areas such as attitudes to 'race' and racism (Wilkins, 1999, pp. 218–220).

The initial teacher education sector in the UK has a very poor record in attracting ethnic minority students, and this sample unfortunately reflects the national recruitment pattern (Tables 16.2 and 16.3). This problem has been recognised for

Table 16.1 Age of respondents

Age	Frequency	%
23 and under	244	58
24–28	100	24
29 and over	74	18

Table 16.2 Ethnic identification

Self-identification of respondent	No. of respondents	%
White UK	376	90
Asian Indian	6	1
Asian Pakistani	3	1
Asian Bangladeshi	1	<1
Asian Chinese	2	1
Black UK Afro-Caribbean	6	2
Black UK Asian	3	1
Black UK Chinese	3	1
Other	18	4
Total	418	

Table 16.3 Breakdown of those responding 'other' in Table 16.2

Self-identification of respondent	No. of respondents	%
White European	1	6
White non-European	10	59
Arabic	3	18
'Mixed race' UK	2	12
Welsh	1	6
No response	1	6
Total	18	

Note:
The categories included are those used by GTTR on their application forms.

many years, and was acknowledged as such by the influential Swann Report (DES, 1983), yet recruitment patterns have remained largely unchanged (see, for instance, GTTR, 1996). The proportions were very similar at both institutions, despite the fact that one is based in a region with one of the largest ethnic minority populations in the UK. Clearly, this has an impact on the research, given the nature of the issues discussed, although the demographic profile of this cohort broadly represents that of the teaching profession in the UK today, and therefore it is possible to draw tentative inferences from the views expressed in this cohort about wider views amongst entrants to the profession.

Discussion of findings

Attitudes to 'race'

Analysis of the questionnaire responses clearly indicates that most students are aware of racism as a major social issue, with over half agreeing with the view that there was 'a lot' of racism towards British-Asian and British-Afro-Caribbean people (Table 16.4). This matches other research findings from the last decade (see Young, 1992), and is consistent with responses to other statements, such as those exploring perceptions of racism in the criminal justice system (see Table 16.7 and Table 16.8(c) and (d)).

However, when the responses are examined more closely, a more complex pattern emerges. When asked in the questionnaire about whether they thought the amount of racism in Britain was increasing or decreasing, almost one-third of the samples were unable to answer, and those who could respond gave no clear picture (Table 16.5).

When we look further, a clear contradiction can be detected in the responses to a number of the questions raised in this study, as illustrated by the results in Table 16.6. Although a clear majority acknowledge the existence of racism in British society, only around a quarter of the sample categorically acknowledge institutional racism in certain key areas, stating that they thought the state gave 'too little' help to black people, in terms of housing, employment, etc. Almost 40 per cent of the sample gave an uncertain response to this question, whilst a small number (6.5 per cent) believe the state gives too *much* support to black people. The significance of this group (there appears to be a small minority (a core of around 5 per cent) of the sample who consistently have a negative or hostile attitude towards black people) is discussed later.

Table 16.4 Racism in Britain (% response)

	A lot	A little	Hardly any	Not sure
Racism towards Asian people	58	35	2	5
Racism towards African-Caribbean people	52	37	6	6

Table 16.5 Change in levels of racism (% response)

More than 5 years ago	The same	Less than 5 years ago	Not sure
14	32	26	28

Table 16.6 State help to black people (% response)

Too much	About right	Too little	Not sure
7	29	28	37

The issue of racism is an emotive one and almost all the students interviewed held strong views of one kind or another, with the majority seeing racism as an objectionable phenomenon caused largely by ignorance and fear. There was a strong feeling that there was a generational factor in operation. A number of the students argued that younger people were much more likely to be tolerant of people of different cultural or ethnic backgrounds, although this does appear to contradict the questionnaire results about changing levels of racism. These had indicated a feeling that racism had *not* significantly declined over recent years, which logically would have been the case if Britons were becoming progressively more tolerant. Suspicion amongst the white community of those with different lifestyles was undoubtedly seen as the primary cause of racism:

> I guess they feel threatened . . . mainly, it happens because of the way race gets used as an excuse, and black people end up as the scapegoats, people think that they are going to lose their jobs . . . they get scared, and some people will use colour as a way out, of explaining things . . . but there is also just the thing about being different.

For most of these students, a major reason for this fear and prejudice was simply the lack of exposure to diverse cultural experiences, and many explicitly stated that through the very fact of Britain becoming a more multicultural and ethnically diverse society, a reduction in this prejudice would result:

> it's just ignorance really, lack of exposure to other cultural influences. If you only hear about people second-hand, you tend to end up with stereotypes, with a really exaggerated, one-sided view . . . I went to school in South London, so always spent a lot of time with other cultures . . . I think I have a

Table 16.7 Race and criminal justice system: suppose two people, one
white and one black, each appear in court charged with
a crime they did not commit. What do you think are their
chances of being found guilty? (% response)

White person more likely to be found guilty	Both have same chance	Black person more likely to be found guilty
4	33	63

> reasonable insight . . . I don't think a lot of white people have any idea what
> it's like to be black in this country.
>   I think younger people are different, mainly because they've been brought
> up in multiracial communities, they've had black friends and been to school
> with them since they can remember, you know? We don't have the same hang
> ups . . . so they're trying to fuel the fires and whip up votes . . . it might cause
> resentment with a few, but most people see through it.

Although a significant number of the students referred in the questionnaire
responses to institutional manifestations, such as the injustices inherent within
the criminal justice system (see Table 16.7), the emphasis when exploring the issue
through interviews seemed to rest more on personal prejudice. Of course, these
interviews took place before the MacPherson Inquiry, and responses may well
be significantly different now. However, on current evidence, the views of the students interviewed are strikingly in accord with that of curriculum guidelines for
citizenship education, that racism is most effectively tackled at an individual level.
      The limitations of this individualised view are clear. It does little to challenge,
and can indeed reinforce stereotypes; there is little to suggest that the anthropological study of the world's major religious faiths, or the use of literature from non-
European and non-white cultures has had a significant impact on racism in Britain
(Gaine, 1995, pp. 2–3). Yet, the assumption that prolonged exposure to other cultural influences, the mere fact of living in a multicultural society, is itself sufficient
to promote understanding and a harmonious environment was widespread
amongst the students interviewed. Only one student made explicit links with socio-
economic factors, comparing the relatively harmonious state of race relations in
their teaching placement school with the more troubled experience of a time spent
in a school before beginning their training:

> It's obviously an economic thing. The school where I am now, it's very middle
> class, a very nice part of [*placement city*], top of the league table [published
> standardised academic test results] . . . the school in [*home town*] was
> innercity, and bottom of the league tables . . . The PSE [*Personal, Social
> Education*] thing, in our school, it's a very good department, and I'm not sure
> how the school in [*home town*] dealt with PSE, citizenship, I'm not sure there
> was any . . . also, the mix was different, the number of ethnic minorities was
> much higher in [*home town*].

The interviews did include a small number of responses in respect of attitudes to
'race' and culture from students whose views were disturbing. One primary student,
who had attended university in a city with a large non-white population, expressed
openly hostile attitudes towards the British Asian community. The bulk of the

interview revolved around the issue of race relations as it was obviously a particularly resonant one for this student. Many of the views were openly racist, and would be considered by most teachers as completely unacceptable in their profession, following a fairly standard line of racist rhetoric about black people being largely responsible for crime, and for a failure to integrate into the host community:

> they make it clear, [*home town*] Asians are Asian, they have absolutely no bones about it . . . about half of them will *not* speak English. You've got a lot of children that are UK-born Asians and they are the ones we have a lot of problems with . . . because they want the best of both worlds. They're going to have difficulties integrating properly because they can't choose.

This perceived attitude of young Asians was in turn cited as the cause of resentment and fear amongst the white population:

> They're afraid when they're on the streets. But mainly they resent them because they don't work. None of them work, they all live off the State . . . basically it's just two different cultures that clash. They just can't mix.

Another student displayed a strong resentment against what they saw as the favourable treatment given to ethnic minorities:

> I think one of the big causes of trouble in recent years, is . . . the government is racist towards white people, in some ways . . . I mean, where I lived, we tried to get money for a youth club, and the Council wouldn't give it to us, they said they hadn't got the money . . . but, next thing, they gave a load of money for an Asian community centre, and no whites were allowed in . . . definitely think that positive discrimination has gone too far . . . some coloured people tend to get a chip on their shoulder about racism, and all this PC [*political correctness*] makes them worse.

Clearly, the views of these students are extreme ones, although they do represent a small but distinct minority strand within the larger cohort, supporting the findings of an earlier survey with student teachers (Cohen, 1989). The questionnaire responses relating to issues of 'race' (and a range of other social issues: gender, sexual morality, etc.) seem to indicate a small minority whose world view contrasts strongly with the generally pluralist, 'inclusive' social attitudes and values of the majority (Table 16.8).

The fact that 1 in 10 students agreed that 'the number of black people living in Britain causes unemployment problems', and almost as many made the link with black people and crime levels is deeply disturbing. Possibly even more so is that a quarter feel that 'people of different races living together inevitably leads to tension' and that 'black people do not make enough effort to embrace British culture'.

The views expressed by these students stem not from the 'new cultural racism' described by Barker (1981), but demonstrate the persistence of the 'old' biological racism of negative stereotypes and 'signifiers of difference', mirroring research in the late 1980s amongst school-age children in the 1980s (Gaine, 1995, pp. 2–8). Whilst the views of this small minority are clearly worrying, the widespread perception of racism as being a matter of personal prejudice caused by ignorance may be of more significant concern in the long term. This perception implicitly suggests that racial harmony and social justice in British society will somehow

Table 16.8 Race relations (% response)

	Agree	Neither agree nor disagree	Disagree	Not sure
(a) People of different races living together inevitably leads to tension	24	15	59	2
(b) Right-wing extremists are largely responsible for increasing racial tension	52	17	22	9
(c) The police are prejudiced against black people	37	28	28	7
(d) The police do not take racist attacks seriously enough	49	14	24	13
(e) The number of black people living in Britain causes unemployment problems	12	12	73	3
(f) White people are too suspicious of people who are different	53	22	23	2
(g) Black people do not make enough effort to embrace British culture	23	25	47	6
(h) Black people are largely responsible for the increase in crime	8	11	77	4
(i) Negative stereotyping in the media is a major cause of racist attitudes	57	17	20	6
(j) Positive discrimination in favour of ethnic minorities has gone too far, causing resentment amongst white people	37	23	32	9
(k) Many black people are still denied opportunities in life because of racism	69	9	15	7

evolve naturally through the process of cultural exposure, by the very fact that people of different ethnic backgrounds are living in close proximity, they will automatically become more tolerant. This view, fostered by the traditional multicultural approach of education through cultural understanding, is clearly not borne out by evidence of this study, which suggests that without an understanding of the social structures which create the individual prejudice through which racism is manifested, teachers are unlikely to play a major part in challenging racism. Teachers must be equipped to challenge the causes of racism, not simply the symptoms.

The 'political correctness backlash'

The responses to this section of the questionnaire suggest a considerable degree of ambivalence about the issue of 'race'. This must be set in the context of the political climate of recent years, and in particular, the educational debate, with a distinct shift from the broadly progressive, egalitarian approach of the 1970s and the traditionalist agenda of the 1980s. The tone of the debate in recent years has often been confrontational, with successive governments hostile to the 'progressive' (generally egalitarian, socially transformative) approach of the educational establishment. This hostility has been supported in the media and in popular culture; 'PC-bashing', since the early 1980s, when regular tabloid press 'loony-left scandals' of 'positive discrimination' were uncovered. 'Race spies', children banned from singing 'Baa, Baa, Black Sheep' and a host of other stories from this era are now part of the popular mythology of 'progressive education'. Mythology is a deliberately chosen term, for the vast majority of stories were either complete fabrications or grossly distorted versions, promoted in a media sympathetic to the agenda of the radical right. The assault on egalitarianism in education began with the Black Papers in the 1970s and was continued throughout the 1980s by groups such as the Hillgate Group (see, e.g. Palmer, 1986), in what has been described as a 'discourse of derision' (Balls, 1990, pp. 32–42).

The cultural shift has been profound and long-lasting. At the time of writing, Section 28, the discriminatory law inhibiting free discussion of homosexuality in schools (His Majesty's Stationery Office [HMSO], 1989), is still in place, twenty-two years after its introduction. Meanwhile, the current Secretary of State for Education makes no secret of his distaste for any concern in education outside the narrow context of the raising of academic standards. It is not surprising, perhaps, that in this climate, the issue of 'political correctness' is high amongst the concerns of the students interviewed in this research.

Several comment on being exposed to 'too much stuff about equality', both during their own schooling and during their PGCE course. One student commented on anti-sexist and anti-racist ideas being 'shoved down his throat', and felt that most students held similar views:

> it was always one or two students getting involved, and the rest either just . . . switched off . . . or being hostile . . . by not turning up for sessions, not taking part, or by making facetious comments, or just rejecting whatever came their way.

For this generation of student teachers, this shift in political culture appears to have had a measurable effect, even amongst those individuals whose general world view is broadly sympathetic towards a 'liberal-progressive' model of education. Interestingly, however, Table 16.9 highlights a disparity between the respondents' attitudes towards 'positive discrimination' when applied to different issues. Whereas over a third of respondents feel that there is 'too much' discrimination in favour of black people, less than one in six feel the same way about discrimination

Table 16.9 Attitudes towards 'positive discrimination' (% response)

	Agree	Neither agree nor disagree	Disagree	Not sure
Positive discrimination in favour of ethnic minorities has gone too far, causing resentment amongst white people	37	23	32	9
Positive discrimination in favour of women has gone too far, causing resentment amongst men	16	24	53	7

in favour of women. This, of course, might simply be caused by the fact that this cohort, whilst overwhelmingly white, is also predominantly female.

Implications

Despite the evidence of problematic social attitudes from a small minority of this cohort of student teachers, this study suggests that the majority of respondents are fundamentally predisposed towards a society based on mutual respect and tolerance. However, there is little indication of a deeper understanding of the social processes that create and reinforce racism. Teachers clearly need this understanding in order to challenge it through their teaching. For teacher educators, this must give cause for concern, given the ever-increasing pressures within initial teacher training where there is precious little time for exploring the social contexts of education in a way that will develop this understanding amongst students. In England, the recently introduced National Curriculum for Initial Teacher Training, dominated by the 'deficit model' of the standards set out in Circular 4/98 (Department for Education and Employment [DfEE], 1998), effectively restricts the critical reflective dimension in favour of a narrowly functionalist model of professional induction. The students taking part in this research felt constrained by the rigours of their training, and it seems inevitable that this will become more apparent as student teachers work in an increasingly demanding training environment.

However, this political climate of teacher training contrasts somewhat with the wider issues currently under debate, where education for citizenship and values is a central concern. With the 'social agenda' of schooling high on the national policy agenda, the relevance of the findings reported here is obvious, when set against the findings of the MacPherson (1999) and Crick Reports (AGECTDS, 1998). Education for citizenship should be concerned with negotiating the tension between the desire for social cohesion, the strengthening of 'civic bonds', and the need to incorporate the complex and diverse demands of a pluralist society. Anti-racism should be a key focus for citizenship education. The evidence of this study might point towards a cautious optimism, in that most respondents are fundamentally predisposed towards a society based on mutual respect. However, the presence of a significant minority displaying intolerant values, together with the ambivalence of a larger portion of the sample to other key indicators, suggest that this is an issue which requires careful consideration by initial teacher training institutions.

Initial teacher education should aim to foster a critically reflective approach to all aspects of the curriculum, especially themes such as citizenship, which lie within the social domain. After a period where the political climate has made it difficult for teachers to seriously address issues of structural social inequalities, the tide has begun to turn. The Crick committee report has raised the profile of the social role of schooling, and so provides an opportunity for schools to address social issues in a systematic way through the curriculum. However, the anti-racist agenda appears to have been sidelined in order to make citizenship education more palatable.

This research clearly indicates the danger of this approach. If teachers are not encouraged to confront issues such as racism, and are supported through their training to develop a critically reflective approach to social issues in education, then it is unlikely that an anti-racist dimension will be consistently incorporated into classroom practice. This lesson was conclusively learnt as a result of the MacDonald Inquiry into the racist murder of 14-year-old Ahmed Iqbal Ullah. The Report concluded that school policies predicated on the belief that racism was the manifestation of individual prejudices rather than 'institutional' were 'symbolic rather than real' and therefore doomed to failure (MacDonald *et al.*, 1989, pp. 346–347). Similarly, teacher education has consistently failed to take account of the needs of students in both the structure and content of its provision in respect of issues of 'race', gender and class issues (see, e.g. Commission for Racial Equality [CRE], 1989; Menter, 1989; Clay *et al.*, 1991; Siraj-Blatchford, 1993).

Teacher recruitment and retention from ethnic minorities is as important an issue as the nature and scope of the curriculum. However, whilst the number of black students entering teacher education remains at its present level, then the anti-racist message will struggle to be heard, and black students will continue to be a marginalised minority, often facing openly racist attitudes and practices (Siraj-Blatchford, 1993, pp. 29–30). A multifaceted approach is needed, with a greater commitment at national and institutional level to widen access to teacher education, a change in institutional ethos to incorporate this wider base of entrant, and a teacher education curriculum based on a critically transformative notion of education; one which sees the role of the teacher as a 'transformative intellectual' (Hill, 1989, pp. 21–22). Whilst these concerns may seem out of step with the political climate in which the Teacher Training Agency (TTA)[1] operates, models for good anti-racist practice in education do exist, and these are extensively reviewed elsewhere (Clay and George, 1993; Gaine, 1995). The introduction of the QCA guidelines (QCA, 1999) for the teaching of citizenship provides a shift in emphasis, and whilst they minimise the relationship between citizenship education and anti-racist education, there is a clear opportunity for educators to address both issues in a coherent way.

However, whilst teacher education struggles to balance the need for students to develop critical reflectiveness and the mechanistic demands of the TTA, a radical approach is unlikely to permeate into schools. As with teacher education institutions, schools need to address the aims of anti-racism and citizenship education through a holistic approach to school organisation and management, ethos and curriculum. This was the message of the MacDonald Inquiry into the murder of Ahmed Iqbal Ullah (MacDonald *et al.*, 1989), and is confirmed by the major study into the management and practice of schools in addressing racism (Gillborn, 1995). The findings of this research indicate that whilst the introduction of the National Curriculum and the increased standardisation of academic testing in schools offer little encouragement to those engaged in anti-racist education, many teachers remain committed to the pursuit of egalitarianism and social justice through education (Gillborn, 1995, pp. 191–192). Through building strong links with local communities to address local concerns, through placing 'managing for change' at the centre of the school structure, incorporating the socially transformative agenda of schooling into both staff development and curriculum planning, it is possible to work even within the highly restrictive culture of education today.

Clearly this is an ambitious agenda, and one which requires a highly committed teaching profession prepared to engage critically with the policy issues presented to them. However, this simply reinforces the need to focus on these challenging issues in teacher education. Teacher education should address citizenship as a contested notion that confronts issues of social inequality and injustice head-on. As teacher educators, we need to engage our students with the sometimes conflictual nature of society and to enable them to see themselves as social agents of change. Only then can citizenship education be employed as a tool for change, enabling children to see *themselves* as social agents who will shape society in future generations.

Note

1   The TTA is the Government organisation with responsibility for teacher recruitment and training.

References

Advisory Group on Education for Citizenship and the Teaching of Democracy in Schools (AGECTDS) (1998) *Education for Citizenship and the Teaching of Democracy in Schools* (London, Qualifications and Curriculum Authority).

Balls, S. J. (1990) *Politics and Policy Making in Education: Explorations in Policy Sociology* (London, Routledge).

Barker, M. (1981) *The New Racism* (London, Junction Books).

Bhavnani, K. K. and Bhavnani, R. (1985) Racism and resistance in Britain, in: D. Coates, G. Johnston and R. Bush (eds) *A Socialist Anatomy of Britain* (Cambridge, Polity Press).

Carrington, B. and Short, G. (1996) Who counts; who cares? *Educational Studies*, 22 (2), pp. 203–224.

Clay, J. and George, R. (1993) *Moving beyond Permeation: Courses in Teacher Education* (Buckingham, Open University Press).

Clay, J., Gadhia, S. and Wilkins, C. (1991) Racism and institutional inertia: a 3D perspective of initial teacher education (disillusionment, disaffection and despair), *Multicultural Teaching*, 12.

Cohen, L. (1989) Ignorance, not hostility: student teachers' perceptions of ethnic minorities in Britain, in: G. Verma (ed.) *Education for All: A Landmark in Pluralism* (Lewes, Falmer Press).

Cole, M. (1989) Class, gender and 'race', in: M. Cole (ed.) (1989) *Education for Equality: Some Guidelines for Good Practice* (London, Routledge).

Cole, M. (1992) British values, liberal values or values of justice and equality: three approaches to education in multicultural Britain, in: J. Lynch, C. Modgil and S. Modgil (eds) *Cultural Diversity and the Schools, vol. 3: Equity or Excellence? Education and Cultural Reproduction* (London, Falmer Press).

Cole, M. (1997) Equality and primary education: what are the conceptual issues? in M. Cole, D. Hill and S. Shan (eds) (1997) *Promoting Equality in Primary Schools* (London, Cassell).

Cole, M. (1998) Racism, reconstructed multiculturalism and antiracist education, *Cambridge Journal of Education*, 28, pp. 37–48.

Commission for Racial Equality (CRE) (1989) *Words or Deeds? A Review of Equal Opportunities Policies in Higher Education* (London, CRE).

Crewe, I. (1996) *Political Communications: The General Election Campaign of 1992* (Cambridge, Cambridge University Press).

Department for Education and Employment (DfEE) (1998) *Teaching: High Status, High Standards: Requirements for Courses of Initial Teacher Training* (London, DfEE).

Department of Education and Science (DES) (1983) *Education for All* (London, HMSO).

Department of Education and Science (DES) (1985) *Education for All: Final Report of the Committee of inquiry into the Education of Children from Minority Groups* (London, HMSO).

Epstein, D. (1993) *Changing Classroom Cultures: Antiracism, Politics and Schools* (Stoke-on-Trent, Trentham Books).

Gaine, C. (1995) *Still No Problem Here* (Stoke-on-Trent, Trentham Books).

Gillborn, D. (1995) *Racism and Antiracism in Real Schools* (Buckingham, Open University Press).

Graduate Teacher Training Registry (GTTR) (1996) *Annual Statistical Report* (Cheltenham, GTTR).

Her Majesty's Stationery Office (1989) *Local Government and Housing Act* (London, HMSO).

Hill, D. (1989) *Charge of the Right Brigade: The Radical Right's Attack on Teacher Education* (Brighton, Institute of Education Policy Studies).

Hill, D. and Cole, M. (eds) (1998) *Promoting Equality in Secondary Schools* (London, Cassell).

Hill, D., Cole, M. and Shan, S. (eds) (1997) *Promoting Equality in Primary Schools* (London, Cassell).

Hillcole Group (1991) *Changing the Future: Redprint for Education* (London, Tuffnell Press).

Hillcole Group (1997) *Rethinking Education and Democracy: A Socialist Alternative for the Twenty-First Century* (London, Tuffnell Press).

Jeffcoate, R. (1984) *Education and Cultural Pluralism* (Lewes, Falmer Press).

Jowell, R., Curtice, J., Brook, L. and Ahrendt, D. (eds) (1996) *British Social Attitudes: The 13th Report* (Aldershot, Gower).

MacDonald, I., Bhavnani, T., Khan, L. and John, G. (1989) *The Burnage Report: Murder in the Playground* (London, Longsight Press).

MacPherson, W. (1999) *The Stephen Lawrence Inquiry* (London, HMSO).

Menter, I. (1989) Teaching practice stasis: racism, sexism and school experience in initial teacher education, *British Journal of Sociology*, 10, pp. 459–473.

Modgil, S., Verma, G., Mallick, K. and Modgil, C. (1986) *Multicultural Education: The Interminable Debate* (Lewes, Falmer Press).

Mohood, T. (1992) On not being white in Britain: discrimination, diversity and commonality, in: M. Leicester and M. Taylor (eds) *Ethics, Ethnicity and Education* (London, Kogan Page).

National Curriculum Council (NCC) (1990) *Curriculum Guidance 8: Education for Citizenship* (London, NCC).

Palmer, F. (ed.) (1986) *Antiracism – an assault on education and value* (London, Sherwood Press).

Parekh, B. (1986) The concept of multicultural education, in: S. Modgil, G. Verma, K. Mallick and C. Modgil (eds) *Multicultural Education: The Interminable Debate* (Lewes, Falmer Press).

Qualifications and Curriculum Authority (QCA) (1999) *The Review of the National Curriculum in England, the Secretary of State's Proposals* (London, QCA).

Scruton, R. (1986) The myth of cultural relativism, in: F. Palmer (ed.) *Antiracism: An Assault on Education and Values* (London, The Sherwood Press).

Short, G. and Carrington, B. (1996) Antiracist education, multiculturalism and the new racism, *Educational Review*, 48, pp. 65–77.

Siraj-Blatchford, I. (ed.) (1993) *'Race', Gender and the Education of Teachers* (Buckingham, Open University Press).

Skinner, G. and MacCullum, A. (2000) Values education, citizenship and the challenge of cultural diversity, in: R. Bailey (ed.) (2000) *Teaching Values and Citizenship across the Curriculum: Educating Children for the World* (London, Kogan Page).

Stone, M. (1981) *The Education of the Black Child in Britain: The Myth of Multiracial Education* (London, Fontana).

Troyna, B. (1993) *Racism and Education: Research Perspectives* (Buckingham, Open University Press).

Wilkins, C. (1999) Making 'good citizens': the social and political attitudes of PGCE students, *Oxford Review of Education*, 25, pp. 217–230.

Wilkinson, H. and Mulgan, G. (1995) *Freedom's Children: Work, Relationships and Politics for 18–34 year olds in Britain today* (London, Demos).

Young, K. (1992) Class, race and opportunity, in: R. Jowell, L. Brook, G. Prior and B. Taylor (eds) British Social Attitudes: the 9th report (London, SCPR).

CHAPTER 17

MENTORS' PERCEPTIONS OF THEIR ROLES IN SCHOOL-BASED TEACHER TRAINING IN ENGLAND AND GERMANY

Marion Jones

Introduction

In England as in Germany, mentoring constitutes a central element in the partnership established between schools and training institution. But there is no agreement on the precise interpretation of this role. Definitions range from simply 'being there' (Feiman-Nemser *et al.*, 1993) to providing 'active assistance for student teachers' (Tomlinson, 1995). The conceptual framework underpinning this study draws on research and documents concerned with the role of the mentor in relation to trainee teachers and their professional development rather than the often additionally assigned role of 'bureaucrat' or 'supervisor' (Watkins and Whalley, 1993).

In Germany, the idea of preparing professionals is central to the training process of beginning teachers and is described as 'preparatory service for teaching' (*Vorbereitungs-dienst für das Lehramt*). The philosophy underpinning this model is centred on the concept of developing reflective professionals rather than training in a technical sense which focuses on the learning of new skills (Ballantyne *et al.*, 1995, p. 301), and as such it provides the framework for 'a relationship based on mutual trust and respect' (Bolam *et al.*, 1996, p. 44) that 'bind mentor and intern together' (Abell *et al.*, 1995, p. 179). In England, however, the role of the mentor is more diverse and can be located within different conceptual paradigms which are reflected in the three models of mentoring presented by Maynard and Furlong (1993):

- the 'apprenticeship model' within which the mentor acts as the master teacher to be emulated;
- the 'competence model' according to which the mentor relates training and assessment to pre-determined standards of practice;
- the 'reflective model' within which the mentor adopts the role of the 'critical friend' who assists in the evaluation of teaching.

Aims and objectives of this study

During the past ten years mentoring in school-based teacher training in England has undergone dramatic changes concomitant with the challenge of new duties and responsibilities. The new diversity and complexity of the mentor role has increased the potential for conflicts to arise between the different aspects of mentoring. It is therefore the purpose of this study to investigate mentors' perceptions of their role in England and Germany in order to gain a better understanding of how the different aspects of mentoring affect their relationship with, and the professional development of, trainee teachers. By identifying similarities and differences in mentors' behaviour and their understanding of themselves as participants in the training process, answers are sought to the following questions.

1   How do English and German mentors perceive their respective roles?
2   What aspects of similarity and difference can be identified between the two systems?
3   In what way and to what extent do aspects of the mentor role enhance or impair the professional development of trainee teachers?

Method

The sample

The sample of mentors was composed as follows:

- twenty-five English mentors from state comprehensive schools in partnership with Edge Hill College of Higher Education;
- twenty-five German mentors from *Hauptschulen* (non-selective state secondary schools) linked with teacher training institutions (*Lehrerseminare*) in Baden-Württemberg and Bavaria, Germany.

The selection of the sample was guided by practical considerations such as gaining access to data within the constraints of time, funding and logistics and was based on the fact that the model of school-based teacher training for the *Hauptschule* is more akin to the programme of Initial Teacher Training in England than that of the selective *Realschule* (technical orientation) or the *Gymnasium* (grammar school) (Kappler and Reichart, 1996).

Data collection

In order to obtain responses to the research questions a qualitative approach was adopted. Information on mentors' perceptions of their roles was gathered by means of questionnaires consisting of structured and open-ended questions. All fifty questionnaires were completed and the anonymity of respondents' identities was assured by use of pseudonyms in the form of English and German forenames. Through recorded interviews with a small group of volunteers it was hoped to gain a deeper insight into mentors' written responses. Supplementary information was gathered by means of informal group discussion with mentors in England and Germany and documentary evidence such as guidelines on assessment criteria and procedures. The collection of data in England was relatively unproblematic. In my role as college tutor I had unrestricted access to the mentors in our partner schools and enjoyed their trust and support. In contrast, a complex operation was required in Germany. By employing the strategy of snowball sampling (Cohen and Manion, 1994), I took advantage of contacts I had established with colleagues, mentors and trainee teachers at a teacher training institution during a previous visit, when I investigated trainee teachers' perspectives of school-based training (Jones, 2000). In order to complete the collection of data within the four days allocated, I arranged meetings with individual mentors in schools, public places and at home, at their convenience. By accommodating their individual preferences regarding the time and venue of the interview I assumed that the respondents' cooperation would be enhanced, but was equally aware of the need to make some further investment in terms of a reciprocal arrangement to secure their trust. In an effort to achieve this ambitious goal I adopted the strategy of providing some common ground between myself and my respondents. This was intended to serve as a basis for establishing the level of rapport and trust required to express their views and feelings freely without fear of possible repercussions or misunderstandings on my part. In sharing personal information about my cultural background and professional experience as a teacher and mentor I hoped that the respondents would be able to perceive me in the role of fellow professional rather than the researcher from England.

Data analysis

The analysis of data centred on two key aspects: the mentor role and mentor attributes. In Questions 1 and 2 of the questionnaire mentors were asked to select from a list of roles, those which they felt they performed and to identify mentor attributes which they believed to have a positive influence on their relationships with the trainee teacher. To avoid the omission of relevant information as a result of a predetermined conceptual framework reflecting the researcher's bias, mentors were asked to list any additional roles or attributes they considered important but which were not included in the questionnaire. Applying the principle of 'selection by frequency', mentor roles and attributes within each sample were placed in rank order according to their cumulative scores (Tables 17.1 and 17.2). In Question 3 mentors were asked to identify factors that had a negative influence on their relationship

Table 17.1 Perceived mentor roles (selection by frequency)

English sample (25 mentors)	Ranking	German sample (25 mentors)
Adviser (24)	1	*Berater* (adviser) (24)
Trainer (22)	2	*Kollege* (colleague) (22)
Assessor (19)	3	*Partner* (partner) (17)
Counsellor (17)	4	*Lehrer* (teacher) (12)
Model (17)		
Colleague (12)	5	*Beurteiler* (evaluator) (11)
Teacher (10)	6	*Vorbild* (model) (10)
Partner (7)	7	*Ausbilder* (trainer) (7)
		Freund (friend) (7)
Friend (5)	8	*Ansprechpartner** (sounding board) (6)
Supporter* (1)	9	*Betreuer* (coach) (4)
	10	*Begleiter* (companion) (3)
	11	*Prüfer* (assessor) (1)

Note:
* Cited in addition to the range of roles provided.

Table 17.2 Mentor attributes that enhance the trainee–mentor relationship (selection by frequency)

English mentors (25)	Rank order	German mentors (25)
Support (25)	1	*Ehrlichkeit* (honesty) (20)
Constructive criticism (22)	2	*Konstruktive Kritik* (constructive criticism) (18)
Practical experience (12)	3	*Kollegialität* (collegiality) (15)
Patience (9) Honesty (9) Collegiality (9)	4	*Fachkompetenz* (subject competence) (13)
Reliability (8)	5	*Unterstützung* (support) (11) *Toleranz* (tolerance) (11) *Zuverlässigkeit* (reliability) (11)
Organisational skill (7)	6	*Erfahrung* (experience) (10)
Tolerance (4)	7	*Sinn für Humor* (sense of humour) (6)
Sense of humour (3)	8	*Geduld* (patience) (4)
Status within the school (0)	9	*Status in der Schule* (status within the school) (0) *Organisationstalent* (organisational skill) (0)

with trainees, while in Question 4 they were invited to make suggestions as to how these shortcomings could be minimised. While the structured approach in Questions 1 and 2 produced a clear indication of the differences and similarities of mentors' perceptions in each sample, Questions 3 and 4 in combination with individual interviews and group discussion offered the scope to explore their individual experiences and opinions further and thus provide the depth and detail required for the interpretation of the data.

Limitations

Having spent the first half of my life in Germany, I have had extensive experience of the German education system as a pupil, university student and trainee teacher. To a similar extent, although in different capacities, I have been involved in English education for an equally long period as a trainee teacher, teacher, mentor and PGCE tutor. As a result of my bicultural background I have acquired the linguistic, cultural and professional knowledge and understanding that allows me to gain access to both systems with relative ease and to approach the research question from more than one perspective. However, I was not complacent in thinking that this dual perspective could guarantee the absence of bias and that the collection and interpretation of data would be unaffected by my own preconceived ideas and opinions I had acquired through my experiences in the two cultural settings. In order to minimise the influence of my bias on the research process and enhance the validity and reliability of findings I adopted the following strategies.

First, all respondents were assured of their anonymity, informed about the purpose of the study and given a brief description of my biographical background. For, in the same way as the researcher's bias can influence the reliability of data, the respondents may provide information through a filter coloured by their relationship with the researcher. I was aware that the way in which the English mentors responded to me as the researcher could not be entirely free from their perceptions of me as the college tutor and colleague with whom they had been working in partnership for several years. In contrast, for their German counterparts I represented the researcher from higher education and the foreigner from England. By assuring respondents that their identities would be protected, I hoped to minimise the effect of over-familiarity on the one hand and lack of familiarity on the other and to ensure that they would trust me sufficiently to forward accurate, reliable information.

Second, data collection (questionnaire, interview, informal discussion) was not exclusively determined by the researcher's conceptual framework but provided opportunities for additional data to emerge. This strategy was of particular importance in connection with the mentor roles provided in Question 1 of the questionnaire, where literal translation failed to provide a reliable tool in the mapping of culturally specific concepts. For example, the translation of the term 'counsellor' presented itself as problematic. As the literal translation of '*Berater*' (Langenscheidt, 1995) denotes the role of 'adviser', it is not associated with the concept of 'counselling' as it is understood by the English language community. A relative modern concept, it is located in the domain of social support services that provide counselling for emotional and personal problems, but is not used in the context of professional development and learning. Instead, the term '*Betreuer*' was included in the German list of mentor roles, approximating the concept of 'coach' or, according to the dictionary definition, describing a person 'who looks after someone' (*der sich um jemanden kümmert*) (Wahrig, 1997). It is interesting to note that only four mentors perceived themselves in this role.

Similar to 'counselling', the concept of 'partnership' had to be examined more closely in relation to the different cultural and professional contexts to establish the extent to which an equation of the term across cultural and professional boundaries could be problematic. While in England the concept of 'partnership' plays a key role in the contractual arrangement that exists between a school and the higher education institution, in Germany it is understood to provide the basis for a collaborative relationship between trainee and mentor. To avoid any misinterpretations it was pointed out to both samples of respondents that the items listed on the questionnaire referred exclusively to those roles mentors believed themselves to perform in relation to their trainee teachers.

While the two samples of participants involved in this cross-cultural study cannot generate the breadth of data required to represent all mentors' perceptions in England and Germany, they can at least provide us with an insight into their experiences within the trainee–mentor relationship. Owing to the limitations of this study the findings are not unique. However, they synchronise with and reflect other research undertaken in the field of mentoring in school-based teacher training (Wildman, 1992; Feiman-Nemser *et al.*, 1993; McIntyre and Haggar, 1993; Maynard and Furlong, 1993; Dormer, 1994; McLaughlin, 1994; Abell *et al.*, 1995; Ballantyne *et al.*, 1995; Lee and Wilkes, 1995; Yau, 1995; Veenman *et al.*, 1998).

Fieldwork findings and discussion

Through the comparison of scores attached to individual mentor roles and attributes (Tables 17.1 and 17.2) areas of congruency as well as of divergence become apparent. The data suggest that mentoring is perceived as a role that can be defined generically across cultural boundaries, but at the same time bears culturally specific traits which manifest themselves in the way emphasis is placed on different aspects inherent in the mentor role. The study focuses on those roles and attributes where a high correlation or divergence of scores can provide the ground for critical discussion. Mentors' position within the training partnership as well as the professional knowledge to which they refer in their work with trainee teachers are examined in relation to the way in which they perceive themselves as mentors. Furthermore, by giving them a voice in the form of direct speech statements, findings are presented from their perspectives and used in the interpretation of data against the backdrop of the professional framework and cultural setting within which they operate. By adopting a multi-faceted, cross-cultural approach it is the aim of this study that the conclusions drawn are used to generate discussion in relation to aspects which have been identified as problematic and are considered in the evaluation of our policies and practices employed in school-based teacher training in England.

Advising constructively and critically

In both samples 'adviser' emerges as the role most frequently quoted, reflecting the findings of a previous study in which trainee teachers in England and Germany reached a similar consensus (Jones, 2000). German mentors in particular describe the role of adviser as enjoyable in terms of sharing professional experience and expertise with the trainee, while English mentors perceive it as essential in the light of problems that can arise in their absence.

> Mary: Students who did not have a mentor . . . did not know who to go to when they wanted advice. And no member of staff is willing to sit down . . . giving them advice or whatever.

The high correlation between English and German mentors' scores of 'adviser' is mirrored by the frequency with which 'constructive criticism' is cited as the second most important mentor attribute. Trainee teachers regardless of their cultural background consider this an essential ingredient in their preparation for teaching (Jones, 2000), although closer analysis reveals differences in interpretation. While mentors in England place emphasis on 'support', their German counterparts stress the importance of being 'honest'. The divergence in mentor perceptions illustrates the tension inherent in the mentor role, which manifests itself in the way in which mentors manage to balance the elements of 'honesty' and 'support'.

> Mary: It is very hard . . . to be positive without not being honest. There is a fine line between being positive and being critical and being honest.
>
> Angelika: *Bei einer Fortbildung sollten wir Kriterien aufstellen – und da kam genau dieser Punkt an die erste Stelle: die Ehrlichkeit ist das ganz Entscheidende.*
> (At a training seminar we were asked to devise criteria – and this point was identified as the most important one: honesty is of the highest priority.)
>
> Andreas: *Die 'konstruktive Kritik' . . . man muss auch jemandem wirklich auch mal was sagen können, ganz ehrlich sagen können.*
> ('Constructive criticism' . . . it must be possible to tell them something, tell them in all honesty.)

Lending support honestly

Generally, though, all mentors regardless of their cultural background believe that 'constructive criticism' is a prerequisite in the learning process. However, they differ in their views on how it is to be dispensed. In contrast to their German counterparts, English mentors tend to propagate the importance of being supportive over being honest. The inversion of the respective scores attached to these attributes suggests that within each cultural context 'honesty' and 'support' occupy different positions of value and relevance. As pointed out by Tomlinson, 'getting on with people, helping them and working with them are activities that people (perhaps especially the British) have traditionally tended to take for granted' (1995, p. 58). This may not equally be the case in Germany where criticism is generally expressed more generously and frankly than in England.

In addition to socio-cultural idiosyncrasies, structural factors are equally significant in influencing the trainee–mentor relationship. For example, in England the role of 'assessor' can generate tension in the mentor–trainee relationship, particularly when assessment is closely related to predetermined outcomes. This is less likely to occur in Germany where the concept of collaborative partnership provides the key ingredient. In order to alleviate anxieties experienced by the trainee, mentors in England may be particularly supportive and may be more reluctant than their German counterparts in being honest with their trainees. It would be misleading, though, to assume that being supportive equates with acting as a 'friend', for both English and German mentors award this role little significance. And yet, the importance of the social aspect in the mentor–trainee relationship must not be underestimated. In this sense Tickle (1993) attribute the affective dimension of learning equal weighting with the technical skills required. But as Abell explains, 'in general, mentors view their job as taking "the raw goods" that university sends them and helping fledgling teachers develop and evolve into a finished product' (Abell *et al.*, 1995, p. 178). The idea of having to deliver the 'finished product' exerts pressure on English mentors. Throughout the training process they are aware of the fact that the quality of their trainees is monitored, evaluated and assessed in relation to the standards laid out in DfEE *Circular* 4/98. The conflict arising out of the different demands made on the mentor is particularly poignant in the English system as the following comments illustrate:

> Jane: Yes, you can be friendly to them, but at the same time there is a certain distance between you, because obviously . . . you are their teacher in a way.
>
> Keith: It is very difficult working with a student who is not working hard enough. It is difficult to be friendly when you are responsible for them.

According to these statements the concept of 'friend' should be understood in terms of the concept of a 'critical friend' (Crossland, 1991) or 'listening friend' (Nolder *et al.*, 1994), someone who is prepared to support a trainee's professional development through the provision of honest, constructive criticism.

The model to be discussed

Although 'modelling' is not perceived to be one of the more dominant aspects of mentoring, it is understood to play a part in the development of basic teaching skills and setting of standards in professional behaviour.

> Keith: Well, there are some basic skills and practices which are recognised as being more successful than others. And if you can just concentrate on those, at least initially, and then see how things progress from there.

Heinz: *Das ist mir wichtig Vorbild im dienstlichen Verhalten.*
(That is important to me, a model in professional behaviour.)

At the same time, mentors are aware of their limitations in performing the role of 'model' adequately and take a sceptical view of a model of learning that is based on emulation of the experienced practitioner. German mentors are particularly concerned when this approach is used in conjunction with a catalogue of pre-scribed competences, providing a recipe for good practice, a *Rezeptologie* as one *Seminardirektor* (Director of training institution) described it. Such a manual gives guidance in the employment of strategies and techniques in a linear, technicist fash-ion, but leaves little scope for the development of flexibility, creativity and initia-tive. The value of such an approach remains questionable, as it discourages trainees from taking risks through experimentation and developing their own the-ories on the basis of critical reflection. The following comments reflect English and German mentors' reluctance to assume authority over the rights and wrongs in teaching and instead advocate diversity of style and approach.

Keith: Every teacher teaches differently and I don't want to push any of the points.

Asked whether she considers herself a role model, one German mentor declines categorically.

Birgit: *Das hasse ich. Mein Problem ist zu sagen: 'Mach das. Das ist richtig.' Das würde ich nie sagen. Ich hab' da immer meine Bedenken. Ich glaube, das tut keiner von uns.*
(I hate that. My problem is to say: 'Do that. This is right.' I would never say that. I always have my reservations. I don't believe any of us does that.)

In contrast, mentors who do perceive themselves as 'model' present a differentiated view of modelling by locating it within specific stages of the training process.

Mary: Certainly in the first, the Serial Practice, you are providing a model. Frequently, I have a student watching me. You aren't going to give good lessons every time. But certainly I will draw attention to the mistakes, where do you think I went wrong? What do you think I could have done? So, partly I am a model for discussion and hopefully give them some ideas.

Helga: *Und genauso wichtig finde ich auch, dass man mal einen schlechteren Stil an den Tag legt, dass sie das auch mal sieht, einfach. Und dann kann man hinterher das durchdiskutieren, einfach, dass sie genau sieht, aha, das war jetzt frontal, da hat überhaupt keiner mehr aufgepasst.*
(And equally important I believe is when one does not perform as well, that she [the trainee] simply sees this as well. And then this can be discussed after-wards, so that she can see exactly, ah, that was talking at the pupils, nobody paid attention any longer.)

Mary's interpretation of her role promotes a realistic rather than an idealistic concept of modelling and should serve mentors as a warning against playing 'the role of "craft master" of old who usually produced replicas of himself rather than independent and reflective practice' (Adams and Tusiewicz, 1995, p. 30). There is also the danger of trainee teachers over-emphasising the role of the 'model', as the following comment illustrates:

> Heinz: *Hier gibt es Spannungsfelder, weil viele Lehramtsanwärter glauben, sie könnten über reines Beobachten sich das aneignen.*
> (There are areas of tension here, because many trainee teachers believe that they can acquire that simply through observation.)

So far English and German mentors have reached a high level of consensus. They express a clear preference for performing the role of 'adviser', but adopt a cautious view in respect of acting as the trainee's 'friend' or 'model'. Further examination of data will, however, reveal that their perceptions diverge significantly where the roles of 'trainer', 'partner' and 'assessor' are concerned.

Partners within the partnership

Although the concept of 'partnership' occupies a central position in both training systems, it involves different agents. While in England it is primarily defined on the basis of a contractual arrangement that exists between school and training institution, in Germany mentors use the term to describe their relationship with the trainee teacher in the learning process rather than with the visiting tutor from the associated training institution. Their main concern is the trainee's development and welfare, although they may have some influence in the production of the final practice report, if required. Consequently, their position in the overall organisation and delivery of the training programme as well as in the assessment of teaching competence is rather peripheral. Unlike their English counterparts, they are not expected to engage in collaboration with representatives of the validating body, the *Seminar*, but their opinion and judgement may be sought depending on the quality of individual relationships that have been established between mentor and tutor. Within this framework the German mentors perceive their main task to be in supporting trainees in the practical aspects of their professional development which can best be achieved by adopting a partnership approach.

> Angelika: *Also am optimalsten ist er, wenn er eigentlich mehr . . . wie ein Partner ist. Weil dann fruchtet die Arbeit . . . , also ist am effektivsten.*
> (Well, the maximum effect is achieved when he [the trainee] is more of . . . a partner. Because then the work pays off . . . , is at its most effective.)

Similarly, the significance of using the appropriate form of address, formal versus informal, emphasising the element of collegiality that is to be developed is explained by another mentor.

> Andreas: *'Die Sie-Form! Ja, wir haben in einer Fortbildung auch darüber gesprochen. Etwa 80% der Betreuungslehrer sagen, "wir sind Kollegen, wir gehen auf die Du-Form", während der Seminarleiter ja grundsätzlich immer in der Sie-Form bleibt.'*
> (The *Sie* address! Yes, we also discussed this at one of our in-service training sessions. About 80% of mentors say 'we are colleagues, we use the *Du* address', whereas the *Seminar* tutor always and in principle maintains the *Sie* address.)

In England where the statutory framework allocates to the mentor the status of 'assessor' and to the trainee that of 'the one to be assessed', a minority of mentors perceive themselves as the trainee's partner. In contrast, almost three-quarters of the German sample identify themselves with this role. One of the reasons for these divergent views may be related to the fact that the assessment of trainee teachers in Germany is conducted and controlled exclusively by agents external to the school, a process which generally strengthens a school's *esprit de corps*, uniting mentors and trainee teachers alike. Another explanation might be sought in the way in which German teachers attach particular importance to the principles of collegiality and equality, key characteristics of a profession that is structured in terms of teachers' years of experience rather than according to a hierarchy of managerial responsibilities or appraised competence. The findings of this study indicate that English mentors are less likely to perceive their trainees as colleagues, which is not surprising in view of the differences in status that exist between trainee teachers in England and in Germany. First, unlike their German counterparts, English trainees are assessed by their mentor, although not exclusively so. Second, the pupils they teach are 'on loan' from other colleagues or from the mentor, while trainee teachers in Germany bear sole responsibility for the classes they are allocated and receive adequate remuneration for services rendered (Ministerium für Kultus und Sport Baden-Württemberg, 1984; Staatsministerium für Unterricht, Kultus, Wissenschaft und Kunst, 1987). The essential weakness of such a mentorship model is highlighted by Adams and Tusiewicz (1995, p. 43) in that it places the trainee in the 'client' position in another's territory at a disadvantage resulting in 'an uneven distribution of power'. Consequently, feelings of dependency and inferiority can impair the mentor–trainee relationship as described by an English trainee teacher in Chai Kim Yau's study: 'At the end of the day it is going to be her [the mentor] . . . you just get the feeling she's the person to suck up to . . . she's the one' (1995, p. 46). It remains to be seen in what way the recent introduction of a training salary for postgraduate trainee teachers in England to take effect from September 2000 will affect their status as perceived by themselves and their mentors and to what extent it will influence the relationship between them.

Similar feelings of concern are expressed by German trainee teachers in relation to their *Seminar* tutor acting as their assessor (Jones, 2000), providing corroborating evidence in support of the argument that there is a need to develop a more democratic model of learning within the mentor–trainee relationship. In this vein McIntyre and Haggar (1993) propose a concept of 'developed mentoring' which promotes the effective use of teachers' expertise for the development of 'collaborative teaching' (1993, p. 94). Such an approach not only consists of modelling effective teaching behaviour, but involves the sharing of ideas, resources and cooperative planning (Ballantyne *et al.*, 1995, p. 300). In this sense, German mentors perceive themselves as '*Begleiter*' (companion) and '*Ansprechpartner*' (someone who is there to listen to you), approximating Feiman-Nemser's notion of the 'active listener' or 'sounding board for novices' ideas' (1993), as someone who first and foremost has the responsibility to promote reflection, not as 'a trainer in routinised skill and knack' (McLaughlin, 1994, p. 151).

The mentor as assessor – conflicting roles

In contrast to English mentors who rate assessment as one of their main responsibilities, their German counterparts ascribe minor importance to these roles.

> Angelika: *Bewerten und benoten . . . und prüfen tun wir überhaupt nicht.* (Awarding grades . . . and examining is not at all what we do.)

Consequently, their attention is primarily focused on the learning process itself and on providing evaluative feedback and support.

> Jutta: *Da spricht man zwar bewertend, aber wir haben überhaupt keinen Einfluss auf irgendwelche Noten.*
> (True, we use evaluation in our talks [with the *Seminar tutor*] but we don't have any influence on any grades.)

While in England emphasis is placed on the aspect of continuity with regard to learning and assessment, the German system segregates these processes in terms of time, place and personnel. It distinguishes between informal evaluation for the purpose of diagnosis, target setting and measuring of progress by the mentor, and formal, summative assessment by the *Seminar* tutor and external examiners. English mentors, however, believe that their direct involvement in assessment is vital in order to maximise reliability and accuracy in the assessment of trainees' competence.

> Jane: We have a pretty good picture of what the student is achieving.
>
> Mary: It is not fair to judge someone on three, four or five lessons. And there is a lot more to schools and to training than just the occasional lesson.

Although German mentors are obliged to provide feedback on their trainees' overall performance to the *Seminar* tutor, it is not guaranteed that their comment will influence the final grade. Furthermore, the grade awarded for teaching competence does not provide a differentiated picture of a trainee's competence as it relies on a snapshot impression obtained on the day of the exam (*Lehrprobe*). Ironically, it is the mentor who could provide detailed information on a trainee's typical performance and enhance the consistency of evidence produced that is excluded from the assessment process. The following comment reflects the dissatisfaction felt over this procedure:

> Birgit: *So wie das bei uns ist, finde ich nicht sehr gut. Einfach deswegen, weil von den Lehrproben auch sehr viel abhängt . . . Und es kommt sehr viel darauf an, was für ein Thema ich hab' in dieser Stunde. Und was hatte die Klasse davor? Aber hier ist es ja nicht einmal eine Durchschnittsnote, sondern es ist ja die letzte. Hier ist es der LB, der das bewertet und ein Schulrat, der mich noch nie gesehen hat. Die Mentoren haben da gar nichts mitzureden . . . Man hat einen unheimlichen Stress.*
> (I don't find it good, the way it is here. Simply because a lot depends on these practical exams [lesson observation] . . . And a lot depends on the topic I have been given for this lesson. And what did the class have before? But here it is not the average grade, but it is the final grade. Here it is the tutor, who does the assessment and an external examiner who has never seen me before. Mentors have no say in it. The stress is enormous.)

Most German mentors agree that continuous assessment as practised in England is preferable to the 'snapshot' approach.

> Heinz: *Also ich finde so eine Langzeitbeobachtung, egal wer nun letztendlich die Note festlegt . . . für die ehrlichere . . . humanere Art . . . und zuverlässiger, denn diese nervliche Belastung ist extrem hoch.*
> (Well, I find continuous assessment, regardless of who is the assessor, . . . more honest . . . humane . . . and reliable, for the stress is extremely high.)

Apart from incorporating the aspect of continuity, assessment in England is based on a wide range of perspectives including those of all the individuals contributing to the training process; that of the mentor who also takes into account other teachers' evaluations of the trainee's performance with their classes; as well as that of the Professional Mentor whose assessment is of a more general, less subject-specific nature. Last, but certainly not least, the visiting tutor from the higher education institution in partnership with the school plays a significant role in the coordination and moderation of the final report, bearing ultimate responsibility for the quality of the validation process. In spite of the different perspectives that can thus be accommodated in an attempt to enhance the accuracy of assessment, English mentors' opinion is not quite as unanimous as may be expected. While the majority welcome their direct involvement in the assessment of trainees, only one mentor would like to disassociate herself from this responsibility and would prefer it if visiting tutors did the 'dirty work'.

In contrast, their German counterparts are unanimous in their verdict that the aspect of assessment impairs the quality of mentoring. Not only do they believe that it has a detrimental effect on their relationship with the trainee, they also fear that it restricts trainees in developing their own style and creativity owing to fear of assessment. Similar feelings are expressed by mentors in a study conducted by Dormer (1994, p. 130). They claim that assessment undermines the relationship with trainees, as they are not able to admit weaknesses. Furthermore, the potential value of the so-called 'bad lessons' highlighted by Bramaed *et al.* (1994, p. 156) could be jeopardised.

> Gisela: *Für mich ist es sehr angenehm, wirklich als Berater/Partner . . . da zu sein . . . , das heißt, der Lehramtsanwärter darf wirklich ausprobieren und darf Fehler machen.*
> (For me it is very pleasant, really to be there as an adviser/partner; that is, the trainee teacher can really try out things and make mistakes.)

Those English mentors who justify their role as 'assessor' from a pedagogical point of view also welcome the increased status and influence they associated with it.

> Keith: It's an ideal situation to see how successful a teacher is. It certainly makes it more, as if you were doing a worthwhile job. At least you have a say in what happens with the student. I think that the mentor needs to feel that he is doing something important and that what he says or does will affect some kind of decision.

> Jane: You are judging all the time. And I think that you are able to do that. Yes, I suppose it does make your position important . . . and I think, because they actually spend so much time in school, we have a pretty great picture of what the student is achieving.

Parity within the training partnership

German mentors agree that their marginalisation in the assessment of trainees is unsatisfactory. They believe that the current practice of divided responsibilities in assessment and training is problematic in that the mentor's overview is hardly taken into consideration. Consequently, isolated, untypical mistakes on the day of assessment may be accepted as evidence for a trainee's overall performance and distort the overall impression. On the other hand, mentors in both samples concede that the involvement of an external examiner can increase the level of impartiality and allow mentors the space to develop trusting, honest relationships with their trainees, which are unaffected by the status of the mentor and the ubiquitous threat of assessment.

> Mary: I don't enjoy being the assessor . . . because there is conflict between . . . on the one hand you are trying to be positive . . . but at the end of the day, if the lesson was a disaster, it is very hard to say 'Your lesson was a disaster'.
>
> Angelika: *Ich bin persönlich froh, dass ich nicht beurteilen muss, weil es eben so schwierig ist . . . Man will für seinen Referendar einfach das Beste. Und so ist man eigentlich ja gar nicht richtig objektiv. Also ich persönlich würde es dann vielleicht sogar ablehnen, Referendare zu nehmen. Ich würde es als zusätzliche Last und Verantwortung empfinden, . . . ob . . . in der heutigen Zeit, wo's so wenig Lehrerstellen gibt, der jetzt eineAnstellung bekommt oder nicht.*
> (Personally I am glad that I don't have to assess . . . One simply wants the best for one's trainee. And therefore one is not really properly objective. Well, I personally would probably even refuse to have a trainee. I would experience it as an additional burden and responsibility . . . if . . . in these times of high unemployment amongst young teachers the trainee would find employment or not.)
>
> Gisela: *Ich persönlich finde es gut, wenn man nicht beurteilt. Zum einen kennt man den Lehramtsanwärter zwar am besten, aber das Verhältnis wird, glaube ich, beeinträchtigt.*
> (Personally, I find it good, when one does not assess. True, one knows the trainee best, but the relationship will be, I believe, impaired.)

The difficulty of reconciling the conflicting demands of mentoring is highlighted in studies by Yau (1995) and Shaw (1992) and is described by Smith and Alred who state: 'There is a world of difference between being a mentor, a supervisor and an assessor' (1993, p. 113).

Wisdom in practice versus prescriptive standards

The marginalisation of German mentors in the assessment of trainee competence is further exacerbated by the lack of transparency regarding the assessment criteria used by external examiners and tutors. Mentors would therefore welcome a set of clearly defined criteria to serve them as points of reference. Although the *Seminar* issues guidelines for lesson evaluation, mentors' knowledge of them is vague. Guided by a general framework of key points and by drawing on their professional knowledge and experience, German mentors devise their own evaluation criteria without any mechanisms of standardisation and moderation involved in the evaluation of trainee teachers' performance.

> Hanna: *Nee, also die Mentoren innerhalb der Schule haben sich bisher noch nie zusammengesetzt. Also von daher entwickelt jeder dann so sein eigenes Konzept.*
> (No, the mentors within the school have never had a meeting yet. Well, consequently, everyone, sort of, develops their own system.)

Franz: *Ja, also ich mach' mir selber einen Kriterienkatalog für die Unterrichtsbesuche.*
(Yes, well, I make up my own catalogue of criteria for lesson observations.)

In contrast, mentors and trainees in England are well aware of the prescribed standards, which serve them as points of reference in their assessment of their trainees, although opinion about their practical value remains divided.

Keith: It really needs for me every time to look at the criteria . . . you really need to look at them regularly.
Interviewer: Would you feel it is a useful reference?
Keith: Yes, certainly, obviously.

Not everybody lends their wholehearted support to this procedure.

Jane: . . . there are so many little categories . . . to actually grade each one, I think, is particularly difficult. An overall grade might be better.
. . . go[ing] through each of those little tiny statements and read them over and over again to try and understand what they actually mean, I think, you know it's quite, it's very time consuming.
. . . the profile has been a pain . . . It has been, you know, really cumbersome to fill in. It just takes forever to fill in.

The concerns expressed by some English mentors are echoed by their German counterparts who doubt whether a catalogue of seventy or so discrete, narrowly defined standards can provide a reliable means to assess teacher competence. Instead they fear that such an itemised system of prescribed teacher behaviour may divert attention away from overall competence, supporting Whitty's belief that 'assessing the whole often does seem to be more than the sum of the parts' (1994, p. 33).

Andreas: *Also bei uns ist das schon eher das Gesamtbild – also dass man sagt, 'das ist ein Lehrer, der kann mit der Klasse umgehen . . . der kann mit Menschen umgehen'.*
(Well, here it is more a matter of the overall picture – well, of saying 'this is a teacher who can get on with the class, . . . who can get on with people'.)

This view encapsulates the belief that teacher competence can be evaluated globally and intuitively. Feiman-Nemser describes such an ability as 'wisdom in practice' (1993, p. 153), a quality which is at present downplayed in favour of procedural knowledge, as a result of mentoring being promoted as a technical activity that can be controlled by applying specific strategies and techniques.

Two questions arise in light of the prescriptive nature of the standards listed in Circular 4/98.

1 Can English mentors free themselves sufficiently from these standards to evaluate overall competence rather than concentrating their attention on discrete items of narrowly defined behaviour?
2 Can trainees be granted the space and freedom required to develop as 'reflective practitioners' (Schön, 1983, 1987)?

If the answers to these questions were to be a firm 'No', then the framework would merely constitute a collection of 'quick fix' recipes. This is indeed a concern voiced by German mentors who are opposed to the idea of providing beginning teachers with a manual that may lull them into a false sense of security and lead to a superficial preoccupation with 'surface behaviour' at the expense of understanding the reasons for decisions taken and strategies employed (Bullough and Gitlin, 1991, p. 43; Tomlinson, 1995, p. 148). Although they accept that the standards are an attempt to improve clarity and transparency for all parties involved in assessment, they are concerned that it might invite a 'spurious precision'. For, as Norris concludes, 'there is nothing as imprecise as precision' (1991, p. 334). Similarly, Semler (1993) maintains that objective-led outcomes which attempt to quantify desirable outcomes and identify and measure deficiencies often lead to over-bureaucratic, cosmetic and sterile procedures that can engender defensive or hostile responses, and lead to a tendency to avoid problems honestly and forthrightly.

Furthermore, the diverse contexts of teaching raise issues of flexibility and transferability which must be addressed. In light of the highly individualised settings in which teaching occurs, it is questionable whether competences can be decontextualised (Williams, 1994). The following mentor comment draws attention to the fact that schools cover a wide spectrum of ethnic mixes with different demands made on the teacher.

> Angelika: *In Schulen mit hohem Ausländeranteil ist vielmehr die Pädagogik gefragt, wie in Schulen, . . . wo dann kein einziges Ausländerkind drin ist. Da hat man ganz andere Probleme . . . da muss der Lehrer ganz anders funktionieren.*
> (In schools with a high proportion of foreigners pedagogical skills are required to a greater extent than in schools where there isn't a single foreign child. There one has completely different problems . . . there the teacher must function completely differently.)

A standard approach to training and assessment must therefore not ignore the fact that all schools are different and so are the teachers who work within them.

> Angelika: *. . . die Flexibilität fehlt für mich da. Weil's einfach so unterschiedlich ist, wie eigentlich das Lehrerbild sein muss, von den örtlichen Gegebenheiten, wo man eben unterrichtet.*
> (. . . the element of flexibility is missing in my opinion. Because it is simply so different, the way the concept of being a teacher according to the local circumstances, where one teaches.)

Lack of flexibility and openness are identified by German mentors as issues which arise in a training situation that is closely linked to continuous assessment, based on a catalogue of defined standards and involving the mentor as the assessor. The reason for not subscribing to such a model of training is explained by one director of a teacher training institution.

> Seminardirektor M: *Es findet keine Beurteilung statt . . . wir wollen keine Prüfungssituation . . . weil wir dann die Orientierung an mir haben.*
> (Assessment does not take place . . . we don't want an assessment situation . . . because then they will orientate themselves on me.)

In the same vein Eraut (1994) maintains that trainee teachers must be able to develop their own theories and relate them to practice and public theories. 'Without it they will become prisoners of their own school experience, perhaps the competent teacher of today, certainly the ossified teacher of tomorrow' (Eraut, 1994, p. 94).

Conclusions

By adopting a cross-cultural perspective it is the aim of this study to evaluate current practice in school-based initial teacher training as perceived by mentors in England and Germany. On the basis of the findings a number of issues can be distilled in relation to the tensions inherent in mentoring. Influenced by the structural as well as the cultural factors of the respective settings, mentors perceive the various aspects of their roles differently, but also show convergence in some of their interpretations. A high level of agreement is reflected in their perception of their main role as the trainee's 'adviser', whereas divergent views emerge in relation to their responsibilities as 'assessor', 'trainer', 'partner' and 'model'. One of the key issues raised in this study relates to the question of the way in which the aspect of assessment impacts on the trainee–mentor relationship and the trainee's professional development in general. The pertinence of this question becomes apparent in the light of increased government control exercised during the past decade, which manifests itself in a highly prescriptive statutory framework and in rigorous inspection of all providers of initial teacher training. Even now, during the second cycle of Ofsted inspections, the assessment of trainees' competence by mentors and tutors remains one of the major challenges begging further investigation. However, a more detailed examination of this issue would exceed the limitations of this study which is primarily concerned with mentors, perceptions of their roles, one of which is closely linked to the process of assessment.

While the concept of continuous assessment can enhance the reliability, fairness and accuracy in judging trainees' competence, the power differential between assessor and assessee, that is, mentor and trainee, can seriously interfere with the development of a trusting and honest relationship. Similarly, the catalogue of standards (DfEE 4/98), which serves as a point of reference in the measurement and standardisation of teaching competence, can evoke feelings of intimidation and fear of failure. Where this is the case, it remains questionable whether such a framework can assist trainees in adopting a creative approach in order to develop the ability to teach a diverse body of learners across a multitude of contexts. It is conceivable that the ubiquitous threat of assessment inevitably discourages less confident trainees from exploring alternative, slightly more risky strategies, thereby promoting an uninspired, 'play-it-safe' attitude. However, such concern must not lead to a depreciation of the value attached to critical evaluation and reflection. On the contrary, if we accept that teaching is a 'problem solving activity' (Stones, 1984, p. 53) then we cannot rely exclusively on a technicist approach defined by a catalogue of prescribed patterns of surface behaviour. For each classroom experience is unique and makes complex demands on teachers in regard to the way in which they respond to unexpected situations appropriately. To succeed they need not only to build up a repertoire of reliable survival tactics, but to venture beyond the safety of a teacher manual in their endeavour to develop into reflective and reflexive practitioners (Schön, 1983, 1987). In view of the present preoccupation with gradings and league tables, the caveat expressed by Stones sixteen years ago has never appeared to be more poignant than in the present culture of measuring learning outcomes. For 'there is an insidious assumption that assessment by itself elevates standards' (1984, p. 90).

In a climate of total quality control mentors may feel reluctant to allow trainees sufficient leeway in exploring different styles and approaches and may exclusively refer to the standards as set out in *Circular* 4/98 as the ultimate goal to be achieved on completion of the PGCE year. Leading trainees to believe that this would be the end of their journey after which they will emerge as fully fledged teachers is irresponsible and dangerous. Not only can it block any initiative to reach beyond these boundaries during the training process, it can also result in a loss of confidence when newly qualified teachers in their first year of practice are confronted with new, unexpected situations for which they feel ill-prepared. It is therefore vital to emphasise that achieving these standards can only constitute a starting point on the long and never-ending route of continued professional development, a fact which is reinforced by the recent introduction of a statutory induction period by the end of which newly qualified teachers have to have their status confirmed.

It is therefore vital that trainees not only develop an extensive repertoire of teaching strategies and techniques but also acquire a sound knowledge and understanding of the principles underlying learning against which to check their actions and decisions taken in specific classroom situations. Although the significance of mentors providing models of good practice remains undisputed, the sole reliance on this resource could result in a simplistic, narrow model of training within which the mentor's subjective views and professional bias are not challenged. Even if the issue of bias is addressed by including a multitude of models, there is a danger that trainees could be overwhelmed by the sheer volume and quality of 'good teaching' and consequently lose confidence in their own ability or the desire to develop an individual style and discover new ground. To provide sufficient stimulus and input in the form of realistic examples, mentors must possess the confidence to act as models to be emulated as well as admit their fallibility. By allowing trainees access to their own practice, including its strengths and weaknesses, they can provide a platform for critical, constructive dialogue and evaluation between themselves and their trainees. Within such a democratic culture of collaboration and trust the general principles pervading teaching and learning and how they manifest themselves in the use of concrete situations can be discussed and be taken into account at each stage of the evaluation cycle of planning, teaching and reflection.

In addition to mastering the technical aspects of teaching, trainees must also be adequately equipped to enable them to respond appropriately to the complex and unpredictable mechanisms underlying human interaction. Only then will they be in a position to manage the conflicting demands made upon them by pupils, teachers, managers, parents and government agents within a postmodern society where social, economic and cultural changes continuously impinge on all our lives. Tips for teachers or emulating the 'master of old' can no longer suffice. Instead, the role of the mentor has become more versatile and multi-faceted than ever before. The danger, however, is that as a result of ever-increasing demands made upon teachers, mentors may succumb to the temptation of following the simplistic, but highly prescriptive route of a technicist approach without venturing outside its boundaries for the occasional journey of discovery. If our aim is to develop critical thinkers and active agents who can bring about an improvement in the education of our children, then we must encourage trainees to be inquisitive, allow them to take risks and promote a commitment to contribute to the welfare of the local, national and global community. Granted, these attributes may surpass the statutory requirements, but they are essential qualities to be developed if our trainee teachers are to become reflective and reflexive practitioners, operating not only within the confines of *Circular* 4/98 but also in relation to the rapidly changing world around them.

Finally, the irony emanating from this study is encapsulated in the German mentors' desire for greater democratization within their training partnership and increased transparency in the assessment process, as is the case in the English system. However, such a package would come complete with the demands for increased accountability and centralised control which in turn would reduce the freedom which mentors in Germany at present enjoy in their work with trainee teachers.

References

Abell, S. K., Dillon, D. R., Hopkins, C. J., McInerney, W. D. and O'Brien, D. G. (1995) 'Somebody to count on': Mentor/intern relationships in a beginning teacher internship program, *Teaching and Teacher Education*, 11(2), pp. 173–188.

Adams, A. and Tusiewicz, W. (1995) *The Crisis in Teacher Education: A European Concern?* (London, Falmer Press).

Ballantyne, R., Packer, J. and Hansford, B. (1995) Mentoring beginning teachers: a qualitative analysis of process and outcomes, *Educational Review*, 47(3), pp. 297–307.

Bolam, R., MaCmahon, A., Pocklington, K. and Weindling, D. (1996) Mentoring for new headteachers: recent British experience, *Journal of Educational Administration*, 33(5), pp. 29–44.

Bramaed, R., Hardman, F., Leat, D. and McManus, E. (1994) The importance of 'Bad Lessons', in: I. Reid, H. Constable and R. Griffiths (eds) *Teacher Education Reform: Current Research* (London, Paul Chapman).

Bullough, R. V. and Gitlin, A. D. (1991) Educative communities and the development of the reflective practitioner, in: B. R. Tabachnich and K. Zeichner (eds) *Issues and Practices in Inquiry-Orientated Teacher Education* (London, Falmer Press).

Cohen, L. and Manion, L. (1994) *Research Methods in Education* (fourth edn) (London, Routledge).

Crossland, H. (1991) A competency-based approach to teacher development at the induction phase (unpublished course notes, University of Plymouth).

DES (1991) *School Based Initial Teacher Training in England and Wales* (HMI Report, HMSO).

DfEE (1998) *High Status, High Standards*, Circular 4/98 (London, Teacher Training Publications).

Dormer, J. (1994) The role of the mentor in secondary schools, in: M. Wilkin and D. Sankey (eds) *Collaboration and Transition in Initial Teacher Training* (London, Kogan Page).

Eraut, M. (1994) The acquisition and use of educational theory by beginning Teachers, in: G. Havard and P. Hodkinson (eds) *Action and Reflection in Teacher Education* (Norwood, N. J., Ablex).

Feiman-Nemser, S., Parker, M. B. and Zeichner, K. (1993) Are mentor teachers teacher educators?, in: D. McIntyre *et al.* (eds) *Mentoring* (London, Kogan Page).

Jones, M. (2000) Trainee teachers' perceptions of school-based training in England and Germany with regard to their preparation for teaching, mentor support and assessment, *Mentoring and Tutoring*, 8(1), pp. 63–80.

Kappler, A. and Reichart, S. (eds) (1996) *Facts about Germany* (Frankfurt am Main, Societüts-Verlag).

Langenscheidt (1995) *Langenscheidt's New College German Dictionary*, German–English, completely revised edition (Berlin, Langenscheidt KG).

Lee, S. and Wilkes, J. (1995) Mentoring and the professional development of teachers, *Mentoring and Tutoring*, 3(2), pp. 33–38.

McIntyre, D. and Haggar, H. (1993) Teachers' expertise and models of mentoring, in: D. McIntyre *et al.* (eds) *Mentoring: Perspectives on School-Based Teacher Education* (London: Kogan Page).

McLaughlin, T. H. (1994) Mentoring and the demands of reflection, in: M. Wilkin and D. Sankey (eds) *Collaboration and Transition in Initial Teacher Training* (London, Kogan Page).

Maynard, T. and Furlong, J. (1993) Learning to teach and models of mentoring in: D. McIntyre, H. Hagger and M. Wilkin (eds), *Mentoring: Perspectives on School-Based Teacher Education* (London, Kogan Page).

Ministerium für Kultus und Sport Baden-Württemberg (1984) *Kultus and Unterricht. Verordnung des Kultusministeriums über den Vorbereitungsdienstund die Zweite Staatsprüfung für das Lehramt an Grund- und Hauptschulen GHPO II* (Regulations for the training and examination requirements for teachers at Grund- and Hauptschulen) (Villingen-Schwenningen, Neckar-Verlag).

Nolder, R., Smith, S. and Melrose, J. (1994) *Working Together: Roles and Relationships in the Mentoring of Mathematics Teaching* (London, Falmer Press).

Norris, N. (1991) The trouble with competence, *Cambridge Journal of Education*, 21(3), pp. 331–341.

Schön, D. (1983) *The Reflective Practitioner: How Professionals Think in Action* (New York, Basic Books).

Schön, D. (1987) *Educating the Reflective Practitioner: Toward a New Design for Teaching and Learning in the Professions* (San Francisco, Jossey-Bass).

Semler, R. (1993) *Maverick* (London, Century Press).

Shaw, R. (1992) *Teacher Training in Secondary Schools*, Educational Management Series (London, Kogan Page).

Smith, R. and Alred, G. (1993) The impersonation of wisdom, in: D. McIntyre *et al.* (eds) *Mentoring* (London, Kogan Page).

Staatsministerium für Unterricht, Kultus, Wissenschaft und Kunst (1987) Neufassung der Lehramtsverordnung 2 (Revised regulations for teacher training 2) (*Bayerisches Gesetz- und Verordnungsblatt*, München).

Stones, E. (1984) *Supervision in Teacher Education* (London, Methuen and Co).

Tickle, L. (1993) The wish of Odysseus? New teachers' receptiveness to mentoring, in: D. McIntyre *et al.* (eds) *Mentoring* (London, Kogan Page).

Tomlinson, P. (1995) *Understanding Mentoring* (Buckingham, Open University Press).

Veenman, S., De Laat, H. and Staring, C. (1998) Evaluation of a coaching programme for mentors of beginning teachers, *Journal of In-service Education*, 24(3), pp. 411–427.

Wahrig, G. (1997) *Deutsches Wörterbuch* (*German Dictionary*), rev. edn R. Wahrig-Burfeind (ed.) (Gütersloh, Bertelsmann Lexikon Verlag).

Watkins, C. and Whalley, C. (1993) Mentoring beginning teachers: issues for schools to anticipate and manage, *School Organisation*, 13(2), pp. 129–138.

Whitty, G. (1994) The use of competences in teacher education, in: A. Williams (ed.) *Perspectives on Partnership* (London, Falmer Press).

Wildman, T. M. (1992) Teacher mentoring: an analysis of roles, activities and conditions, *Journal of Teacher Education*, 43(3), pp. 205–213.

Williams, A. (1994), Roles and responsibilities in initial teacher training – student views, in A. Williams (ed.) *Perspectives on Partnership* (London, Falmer Press).

Yau, C. K. (1995) From a student standpoint: my views on mentoring, *Mentoring and Tutoring*, 3(2), pp. 45–49.

CHAPTER 18

TEACHER STRESS
Directions for future research

Chris Kyriacou

Introduction

In 1977, I published a review of research on teacher stress in *Educational Review* (Kyriacou and Sutcliffe, 1977). As far as I know, that was the first time the term 'teacher stress' had appeared in the title of a chapter. Since then teacher stress has become a major topic of research throughout the world. The purpose of this chapter is to suggest some directions for future research on teacher stress.

I first became interested in the topic of teacher stress when I started out as a teacher of mathematics in a secondary school in London in 1972. The school I joined served a disadvantaged community and as a result all teachers in the school received an enhancement to their salary, which was called a 'social priority allowance'. The intention of this salary enhancement was to reduce the high rate of teacher turnover that was typical in schools serving deprived areas. When I arrived at the school my colleagues jokingly referred to this allowance as a 'stress allowance'. This got me interested in the notion that teachers in such schools may be facing particular difficulties that were causing them to experience high levels of stress. However, when I looked for research literature on this, there was virtually nothing to be found. There have, of course, always been references made over the centuries to the fact that teachers may become upset and frustrated by aspects of their work, but by 1972 very few researchers had yet made specific use of the term 'stress' in the context of teachers and teaching.

More generally, the term 'stress' was becoming widely used in the social sciences following the pioneering work on psychological stress by Selye in the 1950s (Selye, 1956). In the 1960s, studies began to appear making reference to teachers' concerns and anxieties, including several studies which focused on student teachers. In addition, studies of job satisfaction in teachers began to identify the sources of dissatisfaction. However, it was not until the mid-1970s that publications referring directly to 'stress in teaching' began to appear in reasonable numbers (see Coates and Thoresen, 1976; Dunham, 1976; Kyriacou and Sutcliffe, 1977). During the 1980s the number of studies reporting on teacher stress grew rapidly (Kyriacou, 1987; Cole and Walker, 1989). By the end of the 1990s the research literature on teacher stress had become voluminous (Travers and Cooper, 1996; Dunham and Varma, 1998; Vandenberghe and Huberman, 1999; Kyriacou, 2000).

Definitions and models of teacher stress

Teacher stress may be defined as the experience by a teacher of unpleasant, negative emotions, such as anger, anxiety, tension, frustration or depression, resulting from some aspect of their work as a teacher. This is the definition I adopted when I first started to do research on teacher stress in the 1970s and is very much in line with the definitions most widely used by other researchers. My definition was linked to a model of teacher stress that I developed (Kyriacou and Sutcliffe, 1978a) which essentially viewed stress as a negative emotional experience being triggered by the teacher's perception that their work situation constituted a threat to their self-esteem or well-being.

However, other definitions and models of stress abound. Some researchers have used the term stress to refer to the level of pressure and demands made on an individual and have used the term 'strain' to refer to the reaction to such stress. Other researchers have defined stress in terms of the degree of mismatch between the demands made upon an individual and the individual's ability to cope with those demands. In addition, a number of researchers have focused on the notion of teacher burnout, which is seen to be a state of emotional, physical and attitudinal exhaustion which may develop in teachers who have been unsuccessful in coping effectively with stress over a long period (Guglielmi and Tatrow, 1998; Vandenberghe and Huberman, 1999).

Researching teacher stress

The most widespread measure of teacher stress has been the use of self-report questionnaires. On the one hand, there are those which have employed a single item measure which ask teachers to rate their overall level of stress on a single response scale. A widely used example of this is that used in my own research, where teachers were asked to respond to the question 'In general, how stressful do you find being a teacher?' on a five point scale labelled 'not at all stressful', 'mildly stressful', 'moderately stressful', 'very stressful' or 'extremely stressful' (Kyriacou and Sutcliffe, 1978b). On the other hand, there are those which summate the teachers' responses to a list of items. An example of this is the teacher – event stress inventory, which is based on summating both the frequency of occurrence of a list of sources of stress with the degree of stress each of these items is reported to generate (Kyriacou and Pratt, 1985).

Some researchers have made use of measures of mental and physical ill-health (such as questionnaires of general health and early retirements due to ill-health), behavioural indices of stress (such as absenteeism, loss of temper and sleeplessness) and physiological indices (levels of hormones in the urine associated with stress and levels of heart rate during lessons).

Whilst questionnaire surveys have been the most widely used approach adopted to explore teacher stress, other studies have included interview surveys, case studies and studies using physiological indicators of stress. In addition, a number of studies have used powerful statistical techniques to identify causal pathways linking the different variables involved in teacher stress (Tellenback *et al.*, 1983; Worrall and May, 1989).

The prevalence of teacher stress

Survey data certainly indicates that teaching is one of the 'high stress' professions (Travers and Cooper, 1996; Dunham and Varma, 1998; Kyriacou, 2000).

Questionnaires asking teachers to rate their experience of stress at work typically indicate that about a quarter of schoolteachers regard teaching as a 'very or extremely stressful' job.

One of the most interesting studies reported is that of Huberman (1993). His study was based on 160 interviews with high school teachers in Switzerland. What made his study so interesting was that he compared the ways in which teachers of differing lengths of experience viewed their working life and thereby identified some key stages and associated worries and frustrations that teachers typically seemed to experience as their careers developed. The study indicates that most teachers seem to encounter a period of self-doubt, disenchantment and reassessment, in which their concerns are either resolved with them continuing with their career as a teacher or their deciding to leave. Huberman reports that amongst the most common motives cited for leaving teaching were fatigue, nervous tension, frustration, wear and tear, difficulties in adapting to pupils, personal fragility and routine. The notion of 'wear and tear' here is also evocative of studies elsewhere which have indicated that prolonged stress can lead to teacher burnout.

The main sources of stress facing teachers

Studies reporting sources of teacher stress (see e.g. Travers and Cooper, 1996; Benmansour, 1998; Pithers and Soden, 1998) indicate that the main sources of stress facing teachers are as follows:

- teaching pupils who lack motivation;
- maintaining discipline;
- time pressures and workload;
- coping with change;
- being evaluated by others;
- dealings with colleagues;
- self-esteem and status;
- administration and management;
- role conflict and ambiguity;
- poor working conditions.

It is important to bear in mind, however, that the main sources of stress experienced by a particular teacher will be unique to him or her and will depend on the precise complex interaction between their personality, values, skills and circumstances. As such, whilst we can highlight the most common sources of stress for teachers in general, we must take care not to overlook the specific concerns of individuals. In addition, however, there are differences in the main sources of teacher stress between countries based on the precise characteristics of national educational systems, the precise circumstances of teachers and schools in those countries and the prevailing attitudes and values regarding teachers and schools held in society as a whole.

For example, Chan and Hui (1995) have explored teacher burnout in a study of 415 Chinese secondary school teachers in Hong Kong. They observed that previous studies of teachers in Hong Kong have indicated that one of the major sources of stress was having too heavy a workload. Many teachers in Hong Kong have been given additional duties in school guidance work as part of moves to improve the quality of guidance in Hong Kong schools. As such, in their study they looked to see whether these guidance teachers reported more stress than non-guidance teachers. Surprisingly, they found that despite the guidance teachers reporting a higher level of workload, they did not report a higher level of burnout. Moreover, they reported a greater sense of personal achievement compared with the non-guidance teachers. Presumably, guidance teachers are teachers who value this type of work. As such, this study suggests that even in a context of feeling overloaded, taking on additional duties in a valued area of work need not create more stress, and may indeed enhance job satisfaction.

Coping with teacher stress

Individual coping strategies fall into two main types: direct action techniques and palliative techniques.

Direct action techniques refer to things that a teacher can do to eliminate the source of stress. This involves the teacher in first of all getting a clear idea of what the source of stress is and then carrying out some form of action that will mean that the demands which are causing the stress can be successfully dealt with in future or changing the situation in some way so that the demands no long occur. Direct action techniques may involve simply managing or organising oneself more effectively; it may involve developing new knowledge, skills and working practices; it may involve negotiating with colleagues, so that aspects of one's situation are changed or dealt with by others.

Palliative techniques do not deal with the source of stress itself, but rather are aimed at lessening the feeling of stress that occurs. Palliative techniques can be mental or physical. Mental strategies involve the teacher in trying to change how the situation is appraised. Physical strategies involve activities that help the teacher retain or regain a sense of being relaxed, by relieving any tension and anxiety that has built up.

Studies of how teachers cope with stress (see e.g. Borg and Falzon, 1990; Cockburn, 1996; Benmansour, 1998) indicate that the most frequent coping actions used by teachers are as listed here:

- try to keep problems in perspective;
- avoid confrontations;
- try to relax after work;
- take action to deal with problems;
- keeping feelings under control;
- devote more time to particular tasks;
- discuss problems and express feelings to others;
- have a healthy home life;
- plan ahead and prioritise;
- recognise ones own limitations.

As can been seen, this list reflects the mix of direct action and palliative techniques described earlier. A particularly interesting study was reported by Griffith *et al.* (1999), who conducted a questionnaire survey of 780 primary and secondary school teachers in London. Their data indicate that both the presence of social support and the use of effective coping behaviour can affect the teacher's perception of stress. Their findings highlight the importance of recognising that a teacher's perception of the demands made upon him or her is itself influenced by the degree of stress being experienced and that social support and successful coping can create a virtuous circle whereby the same 'objective' situation can begin to appear to be less demanding to the teacher.

What schools can do to reduce teacher stress?

As well as individual coping actions that a teacher can take, a number of studies have highlighted the importance of working in a school where a positive atmosphere of social support exists (Sheffield *et al.*, 1994; Punch and Tuetteman, 1996). This enables teachers to share concerns with each other, which can lead to helpful suggestions from a colleague that the teacher can implement or action by colleagues that resolves the sources of stress. Often, simply sharing problems or engaging in some social activity with colleagues during break periods can effectively help dissipate the feelings of stress.

Teachers and senior managers in schools also need to give thought to the way in which they may be creating unnecessary sources of stress through poor management. For example, a senior manager can set unrealistic targets for the completion of certain tasks or fail to communicate adequately with others, which then gives rise to avoidable problems.

A very important development in reducing teacher stress comes from the need to think more in terms of what characteristics make for healthy organisational functioning and then to develop individual and organisational practices to come into line with these, so that staff stress can then be reduced almost as a by-product of this (Rogers, 1996; Cartwright and Cooper, 1997; Education Service Advisory Committee, 1998). Characteristics of a healthy school are listed as follows:

* good communication between staff;
* a strong sense of collegiality;
* management decisions based on consultation;
* consensus established on key values and standards;
* whole school policies in place;
* role and expectations clearly defined;
* teachers receive positive feedback and praise;
* good level of resources and facilities to support teachers;
* support available to help solve problems;
* policies and procedures are easy to follow;
* red tape and paperwork is minimised;
* additional duties are matched to teachers' skills;
* building environment is pleasant to work in;
* senior management makes good use of forward planning;
* induction and career development advice is given.

In addition, some schools are able to make counselling services available to members of staff who are experiencing high levels of stress. An important innovation in the UK has been the establishment of a telephone 'helpline' for teachers, called 'teacherline' (TBF, 2000; see also their website at www.teacherline.org.uk). This service, which is funded by the government, local education authorities and teacher unions, enables any teacher to receive free telephone counselling for stress-related problems.

The effectiveness of teacher stress workshops

Over the years a number of teachers have taken part in in-service workshops aimed at helping them to reduce their level of experienced stress. Such workshops typically focus on helping teachers to develop a mix of direct action and palliative techniques and also helping teachers individually and the school as a whole to develop methods of working which will minimise the occurrence of unnecessary sources of stress. A common feature of such workshops is training in the use of relaxation exercises as a palliative technique. Roger and Hudson (1995) have argued that a key feature in prolonging the experience of stress is a tendency for emotional rumination, which serves to maintain the feelings of tension and upset engendered by the source of stress. They have thus pointed to the need to help individuals develop greater 'emotion control' by terminating such rumination and thereby enabling palliative techniques to be more effective. However, the most important thing to recognise about effective coping strategies is that each teacher has to discover what strategies work best for them.

Directions for future research

Given the vast literature on teacher stress, it is no mean task to highlight areas for future research. However, I would suggest the following five:

(1) There will certainly always be a need for studies to continue to explore the prevalence of teacher stress, the sources of teacher stress and the coping actions used by teachers. Such studies are needed to update our data in this field and to explore trends and changes. In particular, it can alert us to changes in schools that are generating high levels of stress that need to be addressed. Certainly, in many countries schools have undergone periods of rapid change affecting teaching methods, the content of the school curriculum and assessment procedures. Changes in how the quality of teachers' work is monitored have also occurred. As such, the ability to cope with change has become increasingly important if teachers are to cope successfully with the demands made on them. Particular research is needed on the stress generated by coping with change, so that such research can provide governments and policy makers with an ongoing critique of how various educational reforms impact on teachers' experience of stress.

(2) Perhaps the most interesting aspect of teacher stress that requires research attention is the part that successful coping with stress plays as a teacher's career develops. The seminal work of Huberman (1993) focused attention on how teachers often face a mid-career crisis which involves them having to reassess their career aspirations. Similarly, the study of Cherniss (1995) explored reasons why some teachers are able to avoid burnout. There is little doubt that one of the major problems facing the teacher profession is the large number of teachers who decide to leave the profession after only a few years of service and those who continue but who become disaffected. Studies of teachers who have been teaching between five and ten years, may serve to highlight the features that may explain why and how some teachers are more able to successfully negotiate periods of career reappraisal and retain a positive commitment to the work.

(3) There are still aspects of the stress process that require further attention for a fuller understanding to occur. In particular, an important distinction needs to be made between stress triggered by difficult or excessive demands being made on a teacher (e.g. having to mark too many scripts within a day or dealing with a pupil who persistently refuses to behave) and stress being triggered by concerns linked to one's self-image (e.g. being overlooked for promotion or not being allocated an important task). These two types of trigger may often

overlap; for example, having to deal with a pupil who misbehaves may not only be very demanding but may also undermine one's self-image. Nevertheless, there is a need to more fully understand whether the stress process may differ in certain ways in relation to these two types of triggers and the implications any such differences may have for coping actions.

(4) Research is also needed in the area of assessing the effectiveness of particular intervention strategies to help teachers and schools reduce teacher stress. The work of Roger in the area of training people in emotion control seems to be of particular importance (Roger and Hudson, 1995). They argued that stress can often be induced and sustained unnecessarily by a propensity to ruminate over events, sometimes working oneself into a state of annoyance or upset hours or days after the event concerned has occurred. Effective emotion control enables teachers to direct their thinking to future events and tasks in a more productive manner. Similarly, research on action that can be taken by senior managers in a school to reduce teacher stress is also needed. In this area I would highlight the need for more research on the way aspects of school leadership and school organisation impact on teachers. A supportive leadership style which takes account of ways in which feedback to teachers on their performance needs to be encouraging, and may do much to mitigate teacher stress. In addition, organisational arrangements which can minimise the occurrence of unnecessary pressures on teachers may also help mitigate teacher stress. Research on such features is needed to clarify how such intervention strategies can be made more effective.

(5) Finally, a relatively neglected area of research to date has been the impact of teacher–pupil interaction and classroom climate on teacher stress. The point has often been made that teacher stress can sometimes undermine teachers' feelings of goodwill towards pupils and lead teachers to overact with hostility towards pupils when pupils produce poor work or misbehave. This, however, is only part of the story. Research is needed to further explore how a classroom climate is established and maintained and how levels of teacher stress and pupil stress may affect teacher–pupil interactions. In some cases, a positive classroom climate may serve to act as a buffer in preventing teacher stress and pupil stress occurring. We need to know more about how and why external demands and pressures on teachers and pupils may undermine positive teacher–pupil interaction in some classes but not in others.

Conclusion

Research on teacher stress has established itself as a major area of international research interest. As we look towards future research we need to consider directions of research that are likely to be of particular importance or productive. It is hoped that the suggestions made in this chapter will aid such a reflection.

References

Benmansour, N. (1998) Job satisfaction, stress and coping strategies among Moroccan high school teachers, *Mediterranean Journal of Educational Studies*, 3, pp. 13–33.

Borg, M. G. and Falzon, J. M. (1990) Coping actions by Maltese primary school teachers, *Educational Research*, 32, pp. 50–58.

Cartwright, S. and Cooper, C. L. (1997) *Managing Workplace Stress* (London, Sage).

Chan, D. W. and Hui, E. K. P. (1995) Burnout and coping among Chinese secondary school teachers in Hong Kong, *British Journal of Educational Psychology*, 65, pp. 15–25.

Cherniss, C. (1995) *Beyond Burnout: Helping Teachers, Nurses, Therapists and Lawyers Recover from Stress and Disillusionment* (London, Routledge).

Coates, T. J. and Thoresen, C. E. (1976) Teacher anxiety: a review with recommendations, *Review of Educational Research*, 46, pp. 159–184.

Cockburn, A. D. (1996) Primary teachers' knowledge and acquisition of stress relieving strategies, *British Journal of Educational Psychology*, 66, pp. 399–410.

Cole, M. and Walker, S. (eds) (1989) *Teaching and Stress* (Buckingham, Open University Press).

Dunham, J. (1976) Stress situations and responses, in NAS/UWT (eds) *Stress in Schools* (Hemel Hempstead, NAS/UWT).

Dunham, J. and Varma, V. (eds) (1998) *Stress in Teachers: Past, Present and Future* (London, Whurr).

Education Service Advisory Committee (1998) *Managing Work-related Stress: A Guide for Managers and Teachers in the Schools*, 2nd edn (London, HMSO).

Griffith, J., Steptoe, A. and Cropley, M. (1999) An investigation of coping strategies associated with job stress in teachers, *British Journal of Educational Psychology*, 69, pp. 517–531.

Guglielmi, R. S. and Tatrow, K. (1998) Occupational stress, burnout and health in teachers: a methodological and theoretical analysis, *Review of Educational Research*, 68, pp. 61–99.

Huberman, M. (1993) *The Lives of Teachers* (London, Cassell).

Kyriacou, C. (1987) Teacher stress and burnout: an international review, *Educational Research*, 29, pp. 146–152.

Kyriacou, C. (2000) *Stress-busting for Teachers* (Cheltenham, Stanley Thornes).

Kyriacou, C. and Pratt, J. (1985) Teacher stress and psychoneurotic symptoms, *British Journal of Educational Psychology*, 55, pp. 61–64.

Kyriacou, C. and Sutcliffe, J. (1977) Teacher stress: a review, *Educational Review*, 29, pp. 299–306.

Kyriacou, C. and Sutcliffe, J. (1978a) A model of teacher stress, *Educational Studies*, 4, pp. 1–6.

Kyriacou, C. and Sutcliffe, J. (1978b) Teacher stress: prevalence, sources and symptoms, *British Journal of Educational Psychology*, 48, pp. 159–167.

Pithers, R. T. and Soden, R. (1998) Scottish and Australian teacher stress and strain: a comparative study, *British Journal of Educational Psychology*, 68, pp. 269–279.

Punch, K. F. and Tuetteman, E. (1996) Reducing teacher stress: the effects of support in the work environment, *Research in Education*, 56, pp. 63–72.

Roger, D. and Hudson, C. (1995) The role of emotion control and emotional rumination in stress management training, *International Journal of Stress Management*, 2, pp. 119–132.

Rogers, W. A. (1996) *Managing Teacher Stress* (London, Pitman).

Selye, H. (1956) *The Stress of Life* (New York, McGraw-Hill).

Sheffield, D., Dobbie, D. and Carroll, D. (1994) Stress, social support and psychological and physical wellbeing in secondary school teachers, *Work and Stress*, 8, pp. 235–243.

TBF (2000) *Managing Stress in Schools: Teacherline First Report* (London, TBF, The Teacher Support Network).

Tellenback, S., Brenner, S. and Lofgren, H. (1983) Teacher stress: exploratory model building, *Journal of Occupational Psychology*, 56, pp. 19–33.

Travers, C. J. and Cooper, C. L. (1996) *Teachers Under Pressure: Stress in the Teaching Profession* (London, Routledge).

Vandenberghe, R. and Huberman, A. M. (eds) (1999) *Understanding and Preventing Teacher Burnout: A Sourcebook of International Research and Practice* (Cambridge, Cambridge University Press).

Worrall, N. and May, D. (1989) Towards a person-in-situation model of teacher stress, *British Journal of Educational Psychology*, 59, pp. 174–186.

Teachers and Teaching
Theory and Practice

INCREASING TO 6 ISSUES IN 2004

EDITOR

Christopher Day, *University of Nottingham, UK*

Supported by an International Editorial board

Teachers and Teaching: Theory and Practice provides an international focal point for the publication of research on teachers and teaching, in particular on teacher thinking. It offers a means of communication and dissemination of completed research and research in progress, whilst also providing a forum for debate between researchers. This unique journal draws together qualitative and quantitative research from different countries and cultures which focus on the social, political and historical contexts of teaching as work. It includes theoretical reflections on the connections between theory and practice in teachers' work and other research of professional interest. The journal represents the latest phase in the development of the International Study Association on Teachers and Teaching (ISATT), a worldwide association of researchers, teacher educators and teachers.

This journal is also available online.
Please connect to www.tandf.co.uk/online.html for further information.

To request a sample copy please visit: **www.tandf.co.uk/journals**

SUBSCRIPTION RATES
2004 - Volume 10 (6 issues)
Print ISSN 1354-0602
Online ISSN 1470-1278
Institutional rate: US$655; £397
(includes free online access)
Personal rate: US$198; £120 (print only)

Carfax Publishing
Taylor & Francis Group

- -

ORDER FORM
ctat

PLEASE COMPLETE IN BLOCK CAPITALS AND RETURN TO THE ADDRESS BELOW

Please invoice me at the ❏ **institutional rate** ❏ **personal rate**

Name _____

Address _____

_____

_____

Email _____

Please contact Customer Services at either:

Taylor & Francis Ltd, Rankine Road, Basingstoke, Hants RG24 8PR, UK
Tel: +44 (0)1256 813002 **Fax:** +44 (0)1256 330245 **Email:** enquiry@tandf.co.uk **Website:** www.tandf.co.uk

Taylor & Francis Inc, 325 Chestnut Street, 8th Floor, Philadelphia, PA 19106, USA
Tel: +1 215 6258900 **Fax:** +1 215 6258914 **Email:** info@taylorandfrancis.com **Website:** www.taylorandfrancis.com